An End to Silence

An End to Silence

Uncensored Opinion in the Soviet Union

FROM ROY MEDVEDEV'S UNDERGROUND
MAGAZINE *Political Diary*

EDITED AND WITH INTRODUCTIONS BY
STEPHEN F. COHEN

TRANSLATED BY GEORGE SAUNDERS

W · W · NORTON & COMPANY
NEW YORK · LONDON

Anonymous: "Confrontation at the Coffin," pages 217–20 in *Survey*, summer 1972. Reprinted by permission.

"The Jewish Question in the USSR: Theses," pages 588–94 in *The Political, Social and Religious Thought of Russian Samizdat*, edited by Michael Meerson-Aksenov and Boris Shragin. Reprinted by permission of Nordland Publishing International, Inc.

Veniamin Kaverin: "Open Letter to Konstantin Fedin," pages 279–81 in *In Quest of Justice*, edited by Abraham Brumberg. Reprinted by permission of Praeger Publishers.

Lev Kopelev: "The Stalin Cult Has Been Destroyed," pages 320–22 in *In Quest of Justice*, edited by Abraham Brumberg. Reprinted by permission of Praeger Publishers.

"Protest and Reprisal: The Case of Valeria Gerlin," pages 340–49 in *In Quest of Justice*, edited by Abraham Brumberg. Reprinted by permission of Praeger Publishers.

Viktor Sosnora: "Letter by V. A. Sosnora," pages 221–23 in *Survey*, summer 1972. Reprinted by permission.

Georgy Vladimov: "Letter from G. Vladimov to Presidium of the Fourth Soviet Writers' Congress," pages 94–96 in *Solzhenitsyn: A Documentary Record*, edited by Leopold Labedz. Copyright © 1970 by Leopold Labedz. Copyright © 1971 by Harper & Row, Publishers, Inc. Reprinted by permission of the publisher.

Burgess

DK
267
.M413
1982

c. 1

Library of Congress Cataloging in Publication Data
Cohen, Stephen Frand (ed.),1938–
    An end to silence.
    Includes index.
    1. Soviet Union—Politics and government—1936–
1970—Addresses, essays, lectures. 2. Soviet
Union—Politics and government—1953– —Addresses, essays, lectures. 3. Underground literature—
Soviet Union—Addresses, essays, lectures.
4. Dissenters—Soviet Union—Addresses, essays,
lectures. I. Cohen, Stephen F. II. Politicheskii
dnevnik.
DK267 .M413 1982   947.084'2   81–3987
ISBN 0–393–01491–6   AACR2

W. W. Norton & Company, Inc. 500 Fifth Avenue, New York, N.Y. 10110
W.W. Norton & Company Ltd. 25 New Street Square, London EC4A 3NT

1 2 3 4 5 6 7 8 9 0

Contents

4 Currents of Soviet Opinion and Dissent   207

5 August 1968: The Winter of Communist Reform   277

6 Toward a Moscow Spring?   297

Editor's Preface:
Roy Medvedev and
Political Diary

W ESTERN MISPERCEPTIONS of the Soviet Union usually are the result of gray stereotypes that obscure diversity and complexity. This book is the product of the multicolored realities of Soviet political life since Stalin's death in 1953.

The book's contents are drawn from an unusual underground publication, *Political Diary,* a monthly bulletin—journal or magazine are also appropriate characterizations—that circulated secretly among a small group of people between October 1964 and March 1971. *Political Diary*'s readers included prominent intellectuals in the Soviet Establishment as well as dissidents. Its creator and editor was Roy Medvedev, the now famous historian and political dissident, who tells the inside story of *Political Diary* in a special introduction to this book.

Political Diary is an extraordinary example of Soviet samizdat, or "self-published" typescripts that circulate from reader to reader in defiance of official censorship. Though the device probably is as universal and old as censorship itself, samizdat became a mass phenomenon in the Soviet Union only in the second half of the 1960s. It sprang up to express the uncensored views not only of political dissidents but of a larger segment of the Soviet intelligentsia that had been emboldened, after Stalin's long reign of terror, by Khrushchev's reforms of 1953–64, and then frustrated by the conservatism of Khrushchev's successors. Samizdat output has diminished since the mid-1970s, but it remains, despite official repression, a regular feature of Soviet political and intellectual life. It has put into circulation thousands of separate items, from one-page protests to full-scale books and periodicals such as *Political Diary*.

The importance of samizdat and open dissent in the Soviet Union should be understood properly. Public assertion of political liberties, especially the samizdat principle of free expression, is a significant development in a country where for decades citizens, including the once outspoken Russian intelligentsia, were silenced by terror. The Soviet government no longer can abuse power without adverse publicity or monopolize public opinion. But it is also clear that these dissident activities involve only a tiny minority of the populace, which is overwhelmingly conformist; they do not represent a direct political threat or alternative to the government.

Samizdat has, however, another and perhaps larger political importance. It is in these "publications" that an uncensored debate about the political past, present, and future of the Soviet Union is finally taking place, and thus where the nation's diverse traditions, social currents, and political spectrum have emerged in open conflict. Samizdat has shattered the official myth, and the Western illusion, of a "monolithic" Soviet system and society. It has brought into view a stunning array of Soviet political trends and outlooks, ranging from left to right, liberal to neofascist, orthodox Marxism-Leninism to Russian Orthodox religion.

Nor, as we shall see in this book, do these samizdat currents exist in isolation from the official political system. Many of the rival political trends among dissidents—Marxist, liberal, Slavophile, protofascist, for example—exist also, in subterranean ways, inside Soviet officialdom, and even inside the ruling Communist Party. Conflicting political outlooks stated openly by samizdat writers can be found, for example, in muted form, in official censored publications as well; indeed, since the 1960s, many Soviet writers have contributed to both the official press and to samizdat. In this respect, officialdom and samizdat are not worlds apart but, to use the imagery suggested by a former insider, the "upstairs" and "downstairs" of Soviet political ideas.[1] And for this reason, the growing body of uncensored literature provides a wealth of information about both the society below and the Establishment above.

Political Diary occupies a special place in the history of samizdat. It was the first successful effort to establish a regular uncensored periodical or journal. When Roy Medvedev decided to stop publication in 1971, after almost seven years and eighty monthly issues, it was also the most long-lived. (That honor now belongs to the underground news bulletin *Chronicle of Current Events,* which began in 1968 and continues to appear more or less bimonthly.) *Political Diary*'s secrecy, which distinguished it from samizdat publications that sought wide circulation, helps to explain its relative longevity. Until Medvedev made eleven issues available to Western correspondents in 1971, *Political Diary*'s existence seems to have been completely unknown outside its select circle of some forty to fifty readers, even to the KGB. Even then, the identity of its editor remained generally unknown until 1975.[2]

1. Alexander Yanov, *The Russian New Right: Right-Wing Ideologies in the Contemporary USSR* (Berkeley, 1978), p. 15.
2. After Roy Medvedev ended publication of *Political Diary* in March 1971, his brother, Zhores, gave eleven issues to two American correspondents in Moscow, but without divulging the

Most important, *Political Diary* is the only uncensored journal known to have originated as Party samizdat, edited and read mainly by members of the Soviet Communist Party or by Establishment intellectuals close to it. Created immediately after Khrushchev's overthrow in October 1964, amid fears that the new leadership would turn back his anti-Stalinist reforms, *Political Diary* quickly developed into a thick journal with two corollary purposes, which made it a uniquely rich source of information about Soviet affairs.

The first purpose was to promote, in the context of "creative Marxism," the cause of anti-Stalinism and democratic socialist reform inside the Communist Party. *Political Diary*'s goal was the democratization of the whole Soviet system. Its perspective was the possibility of liberal reform from above and thus the necessity of working for reform inside the political system. *Political Diary* therefore tried to function, in the areas of ideology and policy ideas, as an embryonic loyal opposition. (All such opposition had been ruthlessly banned in the Soviet Union since the end of the civil war in 1921.) In this respect, *Political Diary* was a samizdat, or "downstairs," counterpart of *Novy mir* (New World), the official Soviet monthly that represented anti-Stalinist, liberal opinion inside the Establishment in 1956–70. The common cause of these otherwise disparate journals, one edited by a high Soviet official and enjoying a circulation of 100,000, the other having perhaps fifty secret readers, and their relationship, is one theme of this book.

Political Diary persisted in its loyalist orientation, even as the cause of anti-Stalinism and liberal reform suffered crushing defeats, from Moscow to Prague, throughout the late 1960s, and even after Roy Medvedev himself was expelled from the Communist Party in 1969. The result, as is clear from Medvedev's introduction and the contents of this book, was unique access to official Soviet sources—to historical and contemporary documents, officials, and privileged information, which then passed, through *Political Diary*, into the realm of samizdat.

The second function of *Political Diary* evolved with the politics of the Soviet 1960s. Along with his Marxist convictions, Medvedev, as editor, was faithful to democratic principles of free expression and pluralism. He collected and filled his uncensored journal with the growing volume of dissident opinion at large, especially protest statements of the emerging movement for civil rights. *Political Diary* grew into a thick monthly anthology of Soviet samizdat. Most of the best-known writings of the period, but also many otherwise obscure ones, ap-

---

editor's identity. The correspondents published featured stories on the journal, with excerpts, in the *New York Times* and the *Washington Post* of August 22, 1971. Longer excerpts were published in the journal *Survey* (summer 1972, pp. 209–23). In 1972, these eleven issues were published in Russian, in one thick volume, by the Alexander Herzen Foundation in Amsterdam, again without the editor's identity. In 1975, the Herzen Foundation published another eight issues of *Political Diary*, obtained from Zhores Medvedev, who identified his brother as the editor in a foreword to this volume. See *Politicheskii dnevnik*, vols. 1 and 2 (Amsterdam, 1972 and 1975).

peared in its pages. Readers of *Political Diary* thus obtained a unique documentary record of ongoing events and the spectrum of educated public opinion, which was unavailable from the official press or from unsystematic access to samizdat. In this way, the journal served its reformist purpose of enlightening Establishment officials and intellectuals. Several, including Andrei Sakharov, owed their initial familiarity with uncensored literature, and their early dissident education, to *Political Diary*, which even today, a decade after it ceased publication, remains the fullest Soviet source of samizdat.[3]

Political Diary was the creation of a remarkable and representative figure in contemporary Soviet politics. Now a silver-haired, ruddy-faced man of fifty-five, with a bemused look and ironic sense of humor, Roy Medvedev emerged above ground, out of Soviet officialdom, in 1971, when he published abroad his first samizdat books and became a leading dissident spokesman. His life and career reflect the intensely historical nature of Soviet political life, particularly the legacy of the terror-ridden Stalinist past.

Roy Medvedev and his twin brother, Zhores, the equally well-known dissident writer and biochemist who now lives in exile in London, were born in 1925. Their lives as anti-Stalinists began on a night in August 1938, when the twelve-year-old brothers lost their father to Stalin's terror. As happened to so many people in those terrible days, Aleksandr Medvedev, a middle-level army officer and Communist Party professor of philosophy, was arrested in the family's Moscow apartment and convicted on false charges, which included a denunciation by a former university colleague. He was sent to an Arctic labor camp, where he died in 1941, at the age of forty-two.

Their father's fate was a searing family experience that shaped the Medvedev brothers' future careers as reformers inside the system and then as dissidents.[4] Evicted from their Moscow apartment, they were raised by their mother, a musician, in south Russia and Soviet Georgia. After serving in the Soviet army in World War II, both managed to obtain the equivalent of a doctoral education, Roy in pedagogy at Leningrad University, and Zhores in biochemistry. But as children of an "enemy of the people," they were stigmatized politically and limited professionally until 1956, when their father was legally exonerated, along with thousands of other victims, as part of Khrushchev's de-Stalinization policies. That year, Roy joined the Communist Party and, in 1957, was able to move to

3. See Roy Medvedev's introduction below. Sakharov, who received samizdat material from Roy and Zhores Medvedev in the 1960s, including their own writings, later wrote, "Whatever my subsequent disagreements with the Medvedevs on matters of principle, I cannot minimize their role in my own development." *Sakharov Speaks* (New York, 1974), p. 35.

4. This biographical information is from Zhores Medvedev, "Rasskaz o roditeliakh," *Novyi zhurnal*, no. 112 (1973), pp. 190–207; and Roy Medvedev and Zhores Medvedev, *In Search of Common Sense* (New York: W. W. Norton, forthcoming 1982).

Moscow. Both brothers had prestigious official careers during the next fourteen years. Roy became deputy editor in chief of a major publishing house and then a senior research associate and department head at an institute of the Academy of Pedagogical Sciences, while Zhores achieved similar standing as a scientist.

But neither official status nor Khrushchev's limited reforms satisfied the brothers' radical anti-Stalinism, which was leading them to democratic ideas. As early as 1962, Zhores had completed and put into samizdat circulation an exposé of a still forbidden subject, Stalin's reign of terror in Soviet science.[5] Meanwhile, Roy began underground research for his monumental study of the whole Stalin era, *Let History Judge: The Origins and Consequences of Stalinism.* These activities brought the brothers into friendly contact with such high-ranking liberals in Soviet officialdom as Aleksandr Tvardovsky, the editor of *Novy mir,* and the nuclear physicist Sakharov. Their founding of *Political Diary* in 1964 was another stage in their development as Establishment reformers, but a step that brought them up against the limits of the system.

They were driven outside, into open dissent, by the pro-Stalinist and repressive policies of the post-Khrushchev leadership. Samizdat circulation of *Let History Judge* led to Roy's expulsion from the Communist Party in October 1969.[6] In 1970, Zhores was dismissed from his research position, arrested, and confined in a mental hospital for three weeks, until a public campaign by Establishment liberals and dissidents, organized by Roy, won his release. Threatened with arrest himself, Roy disappeared from Moscow for several months in 1971–72.[7] Still, the brothers showed no desire to turn back. In 1971, they published abroad, in defiance of official warnings, *Let History Judge* and their coauthored account of Zhores's incarceration, *A Question of Madness,* which made them known around the world. That same year, Roy resigned his official research position, closed down the underground *Political Diary,* and turned, openly and full-time, to the life of a nonconformist historian and political dissident.

Despite police harassment of his family, searches of his Moscow apartment, the confiscation of his archives, periodic interrogations, and more threats of arrest, he has been amazingly prolific in both roles. Medvedev's historical writings now include six books.[8] Based on a wealth of unpublished manuscripts and oral testimonies obtained through his contacts with Old Bolsheviks and sympathetic officials, they are pioneering works of uncensored research and indispensable reading for a knowledge of Soviet history. They have been widely translated abroad, establishing his international reputation as a major historian.

5. Zhores A. Medvedev, *The Rise and Fall of T. D. Lysenko* (New York, 1969).
6. See Roy Medvedev, *On Soviet Dissent: Interviews with Piero Ostellino* (New York, 1980), chap. 3.
7. See Medvedev and Medvedev, *In Search of Common Sense.*
8. *Let History Judge* (New York, 1971); *Khrushchev: The Years in Power* (New York, 1976), written with his brother, Zhores; *Problems in the Literary Biography of Mikhail Sholokhov* (New York, 1977); *Philip Mironov and the Russian Civil War* (New York, 1978), coauthored by Sergei Starikov; *On Stalin and Stalinism* (New York, 1979); and *The October Revolution* (New York, 1979).

Medvedev's dissident writings on contemporary political affairs are equally prolific but more controversial. For ten years, while protesting official abuses at home and abroad, he has been the foremost advocate of liberal Marxist reform and democratic socialism, including a multiparty system, in the Soviet Union. These ideas, set out most fully in his *On Socialist Democracy,*[9] have won for him the admiration of many left and liberal intellectuals in the West, including Euro-Communists, but also the hostility of those Soviet dissidents and émigrés who dislike his socialist views and gradualist tactic of supporting like-minded reformers still inside the system. They have also disagreed with him bitterly on international politics. While many dissidents, including his former friend and ally Sakharov, have called for hard-line American policies as a way of imposing civil-rights reforms inside the Soviet Union, Medvedev has insisted that détente is the only policy and international environment conducive to Soviet liberalization.[10]

Stranded between a conservative Soviet leadership and a dissident community that has lost its reformist hopes, Roy Medvedev has become an increasingly solitary voice. Nor can he find much comfort in Russia's historical traditions, which have usually fostered political extremism and victimized reformers. And yet, while candidly realistic about the setbacks of the 1970s, Medvedev remains "optimistic" about the development of social forces that will favor liberalization and the advent of a more reform-minded generation of Soviet political officials. Somehow resisting both despair and euphoria, he still believes that a dissident's proper role is to encourage a dialogue with officialdom and "initiative from 'above'." He sees no other way out of the Soviet past and present.[11] Only future events will tell us whether this perspective, first developed in *Political Diary,* is the augury of a Moscow Spring or the illusion of a Don Quixote.

Rich materials are an editor's luxury and problem. In preparing this book, I have had access to thirty complete issues of *Political Diary* and the partial contents of another eleven. Their dates of publication extend from October 1964 to December 1970. Nineteen of the full issues were published in Russian, in two volumes, by the Alexander Herzen Foundation in Amsterdam, which received them from the Medvedev brothers.[12] Typescript copies of the other twenty-two complete and partial issues were made available to W. W. Norton and Company, the American publisher, by Zhores Medvedev. Therefore, I had at my disposal approximately half of *Political Diary*'s run. (The full contents of these issues are listed in the Appendix to this book.) But even half represented a very large and

9. New York, 1975. See also his *Political Essays* (Nottingham, 1976); *On Soviet Dissent;* and *In Search of Common Sense.*
10. See *Détente and Socialist Democracy: A Discussion with Roy Medvedev* (New York, 1976).
11. See Medvedev, *On Soviet Dissent.*
12. See above, note 2.

rich body of materials, equal to about 3,000 tightly printed book pages, and thus a major problem of selection.

I alone have been responsible for deciding which materials should go into the book. Instead of a simple miscellany with no overall design or theme, or several kinds of more specialized volumes that could be based on *Political Diary*'s far-ranging contents, I decided to adopt the journal's own broad concern with the relationship between the Stalinist past, the Soviet present, and the future. Accordingly, the book is organized into chapters that proceed chronologically and thematically—from revelations about the Stalinist past to disagreements about responsibility for those crimes, the struggle between anti-Stalinism and neo-Stalinism, the flowering of samizdat and open dissent, and the question of the future. This design has enabled me, I hope, to capture many important themes of a turbulent period in Soviet political life, and to include *Political Diary*'s most interesting authors and materials. Most of the selections have not appeared previously in English, or at least not so fully.

To place the materials in context, I have written a long introduction on a central theme of modern Soviet politics, "The Stalin Question since Stalin," and short introductions to each chapter and selection. For the latter, I often drew upon unique information gathered by Roy Medvedev for *Political Diary*'s own commentaries. Most of the authors and documents published here speak for themselves, even to a reader with little knowledge of Soviet affairs. Where annotation has been necessary, I have tried to be brief, using brackets in the text or, infrequently, footnotes. All bracketed commentary and footnotes are mine, unless otherwise indicated. I have also provided first names, in place of the customary Russian initials, wherever possible. In those cases in which I abridged or retitled a document, this is stated in the appropriate introduction. I decided against using ellipses to indicate abridgments, except in a few places where long substantive cuts were made; so many inexplicable ellipses appear in the original text of *Political Diary* that the practice here would have been ungainly. Instead, I have usually omitted all ellipses. Scholars who worry about these omissions can consult the Russian originals.

The book is translated, except for a few items, by my friend George Saunders, who also advised me in invaluable ways in my editorial work. In spelling Russian names and titles, he has used the system most accessible to general readers—that is, one with no diacritical marks and with *y* rather than *i* or *ii* in the appropriate places. Thus we have Pyotr Yakir (not Pëtr Iakir), Baitalsky (not Baital'skii), Plyushch (not Pliushch), Krupskaya (not Krupskaia), and Aganbegyan (not Aganbegian). Likewise, the *y* usually appears when there is a palatalization between vowels, as in Fadeyev and Chalmayev. There are two occasional exceptions: first, where a different spelling already has been established in English usage, such as Lydia (not Lidiya) Chukovskaya, Eugenia (not Yegeniya) Ginzburg, Joseph (not Iosif) Stalin, and Leon (not Lev) Trotsky; and, second, in my own footnotes, where I have cited Russian titles according to the Library of

Congress system of transliteration, to assist readers who want to locate the item.

Finally, I want to thank other friends who helped me in important ways—James Mairs (my editor at W. W. Norton), Zhores Medvedev, Robert C. Tucker, Vera Dunham, Susan Mlot, and Vladimir Brovkin. I am grateful also to the John Simon Guggenheim Memorial Foundation, the Rockefeller Foundation, and the Center of International Studies at Princeton University, which supported my work at different stages. Indiana University Press, Nordland Publishing Company, Praeger Publishers, and the journal *Survey* granted permission to reprint here some translations under their copyright.

STEPHEN F. COHEN

New York City
January 1981

Introduction

How Political Diary *Was Created*

BY ROY MEDVEDEV

The typewritten or samizdat magazine, which later was given the name *Political Diary*, originated as an information bulletin in the fall of 1964 and continued until early 1971. It was not very large at first, 25 to 30 pages of typescript altogether. But by 1968–69, most issues were as large as 100 to 200 pages, single-spaced—that is, the size of a book.

The main topics of discussion in the first several issues were Khrushchev's ouster from his leadership posts in the Party and government and the increasingly insistent attempts to rehabilitate Stalin. Gradually the subject matter and the structure of the magazine expanded and grew more complex. Such regular sections of the magazine were established as "Survey of Main Events of the Month," "Letters, Articles, and Manuscripts," "From Literary Life," "From the Past," "Notes on Economic Questions," and "Nationality Problems." In 1968–69, the magazine's attention focused mainly on the events in Czechoslovakia

Political Diary had no formal editorial board or staff. I was the sole editor, compiler, and the author of all the commentaries, articles, and reports that appeared without any signatures. Many other people, however, helped in the collection of information, the preparation and preliminary discussion of certain materials, and the retyping, distribution, and safekeeping of the magazine. Unfortunately, at this time, I can only name a few of them.

From the very beginning, Yevgeny Petrovich Frolov gave unstinting help. Frolov was a veteran Party member who in 1964 held a responsible position on the editorial staff of *Kommunist* [the theoretical magazine of the Central Committee]. He had a complex and contradictory life. Before World War II, he worked in the Central Committee apparatus and knew personally all the top figures in the Party leadership—including Bukharin, Molotov, Yezhov, Kaganovich, Suslov, Mikoyan, Malenkov, and Lozovsky. In 1937–38, Frolov took part in the repressions, and during the war he was head of a department of SMERSH* in a tank corps. After the war, he was one of the leaders of the Cominform [the international Communist organization dominated by the Soviet Union], and to judge from some of the documents in his personal archives (which I was asked to go through after his death in 1967), he was indirectly involved in the arrests of a number of prominent Cominform officials in 1949–50. However, his personal notes, letters, and diaries make it clear that he came to feel profound remorse for his deeds of the past. Thus Frolov not only

---

*A special division of the security police whose task was to track down and punish alleged enemies of the Soviet Union among Soviet citizens who had been outside the government's control during World War II.

welcomed the changes of 1953–54 with great enthusiasm but even before the Twentieth Party Congress, in 1956, he won the release from camp and the rehabilitation of a dozen or more Party officials he had known well.

As early as 1956, Frolov began making copies of certain important documents and confidential letters that came into his hands temporarily. (He then was secretary of the Party organization for the editorial staff of *Kommunist.*) He showed these materials to some of his friends. For example, I obtained from him two copies of a typescript of Khrushchev's secret speech to the Twentieth Congress. Before returning the text to the Party District Committee, Frolov had locked himself in his office all night and retyped the entire speech on his own typewriter, a twelve-hour job. He not only supported the idea of publishing an unofficial information bulletin, but from 1956 to 1966 he placed a large quantity of materials of the most varied kind at my disposal.

Four other Old Bolsheviks who are no longer alive similarly supported me with their counsel and with materials to which they had access. These were P. I. Shabalkin, A. M. Durmashkin, I. P. Gavrilov, and A. Ye. Yevstafyev.

In 1966, a young physicist from Obninsk, Valery Pavlinchuk, began to play a very important role in producing *Political Diary.* At the time, he was a major influence among the scientists at Obninsky, and in 1967 he was expelled from the Party for circulating samizdat. In early 1968, he became friends with Pavel Litvinov and Pyotr Grigorenko [two prominent dissidents in Moscow] and was one of the founders of another [samizdat] information bulletin, the *Chronicle of Current Events,* which was intended for the widest possible dissemination. Nevertheless, Pavlinchuk continued to help gather material for *Political Diary.* Unfortunately, he developed a severe illness in the summer of 1968 and died, though he was only about thirty years old.

Other people who helped me greatly with advice and materials were M. A. Solntseva, Raissa Lert, Valentin Turchin, Suren Gazaryan, Mikhail Yakubovich, and several more. The widow of Ilya Ehrenburg placed a number of important documents at my disposal, as did the writer Yelizaveta Drabkina. (Drabkina's material formed the basis for my article on Sverdlov's family.) Similar assistance came from the writers Aleksandr Bek, A. K. Gladkov, and Boris Yampolsky.

Political Diary was a monthly publication, though in the summer months and in 1965 I published double issues several times. During the month, I would gather a wide variety of material in a special folder—memoranda, samizdat texts, and the most interesting articles from certain magazines and newspapers. At my request, several friends would read through all the sociopolitical and literary journals for the current month and send or bring me the most interesting excerpts, also providing brief notes on literary works that had been published. At the end of the month, I would sit down at the typewriter and in three to five days compose the next issue of the magazine. Then it would be retyped by my friends, with a maximum of five copies. I did not want the magazine reproduced in greater quantity than that. Comrades would come to my home to read the magazine or to the homes of others where sets of *Political Diary* were kept.

After three or four months, I would reread each issue and reedit it thoroughly, adding new materials and documents to all sections. After this, a professional typist would retype the magazine, once again in five copies only. I kept the first typed copy at my home and distributed the rest to my friends for safekeeping —and so that they could read and discuss it. My brother, Zhores, who of course was my main helper in all matters (as I was for him), made three photocopies of each issue, which were stored in different places.

Political Diary was not intended for wide circulation. Its existence was known • to, and it was read (more or less regularly) by, only forty or fifty people. This was one of the major differences between it and such samizdat information bulletins as the *Chronicle of Current Events.* I am sometimes asked what the sense was of producing a magazine that would not have the widest possible circulation. I would sometimes ask myself that question too. But, first, under the conditions that existed in our country (and exist to this day), wide distribution would immediately leave the magazine open to attack by the authorities. The magazine would no longer be "confidential," it would be easy to trace, and its editor and supporters (who were not known at that time outside a restricted circle of Soviet intellectuals) could easily be forced to stop publication. As we know, the *Chronicle of Current Events* immediately came under attack by the punitive agencies and since then has had to change its "editorial board" many times. But the *Chronicle*'s objective was simpler—to inform public opinion of the numerous cases of human-rights violations, the status of various political prisoners, and so on.

The *Political Diary* had a broader aim—to develop and elaborate various theories and conceptions. Moreover, it was not a "nonparty" publication. Its aim was not only to inform but to criticize, analyze, study reality, and so forth. And it was not possible to change frequently the editorial board; in those days there were only a few people who could carry out this work.

Moreover, far from seeking to expand our readership, we wished to make a strict selection and include only those people who themselves wanted to do creative political work and develop Marxist theory, as well as certain writers and other prominent representatives of the intelligentsia, around whom circles of creatively minded people had gathered in those years. Nevertheless, it is a fact that we consciously restricted our magazine's potential political influence; on the other hand, we made it possible for the magazine to exist and evolve. And when (in our opinion) the time was ripe in 1971, Zhores and I decided not only to make the fact of *Political Diary*'s existence widely known, but also to have eleven issues published abroad. A well-informed individual communicated to me the fact that when long articles about the existence of *Political Diary* appeared in the *New York Times* and the *Washington Post* and certain articles from the magazine were broadcast by the BBC and other foreign stations with Russian-language services, it came as a complete surprise to the KGB departments responsible for such matters. This means that among those forty or fifty persons who regularly (or irregularly) read my bulletin, there was not a single informer.

About forty issues of *Political Diary* have been published in Russian, or made available for publication, in the West.[1] The remaining issues are not particularly interesting for a number of reasons. Some of them contain material that has already been published abroad and is well-known to people interested in these matters—for example, Solzhenitsyn's letter to the Fourth Soviet Writers' Congress, Sakharov's *Progress, Coexistence, and Intellectual Freedom,* the open letters of Lydia Chukovskaya, Pyotr Grigorenko's letter on Aleksandr Nekrich's book about Stalin and World War II, and Anna Akhmatova's narrative poem *Requiem.* In *Political Diary,* I also published articles that were early variants of chapters in my book *On Socialist Democracy,* Zhores Medvedev's book *International Cooperation among Scientists,* and our joint work *Khrushchev: The Years in Power.* Many of the brief notes in the historical sections of *Political Diary* were used in my book *Let History Judge.* There is, of course, no need to reprint this material.

Among those who read *Political Diary,* though not regularly, were Aleksandr Tvardovsky, Mikhail Romm, and Boris Astaurov, not to mention a number of other prominent writers and scientists. I should make special mention of Fyodor Korolev, a member of the presidium of the Academy of Pedagogical Sciences, who died a few years ago. After the Twenty-second Party Congress in 1961, he himself proposed to write a book about Stalin and the special traits of the Soviet bureaucracy. He gathered the material for it but was unable to carry out his plan. Since I also worked at the Academy of Pedagogical Sciences, I could, without attracting anyone's attention, meet with Korolev and discuss any question. A man of great generosity, he frequently gave me large sums of money, which were indispensable for the retyping of *Political Diary,* my book *Let History Judge,* and many samizdat materials. He also helped store materials that I did not want to keep in my home.

In 1968, Andrei Sakharov was a regular reader of the bulletin. In his autobiographical essay, he referred to *Political Diary* as "a supposedly secret publication," a samizdat magazine for higher Party officials.[2] At that time, Sakharov had not yet seen the Amsterdam edition of *Political Diary* and could not understand how his discussion with Ernst Henry on the problems of disarmament found its way into the magazine. The explanation is that the words *Political Diary* did not appear on any of the issues of our information bulletin. The first page carried only the month and the year, e.g., "October 1968" or "March 1967." Among ourselves we called the publication *Mesyatsy* (Months). The phrase *Political Diary* was added later as a title for the issues that were sent abroad for publication. As for the dialogue between Sakharov and Ernst Henry, the text was given to me by Sakharov personally after we made each other's acquaintance in 1967, just as he gave me a number of other interesting documents from his personal archives.

1. See above, p. 12.
2. *Sakharov Speaks* (New York, 1974), p. 36.

For my part, I introduced him to many samizdat materials from my archives.

My friends considered *Political Diary* a useful and necessary publication and gave me all the help they could. Most of all, however, I found this work useful to myself; it helped me clarify my own views on a wide variety of events, to express my thoughts and opinions without looking over my shoulder at any "internal" censor or other editor. Nevertheless, much time and effort was required to prepare each issue. Despite material assistance by Korolev and several other friends, almost half my earnings from the Academy were spent on the retyping of the magazine and the several variants of *Let History Judge*. I stopped publication and my work on the magazine simply because I grew tired of it.

In an issue of the magazine *America,* I once read an article on the fate of small magazines in the United States. These are published by private individuals at their own expense with the simplest printing equipment, technology that is accessible to anyone in the United States. For the most part, these publications contain literary works, usually short stories and poetry. Individual enthusiasts will put them out for several years. But then they will be discontinued, primarily because the editor-publishers grow tired of working at night and spending all their free time on these projects; moreover, they find the substantial costs of this type of publication impossible to meet over a long period of time. Very few of these "private" journals and small papers continue for as much as ten to fifteen years, their usual life span being four to five.

That is what happened with *Political Diary.* I needed a respite. After a few years, however, my friends and I felt a powerful urge to revive our publication. This time, we decided not to put out a relatively small information bulletin but a large one—or as we say in the Soviet Union, a "thick journal." We gave it the title *Twentieth Century.* [3] Selected materials from it have recently been published in the West (in Russian, French, German, and English) and in Japan.

October 1, 1976
Moscow

3. Ten issues of *Dvadtsatyi vek* (Twentieth Century) were edited in Moscow in 1975–76, until threats by the Moscow city prosecutor closed down the journal. A selection of materials from these issues was published under the same title in Russian, in two volumes, in London in 1976 and 1977. For a selection in English, see Roy A. Medvedev, ed., *The Samizdat Register* (New York, 1977) and *The Samizdat Register II* (New York, 1981).

The Stalin Question since Stalin

BY STEPHEN F. COHEN

His Thirty Years of Power
Of Majesty and Misfortune.
      —Boris Slutsky

Tell me your opinion about our Stalinist past,
and I'll know who you are.
      —Moscow 1977

It has been called the "accursed question," like serfdom in prerevolutionary Russia. Stalin ruled the Soviet Union for a quarter of a century, from 1929 to his death at the age of seventy-three in 1953. For most of these years, he ruled as an unconstrained autocrat, making the era his own—*Stalinshchina*, the time of Stalin. The nature of his rule and the enduring legacy of Stalinism have been debated in the Soviet Union for more than another quarter of a century, first in the official press and since the mid-1960s in samizdat writings. And yet it remains the most tenacious and divisive issue in Soviet political life—a "dreadful and bloody wound," as even the government newspaper once admitted.[1]

The Stalin question is intensely historical, social, political, and moral. It encompasses the whole of Soviet and even Russian history. It cuts across and exacerbates contemporary political issues. It calls into question the careers of a whole ruling elite and the personal conduct of several generations of citizens. The Stalin question burns high and low, dividing leaders and influencing policy, while generating bitter quarrels in families, among friends, at social gatherings. The conflict takes various forms, from philosophical polemics to fistfights. One occurs each year on March 5, when glasses are raised in households across the Soviet Union on the anniversary of Stalin's death. Some are loving toasts to the memory of "our great leader who made the Motherland strong." Others curse "the greatest criminal our country has known."[2]

These antithetical toasts reflect the history that inflames and perpetuates the Stalin question. Historical Stalinism was, to use a Soviet metaphor, two towering and inseparable mountains: a mountain of national accomplishments alongside

---

1. Konstantin Simonov, "O proshlom vo imia budushchego," *Izvestiia*, November 18, 1962.
2. The last statement is by Pyotr Yakir; see below, p. 61. For an example of the other sentiment, see Aleksandr I. Solzhenitsyn, *The Oak and the Calf* (New York, 1980), p. 224. Western visitors have witnessed all of these manifestations of the Stalin question. For recent examples, see David K. Shipler's reports in the *New York Times*, November 26, 1977, and December 3, 1978.

a mountain of crimes. The accomplishments cannot be lightly dismissed. During the first decade of Stalin's leadership, memorialized officially as the period of the first and second five-year plans for collectivization and industrialization, a mostly backward, agrarian, illiterate society was transformed into a predominantly industrial, urban, and literate one. For millions of people, the 1930s were a time of willingly heroic sacrifice, educational opportunity, and upward mobility. In the second decade of Stalin's rule, the Soviet Union destroyed the mighty German invader, contributing more than any other nation to the defeat of fascism; it also acquired an empire in Eastern Europe and became a superpower in world affairs. All this still inspires tributes to the majesty of Stalin's rule. It is the reason that even a humane and persecuted dissident can say, "The Stalinist period has its legitimate place in history and I don't reject it."[3]

But the crimes were no less mountainous. Stalin's policies caused a Soviet holocaust, from his forcible collectivization of the peasantry in 1929–33, to the relentless system of mass terror by the NKVD or MGB (as the political police was variously known) that continued until his death. Millions of innocent men, women, and children were arbitrarily arrested, tortured, executed, brutally deported, or imprisoned in the murderous prisons and forced-labor camps of the Gulag Archipelago. No one has yet managed to calculate the exact number of deaths under Stalin. Among those who have tried, twenty million is a conservative estimate.[4] Nor does this figure include millions of unnecessary casualties that can be blamed on Stalin's negligent leadership at the beginning of World War II, or the eight million souls (another conservative estimate) who languished in his concentration camps every year between 1939 and 1953. Judged only by the number of victims, and leaving aside important differences between the two regimes, Stalinism created a holocaust greater than Hitler's.

Most of the Stalin controversy pivots on this dual history. The pro-Stalin argument, of which there are primitive and erudite versions among Russians, builds upon the proverb "When the forest is cut, the chips fly." It insists that "Stalin was necessary."[5] The sacrifices—they are usually termed "mistakes" or "excesses" and are said to be exaggerated—were unavoidable, it is argued. The

3. Andrei Sinyavsky in Max Hayward, ed., *On Trial* (New York, 1966), p. 98. For a similar dissident view, see A. Mikhailov quoted in Medvedev, *On Socialist Democracy* (New York, 1975), p. 398.

4. For conservative estimates, see Robert Conquest, *The Great Terror: Stalin's Purge of the Thirties* (New York, 1968), pp. 525–35; and his *"The Great Terror Revised,"* Survey 17, no. 1 (1971): 93. Several samizdat historians and demographers give considerably higher figures. For example: Anton Antonov-Ovseyenko, *The Time of Stalin: Portrait of a Tyranny* (New York, 1981), pt. 2, chap. 15; M. Maksudov, "Losses Suffered by the Population of the USSR 1918–1958," in Roy Medvedev, ed., *The Samizdat Register II* (New York, 1981), pp. 220–76; and the findings of Iosif Dyadkin reported in James Ring Adams, "Revising Stalin's Legacy," *Wall Street Journal*, July 23, 1980. Similarly, see I. Kurganov, "Tri tsifry," *Novoe russkoe slovo*, April 12, 1964.

5. See Giuseppe Boffa, *Inside the Khrushchev Era* (New York, 1959), p. 68; Solomon Slepak quoted in the *New York Times*, November 26, 1977; and Antonov-Ovseyenko, *The Time of Stalin*, epilogue.

economic advantages of collectivized agriculture made rapid industrialization possible. Repression eliminated unreliable, alien, or hostile elements and united the country under Stalin's strong leadership. These events prepared the nation for the great victory over Germany and achieved its great-power status. In this version of the past, Stalin is exalted as a great builder, statesman, and Generalissimo.[6]

Anti-Stalin opinion says just the opposite: "Yes, there were victories, not thanks to the cult [of Stalin], but in spite of it."[7] The brutality of collectivization did more harm than good; there were other and better ways to industrialize. Mass repressions were both criminal and dysfunctional. They decimated the labor pool and elites essential for national defense, including the officer corps. The atmosphere of terror and corrupt Stalinist leadership caused the terrible disasters of 1941 and made the whole war effort more difficult. Soviet prestige in the world, then and now, would be far greater without the stigma of Stalin's crimes.

These arguments seem historically symmetrical, but they do not explain fully why so many, probably the great majority, of Soviet officials and ordinary citizens alike still speak mostly, or even only, good of Stalin, and thus justify crimes of this magnitude.[8] It is true that official censorship has deprived many citizens of a full, systematic account of what happened. But much of the story did appear, however elliptically, in Soviet publications by the mid-1960s. Moreover, most adult survivors must have known or sensed the magnitude of the holocaust, since virtually every family lost a relative, friend, or acquaintance.[9] Why, then, do not most people share the unequivocal judgment once pronounced, even in censored Soviet publications, upon these "black and bitter days of the Stalin cult"—"there is no longer any place in our soul for a justification of his evil deeds"?[10]

Dimensions of the Stalin Question

Western scholars often treat the problem in narrow political terms. The official anti-Stalinism sponsored by Nikita Khrushchev between 1956 and his overthrow in 1964—de-Stalinization or what Soviet officials called "overcoming the personality cult and its consequences"—is interpreted mainly as having been the result of power struggles in the high leadership, as Khrushchev's tactical

6. As we will see below, this version is standard in present-day Soviet textbooks and novels.

7. Yuri Karyakin, "Epizod iz sovremennoi bor'by idei," *Novyi mir*, no. 9, 1964, p. 235. There are many censored and samizdat studies based on this theme; the fullest and most systematic is Medvedev, *Let History Judge*.

8. Though Soviet opinion on this subject cannot be polled and quantified, all firsthand accounts suggest a majority of pro-Stalin sentiment. More on this below.

9. See Ilya Ehrenburg, "People, Years, Life," *Current Digest of the Soviet Press* (cited hereafter as *CDSP*) 17, no. 23 (June 30, 1965): 10; and Aleksandr Nekrich, *Otreshis' ot strakha: vospominaniia istorika* (London, 1979), p. 120.

10. Simonov, "O proshlom vo imia budushchego"; and, similarly, Karyakin, "Epizod iz sovremennoi bor'by idei," p. 235.

weapon against his opponents. Although Khrushchev was the Soviet leader during these years, he was never an unchallenged dictator in high Party and state councils. He used the Stalin issue for his own political purposes; and, as with most of his other policies, de-Stalinization encountered factional opposition.[11] This circumstance helps to explain Khrushchev's erratic anti-Stalinism, including his sometimes stunning turnabouts.

But the factional explanation alone does not go to the political heart of the Stalin question. Like much Western analysis, it construes Soviet politics too narrowly. Rival factions in the Politburo and Central Committee are part of— and they reflect at the top—larger political forces and currents in Soviet officialdom and society. This has been especially true in connection with the Stalin question, which is rooted in three broad constituencies: social groups with an acute self-interest in any official resolution of the Stalinist past; reformist and conservative elites in other policy areas; and popular attitudes.

Two categories of Soviet citizens had an intensely personal interest in the Stalin question after 1953: victims of the terror and those who had victimized them. Most of the victims were dead, but many remained to exert pressure on high politics. Millions of people had survived—some for twenty or more years— in the camps and remote exile. Most of these survivors, perhaps seven or eight million, were eventually freed after Stalin's death. They began to return to society, first in a trickle in 1953 and then in a mass exodus in 1956. To salvage what remained of their shattered lives, the returnees required, and demanded, many forms of rehabilitation—legal exoneration, family reunification, housing, jobs, medical care, pensions.[12]

Their demands were shared by a kindred group of millions of relatives of people who had perished in the terror. The criminal stigma on these families ("enemy of the people"), many of whom had also been persecuted, kept them from living and working as they wanted. Posthumous legal exoneration, or "rehabilitation," and restitution were therefore both a practical necessity and a deeply felt duty to the dead. These demands of so many surviving victims had enormous political implications, if only because exoneration and restitution were official admissions of colossal official crimes. Still more, some victims demanded a full public exposure of the crimes and even punishment of those responsible.

In addition to its size and passion for justice, the community of victims had direct and indirect access to the high leadership. Returnees from the camps became members and even heads of various Party commissions set up after 1953 to investigate the Gulag system, the question of rehabilitations, and specific crimes of the Stalin years. (One such commission contributed to Khrushchev's anti-Stalin speeches to the Party congresses in 1956 and 1961.) Quite a few

11. See Carl A. Linden, *Khrushchev and the Soviet Leadership, 1957–1964* (Baltimore, 1966); and Michel Tatu, *Power in the Kremlin: From Khrushchev to Kosygin* (New York, 1968).

12. Y. Yefimov, "Pravovye voprosy vosstanovleniia trudovogo stazha reabilitirovannym grazhdanam," *Sotsialisticheskaia zakonnost'*, no. 9, 1964, pp. 42–45.

returnees resumed prominent positions in military, economic, scientific, and cultural life. (Unlike those in Czechoslovakia, however, none rose to the high Party leadership.) Some returnees had personal access to repentant Stalinists in the leadership, such as Khrushchev and Anastas Mikoyan, whom they lobbied and influenced. And other returnees, such as Aleksandr Solzhenitsyn, made their impact in different ways.[13] As a result, by the mid-1950s, victims of the terror had become a formidable source of anti-Stalinist opinion and politics.

Their adversaries were no less self-interested, and far more powerful. The systematic victimization of so many people had implicated millions of other people during the twenty-year terror. There were different degrees of responsibility. But criminal complicity had spread like a cancer throughout the system, from Politburo members who directed the terror alongside Stalin, Party and state officials who had participated in the repressions, and hundreds of thousands of NKVD personnel who arrested, tortured, executed, and guarded prisoners, to the plethora of petty informers and slanderers who fed on the crimson madness. Millions of other people were implicated by having profited, often inadvertently, from the misfortune of victims. They inherited the positions, apartments, possessions, and sometimes even the wives of the vanished. Generations built lives upon a holocaust.[14] The terror killed, but it also, said one returnee, "corrupted the living."[15]

The question of criminal responsibility and punishment, either by Nuremberg-style trials or by expulsion from public life, was widely discussed in the 1950s and 1960s, though public commentary usually was muted or oblique.[16] The official and popular defense that only Stalin and a handful of accomplices had known the magnitude and innocence of the victims was rudely shattered on several occasions. When the venerable writer Ilya Ehrenburg later spoke of having had "to live with clenched teeth" because he knew his arrested friends were innocent, he implied that the whole officialdom above him had also known.[17] It may be true, as even anti-Stalinists report, that ordinary people believed the Stalinist mania about "enemies of the people." But when the poet

13. For examples of returnees in these capacities, see Roy Medvedev and Zhores Medvedev, *Khrushchev: The Years in Power* (New York, 1976), pp. 11, 138–39; Antonov-Ovseyenko, *The Time of Stalin,* epilogue, chaps. 1–2; and Boris Dyakov, *Povest' o perezhitom* (Moscow, 1966).

14. See, for example, Antonov-Ovseyenko, *The Time of Stalin,* pt. 2, chaps. 8, 16; and Medvedev, *Problems in the Literary Biography of Mikhail Sholokhov* (New York, 1977), p. 173. The Soviet government newspaper said this about the terror: "False denunciation frequently became a ladder by which to climb to the top." *CDSP* 16, no. 28 (August 5, 1964): 20.

15. A. Snegov in *Vsesoiuznoe soveshchanie o merakh uluchsheniia podgotovki nauchno-pedagogicheskikh kadrov po istoricheskim naukam, 18–21 dekabria 1962 g.* (Moscow, 1964), p. 270. The cancer of responsibility is a central theme of Solzhenitsyn's two great novels of the terror years, *The First Circle* and *Cancer Ward.*

16. Much material on this theme appeared in *Political Diary;* see below, Chapter 2. The samizdat news bulletin *Khronika tekushchikh sobytii* also reported regularly on the discussion; see Peter Reddaway, ed., *Uncensored Russia* (New York, 1972), chap. 20.

17. See the revealing exchange between Vladimir Yermilov and Ehrenburg in *Izvestiia,* January 30, 1963, and February 6, 1963.

Yevgeny Yevtushenko wrote that the masses had "worked in a furious desperation, drowning with the thunder of machines, tractors, and bulldozers the cries
that might have reached them across the barbed wire of Siberian concentration
camps," he acknowledged that the whole nation had "sensed intuitively that
something was wrong."[18]

Of those who were incontrovertibly guilty, a few committed suicide, a few
were ousted from their posts, a handful of high policemen were tried and executed, and some became politically repentant.[19] But the great majority remained untouched. The remote specter of retribution was enough to unite
millions who had committed crimes, and also many of those who only felt some
unease about their lives, against any revelations about the past and the whole
process of de-Stalinization. "Many people," a young researcher discovered in
1956, "will defend [the past], defending themselves." A great poet who had
suffered commented, "Now they are trembling for their names, positions, apartments, dachas. The whole calculation was that no one would return."[20]

The constituency of the implicated offset pressure by victims. Their confrontation was an explosive ingredient of the Stalin question. It extended into the
Politburo itself. More generally, though, it was a fundamental division within the
country at large. "Two Russias," said Anna Akhmatova, "are eyeball to eyeball
—those who were imprisoned and those who put them there."[21]

The second large dimension of the Stalin question was even more ramifying.
Proposals for change throughout the rigidified Soviet system and stubborn resistance to change became the central features of official political life after Stalin's
death.[22] The conflict between reformers and conservatives was inseparable from
the Stalin question because the status quo and its history were Stalinist. In
advocating change, Soviet reformers had to criticize the legacy of Stalinism in
virtually every area of policy—the priority of heavy industry in economic invest-
ment, the exploitation of collectivized agriculture, overcentralization in management, heavy-handed censorship and a galaxy of taboos in intellectual, cultural,
and scientific life, retrograde policies in family affairs, repressive practices and
theories in law, cold-war thinking in foreign policy.[23] And in order to defend
these institutions, practices, and orthodoxies, Soviet conservatives had to defend
the Stalinist past.

18. Yevgeny Yevtushenko, *A Precocious Autobiography* (New York, 1963), p. 17.
19. See below, Chapter 2.
20. Yuri Trifonov, *Otblesk kostra* (Moscow, 1966), p. 86; and Anna Akhmatova in *Pamiati A.
Akhmatovoi* (Paris, 1975), p. 167.
21. *Pamiati A. Akhmatovoi*, p. 188.
22. I have developed this argument in "The Friends and Foes of Change: Reformism and
Conservatism in the Soviet Union," in Stephen F. Cohen, Alexander Rabinowitch, and Robert
Sharlet, eds., *The Soviet Union since Stalin* (Bloomington, 1980), pp. 11–31.
23. For a case study of this relationship between policy and history, see Moshe Lewin, *Political
Undercurrents in Soviet Economic Debates: From Bukharin to the Modern Reformers* (Princeton,
1974).

Unavoidably, Stalin and what he represented became political symbols for both the friends and foes of change. Soviet reformers developed anti-Stalinism as an ideology in the 1950s and 1960s (as did their counterparts in Eastern Europe), while Soviet conservatives embraced, no doubt reluctantly in some cases, varieties of neo-Stalinism. Khrushchev and his allies established the link in the mid-1950s, when they fused a decade of reform from above with repeated campaigns against Stalin's historical reputation. The Stalin question, they said, pit the "new and progressive against the old and reactionary"; Stalin's defenders were "conservatives and dogmatists."[24] Not all Soviet conservatives actually were Stalinists. But the relationship between attitudes toward Stalin and change was authentic, and it spread quickly to every policy area where reformers and conservatives were in conflict.[25]

Popular attitudes were, and remain, an even larger dimension of the Stalin question. The expression "cult of Stalin's personality" became, after 1953, an official euphemism for Stalinism, but it had a powerful and deep-rooted historical resonance. For more than twenty years, Stalin had been officially glorified in extraordinary ways. All of the country's achievements were attributed to his singular inspiration. Virtually every idea of nation, people, patriotism, and Communism was made synonymous with his name, as in the wartime battle cry "For Stalin! For the Motherland!" His name, words, and alleged deeds were trumpeted incessantly to every corner of the land. His photographed, painted, bronzed, and sculpted likeness was everywhere. Stalin's original designation, "The Lenin of Today," soon gave way in the 1930s to titles of omnipotence and infallibility: Father of the Peoples, Genius of Mankind, Driver of the Locomotive of History, Greatest Man of All Times and Peoples. The word "man" seemed inappropriate as the cult swelled into deification: "O Great Stalin, O Leader of the Peoples, Thou who dist give birth to man, Thou who didst make fertile the earth."[26]

The cult was manipulated from above, but there is no doubt that it had deep popular roots, as did the whole Stalinist system. Many Soviet writers, though they disagree about other aspects of Stalinism, tell us that the Stalin cult was widely accepted and deeply believed by millions of Soviet people of all classes, ages, and occupations, especially in the cities. Of course, many people did not believe, or they believed in more limited ways. But most of the urban populace, it seems clear, were captives of the cult. It became a religious phenomenon—"a peculiar

---

24. N. Saushkin, *O kul'te lichnosti i avtoritete* (Moscow, 1962). See also the resolution against Molotov, Kaganovich, and Khrushchev's other opponents in 1957, in *Kommunisticheskaia partiia sovetskogo soiuza v rezoliutsiiakh i resheniiakh s"ezdov, konferentsii i plenumov TSK*, vol. 7 (Moscow, 1971), pp. 267–73.

25. Their conflicts were reflected in many publications of the 1950s and 1960s, including fiction. An effective way to sample this literature is to read the reform journal *Novy mir* and the conservative journal *Oktyabr*, along with *Political Diary*.

26. Quoted in Suzanne Labin, *Stalin's Russia* (London, 1949), p. 65, which contains a good collection of cult appellations. See also Antonov-Ovseyenko, *The Time of Stalin*, pt. 3, chap. 1.

form of Soviet worship," as one Soviet historian tells us.[27] (Even the Russian Orthodox Church joined the chorus of glorification.[28]) In this deeply personal, psychological, and passionate sense, the nation was Stalinist. An older poet later remembered,

> That name didn't know a smaller measure
> Than that of a deity
> Given by people of deep religious faith.
>
> Just try and find the man who
> Didn't praise and glorify him,
> Just try and find him!

And a younger poet reports, "We are all children of the cult."[29]

When the government assaulted the Stalin cult, first obliquely and then with revelations tht portrayed the "Father of the Peoples" as a genocidal murderer, it caused a traumatic crisis of faith. De-Stalinization "destroyed our faith, tearing out the heart of our world-view, and that heart was Stalin . . ." Revelations about the past meant "not only the truth about Stalin, but the truth about ourselves and our illusions." Many people underwent a "spiritual revolution" and became anti-Stalinists. But it was not easy. Because it forced a person "to reevaluate his own life," it was "hard to part with our belief in Stalin."[30]

So hard that many people did not. For every Soviet citizen who repudiated Stalin and what he represented, there were many more for whom "the figure of Stalin as a theme [remained] an echo of the past in me." A not-so-fictional member of the Central Committee, for example, was only shaken: "No, I cannot judge him. The Party, the people, history can judge him. But not I . . . I am too small for this." Some people continued to love Stalin, but more wistfully: "I remember him as I was taught to look upon him then. I cannot help it now."

27. Medvedev, *On Socialist Democracy*, p. 346. For testimony about belief in the cult, see Lev Kopelev, *The Education of a True Believer* (New York, 1980); Antonov-Ovseyenko, *The Time of Stalin*, pt. 3, chap. 1; Vladimir Osipov, *Tri otnosheniia k rodine* (Frankfurt, 1978), p. 57; Yevtushenko, *A Precocious Autobiography*; Karyakin, "Epizod iz sovremennoi bor'by idei," pp. 236–38; Boris Slutsky, *Rabota* (Moscow, 1964), pp. 106–7; Ehrenburg, "People, Years, Life," pp. 3–11; Abraham Brumberg, ed., *In Quest of Justice* (New York, 1970), pp. 55, 320, 329; Yuri Levada, *Sotsial'naia priroda religii* (Moscow, 1965), pp. 99–126; Medvedev, *Let History Judge*, pp. 362–66, 428–30; and Aleksandr Zinoviev, "O Staline i stalinizme," *Dvadtsat' dva*, no. 10 (December 1979), pp. 128–36.

28. See Father Gleb Yakunin, "Moskovskaia patriarkhiia i 'kul't lichnosti Stalina," *Russkoe vozrozhdenie*, no. 1 (1978), pp. 103–37, and no. 2 (1978), pp. 110–50.

29. The stanzas are from Aleksandr Tvardovsky's "Horizon Beyond Horizon," *Poemy* (Moscow, 1963), pp. 475–76, translated here by Vera Dunham. The line is from Andrei Voznesensky's poem, below p. 184—85.

30. The quotations are from, respectively, Osipov, *Tri otnosheniia k rodine*, p. 57; Karyakin, "Epizod iz sovremennoi bor'by idei," p. 238; Yevtushenko, *A Precocious Autobiography*, p. 123; A. Grebenshchikov, "Zabveniiu ne podlezhat!" *Oktiabr'*, no. 6, 1968, p. 209; and Yevgeny Surkov, "Esli merit' zhizn'iu," *Literaturnaia gazeta*, December 16, 1961. Similarly, see *XXII s"ezd KPSS i voprosy ideologicheskoi raboty* (Moscow, 1962), pp. 215–17, 304–5; and below, Chapter 2.

But others still worshiped him aggressively, "as a great statesman," and resented the revelations. Even after disclosures about the crimes of the past, "cult consciousness" remained widespread, and with it "open or secret servants of this cult." Like the neo-Stalinist poet, they "never grow tired of the call: Put Stalin back on the pedestal!"[31]

The Stalin question has involved, therefore, both struggle for power and the historical life of a whole society, policy conflicts and the personal interests of millions of people, political calculation and passion. All of these factors came into play when Stalin died suddenly, and for many inexplicably, on March 5, 1953.

The Friends and Foes of Official Anti-Stalinism

Stalin's death, by removing the autocrat who had dominated the system, was the first act of de-Stalinization.[32] It also dealt an irreparable blow to the divinity of the cult; gods do not suffer brain hemorrhages, enlargement of the heart, and high blood pressure, as described graphically in the published medical bulletins and autopsy. The state funeral was itself a bizarre blend of old and new. Scores of mourners were trampled to death by a hysterical crowd gathered to view the body, adding to the death toll of Stalin's reign. But new chords were sounded in the eulogies by his successors, or the "collective leadership." They praised Stalin's "immortal name," but significantly less than while he lived. And they ascribed to the Communist Party a role it had not played, except in myth, since Stalin's great terror of the 1930's—the "great directing and guiding force of the Soviet people."[33]

The second important act of de-Stalinization came from the people who had been most constantly vulnerable to the terror: those who had risen highest under it. Khrushchev spoke for the whole ruling elite when he said, "All of us around Stalin were temporary people."[34] Not even Politburo membership had provided protection. Several members had been shot, one as recently as 1950; the wife of another (Molotov) was in prison camp; and the whole Politburo had come under Stalin's morbid suspicion toward the end. Having lived so long under a terroristic and capricious despot, most of his successors were united, probably for the last time, on a major reform: the partial dismantling of the powerful terror machine

31. The quotations are from, respectively, Sergei Smirnov, "Svidetel'stvuiu sam," *Moskva*, no. 10, 1967, p. 29; Vsevolod Kochetov's novel *Sekretar' obkoma*, as quoted in A. Maryamov, "Snariazhenie v pokhode," *Novyi mir*, no. 1, 1962, p. 226; Seymour Topping's report in the *New York Times*, November 2, 1961; Louis Fischer, *Russia Revisited* (Garden City, N.Y., 1957), p. 54; Karyakin, "Epizod iz sovremennoi bor'by idei," pp. 236, 239. For the neo-Stalinist poet, see Feliks Chuyev, below p. 174.

32. This point was developed by Robert C. Tucker, *The Soviet Political Mind*, rev. ed. (New York, 1971), chap. 8.

33. See *Pravda*, March 4–10, 1953. For the funeral, see Yevtushenko, *A Precocious Autobiography*, pp. 84–87. The point about the cult is made by Antonov-Ovseyenko, *The Time of Stalin*, p. 305.

34. Nikita S. Khrushchev, *Khrushchev Remembers* (Boston, 1970), p. 307.

and the restoration of the Communist Party to political primacy. By April 1953, Stalin's last terror scenario, the "Doctors' Plot," had been disavowed. By June, the political police had been brought under Party control; the chief, Lavrenti Beria, had been arrested along with a few henchmen; and a few hundred prominent camp inmates had been released.[35]

None of these partial repudiations of the past extended publicly to Stalin, except by inference. For brief periods in 1953, his name was conspicuously absent from the press and critical comments about an unidentified "cult of personality" began to appear. Clearly, the Stalin question was already under discussion in the new leadership. But the revised version of his official reputation that emerged in 1953–54, and which prevailed until 1956, was still highly laudatory. While no longer the "driver of the locomotive of history," Stalin remained the "great continuer of V. I. Lenin's immortal cause" who had led the Party and the nation in all victories since the 1920s, including the liquidation of "enemies of the Party and of the people." He was transfigured, as one scholar has observed, "from Father of the People to Son of the Party."[36]

But this reformulation of Stalin's greatness was both inadequate and unstable. His status had already become a muted symbol in high-level conflicts over economic policy and other proposed reforms. Professional elites, notably the military, were already pressing to rid their institutional reputation of disgraceful stains left by Stalin's misrule. No less important, pressure was building below, as would continue to be the case, for a more radical reconsideration. A "thaw," allowing tentative expression of once forbidden themes, had begun in intellectual and cultural life. Relatives and friends of high leaders were starting to return from the camps with stories about the millions who still languished there. Petitions on their behalf began to flood state and Party agencies, and thousands of posthumous rehabilitations were already underway. There were, in addition, open rebellions in the remote Arctic camps themselves.[37]

Above all, Stalin's reduced status ironically posed a grave danger for his successors by elevating Marxism-Leninism and the Party system to joint responsibility with him for all past deeds, including the bad ones. The new leadership was eager to take credit for the Party's "historic accomplishments." But the mountain of crimes, already hinted at in public announcements of the trials and

35. See Wolfgang Leonhard, *The Kremlin since Stalin* (New York, 1962), chap. 3: and Medvedev and Medvedev, *Khrushchev*, chaps. 1–2.

36. Robert C. Tucker, "The Metamorphosis of the Stalin Myth," *World Politics* 7, no. 1 (October 1954): 56. See, for example, the articles in *Pravda*, on the anniversary of his death and birth, for March 5, 1954, December 21, 1954, and December 21, 1955. For a detailed study, see Jane P. Shapiro, "The Soviet Press and the Problem of Stalin," *Studies in Comparative Communism* 4, nos. 3–4 (July–October 1971): 179–209.

37. See above, note 35; *The Anti-Stalin Campaign and International Communism: A Selection of Documents*, ed. by the Russian Institute, Columbia University (New York, 1956), p. 38; Jane P. Shapiro, "Rehabilitation Policy and Political Conflict in the Soviet Union, 1953–1964" (Ph.D. diss., Columbia University, 1967), chap. 2; and Aleksandr I. Solzhenitsyn, *The Gulag Archipelago*, vol. 3 (New York, 1978).

execution of Beria and his accomplices, loomed no less large. It was "inevitable," as Khrushchev later recalled, "that people will find out what happened." An anxiety similar to that felt by Tsar Aleksandr II about emancipating the serfs—if this is not done from above, it will be done from below—took shape in the Politburo.[38]

These factors led to the advent of official anti-Stalinism, of which there were two significantly different versions during the Khrushchev years. The first professed a "balanced" view of Stalin's historical role; the second emphasized the criminal dimensions of his rule. Both were adumbrated on that fateful night of February 24–25, 1956; but it was the first that emerged, and prevailed officially until 1961, from Khrushchev's dramatic "secret" speech to a closed session of the Twentieth Party Congress.

Speaking for four hours before some 1,500 hastily reassembled delegates, the country's ruling elite, Khrushchev delivered a stunning blow to the Stalin cult.[39] He assailed Stalin's autocratic rule with vividly detailed accounts of the dictator's personal responsibility for "mass repressions," torture, "monstrous falsifications," and his own glorification. Khrushchev implied that Stalin had arranged the assassination of Sergei Kirov, the Leningrad Party boss whose murder in 1934 had set off the great terror. And he flatly blamed Stalin for a succession of Soviet disasters in World War II. Khrushchev's words, spiked with passages from pleading, agonized letters written by tortured victims in their jail cells, were plain and rarely euphemistic. Nor was his speech really secret. Although never published in the Soviet Union, it was read to thousands of official meetings across the country over the next few weeks. Its general contents became widely known.[40]

Khrushchev's speech was a turning point in the history of the Stalin question. Nonetheless, it rested upon a dual evaluation, or what shortly became known as the "two sides of Comrade Stalin's activity—the positive side, which we support and highly value, and the negative side, which we criticize, condemn, and reject."[41] In particular, Khrushchev's indictment of the dead tyrant was sharply limited in three important ways.

First, it focused on Stalin's "mass terror against Party cadres" and other political elites. This complaint reflected Khrushchev's rise to power as head of the resurgent Communist Party in the 1950s and the still limited nature of his proposed reforms; it maintained silence about the millions of ordinary people who

38. *Khrushchev Remembers*, pp. 342–53.

39. There are several English-language editions of the speech, as translated and released by the U.S. State Department. I have used the one in *The Anti-Stalin Campaign and International Communism*, pp. 1–89. A Russian-language version, designed to look like a Soviet publication but printed in the West, is also in circulation.

40. See Medvedev and Medvedev, *Khrushchev*, p. 70; Leonhard, *The Kremlin since Stalin*, pp. 187–90; and Nekrich, *Otreshis' ot strakha*, p. 140.

41. N. Khrushchev, "For Close Ties between Literature and Art and the Life of the People," *CDSP* 9, no. 35 (October 9, 1957): 6. This approach became standard for a time. See the article on Stalin's birthday in *Pravda*, December 21, 1959.

had perished under Stalin. Second, Khrushchev dated Stalin's criminal misdeeds from 1934. This served to defend Stalin's collectivization campaign of 1929–33, which had brought such agony to the peasantry, as a necessary and admirable act; and, in the same way, it prolonged the ban on discussion of Party oppositions and alternatives to Stalinism before 1929. Finally, Khrushchev avoided the question of widespread criminal responsibility and punishment by defining the abuses narrowly in terms of Stalin and a small "gang" of accomplices, who were already exposed and punished. He insisted, at least publicly, that no surviving Politburo members were guilty.[42] If members of Stalin's leadership were proclaimed to be innocent, the community of victimizers around the country had little to fear.

These limitations, whether of Khrushchev's own doing or forced upon him, were designed to keep the lid on the Stalin question, whose political explosiveness quickly became clear. Reports of Khrushchev's denunciation of "mass repressions" were enough to trigger shock waves across the Soviet empire in Eastern Europe and tumultuous dissension elsewhere in the international Communist movement.[43] (Foreign Communist parties have had a major stake in the Stalin question; their representatives have lobbied the Soviet leadership on both sides of the issue over the years.) There were even outbursts, for and against Stalin, inside the USSR and in the Soviet Communist Party itself.[44]

These events brought a strong reaction in high Soviet circles against Khrushchev's radical revelations. They led to a still more "balanced" evaluation when the first public resolution on the Stalin question, adopted by the Central Committee on June 30, finally appeared on July 2, 1956. Though eclipsed in the early 1960s, this document was resuscitated by Khrushchev's successors more than ten years later.

Reportedly, the long resolution was drafted by the most pro-Stalin members of the Politburo, who had been closest to Stalin and thus had the most to conceal —Vyacheslav Molotov, Lazar Kaganovich, Kliment Voroshilov, and Grigory Malenkov.[45] It condemned the "harmful consequences of the cult of personality," but in terms so euphemistic and self-defensive that Stalin's "many lawless deeds" seemed to add up to little more than "certain serious mistakes," which

---

42. Clearly, the matter gave Khrushchev problems; he touched on it repeatedly. *The Anti-Stalin Campaign*, pp. 31, 39, 59–60, 81–85. Official assurances on this point, presumably in response to pressure, were made informally after the congress. Medvedev, *Let History Judge*, p. 344.

43. See *The Anti-Stalin Campaign*; Leonhard, *The Kremlin since Stalin*, chap. 6; and Paul E. Zinner, ed., *National Communism and Popular Revolt in Eastern Europe* (New York, 1956).

44. See *Politicheskii dnevnik*, vol. 2 (Amsterdam, 1975), p. 67; and David Burg, *Oppozitsionnye nastroeniia molodezhi v gody "ottepeli"* (Munich, 1960). The kinds of dissension inside the Party can be gleaned from a long editorial in *Kommunist*, no. 10, 1956, partially translated in *CDSP* 8, no. 32 (September 19, 1956): 3–4, 31; and an article in *Pravda*, April 5, 1956, partially translated in *CDSP* 8, no. 12 (May 2, 1956): 3–4. A major pro-Stalin demonstration, which was forcibly suppressed, took place in Tbilisi, the capital of Soviet Georgia. See Aleksandr Glezer, "Tbilisi, 1956," *Novoe russkoe slovo*, November 10, 1977; and Faina Baazova, "Tanki protiv detei," *Vremia i my*, no. 30, 1978, pp. 189–204.

45. *The Anti-Stalin Campaign*, pp. 275–306; Medvedev, *Let History Judge*, pp. 344–45.

were "less important against the background of such enormous successes." Latching onto a casual phrase in Khrushchev's speech, the resolution insisted that Stalin's misdeeds had been "committed particularly in the later period of his life," presumably after 1945, thereby obscuring the great terror of the 1930s. Further shock waves of anti-Stalinism, especially uprisings in Poland and Hungary in October and November 1956, reinforced this considerable rehabilitation of Stalin's reputation. Within a year, Khrushchev himself was promoting the "two sides" of Stalin. The "positive" now seemed ascendant.

Outwardly, this remained the Soviet leadership's position on the Stalin question, the extent of official anti-Stalinism, during the next four years.[46] But it was not the whole story. Pressures above and from below, which culminated in the paroxysm of radical anti-Stalinism set off at the Twenty-second Party Congress in 1961, continued to build. In June 1957, with the support of a loyalist Central Committee, Khrushchev defeated a Politburo majority led by Molotov, Kaganovich, and Malenkov, who had tried to oust him as Party chief. Most of the "anti-Party group," as Khrushchev stigmatized his rivals, were expelled from the leadership. In March 1958, Khrushchev consolidated his position as leader by becoming head of state as well.

Behind the scenes, the Stalin question was a major issue in the leadership struggle. Khrushchev and his Politburo opponents clashed directly over his proposal to continue the posthumous rehabilitation of Stalin's prominent victims, in this case the military high command massacred in the late 1930s. When Molotov, Kaganovich, and Voroshilov gave fainthearted consent, Khrushchev, according to his later account, exclaimed, "But it was you who executed these people. . . . When were you acting according to your conscience, then or now?" Khrushchev's version was that of the victor, but there is no reason to doubt his charge that his rivals "were afraid of further exposures of their illegal actions during the period of the personality cult, they were afraid they would have to answer to the Party. It is known, after all, that all of the abuses of that time were committed not only with their support but with their active participation."[47]

The outcome of this explosive issue in 1957 was a compromise. Molotov, Kaganovich, and Malenkov were ousted from the leadership as "conservatives and dogmatists," while the matter of their criminal responsibility, with its potential ramifications for so many other people, was set aside. But by putting the matter on the agenda, Khrushchev had gone beyond even his anti-Stalin speech of 1956.

The "conservative" platform of his defeated opponents was no less central

46. See, for example, the entry on Stalin in *Bol'shaia sovetskaia entsiklopediia*, vol. 40 (Moscow, 1958), pp. 419–24; and the commemoration of his birthdate in *Pravda*, December 21, 1959.

47. *XXII s"ezd kommunisticheskoi partii sovetskogo soiuza, 17–31 oktiabria 1961 goda: stenograficheskii otchet*, 3 vols. (Moscow, 1962), II, 586, 589. Khrushchev's account is generally confirmed by other documents. See Robert Conquest, *Power and Policy in the USSR* (New York, 1961), pp. 321–24.

to the Stalin question. Khrushchev's reformism spread to many areas of policy in the middle and late 1950s, arousing conservative opposition throughout the Party and state apparatuses. Stalin's legacy in economic life was particularly at stake. Khrushchev had encouraged Soviet reformers to develop increasingly radical criticisms of the inefficient hypercentralized system of planning and management. By 1960–61, their proposals, which echoed long-forbidden ideas of the 1920s associated with the disgraced Party opposition led by Nikolai Bukharin, called for measured decentralization, a larger role for the market, and more attention to consumer goods and the plight of collective farmers.[48] To make these ideas into policy required a more far-reaching renunciation of the Stalinist experience. But such ideas threatened a whole class of Soviet officials whose authority and privilege were based on the existing Stalinist system. Both structural reform and de-Stalinization elicited only their fear and hostility.

Meanwhile, the past continued to generate anti-Stalinist heat outside the corridors of power. Millions of camp inmates freed since 1956 were now visible and sometimes clamorous reminders of the holocaust. Exonerations of the dead proceeded slowly, erratically, but persistently, while relatives and various groups demanded much more.[49] Khrushchev's 1956 speech had awakened a segment of the intelligentsia to "duty, honor, and conscience." A deeper cultural "thaw" in 1956–57 included guarded public discussion of past Stalinist abuses and existing ones.[50]

The liberal interlude was short-lived, but anti-Stalinist themes continued to appear mutedly in Soviet belles lettres between 1957 and 1961. Most significantly, the "camp theme," as it later became known, forced its way tentatively but doggedly into Soviet fiction and poetry in the character of the vanished and the returnee. Simultaneously, Stalin's diminished reputation and posthumous rehabilitations were populating nonfictional publications with resurrected generations of victims, or at least representative figures. Names unmentioned for decades, their fates still barely explained, crept slowly back into textbooks, monographs, encyclopedias, journals, and newspapers.[51]

48. See Lewin, *Political Undercurrents in Soviet Economic Debates;* and Linden, *Khrushchev and the Soviet Leadership,* chaps. 3–6.

49. For one such case, see Stephen F. Cohen, "Why Bukharin's Ghost Still Haunts Moscow," *New York Times Magazine,* December 10, 1978, pp. 146–50, 153–58.

50. For the "thaw," see Hugh McLean and Walter N. Vickery, eds., *The Year of Protest, 1956: An Anthology of Soviet Literary Materials* (New York, 1961); and Vladimir Zhabinsky, *Prosvety: zametki o sovetskoi literature 1956–1957* (Munich, 1958). The quotation is from Tvardovsky, *Poemy,* p. 415.

51. For examples of the camp and returnee theme in belles lettres at this time, see Aleksandr Korneichuk, *P'esy* (Moscow, 1961), pp. 537–612; Konstantin Simonov, *Zhivye i mertvye* (Moscow, 1959); V. Kaverin, *Otkrytaia kniga,* pt. 3 (Moscow, 1956); V. Panova, *Sentimental'nyi roman* (1958), in her *Izbrannoe* (Moscow, 1972), pp. 181–334; Nina Ivanter, "Snova avgust," *Novyi mir,* August and September 1959; Tvardovsky, "Za dal'iu—dal'," in his *Poemy,* pp. 363–494. For a discussion, see Vera Aleksandrova, "Vernuvshiesia," *Sotsialisticheskii vestnik,* October 1959, pp. 189–91. The rehabilitation process is examined carefully in Shapiro, "Rehabilitation Policy and Political Conflict in the Soviet Union," chap. 3.

All of these ghosts, and with them the unresolved Stalinist past, were loose
in the country by 1960–61. Silence at the top was being broken by the
"muffled rumble of subterranean strata."[52] In 1956, the writer Konstantin
Paustovsky had decried a class of Stalinist officials whose "weapons are betrayal,
calumny, moral assassination, and just plain assassination." His speech could
not be published.[53] Four years later, Aleksandr Tvardovsky was able to publish
a more constrained but powerfully brooding, guilt-ridden poem on the past,
"This Is the Way It Was," in the Communist Party newspaper. The long
poem anticipated the new anti-Stalinism unleashed a year and a half later. It
lamented those "evil times," when people "passed one by one into the
shadow." It asked, "Who is to blame?" Defending the "mature memory we
cannot escape," Tvardovsky called for an end to silence: "And the truth of
things is standing vigil; there is no way around it. Everything supports it, even
while silence and lies prevail."[54]

The pressure gathering below between 1956 and 1961 should not be interpreted out of context. Profound and loud truth telling, like the larger process of
reform, could be initiated only from above. Khrushchev's role in this drama was
always complex. Already in his late sixties, he was a man of the Stalinist past,
formed by its ethos, proud of its accomplishments, and implicated in its crimes,
though considerably less so than many others.

As a repentant Stalinist after 1953, Khrushchev typified many Soviet officials
and ordinary citizens. He seemed always divided on the Stalin question, even in
the memoirs he dictated privately after his fall, hating and admiring Stalin almost
in the same breath, rounding on radical anti-Stalinists whom he had previously
encouraged. His ambiguity was partly the result of constraints on his power and
his fear of the explosiveness of the Stalin question: "We were scared—really
scared," he said later. "We were afraid the thaw might unleash a flood, which
we wouldn't be able to control and which could drown us." But it derived
also from a division inside Khrushchev. "There's a Stalinist in each of you,
there's even some Stalinist in me," he reportedly told his opponents on one
occasion.[55]

Like that of other politicians who have tried to enter history by rising above
their own pasts, Khrushchev's resolve "to root out this evil" ultimately grew and
gained the upper hand. "Some people are waiting for me to croak in order to
resuscitate Stalin and his methods," he said in 1962. "This is why, before I die,
I want to destroy Stalin and destroy those people, so as to make it impossible to

52. The expression is Solzhenitsyn's. *The Oak and the Calf*, p. 16.
53. It is translated in McLean and Vickery, eds., *The Year of Protest*, pp. 155–59.
54. "Tak eto bylo," *Pravda*, April 29 and May 1, 1960.
55. For the first remark, see *Khrushchev Remembers: The Last Testament* (Boston, 1974), p.
79; the second is quoted in Abraham Rothberg, *The Heirs of Stalin: Dissidence and the Soviet Regime,
1953–1970* (Ithaca, 1972), p. 57. For Khrushchev's attack on people he had encouraged, see Priscilla
Johnson and Leopold Labedz, eds., *Khrushchev and the Arts: The Politics of Soviet Culture, 1962–
1964* (Cambridge, Mass., 1965).

put the clock back."[56] This combination of motives—an attempt to break conservative opposition (which had formed again even in the Politburo), responsiveness to anti-Stalinist sentiment below, and a deep moral purpose—led Khrushchev and his supporters to unveil a second and more radical version of official anti-Stalinism at the Twenty-second Party Congress in October 1961.

The assault on the Stalin cult at that congress differed from Khrushchev's speech at the Twentieth Congress in essential ways. Above all, it was public. For almost two weeks during the anniversary month of the October Revolution, daily newspapers and broadcasts riveted public attention on "monstrous crimes" and demands for "historical justice." Speaker after speaker related lurid details of mass arrests, torture, and murder that had been carried out in every region of the country. The public aspect was enhanced by impassioned congressional resolutions that ordered Stalin's body removed from the Lenin Mausoleum on Red Square—an action called for at lower Party levels as early as 1956—and stripped his name from thousands of towns, buildings, and monuments across the country.[57]

The nature of the new anti-Stalinism was also different. It went beyond Khrushchev's 1956 speech, not to mention the watered-down resolution of June 30, 1956, and opened the way to public criticism, over the next few years, of long-forbidden or sacrosanct historical events. The Party Congress indictment still emphasized Stalin's terror against the Party, but it was extended by several speakers to a more general and truthful "evil caused to our Party, the country, and the Soviet people." Indeed, the Mausoleum resolution spoke simply of "mass repressions against honest Soviet people," which anticipated more fulsome revelations about Stalin's concentration camps that began to appear the next year.[58] Generally, the criminal indictment of Stalin's rule was so harsh and sweeping that it obscured his "positive side" altogether. Published criticism of his collectivization campaign, for example, was underway within a few months.

Most dramatically, Khrushchev and his allies at the congress made criminal accusations against living political figures. They maintained flatly that Molotov, Kaganovich, Malenkov, and Voroshilov were "guilty of illegal mass repressions against many Party, Soviet, military, and Young Communist League officials and bear direct personal responsibility for their physical destruction." Voroshilov was forgiven. But Khrushchev and other speakers demanded that Molotov, Kaganovich, and Malenkov be expelled from the Party, implying they might be put on trial for past crimes. The specter of such trials, inflated by references to "numer-

56. The first quote is from Rothberg, *The Heirs of Stalin*, p. 57; the second is from Tatu, *Power in the Kremlin*, p. 306, n. 2. For a similar statement of Khrushchev's purpose, see the editorial on the congress in *Pravda*, November 21, 1961. For his motives, see also Roy A. Medvedev, "The Stalin Question," in Cohen, Rabinowitch, and Sharlet, eds., *The Soviet Union since Stalin*, pp. 35–44.

57. The resolution on the Mausoleum was announced on October 31, and carried out immediately. *Pravda*, October 31 and November 1, 1961. For earlier demands, see *XXII s"ezd*, III, 121.

58. *XXII s"ezd*, III, 122, 362.

ous documents in our possession" and Khrushchev's call for "a thorough and comprehensive study of all such cases rising out of the abuse of power," sent tremors of fear through the thousands, or millions, who bore "direct personal responsibility."[59]

The Twenty-second Congress inaugurated a remarkable, though short-lived, period in Soviet politics, characterized by an openly acrimonious struggle between friends and foes of de-Stalinization. Khrushchev seems to have sprung his radicalized anti-Stalinism on his opponents at the last moment. Not surprisingly, it met strong resistance throughout Soviet officialdom, which began at the congress itself. Most speakers, including Politburo members, conspicuously refused to go as far as Khrushchev had, particularly on the matter of criminal responsibility. Open and covert opposition to de-Stalinization, symbolized by the unbuilt monument Khrushchev proposed in memory of the terror's victims, continued until his overthrow three years later.[60]

But anti-Stalinists, especially among the intelligentsia, were no less determined. They hoped that the "thaw" of the 1950s would now lead to a real "spring."[61] Emboldened by Khrushchev's initiatives, and despite censorship, powerful adversaries, occasional reprisals, and Khrushchev's wavering support, they provoked a public controversy over the Stalinist past and its legacy more critical and far-reaching than any discussion in the Soviet Union since the 1920s. √ Virtually every criticism of Stalinism that appeared later in samizdat was anticipated in official, censored publications of the early 1960s—in scholarly studies, fiction, and memoirs. Some of this radical anti-Stalinism was necessarily oblique or was expressed on transparently surrogate topics;[62] but much of it was explicit. The result was an impressive body of revelations about the three main episodes of Stalin's rule: collectivization, the great terror, and World War II.

Stalin's reputation as the great Generalissimo of 1941–45, as he titled himself and which became the linchpin of his cult, was the most thoroughly assaulted.

59. Ibid., II, 402, 584. For an analysis of this issue at the congress, see Tatu, *Power in the Kremlin*, pp. 151–57.

60. For Khrushchev's proposal, see *XXII s"ezd*, II, 587. For high-level and rank-and-file opposition at the time of the congress, see Nekrich, *Otreshis' ot strakha*, p. 171; and Alexander Werth, *Russia under Khrushchev* (New York, 1962), p. 340. Anti-Stalinists insisted repeatedly that de-Stalinization was the basic conflict in Soviet political life. See, for example, Maryamov, "Snariazhenie v pokhode"; A. Bovin, "Istina protiv dogmy," *Novyi mir*, no. 10, 1963, pp. 174–90; V. Lakshin, "Ivan Denisovich, ego druz'ia i nedrugi," *Novyi mir*, no. 1, 1964, pp. 223–45; and Karyakin, "Epizod iz sovremennoi bor'by idei." Yevtushenko's poem, "The Heirs of Stalin," published in *Pravda*, October 21, 1962, particularly dramatized the struggle; it is translated in George Reavey, *The Poetry of Yevgeny Yevtushenko, 1953 to 1965* (New York, 1965), pp. 161–65.

61. Yevgeny Yevtushenko, "City in the Morning," *CDSP* 14, no. 29 (August 15, 1962): 17.

62. Surrogate topics included Ivan the Terrible, fascism, Maoism, Franco's Spain, and bureaucratic systems in the West. See, for example, Yefim Dorosh, "Kniga o groznom tsare," *Novyi mir*, no. 4, 1964, pp. 260–63; Yevgeny Gnedin, "Mekhanizm fashistskoi diktatury," *Novyi mir*, no. 8, 1968, pp. 272–75; Yevgeny Gnedin, " "Biurokratiia dvadtsatogo veka," *Novyi mir*, no. 3, 1966, pp. 189–201; Fyodor Burlatsky, *Maoizm ili marksizm?* (Moscow, 1967); and Fyodor Burlatsky, *Ispaniia: korrida i kaudil'o* (Moscow, 1967).

Successors to the military corps he had slaughtered took belated revenge. Official histories, monographs, memoirs, and novels portrayed Stalin as a leader who had decapitated the armed forces on the eve of war, who had ignored repeated warnings of the German invasion and thus left the country undefended in June 1941, who had deserted his post in panic during the first days of combat, and whose capricious strategy later caused major military disasters. The vaunted Generalissimo became a criminally incompetent tyrant who bore personal responsibility for millions of casualties.[63] For millions of veterans who had fought with Stalin's name on their lips, this part of the anti-Stalin campaign was probably the most resented.[64] It was the first to be undone after Khrushchev's fall.

The Stalinist terror and concentration-camp system inspired an even more dramatic body of historical exposé. The most famous example is Solzhenitsyn's novella *One Day in the Life of Ivan Denisovich*, published in 1962, which set off a torrent of articles about the camps. But there were many novels, short stories, biographies, memoirs, films, and plays about the terror, from which emerged a fairly unvarnished picture of the twenty-year holocaust.[65] When the camp theme finally burst into the official press, an elated Tvardovsky, the great anti-Stalinist editor, exclaimed, "The bird is free! . . . The bird is free! . . . They can't very well hold it back now! It's almost impossible now!"[66] He assumed that these revelations would destroy at last the legend of the camps as a small, isolated aspect of the Stalin era. Or as Tvardovsky said of those years in his own poem "By Right of Memory," which was to be denied publication in the Soviet Union,

> And fate made everybody equal
> Outside the limits of the law,
> Son of a kulak or Red commander,
> Son of a priest or commissar.
>
> Here classes all were equalized,
> All men were brothers, camp mates all,
> Branded as traitors every one.[67]

63. See, for example, A. M. Nekrich, *1941 22 iiunia* (Moscow, 1965); Konstantin Simonov, *Soldatami ne rozhdaiutsia* (Moscow, 1964); and Grigory Baklanov, *Iiul' 41 goda* (Moscow, 1965). For an extensive bibliography and analysis, see Seweryn Bialer, ed., *Stalin and His Generals: Soviet Military Memoirs of World War II* (New York, 1969).

64. Werth, *Russia under Khrushchev,* p. 340. The renaming of the great battle site Stalingrad was particularly resented.

65. A few examples: Viktor Nekrasov, "Kira Georgievna," *Novyi mir,* no. 6, 1961, pp. 70–126; Yuri Bondaryev, "Tishina," *Novyi mir,* March through May 1962; Dyakov, *Povest' o perezhitom;* A. V. Gorbatov, "Gody i voiny," *Novyi mir,* March through May 1964; Yuri Dombrovsky, "Khranitel' drevnostei," *Novyi mir,* July and August 1964; Gregory Shelest, "Kolymskie zapiski," *Znamia,* no. 9, 1964, pp. 162–80; A. Vasilyev, "Voprosov bol'she net," *Moskva,* no. 6, 1964, pp. 4–108; Ilya Ehrenburg, *Memoirs: 1921–1941* (Cleveland, 1964) and *Post-War Years: 1945–1954* (Cleveland, 1967). See also the report in Mihajlo Mihajlov, *Moscow Summer* (New York, 1965), pp. 66–85. Innumerable biographies of victims often were especially detailed and candid.

66. Quoted in Solzhenitsyn, *The Oak and the Calf,* p. 46.

67. See below, pp. 66–67.

Such exposés could not be confined to the past. The magnitude of the unfolding picture shattered the corollary fiction that only Stalin and a few accomplices had been guilty. Publicizing the camps meant publicizing the conduct of millions. Face-to-face confrontations between victims and their former tormentors were being portrayed in literature and on the stage.[68] And this raised the question of the menace of present-day Stalinists, "The Heirs of Stalin," as Yevtushenko entitled his stunning poem of 1962—those people who "yearn for the good old days" and "hate this era of emptied prison camps."[69]

If the camp theme was traumatic, the subject of the forcible collectivization of 125 million peasants in 1929–1933 was potentially even more ramifying. Every thoughtful citizen knew that collectivization had been a special national tragedy; it had destroyed not only Soviet agriculture but the traditional life and culture of peasant Russia. "The Stalin brand of collectivization brought us nothing but misery and brutality," as Khrushchev privately admitted.[70] But the legitimacy of the existing collective farm system, a still unworkable and largely unreformed foundation of the whole economic system, rested entirely on the Stalinist legend of collectivization as a spontaneous, voluntary, and benevolent process of the peasants themselves.

By the mid-1960s, Soviet scholars (as well as novelists of village life) had chipped away at this legend by itemizing Stalin's preemptory, coercive measures in the winter of 1929–30, which had unleashed the assault on the countryside, and by revealing suggestions of the mass violence, deportations, and famine that followed. Censorship still required that they characterize these events as partial "excesses." But their cumulative research grew piece by piece into a picture of collectivization as one prolonged, disastrous "excess."[71]

The implications of such a reinterpretation struck at the whole concept of the Stalinist 1930s as a period of "building socialism." At the very least, such historical revelations cried out for radical agricultural reform. At worst, they meant that the entire history of the Stalin era, all the accomplishments of the ruling Party since 1929, had been unworthy, that the martyred Bukharinist opposition of 1928–29 had been right, or even, as one Soviet historian protested, that the October Revolution had been in vain.[72] In any case, such a reinterpretation threatened to open the floodgates of change. Accordingly, one of the first

68. See, for example, S. Aleshin, "Palata," *Teatr*, no. 11, 1962, p. 29; and "Donoschiki na ushcherbe," *Sotsialisticheskii vestnik*, November–December, 1962, p. 163. And for actual cases, N. N., "Donoschiki i predateli sredi sovetskikh pisatelei i uchenykh," ibid., May–June, 1963, pp. 74–76.

69. Reavey, *The Poetry of Yevgeny Yevtushenko*, p. 165.

70. *Khrushchev Remembers* p. 74. This, too, became a major theme in Soviet literature in the 1960s.

71. Most of this research was scattered through scholarly journals, but a representative selection was published in V. P. Danilov, ed., *Ocherki istorii kollektivizatsii sel'skogo khoziaistva v soiuznykh respublikakh* (Moscow, 1963). For a bibliography and a picture of what happened, see Moshe Lewin, *Russian Peasants and Soviet Power: A Study of Collectivization* (New York, 1975).

72. The historian Genkina, as quoted in a private transcript of a meeting of historians at the Institute of History on June 17, 1964.

books banned after Khrushchev's fall was a volume in press that promised even more revelations about what had happened in the countryside in 1929–33.[73]

The sweeping reaction that surged up against this kind of de-Stalinization, though diverse, is not hard to explain. Viewed from higher reaches of power, anti-Stalinism seemed to be out of control. It was challenging the official axiom that Stalinism had been only "an alien growth" and not the essence of the Soviet system for twenty years. By arguing that the "essence of the cult of personality is blind admiration for authority," anti-Stalinists were threatening the existing system of controls.[74]

Alarmed that de-Stalinization was "engendering a negative attitude toward all authority," professional managers of the political system—typified by the political administration of the armed forces, cultural bureaucrats, Komsomol (Young Communist League) leaders, and Party ideologists—launched a counter-campaign, based on a "heroic-patriotic theme," for deference to authority.[75] They were supported by people implicated in past crimes or who were neo-Stalinists for other reasons. They threatened Khrushchev himself with the bludgeon of criminal responsibility, traduced "dismal compilers of memoirs, who . . . unearth long-decayed literary corpses," and eulogized the "heroic" Stalinist 1930s.[76]

It would be wrong, however, to see only power, guilt, and malice in the broad reaction against de-Stalinization. It came also from below, from decent people who were not evil neo-Stalinists but who naturally composed the Soviet conservative majority. For them, ending the terror and making limited restitutions was one thing; desecration of the past and radical reforms in the Soviet order, for which they had sacrificed so much, was quite another. It was too much to ask them "to spit on the history of our country," to see their own life history as "a chain of crimes and mistakes," to allow their children to see them as a generation of " 'fathers' who were arrested and 'fathers' who did the arresting."[77] A middle-

73. Medvedev, *Let History Judge*, p. 101, n. 61.

74. The "alien growth" theory was axiomatic even in radical official critiques such as the one cited here. Saushkin, *O kul'te lichnosti i avtoritete*, pp. 19, 28. An example of deepening criticism of existing authority is Tvardovsky's "Terkin in the Other World," *CDSP* 15, no. 34 (September 18, 1963): 20–30.

75. *Preduprezhdenie pravonarushenii sredi nesovershennoletnikh* (Minsk, 1969), p. 12; and "Glorify the Heroic," *CDSP* 16, no. 5 (February 26, 1964): 3–7.

76. Johnson and Labedz, eds., *Khrushchev and the Arts*, pp. 22–26; and V. A. Kochetov, "Speech," *CDSP* 14, no. 7 (March 14, 1962): 21. For the neo-Stalinist spirit at this time, see Vsevolod Kochetov, *Sekretar' obkoma*, reprinted in his *Sobranie sochinenii*, vol. 4 (Moscow, 1975); V. A. Chalmayev, *Geroicheskoe v sovetskoi literature* (Moscow, 1964); and Ivan Shevtsov, *Tlia* (Moscow, 1964).

77. For these conservative catchphrases, see Ye. Popova and Yuri Sharapov, "After the Big Council," *CDSP* 16, no. 9 (March 25, 1964): 35; "Writers about Books," ibid., 15, no. 4 (February 20, 1963): 30; and Sergei Narovchatov, "Civic Spirit in Our Poetry," ibid. 15, no. 31 (August 25, 1965): 17. The expression "chain of crimes and mistakes" quickly became a favorite neo-Stalinist epithet against anti-Stalinist historians and memoirists. See, for example, "Rech' tov. D. G. Sturua," *Zaria vostoka*, March 10, 1966. For a heartfelt statement of conservative attitudes toward "our years," see Yevgeny Dolmatovsky, "Nashi gody," *Oktiabr'*, no. 11, 1962, pp. 3–12.

aged Soviet citizen in 1964 had grown to maturity during the hard Stalin years; and hard lives breed lacquered memories and conservative political attitudes.

It is impossible to document the role of the Stalin question in the Central Committee meeting that overthrew Khrushchev in October 1964. Official explanations at the time of his ouster did not hold de-Stalinization against him.[78] The main charges that Khrushchev himself had grown autocratic and capricious, and that his bolder reforms were hastily conceived, were substantially true. Nevertheless, Khrushchev was brought down by a conservative swing in official and popular attitudes against his ten-year reformation, of which de-Stalinization had been a substantial part. In this sense, Khrushchev fell victim to the Stalin question, as the new leadership's approach to the Stalinist past soon made clear.

Stalin Rehabilitated

For a decade after Stalin's death, popular and official anti-Stalinism seemed to be an irresistible force in Soviet politics. The powerful resurgence of pro-Stalinist sentiments on both levels since 1964 has seemed no less inexorable. The turnabout is reflected in the career of Aleksandr Solzhenitsyn. In 1964, he was nominated for a Lenin Prize, the Soviet Union's highest literary honor, for his prison camp story *Ivan Denisovich;* ten years later, he was arrested and deported from the country.

Khrushchev's downfall at first encouraged both anti-Stalinists and neo-Stalinists in official circles. The former hoped that the new Brezhnev-Kosygin government would chart a more orderly course of reform and de-Stalinization, while neo-Stalinists sought a mandate to stamp out the "poison of Khrushchevism."[79] Their struggle raged openly and covertly in 1965–66. New anti-Stalinist publications appeared, rehabilitations of Stalin's victims continued, and in October 1965 the leadership legislated a major (and ill-fated) program of economic reform.[80] At the same time, however, influential figures, including Brezhnev himself, began to issue authoritative statements refurbishing Stalin's reputation as a wartime leader, eulogizing the 1930s while obscuring the terror, and suggesting that Khrushchev's revelations had "calumniated" the Soviet Union. Behind the scenes, an assertive pro-Stalin lobby, proud to call itself "Stalinist," took the

78. See Medvedev and Medvedev, *Khrushchev,* pp. 174–76; and the speeches of Suslov and Mikoyan in *Politicheskii dnevnik,* no. 1 (Moscow: Samizdat, October 1964); and *Politicheskii dnevnik,* I, 5–8.

79. A Soviet official in Prague, quoted in *Le Monde* (English-language edition), January 13, 1971.

80. Anti-Stalinist publications in different areas included Nekrich, *1941 22 iiunia;* Dyakov, *Povest' o perezhitom;* Trifonov, *Otblesk kostra;* N. I. Nemakov, *Kommunisticheskaia partiia—organizator massovogo kholkhoznogo dvizheniia (1929–1932 gg.)* (Moscow, 1966); and A. Milchakov, *Pervoe desiatiletie: zapiski veterana Komsomola,* 2nd ed. (Moscow, 1965). For rehabilitations, see Jane P. Shapiro, "Rehabilitation Policy under the Post-Khrushchev Leadership," *Soviet Studies* 20, no. 4 (April 1969): 490–98.

offensive in 1965 for the first time in several years, apparently with Brezhnev's support. Anti-Stalinists were demoted, censorship was tightened, new ideological strictures were drafted, already processed rehabilitations were challenged, and subscriptions to anti-Stalinist journals were prohibited in the armed forces.[81]

The decisive battle in officialdom was over by early 1966. Within eighteen months of Khrushchev's overthrow, official de-Stalinization was at an end, a pronounced reverse pattern had developed, and anti-Stalinism was becoming the rallying cry of a small dissident movement. Two events dramatized the outcome. In February 1966, two prominent writers, Andrei Sinyavsky and Yuli Daniel, were tried and sentenced to labor camps for publishing their "slanderous" (anti-Stalinist) writings abroad. The public trial, with its self-conscious evocation of the purge trials of the 1930s, was a neo-Stalinist blast against critical-minded members of the intelligentsia. Meanwhile, a campaign began against anti-Stalinist historians. The first victim was a Party historian in good standing, Aleksandr Nekrich. He was traduced and later expelled from the Party for little more than restating the anti-Stalinist historiography, developed during the Khrushchev years, of the German invasion of 1941.[82]

These events, and the fear that Stalin would be officially rehabilitated at the Twenty-third Party Congress in March 1966, gave birth to the present-day dissident movement and samizdat literature as a widespread phenomenon. A flood of petitions protesting the Sinyavsky-Daniel trial and neo-Stalinism generally circulated among the intelligentsia; they gathered hundreds and then thousands of signatures, including the names of prominent representatives of official anti-Stalinism under Khrushchev. A pattern developed that has continued. The growing conservative and neo-Stalinist overtones of the Brezhnev regime drove anti-Stalinists from official to dissident ranks and gave the movement many of its best-known spokesmen, such as Andrei Sakharov, Lydia Chukovskaya, Roy and Zhores Medvedev, Solzhenitsyn, Pyotr Yakir, and Lev Kopelev. These people later went separate political ways, but the fallen banner of anti-Stalinism first turned them into dissidents.[83] And this development transformed the Stalin question from a conflict inside the Establishment into a struggle between the Soviet government and open dissidents.

Some dissidents believed that their protests prevented a full rehabilitation of

81. See below, Chapter 3; and *Politicheskii dnevnik* for 1965–1966. The most detailed account of these covert events is Roy Medvedev, "Budet li otmechat'sia v SSSR 100-letie so dnia rozhdeniia Stalina?," *Dvadtsatyi vek,* no. 7 (Moscow: Samizdat, January–March 1976); a shortened version appears in Cohen, Rabinowitch, and Sharlet, eds., *The Soviet Union since Stalin,* pp. 32–49. For pro-Stalinist statements in the press, see S. Trapeznikov in *Pravda,* October 8, 1965; Ye. Zhukov, V. Trukhanovsky, and V. Shunkov in *Pravda,* January 30, 1966; Sturua cited above, note 77; articles on collectivization in *Sel'skaia zhizn',* December 29, 1965, and February 25, 1966; and S. S. Smirnov, "Smert' komsomolki," *Komsomol'skaia pravda,* November 15, 16, 18, and 19, 1966.

82. See Hayward, ed., *On Trial;* and the appendices in A. M. Nekrich, *June 22, 1941* (Columbia, S.C., 1968).

83. In addition to the documents in this book and *Political Diary* for 1965–71, see Brumberg, ed., *In Quest of Justice.* Rothberg, *The Heirs of Stalin,* is a useful history.

Stalin at the Twenty-third Congress, where his name was hardly mentioned. If so, it was a small victory amid a rout. The policies of the Brezhnev government grew steadily into a wide-ranging conservative reaction to Khrushchev's reforms. The defense of the status quo required a usable Stalinist past. Increasingly, only the mountain of accomplishments was remembered in rewritten history books and in the press.

By the end of the 1960s, Stalin had been restored as an admirable leader. Serious criticism of his wartime leadership and of collectivization was banned; rehabilitations were ended and some even undone; and intimations that there ever had been a great terror grew scant. Indeed, people who criticized the Stalinist past (as Khrushchev had done at Party congresses) could now be prosecuted for having "slandered the Soviet social and state system."[84] Dozens of honored anti-Stalinist writers and historians were persecuted or simply unable to publish. Arrests of dissidents grew apace.

If anti-Stalinist reformers in the Establishment still had any hope, it was crushed along with the Prague Spring in August 1968, which had epitomized the anti-Stalinist cause for Soviet anti-Stalinists and neo-Stalinists alike. The language used to justify the Soviet invasion of Czechoslovakia evoked the terroristic ideology of the Stalin years. It soon crept back into domestic publications as well, along with the charge that de-Stalinization was nothing but "an anti-Communist slogan" invented by enemies of the Soviet Union.[85]

Fresh from this triumph, neo-Stalinist officials began a campaign for the full rehabilitation of Stalin's reputation in connection with the ninetieth anniversary of his birth in December 1969. Continuing a trend that had developed since 1967, novels appeared regularly throughout the year, obviously encouraged from above.[86] Plans for a full-scale rehabilitation—including memorial meetings and articles, collections of Stalin's writings, and mass-produced portraits and busts—apparently gained the leadership's approval sometime in mid-1969. Once again, dissidents mounted a protest campaign, as did, privately, a number of foreign Communist leaders.[87] And once again, their victory was small.

---

84. Medvedev, *On Socialist Democracy*, p. 153. New guidelines for history writing were set out in *Kommunist*, no. 4, 1968, pp. 107–14; no. 2, 1969, pp. 119–28; and no. 3, 1969, pp. 67–82. Anti-Stalinists noted despairingly the differences between official histories published under and after Khrushchev. N. Muratov, "Fal'sifikatsiia istorii prodolzhaetsia," *Dvadtsatyi vek*, no. 7 (Moscow: Samizdat, January–March 1976).

85. See, for example, F. M. Vaganov, *Pravyi uklon v VKP(b) i ego razgrom (1928–1930 gg.)*, 2nd ed. (Moscow, 1977); V. V. Midtsev, *Revizionizm na sluzhbe antikommunizma* (Moscow, 1975), pp. 10–11; and below, note 95.

86. See above, note 84. Also, for example, Vsevolod Kochetov's novel *Chego zhe ty khochesh'?* in *Oktiabr'*, September through November 1969; and Aleksandr Chakovsky's *Blokada*, vol. 1 (Moscow, 1969). For the pro-Stalin trend in belles lettres earlier, see Vitaly Zakrutkin, "Sotvorenie mira," *Oktiabr'*, June and July 1967; and M. Sinelnikov, "Otvetstvennost' pered vremenem," *Literaturnaia gazeta*, March 20, 1968.

87. Medvedev, "The Stalin Question," pp. 46–48; and Reddaway, ed., *Uncensored Russia*, pp. 423–24.

Plans for a grand rehabilitation were aborted at the last moment, but people who wanted Stalin back on his pedestal gained far more than they lost. The memorial article that finally appeared in *Pravda* on December 21 was carefully balanced. It credited Stalin's "great contribution" as an "outstanding theoretician and organizer" and leader of the Party and the state; it also condemned his "mistakes," which had led to "instances" of "baseless repressions."[88] But this still marked the first official commemoration of Stalin's birthdate in ten years.

The real meaning of the "balanced" appraisal was soon revealed: a flattering marble bust was placed on Stalin's gravesite just behind the Lenin Mausoleum. The bust did not signify unequivocal rehabilitation or a rebirth of the Stalin cult. But it was rehabilitation nonetheless, largely exonerating Stalin of Khrushchev's criminal indictment. Governments do not erect monuments, even small ones, to people they consider to be criminals.[89] Lest any doubt remained, the Brezhnev leadership also satisfied a long-standing neo-Stalinist demand. It ousted the editorial board of *Novy mir* headed by Tvardovsky, thereby crushing the last bastion of official anti-Stalinism in the Soviet Union.[90]

Stalinist sentiment in Soviet officialdom has grown steadily more fulsome through the 1970s and into the 1980s. With few exceptions, critical analysis of the Stalinist experience has been banished from the official press to small circles of samizdat writers and readers.[91] References to Stalin's "negative" side, to "harm" caused by his personal "mistakes," appeared in two prominent articles officially commemorating the one hundredth anniversary of his birth in December 1979.[92] In the broader context, they seemed to be little more than

88. "K 90-letiiu so dnia rozhdeniia I. V. Stalina," *Pravda*, December 21, 1969. On the other hand, the official 1969 desk calendar commemorated Stalin's birth date with a biographical paragraph that made no mention of repressions.

89. The bust was reported and pictured in the *New York Times*, June 26, 1970. Voroshilov's state funeral earlier in December 1969, which was highly publicized, provided another sign that criminal charges against the old Stalinist leadership had been dropped. Molotov, in obscurity for years, appeared in the honor guard. Ibid., December 6, 1969; and *Washington Post*, December 7, 1969.

90. For the significance of this event, see Vladimir Lakshin, *Solzhenitsyn, Tvardovsky, and Novy mir* (Cambridge, Mass., 1980).

91. The most important *samizdat* writings on the Stalinist past include Medvedev, *Let History Judge;* Solzhenitsyn, *The Gulag Archipelago;* Eugenia S. Ginzburg, *Into the Whirlwind* and *Within the Whirlwind* (New York, 1967 amd 1981); Lydia Chukovskaya, *The Deserted House* (New York, 1967) and *Going Under* (New York, 1972); Antonov-Ovseyenko, *The Time of Stalin;* Zhores A. Medvedev, *The Rise and Fall of T. D. Lysenko* (New York, 1969); Varlam Shalamov, *Kolyma Tales* and *Graphite*(New York, 1980 and 1981); Georgi Vladimov, *Faithful Ruslan* (New York, 1979); Aleksandr Bek, *Novoe naznachenie* (Frankfurt, 1971); Lev Kopelev, *Khranit' vechno* (Ann Arbor, 1975) and *The Education of a True Believer;* Yevgeny Gnedin, *Katastrofa i vtoroe rozhdenie* (Amsterdam, 1977); Nadezhda Mandelstam, *Hope Against Hope* and *Hope Abandoned* (New York, 1974); Aleksandr M. Nekrich, *The Punished Peoples* (New York, 1978); Vasily Grossman, *Forever Flowing* (New York, 1972); A. Zimin, *Sotsializm i neostalinizm* (New York, 1981); Mikhail Baitalsky, *Eto nasha shkola: vospominaniia* (Moscow: Samizdat, 1970); Suren Gazaryan, *Eto ne dolzhno povtorit'sia* (Moscow: Samizdat, 1961); and the samizdat periodicals *Political Diary, Pamiat', Dvadtsatyi vek,* and *Poiski.*

92. "K 100-letiiu so dnia rozhdeniia I. V. Stalina," *Pravda*, December 21, 1979; "Krupnyi vopros istoricheskogo materializma," *Kommunist*, no. 18, 1979, pp. 25–46. Both articles complained

carping asides. In a welter of official mass-circulation publications, Stalin's personal reputation has soared. He is no longer the subject of religious worship, but he is, once again, the great national leader and benefactor who guided the country's fortunes for twenty years. His "devotion to the working class and the selfless struggle for socialism" is unquestioned.[93] Above all, the entire Stalinist era, now the historical centerpiece of the conservative Soviet leadership, has been wholly rehabilitated as the necessary and heroic "creation of a new order." Or as a high official earlier instructed historians, *"All*—and I repeat, *all*—stages in the development of our Soviet society must be regarded as 'positive'."[94]

A coarser, more ominous form of pro-Stalinism has also emerged in official circles since the early 1970s. A variety of publications—including a spate of historical novels, some of them made into prize-winning and popular films—have justified Stalin's terror of the 1930s as a "struggle against destructive and nihilistic elements." Epithets of the terror years—"enemies of the Party and of the people," "fifth column," and "rootless cosmopolitans"—have reappeared in print.[95] (They are popularized still more widely by Party lecturers, whose daily oral propaganda throughout the country does much to set the tone of Soviet political life.) Indeed, by the mid-1970s, odious proconsuls of Stalin's terror had been resurrected as exemplars of official values.[96] And in time for the centenary of Stalin's birth in 1979, neo-Stalinist officials seem even to have achieved, despite rulings under Khrushchev, the rehabilitation of the notorious show trials of the

about persistent Western commentary on the Stalin years and suggested that this was the only reason it was still necessary even to mention the "negative" aspects.

93. The quotation is from the military desk calendar for 1979. For examples of pro-Stalinist writings in the 1970s, see S. Semanov, *Serdtse rodiny* (Moscow, 1977); V. Chikin, *Imiarek* (Moscow, 1977); Ivan Shevtsov, *Vo imia ottsa i syna* (Moscow, 1970) and *Liubov' i nenavist'* (Moscow, 1970); G. A. Deborin and B. S. Telpukhavsky, *Itogi i uroki velikoi otechestvennoi voiny*, 2nd ed. (Moscow, 1975); S. P. Trapeznikov, *Na krutykh povorotakh istorii* (Moscow, 1971); Ivan Stadnyuk, *Voina* (Moscow, 1977); Aleksandr Chakovsky, *Blokada*, 4 vols. (Moscow, 1969–1973) and *Pobeda* (Moscow, 1980); Pyotr Proskurin, *Sud'ba* (Moscow, 1973); Anatoly Ivanov, *Vechnyi zov*, bk. 2 (Moscow, 1977); A. V. Likholat, *Sodruzhestvo narodov SSSR v bor'be za postroenie sotsializma 1917–1937* (Moscow, 1976); Ye. Ambartsumov, et al., "Protiv iskazheniia opyta real'nogo sotsializma," *Kommunist*, no. 18, 1978, pp. 86–104; and V. I. Pogudin, *Put' sovetskogo krest'ianstva k sotsializmu* (Moscow, 1975).

94. *Kommunist*, no. 18, 1979, pp. 41–42; Rudolf L. Tökes, ed., *Dissent in the USSR* (Baltimore, 1975), p. 351.

95. See, for example, S. N. Semanov, "O tsennostiakh, otnositel'nykh i vechnykh," *Molodaia gvardiia*, no. 8, 1970, p. 319; Proskurin, *Sud'ba*, p. 247; Ivanov, *Vechnyi zov*, p. 335; Semanov, *Serdtse rodiny*, p. 63; V. Dolezhal, "Plesen' kontrrevoliutsii," *Literaturnaia gazeta*, June 28, 1978; and several of the items, especially the historical novels, cited above, note 93. Television and film adaptations of the novels by Ivanov and Proskurin won state prizes in 1979. *CDSP* 31, no. 45 (December 5, 1979): 12.

96. See, for example, the commemorative articles about Andrei Zhdanov in *Pravda*, March 10, 1976, and *Kommunist*, no. 3, 1976, pp. 80–86; and the publication of books by one of Stalin's most notorious defamers, David Zaslavsky, *Vintik s rassuzhdeniem* (Moscow, 1977) and *Talant, otdannyi gazete* (Moscow, 1980). Molotov was also rehabilitated. See *Soviet Analyst*, December 12, 1974, p. 4.

1930s, which served as the juridical linchpin of Stalin's terror against the Communist Party itself.[97]

Nor is this pro-Stalin sentiment merely an official artifice manufactured above. It has become a popular phenomenon. The marble bust placed on Stalin's grave site seemed to release popular attitudes constrained, except in his native Georgia, for more than a decade. Ordinary Soviet citizens now admire Stalin openly, speaking longingly of his reign and restoring retrieved or bootlegged replicas of his likeness to their homes, kiosks, and dashboards.[98] "Stalin walks among us, but not only in Tbilisi [the Georgian capital]—in Moscow as well." Another Muscovite reports, "Stalin today is less dead than he was 20 years ago."[99]

Stalin and the Soviet Future

The contemporary resurgence of Stalinist sentiments represents a potential base for more despotic leadership in the Soviet Union, but it does not signify a rebirth of Stalinism. As a system of personal dictatorship and mass terror, Stalinism was the product of specific historical circumstances and a special kind of autocratic personality; these factors have passed from the scene. Today, the Soviet political system is very different, however authoritarian it remains. Neo-Stalinists may press for and even achieve more hard-line policies at home and abroad. But actual "re-Stalinization" would be a radical change opposed by the great majority of Soviet officials and citizens, whose pro-Stalinist sentiments reflect something different—their own deep-rooted political and social conservatism.[100] Indeed, the appeals of neo-Stalinism today are diverse and often contradictory.

Pro-Stalin opinion among high officials is easy to explain. For them, the Generalissimo on his pedestal continues to symbolize their own power and privilege, and to guard against change. Not surprisingly, the main patrons of neo-Stalinist literature are those authorities responsible for the political attitudes of young people and the armed forces. These officials know the truth about the past and thus deserve the harshest judgment of anti-Stalinists: "Knowingly to restore

97. On June 9, 1977, the family of the main defendant at the 1938 Moscow trial, Nikolai Bukharin, was informed that charges against him, which had been officially repudiated under Khrushchev, were again in force. *Khronika zashchity prav SSSR*, no. 27 (July–September 1977), pp. 16–17. See also the favorable comments on the trials of the early 1930s in *Voprosy istorii KPSS*, no. 12, 1979, p. 108.

98. See Hedrick Smith, *The Russians* (New York, 1976), chap. 10; and Viktor Nekipelov, "Stalin na vetrovom stekle," *Kontinent*, no. 19 (1979), pp. 238–43. And why not? A much honored general proudly reported that he kept Stalin's photograph on his desk. S. M. Budyonny, *Proidennyi put'* (Moscow, 1973), p. 404.

99. Quoted in the *New York Times*, December 16, 1979, and December 3, 1978.

100. Thus, overly assertive neo-Stalinists, such as Aleksandr Shelepin, were demoted or deposed in the late 1960s and early 1970s; and Brezhnev himself felt the need to give a public assurance that there would not be a return to mass terror. *Pravda*, June 5, 1977.

respect for Stalin would be to establish something new—to establish respect for denunciation, torture, execution."[101]

But as a broad popular phenomenon, today's pro-Stalin sentiment is something different, even an expression of discontent. On one level, it is part of the widespread resurgence of Russian nationalism, to which Stalin linked the fortunes of the Soviet state in the 1930s and 1940s, and which has reemerged, in various forms, as the most potent ideological factor in Soviet political life. Echoing older ideas of Russia's special destiny, most of these nationalist currents are statist and thus identify with the real or imagined grandeur of the Soviet Russian state, as opposed to the Communist Party, under Stalin. They perpetuate assorted legacies of that era, from pride in the accomplishments of the 1930s and the war years to anti-Semitism and quasi-fascist cults. In this haze of nationalist sentiment, Stalin joins a long line of great Russian rulers stretching back to the early tsars. And the nostalgic cry "Back! Only back!" can mean either.[102]

Such ideas are also the product of contemporary social problems. Varieties of neo-Stalinist opinion cut across classes, from workers to the petty intelligentsia, reflecting their specific discontents in Soviet society.[103] More generally, though, liberalizing trends and other changes in the 1950s and 1960s unsettled many lives and minds; the open discussion of long-standing social problems made them seem new. By the mid-1960s, many officials and citizens saw a reformed, partially de-Stalinized Soviet Union as a country in crisis. Economic shortages, inflation, public drunkenness, escalating divorce rates, unruly children, cultural diversity, complicated international negotiations—all seemed to be evidence of a state that could no longer manage, much less control, its own society. And all cast a rosy glow on the Stalinist past as an age of efficiency, low prices, law and order, discipline, unity, stability, obedient children, and international respect.

Contemporary discontents, the feeling that "we have been going downhill ever since his death," could only enhance Stalin's popular reputation. By the end of the 1970s, official portraits of a largely benevolent chief of state were reinforced below by memories of Stalin as a "strong boss" under whose rule "we did not have such troubles."[104] Little remained to counter this folk nostalgia. While anti-Stalinists have been silenced by censorship, new generations, perhaps 40 percent of the population, have grown up in the post-Stalin era. Raised on parental remnants of the cult, many think that Stalin arrested "20 or 30 people" or "maybe 2,000." When a famous anti-Stalinist told a group of young people

101. G. Pomerants in Brumberg, ed., *In Quest of Justice*, p. 329.

102. Semanov's *Serdtse rodiny* is a classic example. For others and an analysis, see Medvedev, *On Socialist Democracy*, pp. 87–90; and Alexander Yanov, *The Russian New Right: Right-Wing Ideologies in the Contemporary USSR* (Berkeley, 1978).

103. See Viktor Zaslavsky, "The Rebirth of the Stalin Cult in the USSR," *Telos*, no. 40 (summer 1979), pp. 8–16.

104. See Darrell P. Hammer, *USSR: The Politics of Oligarchy* (Hinsdale, Ill., 1974), p. 94; Smith, *The Russians*, pp. 245–49; Nekipelov, "Stalin na vetrovom stekle"; and Shipler's reports in the *New York Times*, November 26, 1977, and December 3, 1978.

that the arrests were "reckoned not in thousands but in millions, they did not believe me."[105]

Outwardly, anti-Stalinism and thus the Stalin question itself appear to have lost their potency as factors in Soviet politics. And yet, there are at least two important reasons why this may be only a temporary condition, or even an illusion created by censorship. One is pragmatic. The reformist cause, despite its defeat in recent years, lives on in Soviet officialdom, mainly because Stalin's institutional legacy—particularly, the hypercentralized economic system—remains the source of so many serious problems.[106] In different political circumstances, as in a time of leadership instability, another leader or faction will reach for the fallen banner of fundamental economic reform. Such a program will require not only renewed criticism of the Stalinist past, but a reformist ideology to overcome widespread conservative resistance to change.[107] And anti-Stalinism remains the only viable ideology of Communist reform from above, as it was under Khrushchev and as it has been in other Communist parties, from Belgrade and Prague to Peking.

The other enduring source of anti-Stalinism is emphasized by the neo-Stalinist complaint against people who *"elevate ethical-moral problems above those of the state and patriotism."*[108] Enthralled by the apparent mountain of achievements, many Soviet citizens (and Westerners, too, it seems) will always admire Stalin as a great leader or "modernizer." But too much has become known for the mountain of crimes to vanish from view, even after all the victims of Stalinism have passed from the scene.

Historical justice is a powerful moral idea that knows no statute of limitations, especially when reinforced by a sense that the whole nation bears some responsibility for what happened.[109] This truth is confirmed by other historical examples. But Russians need look only to the growing body of samizdat literature, where exposés of Stalinism and the idea of a national reckoning "in the name of the present and the future" are kept alive.[110] The timelessness of the Stalin question and the prospect of new generations of anti-Stalinists are explained by a recent samizdat historian: "It is the duty of every honest person to write the truth about Stalin. A duty to those who died at his hands, to those who survived that dark

105. Yevtushenko quoted in Smith, *The Russians,* pp. 247–48. Similarly, see Craig Whitney's report in the *New York Times,* December 29, 1978.

106. I have argued this point more fully in "The Friends and Foes of Change." See above, note 22.

107. Without an ideological justification, new economic reforms will suffer the fate of those of 1965. See Karl W. Ryavec, *Implementation of Soviet Economic Reforms* (New York, 1975), p. 296.

108. V. Chalmayev, "Otbleski plameni," *Moskva,* no. 2, 1978, p. 187.

109. For expressions of this latter view, see *Politicheskii dnevnik,* II, 302–3; the anonymous poem cited in Medvedev, *Let History Judge,* p. 409; Tvardovsky's poems in this book; Hayward, ed., *On Trial,* pp. 66–67; and Pavel Antokolsky's poem in *Russia's Underground Poets* (New York, 1969), p. 7. The popular nature of the Stalin cult is, of course, part of this problem. See above, note 27.

110. *Politicheskii dnevnik,* I, 86. Similarly, see Leopold Labedz, ed., *Solzhenitsyn: A Documentary Record,* enl. ed. (Bloomington, 1973), p. 215; Brumberg, ed., *In Quest of Justice,* pp. 316–18; *Pamiat',* no. 1 (New York, 1978), pp. v–vii; and most of the items cited above, note 91.

night, to those who will come after us."[111] Enough anti-Stalinist themes have forced their way even into the censored Soviet press in recent years to tell us that this outlook still has adherents in the Soviet Establishment as well.[112]

Official censorship can mute the controversy, postpone the historical reckoning, and allow another generation to come to age only dimly aware (though not fully ignorant) of what happened during the Stalin years. But it is also true, as events since Stalin's death have shown, that making the past forbidden serves only to make it more alluring, and that imposing a ban on historical controversy causes that controversy to fester, intensify, and grow politically explosive.

111. Antonov-Ovseyenko, *The Time of Stalin*, p. xviii.

112. See, for example, Chingiz Aitmatov and Kaltai Mukhamedzhanov, *The Ascent of Mount Fuji* (New York, 1975), a play produced in 1973; the reviews of Ivan Stadnyuk's *Voina* in *CDSP* 26, no. 39 (October 23, 1974): 9–10; Yuri Trifonov, "Dom na naberezhnoi," *Druzhba narodov*, no. 1, 1976, pp. 83–168, which was produced as a play in 1979–80; Aleksandr Kron, *Bessonnitsa* (Moscow, 1979); and Fyodor Burlatsky, *Zagadka i urok Nikkolo Makiavelli* (Moscow, 1977). See also the interviews on this question with three Soviet writers—Yuri Trifonov, Bulat Okudzhava, and Vasily Aksyonov—in the *New York Times*, December 16, 1979. (Aksyonov left the Soviet Union in 1980; Trifonov died in Moscow in 1981.)

1

The Crimes
of the Stalin Era

M ASS CRIMES *can be covered up, forgotten, minimized, or seriously disputed for a long time, but not forever—not even in a censored society. For twenty-five years, the mountainous crimes of Stalin's rule were concealed, inside the Soviet Union, by official falsifications and the fearful silence of a terrorized populace. The next twenty-five years brought a historical reckoning of sorts—an irrepressible exposé of these crimes.*

The process of revelations was started by Khrushchev at the Twentieth Party Congress in 1956, and it has been carried on, since the end of official anti-Stalinism in the mid-1960s, by unofficial or samizdat writers. The result is a picture of the Stalinist past that is clear and beyond serious dispute: between 1929 and 1953, Stalin's policies caused the arrest, execution, torture, deportation, and often murderous imprisonment of tens of millions of innocent Soviet people. Stalinism created a Soviet holocaust. Only the exact number of victims and a fully adequate explanation remain uncertain.

The chronology of these mass crimes, leaving aside the question of their origins in the Leninist period, has also come into sharp focus. It began with Stalin's merciless assault on 125 million peasants during collectivization in 1929–33, which was followed by the great terror, or purges, of the 1930s, when millions of officials and ordinary citizens fell victim. War brought another series of mass victimizations, from Stalin's willful unpreparedness for the German invasion in

1941, which cost millions of lives, to his wartime and postwar deportation of several entire nationalities and his imprisonment of millions of Soviet soldiers who had been taken captive by the Germans during the war. Though less dramatic, Stalin's last years constantly threatened to develop into a full-scale replay of the 1930s. A new repression began in Soviet cultural and scientific life in 1947–48. It was followed by a pogromlike campaign against Jewish intellectuals, another political purge of high officials, and another scenario of mass terror (the "Doctors' Plot" of 1952–53), aborted only by Stalin's death. No elite, profession, or segment of the population escaped these twenty-four years of terror. And each wave of victims fed Stalin's far-flung system of prisons, forced-labor camps, and remote exile that Aleksandr Solzhenitsyn has called the Gulag Archipelago.

Many kinds of people came forward, beginning in the 1960s, as samizdat witnesses and chroniclers of these historical crimes—victims and accomplices, famous and obscure, scholars and poets, young and old, Communists and anti-Communists. Most were motivated by a desire to awaken the nation from its collective amnesia, induced by censorship and other factors, and to preserve its memory of what had happened. As a result, a substantial samizdat literature— personal testimonies, archive documents, scholarly research, and belles lettres— appeared on almost every major aspect of the Stalinist terror.

Four general themes emerged from this literature. The crimes of the Stalin years were at least as great as the officially proclaimed achievements. The actual consequences of the terror in various areas of Soviet life, from cultural to military affairs, were disastrous for the country. The treatment of victims, whether in prison cells or the polar concentration camps, was inhuman. And while Stalin personally directed the terror, it operated through a vast mechanism that included not only his highest political associates and notorious police chiefs— Genrikh Yagoda in 1934–36, Nikolai Yezhov in 1936–38, and Lavrenti Beria in 1938–53—but thousands and perhaps millions of other officials and ordinary citizens.

Many samizdat commentaries on the Stalinist past appeared in Political Diary, where historical rethinking was an integral part of ideas about political reform. The selections that follow are only a few of them.

The Stalin Cult Has Been Destroyed
BY LEV KOPELEV

Lev Kopelev (born 1912) is one of the best-known and most admired representatives of the dissident Soviet intelligentsia. A distinguished literary scholar specializing in German literature, he began his political career as an ardent Communist, and Stalinist, in the 1930s and later served as a Soviet army major during World War II. He was arrested in 1945 for protesting abuses by Soviet occupation troops in Germany and spent ten years in Stalinist prisons and labor camps. During his imprisonment, Kopelev met Aleksandr Solzhenitsyn, another political prisoner. Their friendship became a significant factor in the history of Soviet literature. The character Rubin in Solzhenitsyn's novel The First Circle *was based on Kopelev; and Kopelev was instrumental in arranging publication in 1962 of Solzhenitsyn's prison-camp novella* One Day in the Life of Ivan Denisovich. *Kopelev has told his own life story in three volumes of memoirs:* To Be Preserved Forever *(Philadelphia, 1977);* The Education of a True Believer *(New York, 1980); and* Relieve My Sorrow *(in Russian; Ann Arbor, 1981). The following document is from an open letter, written to an Austrian correspondent in November–December 1967, protesting the gradual rehabilitation of Stalin by the post-Khrushchev government. For this and many other protests on behalf of civil liberties, Kopelev was subjected to various forms of persecution, including expulsion from the Soviet Communist Party in 1968 and from the Writers' Union in 1977. He finally left the Soviet Union in 1980.*

Twenty—or even ten—years ago, in ignorance of the facts or in an effort to ease one's mind with dialectical sophistries, one could simultaneously support socialism *and* Stalin; quite honestly, one could praise the achievements of the land of the Soviets and believe in the wisdom of Stalin's policy.

That is no longer possible today.

After everything that became known at the Twentieth and Twenty-second Party congresses, after the publication of the hitherto secret documents of Lenin, after the publication of the eyewitness testimony of hundreds of old Communists, the mythology of the cult of Stalin has been destroyed once and for all.

1. Today it is generally known and has clearly been proved that Stalin's tyrannical and unprofessional intervention in the administration of agriculture during the years 1929–33, as well as in the postwar period, led to extended famines and to the destruction of the economic foundations not only of the individual peasant farms but also of collectivized agriculture.

2. Today it is generally known and has been proved that with Stalin's knowledge, indeed at his command, hundreds of thousands of people, including the overwhelming majority of the commanding officers and generals of the Red Army and the majority of the experienced and trained leaders of industry, were arrested, exiled, murdered, and tortured to death in the years 1935–40. In those years, more Communists were confined in Stalin's prisons and camps than in all the capitalist and fascist countries taken together. Among those shot and condemned as enemies of the people were the overwhelming majority of the delegates to all past Party congresses, the majority of the delegates to the immediately preceding Seventeenth Party Congress of 1934 and of the Central Committee members elected by it, and the overwhelming majority of the members and functionaries of all the Union Republic governments and of all provincial and district Party committees.

3. Today it is generally known and has been proved that Stalin attempted to turn the 1939–41 nonaggression pact with Germany into a treaty of friendship; that, in official documents and speeches, he called the enemies of Hitler imperialist aggressors; and that he in fact forbade all antifascist propaganda.

4. Today it is generally known and has been proved that Stalin, a man who was pathologically suspicious and who even distrusted his oldest and most loyal friends and comrades-in-arms (e.g., Yenukidze, Ordzhonikidze, Postyshev, Tukhachevsky, and others),[1] naively and for quite incomprehensible reasons placed full confidence in the friendship of Hitler, whom he trusted so much that he even set aside numerous warnings that reached him through various channels, ignored the reports of all his agents, and thus condemned our army to its worst defeats and the entire country to frightful losses and sacrifices.

5. Today it is generally known and has been proved that after the war, with Stalin's knowledge and at his command, millions and millions of people were subjected to repressive acts of the most severe kind. Entire peoples—the Volga Germans, the Kalmyks, the Chechens, the Balkars, the Ingushi, the Karachais, and the Crimean Tatars—had their homelands stolen from them and were exiled as nations, as national communities. The overwhelming majority of Soviet citizens who had been taken prisoners of war, as well as of those who had been inmates of fascist concentration camps, were condemned for "high treason." Their tragic fate is embodied in the figure of Ivan Denisovich of Solzhenitsyn's novel.

6. Today it is generally known that Stalin was the one who inspired the defamatory witch-hunt against Yugoslavia and who strove to transplant the methods of the Beria terror, of lies and provocations, to Poland, Bulgaria, Hungary, Rumania, and Czechoslovakia.

---

1. Avel Yenukidze, Grigory (Sergo) Ordzhonikidze, and Pavel Postyshev were high-ranking Bolshevik leaders and Stalin's former allies in the intra-Party struggles of the 1920s. Yenukidze and Postyshev were arrested and executed in the terror of the 1930s; Ordzhonikidze was murdered or forced to commit suicide in 1937. Marshal Mikhail Tukhachevsky was the most illustrious general executed in the military purge of 1937. All four were rehabilitated after Stalin's death.

These are the reasons why the exculpation of Stalin would be tantamount to the defamation of socialism. Today, Stalin can still be defended only by incredibly stupid and naive persons from the ranks of those bureaucrats, in retirement or grown gray in the service, whose thoughts run along the same lines as those of the anecdotal character of Dostoevsky: "If there is no God, what sort of a captain can I be?" or by completely conscienceless, cynical partisans of the jesuitical principle "The end sanctifies the means," who are unable to grasp the fact that Stalin's "means" themselves constitute a negation of the end that is adduced to justify them.

[No. 40, January 1968]

A Posthumous Indictment of Stalin
BY PYOTR YAKIR

The life of Pyotr Yakir (born 1923) is a representative tragedy of Stalinism and its legacy. His father, the illustrious Army Commander Iona Yakir, was arrested and executed along with Marshal Mikhail Tukhachevsky and other Soviet generals in June 1937. Pyotr Yakir, like so many children of "enemies of the people," thereby also became a victim of the terror. Arrested at the age of fourteen, he spent his entire youth in prison camps and exile, as he later related in A Childhood in Prison *(New York, 1972). (Stalin's terror included a 1935 decree that subjected children over twelve to the death penalty.) Released in 1954, Pyotr Yakir eventually returned to Moscow, where he became a graduate student at the Institute of History of the Academy of Sciences. He gained official sympathy during Khrushchev's de-Stalinization campaigns of the early 1960s; a memorial volume about his father, coedited by Pyotr, was published in 1963. During the second half of the 1960s, Yakir became an increasingly outspoken opponent of the neo-Stalinist overtones of the post-Khrushchev government and a founder of the Soviet dissident movement. He was one of the most active and courageous dissidents until his arrest in June 1972. A few months later, in an official and highly publicized spectacle, he recanted his dissident views, and his sentence was suspended. Yakir's repentance remains an enigmatic act. His health already impaired by years of imprisonment, he told friends shortly before his arrest that if he made such a statement, "You will know it will not be the real me." Yakir now lives quietly in Moscow. He wrote the following indictment in March 1969, as an open letter to* Kommunist, *the main journal of the Central Committee of the Soviet Communist Party, which was promoting Stalin's rehabilitation. Even though the document has been abridged here, it is too detailed to be annotated fully; suffice it to say that the many victims listed by Yakir were names known to most Soviet readers.*

Tens of thousands of pages could be written on Stalin's crimes. Ours is a more modest task: using the Criminal Code of the Russian Republic, published in 1966 (the mildest in our history), we will try to show that your journal [*Kommunist*] has come to the defense of a criminal who, on four different counts, deserved death by shooting as well as a total of sixty-eight years imprisonment, to be served under the strictest conditions of detention. The above would apply if the crimes had been committed only once, but since they were committed repeatedly, the penalties should be increased hundreds and thousands of times.

The resolution of the Twenty-second Party Congress [in 1961] states the following: "It is acknowledged to be inappropriate that the sarcophagus containing Stalin's coffin remain any longer in the mausoleum, since Stalin's serious violations of Leninist precepts, *abuse of power, mass repression against loyal Soviet citizens, and other actions during the personality cult* (emphasis added— P.Y.) make it impossible to leave his remains in the Lenin mausoleum."

This resolution was adopted unanimously by the congress on a motion by the Leningrad and Moscow delegations and the delegations of the Ukrainian and Georgian Communist parties. These delegations, in turn, introduced this motion at the request of the working people of their cities and republics. This decision has not been reversed by anyone.

The Criminal Code of the Russian Republic contains articles providing penalties for the acts mentioned in the resolution of the Twenty-second Congress:

1. Abuse of power—a correct and all-inclusive charge—Article 170 [provides for] imprisonment for up to eight years; likewise, for exceeding one's authority or the powers of one's office [a narrower charge], imprisonment for up to ten years, according to Article 171.

2. During the mass repression [referred to in the congressional resolution] people were illegally deprived of their freedom, which is punishable under Article 126, in combination with Article 17, by imprisonment for up to three years. Article 17 of the Russian Republic Criminal Code, "complicity" [on being an accessory to a crime], states the following: "The organizers, instigators, and accomplices in a crime, apart from its perpetrators, are considered to be accessories to the crime." Since it cannot be documented whether Stalin personally carried out a particular misdeed, under this category, as well as in a number of others, we will have recourse to Article 17, for Stalin's role as organizer is obvious, as is confirmed by the documents of the Twenty-second Congress if nothing else: "The postwar repression of 1949–50, like the repression of 1935–37, was carried out either on Stalin's direct orders or with his knowledge and approval."

3. It is known that it was on Stalin's proposal that the decision was made to use physical methods in investigations. This resulted in beatings, deprivation of sleep for as much as seven days at a time, and other kinds of torture, personally witnessed by the author of these lines. (I was arrested in 1937 at the age of fourteen as a member of a family of an "enemy of the people.") These acts are punishable under Articles 113 and 17 by imprisonment for up to three years.

4. A large number of leading officials took their own lives, some through unwillingness to participate in the crimes being committed, as they stated in letters they wrote before their deaths—for example, Sergo Ordzhonikidze; V. Kosior; F. Furer; Pogrebinsky, head of the NKVD in the Gorky region and founder of our rehabilitation communes; Litvin, head of the Leningrad NKVD; Kozelsky, head of one of the NKVD bureaus in the Ukraine; Norin, head of the NKVD special section in Georgia; and many others. A number of those being

persecuted killed themselves as a protest or from fear of torture—[for example,] I. Gamarnik, M. Tomsky, P. Lyubchenko and his wife, V. Lominadze, A. Chervyakov, Rabichev, Adamovich, Lakoba, Firin, and many others. Some who could not bear up under torture committed suicide in prison—[for example,] N. Gololed, I. Garkavy, Nosolevsky, Lapin, and others. All this comes under Article 107 ("instigation to suicide") and carries penalties of imprisonment for up to five years.

5. The mass repression was accompanied by slanders and insults against the victims, their friends and relatives. This was done in the press, on the radio, and at meetings and conferences. Actions of this kind come under Article 130 ("slander," up to five years imprisonment) and Article 131 ("insults," corrective labor for up to one year).

6. For failure to denounce and for having protected his accomplices (Yezhov, Frinovsky, Yagoda, Beria, Ulrikh, Vyshinsky, and tens of thousands of others), Stalin is answerable under Articles 88-1 and 88-2 and subject to imprisonment for from three to five years.

7. Many of the victims of repression were shot or simply killed [in other ways] or died of injuries received during interrogation. Among them were such eminent party figures as Chubar, Kosior, Rudzutak, Postyshev, Eikhe, Voznesensky, Kuznetsov, 110 members of the Central Committee of the Communist Party out of the 139 who were elected at the Seventeenth Party Congress [in 1934], and hundreds of other loyal citizens.

7a. On Stalin's orders, representatives of all the [Bolshevik] oppositions were arrested and in most cases liquidated. Many of them have not been rehabilitated to this day, although the accusations against them were complete fabrications. (None of the defendants in the Zinoviev trial of 1936 or the Pyatakov trial of 1937 have been rehabilitated; five of the twenty-two in the Bukharin trial of 1938 have not been; nor have a number of the defendants in the trials of the early 1930s.)

7b. Stalin had no compunction about annihilating foreign Communists who had taken refuge in our country to escape persecution by fascist, semifascist, and monarchist dictatorships—for example, the Germans H. Remmele, H. Schubert, Heinz Neumann, Werner Hirsch; the Hungarians Bela Kun, Mesan, Gidas, Gabor Farkas, and others; the Bulgarians Stamonyakov, Tanev, and others; the Poles Dombal, Leszczynski, Prochniak, and others; Kh. Pegelman and other Estonians; Sultan-Zadeh and other Iranians; the Yugoslavs V. Copic, D. Serdic, and others; the Swiss Fritz Platten (who had shielded Lenin with his body during the first attempt on Lenin's life) and others. This list could be made much longer, but we think it is sufficient for including this charge in the indictment.

7c. With Stalin's knowledge many leading figures in our intelligence service were liquidated: Berzin, Artuzov, Trilisser, Boky, Uritsky, Borovich, Spiegelglass, Ksenofontov, Peters, Latsis, Kedrov, and others. This seriously weakened our intelligence in the prewar period.

Since we cannot document whether Stalin personally carried out murders, we are compelled to accuse him under Article 17, and more specifically under Article 102 combined with 17 ("premeditated murder with aggravating circumstances," punishable by up to fifteen years imprisonment or death) and Article 66 combined with 17 ("terrorist act": "murder of a government or public figure or of a representative of the state . . . with the aim of undermining or weakening Soviet power," punishable by imprisonment up to fifteen years imprisonment or death).

8. Stalin was the head of state in the period during and after the Great Patriotic War [World War II] when many peoples in our country (the Crimean Tatars, Kalmyks, Chechens, Ingush, Balkars, Koreans, Greeks, Turks, Germans, and others) were victims of forced and illegal deportation from their native lands. These crimes come under Article 74 ("violation of the equality of nations and races," punishable by up to five years imprisonment).

9. In connection with the mass repression, administrative, scientific, and technical cadres in all branches of our industry and agriculture were liquidated or imprisoned, seriously affecting the country's economy. For example, 10 percent less iron ore was mined in 1938 than in 1937, although the plan envisaged an increase. The removal of trained cadres acted as a brake on production. For example, in 1940 out of 153 heads of shops in the metal industry, 75 held this position for less than a year.

The greatest engineers and inventors in the field of military science were physically liquidated, including such figures as G. Langemak, inventor of the [antitank] weapon that later became famous as the Katyusha; L. Kurchevsky, creator of the best recoilless cannon; V. Bekauri, originator of a remote-control radio system for detonating explosives; V. Zaslavsky, a tank designer; N. Smirnov, head of work on radar; I. Kleimenov, head of a research institute on jet engines; M. Leiteizen, founder of the "Interplanetary Travel Society" at the Zhukovsky Academy. And there were many others. Among the enormous number who were imprisoned were A. Tupolev, S. Korolev, A. Berg, V. Glushko, and B. Vannikov, people's commissar of armaments. Some of the greatest scientists and scholars were liquidated, including N. Vavilov, I. Krichevsky, Dogadkin, Tulaikov, Gerasimovich, and Polag. A huge number of others were imprisoned.

These acts may be categorized under Article 69 ("sabotage"—"action or inaction aimed at disrupting industry, transport, agriculture"—punishable by up to fifteen years imprisonment).

10. There were cases of desecration of graves (punishable under Article 22 by up to three years imprisonment). The urn with the ashes of S. S. Kamenev was removed from the Kremlin wall, the urn with the ashes of Yan Gamarnik was stolen, Mikhail Tomsky's grave was destroyed, the tombstone at the grave of Iona Yakir's mother was overturned, and so on.

11. As is known from the secret letter of the Central Committee to the Twentieth Party Congress, and from the recently published novel [*Blokada*] by Aleksandr Chakovsky, Stalin went into hiding on the first day of the war; for

several days none of the leaders of the state could find the commander in chief. This incident would come under Article 247 ("desertion"), which in wartime is punishable by death.

12. In 1939, a long and deep line of well-armed fortifications (called the URy, or "fortified regions") was built along our western borders. After the incorporation of the Baltic republics, western Byelorussia, western Ukraine, Bessarabia, and northern Bukovina, the Soviet border was moved 100 to 600 kilometers west. A decision was made to fortify this new frontier. Without even waiting for construction to begin on the new URy, and over the protests of B. Shaposhnikov, chief of the general staff, all of the old fortifications were dismantled by order of Stalin. This made it possible for the fascist aggressors to move through our territory unimpeded. This seems to us to be criminal negligence, bordering on treason. As for the annihilation of 80 percent of the highest-ranking military leaders and commanding officers, which decapitated the Red Army, that was outright treason (Article 64, the death penalty).

Moreover, military leaders who had fought in the Spanish civil war were arrested in the spring of 1941 and subsequently, in October, shot without trial. Among them were Smushkevich, twice honored as a Hero of the Soviet Union (to whom a monument was erected on February 26 of this year . . .), and other Heroes of the Soviet Union such as Rychagov, Shtern, Chernykh, Ptukhin, Gusev, Proskurov, Pumpur, and Arzhanukhin. Partisan bases on our territory were dissolved; tank formations were disbanded; certain types of automatic weapons, indispensable for the army, were not put into production; and many other such measures were taken.

The millions of victims of the first phase of the Great Patriotic War were the result of this whole complex of crimes committed by Stalin.

13. Apart from what has been stated above, medieval atrocities were committed in our country that do not come directly under the Criminal Code of the Russian Republic but that are crimes against humanity. Under interrogation, people were driven into insanity by beatings and other torture techniques; moreover, perfectly sane people were locked up in mental hospitals.

14. Wives of slain leaders were also arrested and often were shot, for example, the wives of Tukhachevsky, Uborevich, Postyshev, Kosior, Eikhe, Gamarnik, Kork, Chubar, Shelekhes, Agranov, Dybenko, and Vareikis.

15. The minor children of prominent victims of repression were imprisoned or placed in camps, for example, those of Postyshev, Kosior, Lyubchenko, Medved, Kamenev, Garkavy, Bauman, Kadatsky, Tomsky, Sosnovsky, and Popov. Postyshev's eldest son, Valentin, and the sons of Yevdokimov and Lakoba, were shot.

16. In several prison camps, prisoners were shot without trial or investigative procedures (e.g., Garanin's reign of terror in Kolyma).

17. Almost all the former Mensheviks, Anarchists, Bundists, Borotbists, and Right and Left SRs [parties opposed to the Bolsheviks during the revolution],

people who had essentially abandoned politics, were physically annihilated in the 1930s and early 1940s, including [the famous SR] Maria Spiridonova.

18. The author of these lines, having spent part of his prison term in the North Ural MVD camp (1941–42), can testify personally that most of the political prisoners volunteered for the front, and in answer to their request, the authorities condemned them to death by starvation, which aside from the other issues involved, seriously weakened our war effort.

19. On Stalin's orders, our government refused to join the International Red Cross to assist prisoners of war, because under our military code, to be taken prisoner was equivalent to treason. This deprived prisoners of material aid and [international] supervision of their conditions of detention, contributing to the deaths of many loyal persons. (The majority were taken prisoner when wounded and unconscious, or when out of ammunition.)

It has not been our aim to present here all the possible charges against Stalin, but even the ten-thousandth part of his crimes as set forth in the present statement add up to a sizable body of offenses under [the above mentioned] articles. . . . If we examine Article 38 of the Criminal Code ("extenuating circumstances"), we find no grounds for lightening the sentence in Stalin's case. On the basis of Article 39, however ("aggravating circumstances")—which includes "(1) Crimes committed by a person who has already committed a crime"; "(4) Crimes having serious consequences; (5) Crimes committed against a minor, an elderly person, or a defenseless person"; and "(7) Crimes committed with particular cruelty and humiliation of the victim"—we have no doubt of the need to apply Article 39 as well against the accused, J. V. Stalin. It is equally necessary to apply Article 36 against Stalin ("deprivation of military and other ranks, as well as decorations, medals, and honorary titles"), since this is provided for in cases of conviction for especially serious offenses.

On what grounds, then, do the authors of the articles we have mentioned and the editorial staff of the magazine [*Kommunist*] rehabilitate the greatest criminal our country has known in its recent history?

[No. 54, March 1969]

The Son Does Not Answer For the Father

BY ALEKSANDR TVARDOVSKY

*Unlike the other contributors to this chapter, Aleksandr Tvardovsky (1910–1971) and Konstantin Simonov (below) were luminaries rather than victims of the Stalin period. A poet of peasant origin, Tvardovsky is a fascinating figure in Soviet literary and political history. Two long narrative poems—*The Land of Muravia *(1936), a eulogy of collectivization, and especially* Vasily Tyorkin *(1942–45), a folk classic about the ordinary Russian soldier in World War II—brought Tvardovsky enormous popularity and virtually every official honor during the Stalin years. In the 1950s and 1960s, however, he emerged as one of the most important and committed official anti-Stalinists as editor (1958–70) of* Novy mir, *ardent champion of anti-Stalinist writers (especially Solzhenitsyn), candidate member of the Party Central Committee, and as a kind of poet laureate of Khrushchev's de-Stalinization. (One samizdat writer has remarked that these years really should be known as the "era of Tvardovsky.") Embattled to the end, Tvardovsky's position weakened increasingly after Khrushchev's overthrow, as the new regime abandoned anti-Stalinism and many of* Novy mir's *writers were forced into silence or, like Solzhenitsyn, open dissent. By 1970, Tvardovsky and his loyal editorial board had been driven from his beloved* Novy mir. *He died of cancer a year later. Throughout these turbulent political years, Tvardovsky was a man deeply divided between new currents of dissent and his own past, official position, and reformist Communist beliefs—or as his great protégé and former friend Solzhenitsyn tells us, "between his dossier and his soul."[2] Tvardovsky's personal turmoil is reflected in his last known, and most bitter, epic poem,* By Right of Memory. *A draft of this long brooding reflection on Stalinism and its legacy apparently was completed in 1967, but Tvardovsky was denied permission, despite repeated efforts, to publish the most candid parts—"The Son Does Not Answer For the Father" (which follows here) and "Memory" (which appears below, in Chapter 3)—even in his own* Novy mir.[3] *This part, entitled after a few*

Translator's Note: I have not attempted to reproduce in English the regular meter and *a b a b* rhyme scheme of Tvardovsky's Russian verse, but I have tried to convey some of the color, tone, and music of this poem.

2. See Solzhenitsyn, *The Oak and the Calf* (New York, 1980); and, for a different first-hand portrait, Vladimir Lakshin, *Solzhenitsyn, Tvardovsky, and Novy mir* (Cambridge, Mass., 1980).

3. There is contradictory information as to when Tvardovsky began writing *By Right of Memory.* According to Solzhenitsyn, he began writing it just after the Soviet invasion of Czechoslovakia in 1968. (*The Oak and the Calf,* pp. 242–43) According to *Political Diary,* a "first variant" was written in 1967 as a continuation of Tvardovsky's earlier epic poem *Horizon beyond Horizon* and then grew into a separate work composed of a short introduction and three parts. (Unlike the two parts in this

words uttered by Stalin during the terror, includes Tvardovsky's unvarnished
reconsideration of collectivization. It is also an apology to his own father, an
ordinary peasant, or muzhik, who was forcibly dispossessed and deported to
Siberia, along with millions of other so-called kulaks, in the course of this great
rural tragedy.

"The son does not answer for the father."
Eight words. Just count them. Eight exactly.
But what those eight words bear within them,
Young people, you won't grasp so quickly.

Those words were casually tossed off
Within a Kremlin meeting hall
By him who was to all of us
Sole ruler of man's fate on earth,
Whom all the peoples, with rejoicing,
Hailed and proclaimed their father dear.

You of another generation
Could hardly plumb the depths of what
Those brief words' revelation meant
To us, the guiltless guilty ones.

In hellish, fuming midnight meetings
This question never tortured you.
The answer nowadays is simple:
"Your father's not someone you choose."

But in those years and five-year plans
For those with "the rubric" things went hard.
Present your forehead without murmur
To be indelibly stamped.

One had to wear it—that was the law—
With suffering and burning shame,
Always at hand in case the supply
Of class enemies ran short.

Ready for public humiliation always—
And bitterness; at times more bitter,
As when your bosom buddy keeps his eyes
Cast down upon the ground.

---

book, the first part was published in *Novy mir.*) Whatever the case, the forbidden parts 2 and 3 were
circulating in literary circles in the late 1960s. A version identical to that in *Political Diary* found
its way into several European magazines in 1969, a development that Tvardovsky was compelled to
condemn. *Literaturnaia gazeta,* February 11, 1970.

O years of childhood not so pleasant,
The cruel buffeting it meant.
One minute father, the next class enemy.
And mother? They spoke of two class worlds
But nothing was said about mothers.

And here—beyond the flood of years—
Here where you fled in barefoot haste,
You are called "misbegotten spawn,"
And never "son," just "sonnyboy."

And how a young lad manages
To live with such a name attached,
How serves this term of unknown length,
The author of these lines can tell,
Not secondhand, not from some book.

You're here but you're not *from* here, sonny.
What law any more is there for you
When your parent's name has been set down
On the list itself, the unspeakable list?

With that beginning you'd hardly dream
Of trying to enter the charmed circle,
And even your bosom pal is cautious
About shaking your hand.

Then all of a sudden:
"The son does not answer for the father."

The stigma is now removed from you.
A hundred times happy! There you were,
Neither hoping nor dreaming,
And suddenly—no longer guilty at all.

An end has come to your misfortunes.
Stand up tall, don't hide your head.
Thanks to the Father of the Peoples
That he has now forgiven your dad,

Your father by blood. The curse is gone
With shocking ease. As though he had
Just looked around, spied an odd law
He had not known, and canceled it.

The son for the father? Does not answer!
Amen! But a question quickly stirs,
Now that the son has served his time,
Now that he has received these rights,
Could he indeed answer for his father?

Answer—perhaps not with careful science,
Not approaching it from that end,
But merely by recalling perhaps
What kind of hands his father had?

Those hands all calloused, with the fingers
All bent, with knots of veins and sinews,
Which when he sat down at the table
He'd plank down like things that weren't his.

And with those hands like rakes he'd try
To take the handle of a spoon,
Such an evasive little thing,
And wouldn't get it very soon.

Those hands, which he, try as he might,
Could neither open nor clench tight,
Were all one callus, no distinctions.
A kulak—fist? Yes, genuine.

And that was his sole aim (they charged)
For years growing humpbacked over the earth,
Sprinkling it with his unpaid sweat,
And running the dawn into the dusk.

And for my part I'll even add
That maybe when disaster struck
His muzhik's vanity was tickled
A little bit—How terrible!

Yes, maybe in those parts where frost
Clung to the barrack ceiling and walls
He felt a swell of pride that he
Had passed as a kulak just like that.

"A mistake's been made? Don't say a word,"
Perhaps that's how he advised himself.
"If it's like this, it means I was tops,
I was a master; that's what it means."

Or maybe it was with great sadness
He left behind his home and land,
Scorning the blind and savage sentence
Rounded off to the highest year.

And in the crowded cattle car
That carried him beyond the Urals
Perhaps he held himself too proudly
Apart from those whose fate he shared.

Jammed in the heated car with them,
Together trapped in that crude conveyance,
Hiding his tears, he would not let
The children sink into homesickness.

Shielding himself with his hunched back
From others' gloating or sympathy,
Among the Soviet power's foes
He alone stuck up for it.

He'd been its helper, dressed in rags,
Supporting it and fighting for it.
And under it lived well at last
Upon his own long-sought-for land.

Abandoned to his fate by Soviet power,
He did not curse it angrily.
A minor excess isn't crucial
When the great change is here,
He seemed to say.

And he believed: As soon as Comrade
Stalin himself had read his letter
He would set everything to rights
And not be slow in the reappraisal.

Or maybe father sought to solve
His fate some other way than this.
Maybe he thought, If there's no going
Home, we won't go just anywhere.

Maybe he thought, We'll try a sure thing,
We'll get the law to work for us.
Be a good friend, Magnitogorsk,[4]
Enroll us in the working class.

But how and where dad found his moorings
Is not what matters; our subject's the son.
The son does not answer for the father.
Make sure the way is clear for him.

Eight brief words. But years went by
And they were reduced to nothingness.
The title "son of an enemy,"
Despite those words, remained in force.

And fate made everybody equal
Outside the limits of the law,

4. A large iron and steel construction site of the 1930s, where peasants were being turned into industrial workers.

Son of a kulak or Red commander,
Son of a priest or commissar.

An infant with such enemy blood
Was branded from the time of birth,
But still it seemed the country suffered
A shortage of such branded youth.

And not for nothing in bloody wartime
Did some men bless and praise the war.
It did not scorn them for the sin
That seared their souls with bitter bane.
It offered them the right to die
And even win a bit of fame
With those who fought for our dear land.

The field of war provided every
Soldier with the title son.
But there was one dread destiny:
Missing in action, fate unknown.

And after enduring to the full
The road of the cross, half-dead, yet alive,
To pass from one *camp* to another—
To the boom of victory salutes—
With a double brand upon your brow.

On the other hand, without exception
Here classes all were equalized,
All men were brothers, camp mates all,
Branded as traitors every one.

Through all the ages, Motherland,
You never guessed that you would gather
Such a host of "enemies"
Beneath the skies of Magadan.[5]

Nor could you tell how it all began,
How you managed to raise such sons,
Whom now you hold behind barbed wire
In far-off zones, dear Motherland.

Amid the rush of holidays and workdays
Not everybody could recall exactly
By what code addressed to mortal men
The visitor divine had summoned them.

5. A reference to the murderous and infamous Kolyma-Magadan complex of forced-labor camps in the Soviet Arctic.

He said to them: Come follow me,
Come leave thy father and thy mother,
Leave all these passing earthly things,
And dwell with me in paradise.

Proud that we did not believe in God,
But in the name of our own sanctities,
We sternly required this sacrifice:
Renounce thy father and thy mother.

Forget the family whence you came,
Remember this, and do not question:
Your love for the Father of the Peoples
By any other love is lessened.

The task is clear, sacred the cause.
For the shortest way to the highest goal,
Betray your brother as you go
And stab your best friend in the back.

And do not burden your soul with human
Sentiment self-indulgently.
Be bestial in the leader's name
And bear false witness for his sake.

Thankful for any fate, you must
Profess but one thing: He is great.
Whether you be Crimean Tatar,
Steppe-dwelling Kalmyk, or Ingush.

Applaud for every sentence issued,
Those that defy all comprehension.
Denounce the people along with whom
You're driven to exile far away.

And in the choking Exodus,
Not of the Bible, of our times,
Extol the Father of the Peoples,
Highest of all. He knows what's best.

He makes known and self-evident
Every beginning and every end.

The son does not answer for the father.

This is a law which also means
The father must answer—with his head.

But blessed night has now extinguished
All laws for him forever more.
And now he's not the one to answer
Not for the son, not for the daughter.

There at the mute wall of the Kremlin
He luckily has no idea
What a terrible fate for a father
Accompanies his sepulchral sleep.

The sons have long since grown to fatherhood.
But still we all must answer for this father.
As it turns out, we're all being held to account.

And the trial has gone on for decades
And there's still no end of it in sight.

[No. 60, September 1969]

The Terror and the War

BY KONSTANTIN SIMONOV

There are different interpretations of the long literary career of Konstantin Simonov (1915–1979). One is that he became, like Tvardovsky and Khrushchev himself, a sincerely repentant Stalinist. Another is that he bent to whichever Soviet leader and policy prevailed. Under Stalin, Simonov was an enormously successful writer and an important literary bureaucrat; he won five Stalin prizes for his novels, plays, and poetry, while serving as editor of Literaturnaya gazeta *and* Novy mir, *deputy head of the Writers' Union, and candidate member of the Party's Central Committee (1952–56). On the other hand, Simonov was associated with the liberal wing of the Soviet intelligentsia in the post-Stalin 1950s and 1960s, using his authority to criticize the past and to encourage new anti-Stalinist writers, including Solzhenitsyn. But he also remained in good official standing after de-Stalinization came to an end, and indeed until his death in 1979 —a secretary of the Writers' Union, deputy to the Supreme Soviet, and recipient of Lenin prizes. A war correspondent, Simonov had a special attachment to the history of the Soviet army in World War II. It was the subject of his most popular novels, including* Days and Nights *(New York, 1945) and* The Living and the Dead *(New York, 1962). The latter novel was part of a trilogy that did much to destroy Stalin's reputation as an infallible wartime leader. The following essay, again on Simonov's favorite subject, is from a longer article entitled "The Lessons of History and the Conscience of the Writer," which he wrote in 1967 for the scholarly journal* Voprosy istorii *(Problems of History). Such candor on the again sacrosanct Soviet-German war was no longer possible. Simonov's article was rejected and passed into samizdat.*

I would like to go into more detail on the difficult topic of 1937–38, or the Yezhovshchina. That was the name the people simply and concisely gave it—and not after the fact either, not after Stalin's death, but right then and there. Incidentally, those who love evasive formulations about "isolated cases of injustice" and "certain violations" could do worse than to think over the formulation the people used for that time. If it was only a matter of some "isolated" instances, such terms as Yezhovshchina or Oprichnina[6] would never have arisen among the people.

At this point, I wish to discuss 1937–38 only from the viewpoint of its direct

6. The Oprichnina was the personal police force of Tsar Ivan the Terrible. Yezhovshchina refers to the terror of 1936–38.

effect on our lack of preparedness for the war. Unfortunately, people who denounce the shameful events of those years with all their hearts sometimes give too narrow and one-sided a treatment to the way those events affected the subsequent fate of the army. When you read an article in which the names of several military leaders who were killed in 1937 are listed for the nth time and the author comments that if they had lived, the war would have gone differently, you have to wonder how such a writer can actually reduce everything to that.

On one occasion, after reading such arguments, I actually tried to imagine what would have happened. Let us suppose that in 1937 everything else had not occurred, that there had simply been a tragic accident—an airplane on its way to maneuvers carrying Mikhail Tukhachevsky, Iyeronim Uborevich, August Kork, and the other victims of the frame-up trial had crashed. Would this have been a tragic loss? Of course. Would it have harmed the functioning of the army? Unquestionably. Would it have had such far-reaching results four years later, in 1941?

In my thoughts, I asked this question, and answered: No, it would not have. Because a loss of that kind, as tragic as it would have been, would have forced us, according to our revolutionary traditions, to close ranks ever more tightly, and to advance new capable people who had been trained and nurtured by the Party and the Red Army.

No, everything cannot be reduced to a few famous military names of that time. And the possible role they could have played in the war cannot be viewed apart from the context, the atmosphere of the times in which they died, an atmosphere that became much worse because of their deaths and their being branded posthumously as "traitors to the motherland."

First of all, they did not die alone. In their wake and in connection with their deaths, hundreds and thousands of others perished—constituting, to a significant extent, the flower of our army. And they did not simply perish; the consciousness of the majority of our people was that they left the scene with the mark of treason on their brows.

We are not just talking about the losses involved in the deaths of these people. We must also remember what happened in the minds of those who continued to serve in the army, the powerful spiritual blow that was dealt them. We must remember what unbelievable effort it cost the army—at present, I am talking only about the army—to begin to get a grip on itself after such fearful blows.

At the beginning of the war, this process was still under way. The army was caught not only in the most difficult stage of unfinished rearmament but also in a no less difficult period of unfinished restoration of morale and discipline.

If this problem is not analyzed, the reasons for our many inept actions on the eve of and at the beginning of the war cannot be fully understood. I wish to take issue with a tendency that seems to crop up here and there, repeatedly—a tendency to counterpose the cadres who died in 1937–38 with those who willy-nilly were obliged to shoulder the burden of the war.

Some people apparently think they are giving the individuals Tukhachevsky,

Yakir, and others, the credit due them by suggesting that if they had commanded the fronts instead of Kirponos or Pavlov in the first days of the war, things would have gone differently. Such outwardly impressive contrasts seem to me not only light minded but morally irresponsible.

To use the vivid expression of a leading military man, "The war selected our cadres." Some prominent military leaders, living on past laurels and lagging behind the times, proved to be out of touch. Some young commanders hastily promoted before the war also proved to be misplaced.

But the war selected and kept selecting our cadres. And we cannot take the people who headed divisions, armies, and fronts, who retreated to Moscow, Leningrad, Stalingrad, but never surrendered those cities, who after a time went over to the offensive, having learned how to fight, and ultimately smashed the most powerful army in the world, the German army, and reached Berlin—we cannot take these people and counterpose Tukhachevsky or Yakir or the others to them, however high the regard in which we hold their names.

When we speak of the miscalculations of Hitler and the German high command, we should remember that one of the most important was the way they misjudged our cadres. It is true that in 1937–38 these cadres suffered terrible losses. But Hitler and his high command thought the loss irreparable and our army incapable of fighting a major war.

The cadres that survived, however, having undergone the extremely severe test to their morale represented by 1937–38 and not having yet recovered from those trials at the beginning of the war, demonstrated their bravery and their ability to grow and improve. They demonstrated that they were of the same Soviet military school that produced Tukhachevsky, Uborevich, Yakir, and the like. And in the end they accomplished what neither our enemies nor our allies expected—they emerged from this terrible war as the victors.

We do not know and we will never know how Vasily Blyukher or Ivan Belov, Pavel Dybenko or Ivan Fedko would have fought in 1941. We can only discuss that hypothetically. We do know very well, however, that if 1937 had not happened, the summer of 1941 would not have been the way it was, and that is the heart of the matter. If it had not been for 1937, by the summer of 1941 we would unquestionably have been stronger in every respect, including purely militarily above all because our army would have gone to battle against the fascists with thousands and thousands of people in its commanding ranks who were devoted to Communism and experienced in military matters. People who were ripped from their proper places in the army by 1937. And these people would, at the beginning of the war, have constituted more than half of the top command staff and the senior command personnel in our army.

There is no historical requirement that we personalize this huge problem by trying to guess who would have fought where and how in whose place. The important thing is that they would all have fought against fascism. And the war, as it selected our cadres—and it would have selected them, revealing the true worth of all our military leaders—would have done so, first of all, in an incomparably more favorable atmosphere, and, second, there would have been a much broader layer to select from.

A few words on the atmosphere immediately before the war. For people writing about the war, the starting point is important. The complex and contradictory character of the situation at that time is now sometimes reduced to an extremely primitive level. It is presented more or less as follows: After the events of 1937–38 and the war with Finland [in 1940], which opened our eyes to our weaknesses, the army hastened to reorganize itself; a normal atmosphere was established so that it could reorganize successfully. Everything was getting better, and if on top of that Stalin had listened to Richard Sorge[7] and taken the necessary measures, everything would have been all right.

At first glance, it might seem that this is all correct. But that is not so. The actual historical truth is more complex and contradictory.

There is, of course, a lot of truth in this conception. Anyone who had dealings with the army at that time remembers very well how energetically the new leadership of the defense commissariat after the war with Finland sought to bring order into the army and above all to reorganize it so that it would be ready for battle.

And it is true that lessons were drawn from the war with Finland, including the necessity to speed up the introduction of new equipment, which was taking a dangerously long time. But to say that an atmosphere had already been created in the country and the army that was favorable for successfully repelling the foe would be untrue.

Sometimes matters are presented as though in the fall of 1938, after the so-called excesses had been condemned and Yezhov punished for them, Stalin put an end to the previous situation, that no one was declared an enemy of the people any longer, and that people were freed and returned to their former posts, including military personnel. On the one hand, there is some truth to this. A layer of commanders arrested in 1937–38 were returned and some of them commanded divisions, armies, and even fronts during the war.

On the other hand, both in 1940 and 1941 the paroxysms of suspicion and denunciation continued. Not long before the war, when the memorable TASS communique was published half reproaching and half threatening those who gave in to rumors about Germany's alleged hostile intentions, Rychagov, the commander of the air wing of the Red Army; Smushkevich, the chief inspector of the air arm; and Shtern, the commander of the country's antiaircraft defenses—all were arrested and died in prison.

To complete the picture, we must add that at the beginning of the war the former chief of the general staff and the commissar of armaments were also

7. A Soviet intelligence agent in Japan who warned the leadership that the Germans planned to invade the Soviet Union in 1941.

arrested, although, fortunately, they were subsequently freed. That was what the atmosphere on the eve of the war with fascist Germany was like in reality. Stalin stuck to his maniacal suspicions against his own people, which ultimately proved to be a terrible loss paid for extreme vigilance against the enemy.

And now that we have provided ourselves with the real, not the alleged, atmosphere of that time, let us give some thought to what the situation was like for military personnel who, after analyzing the large quantity of data available, concluded that war was about to break out at any moment, contrary to Stalin's unchallengeable opinion, which he placed on a plane higher than reality.

In judging the actions of those people now, many years after, we should remember that we are not talking about the degree of courage required for people to submit their resignations after the emphatic rejection of measures they regarded as the only proper ones. Unfortunately, the situation was not that simple. To counterpose directly one's own views about the coming war to Stalin's meant not to resign but to die—and to be posthumously branded an "enemy of the people." That is what it meant.

Nevertheless—and we know this from many memoirs that confirm one another—there were people who tried, at least to some extent, to make Stalin aware of the real state of affairs and, risking their own lives at every moment, tried to take at least partial measures so that the outbreak of war would not catch us completely by surprise.

Stalin bears the responsibility not only for the fact that he refused, with incomprehensible stubbornness, to consider the most important intelligence reports. He is guilty before the entire country of having created the deadly atmosphere in which dozens of fully competent people, having irrefutable documented evidence of the danger, were denied the opportunity to present to the head of state the full extent of the danger and had no right to take the necessary measures to forestall the threat of war.

The final touch in this tragedy involving the attitude toward military cadres that grew up around Stalin before the war was the charge of treason brought against the commanders of the western front, Pavlov, Klimovsky, and several other generals—among whom, it came out later, were men who died in the first battles of the war and men who conducted themselves with total integrity in the German prisoner-of-war camps.

It is hard to say what drove Stalin to brand these people traitors. Was it calculated to divert the anger and consternation of the people, who never expected war to start that way—to divert it from himself and dump it on them? Or was it genuine suspicion? I think it was both, because it had been typical of Stalin for a long time back to try to explain away failures not as the result of his or others' mistakes but as treason, wrecking, and the like. Later, during the war, he had to give up this habit, although he fell back into it from time to time.

In the course of the war, in the thick of its trials and tribulations, many prewar ideas, slogans, and theories were put to a severe test. The war confirmed some, threw out others, and reestablished the importance of still others that had once been thrown out. It is vital that we who work in literature and are concerned with the history of the war trace how people's psychology, their attitudes toward each other, and their style in directing military operations changed, how something new, produced by the war itself or restored during the course of the war, struggled against the old, the outworn, and the compromised, whose roots went back to 1937–38.

[No. 37, October 1967]

Tales of the Stalin Years

Censorship and terror suppress historical knowledge, but they cannot destroy it. Memory and oral accounts—"living history," as Russians say—live on, even in the most repressive circumstances. With the onset of de-Stalinization and the return of millions of Gulag survivors, including once high officials, a great many firsthand stories about the Stalin years began to circulate orally in Moscow and other large cities. Some of these personal testimonies found their way into official publications, but the essential job of collecting this mass of oral historical information fell to samizdat historians. Much of this work was done, for example, by Roy Medvedev in Let History Judge, *Aleksandr Solzhenitsyn in* The Gulag Archipelago, *and Anton Antonov-Ovseyenko in* The Time of Stalin. *Many such stories, usually brief, episodic, and anonymous, were compiled in* Political Diary. *Those that follow are only a few, mostly about well-known villains and victims of the Stalinist terror.*

According to V. Desnitsky, an old friend of Maxim Gorky and a veteran Party member, Gorky did, indeed, start to write a biography of Stalin at one time. It was generally thought that he had refused outright, but that is not the case. Gorky began his attempt in 1934 or 1935. For several months, he would shut himself up in his study after breakfast and work on the numerous documents that couriers from the Central Committee delivered to him on behalf of Stalin's minions. But one day, when Desnitsky was there, Gorky came out for lunch in a cheerful mood and said, rubbing his hands, "It's coming out too sickly sweet for his taste and he'll have to reject it." After that Gorky did not touch the Stalin material any more.

In the years 1934–36, Gorky's secretaries and guards were fairly blunt about not admitting "undesirables" to see him. One day, the elderly Mikhail Prishvin, a prominent Russian writer who had always avoided political topics, came to see Gorky. But P. P. Kryuchkov, the chief secretary—who many considered an agent of Yagoda—tried to keep him from going in to Gorky's office. Prishvin simply pushed him aside and walked in. When Prishvin remarked on the secretary's behavior, Gorky said in embarrassment, "Oh, didn't you know I was being kept under house arrest?"

[No. 37, October 1967]

In the early 1920s, Aleksei Snegov was first secretary of the Party Committee in Vinnitsa Province (which then included what are now several regions). A conflict arose between Snegov and the Cheka organization for that province, and

Snegov went to Moscow in an effort to have the head of the Cheka in the province removed. For this purpose, Snegov met with Feliks Dzerzhinsky.[8] "I'll give you a solid and reliable man," said Dzerzhinsky. Soon Leonid Zakovsky arrived in Vinnitsa under assignment from Moscow, and Snegov established normal working relations with him. Subsequently Snegov did Party work in Transcaucasia, Siberia, and Leningrad. Zakovsky continued his career in the punitive agencies and after the Kirov assassination was placed in charge of the NKVD's Leningrad administration.

In 1937, it was on Zakovsky's order that Snegov was arrested in Leningrad. Zakovsky personally oversaw "the Snegov case," including the torture administered several times. Snegov was sentenced to be shot, but just at that time Zakovsky himself was arrested. Snegov was exonerated, and Zakovsky himself was shot after extremely savage and refined torture. Snegov did not remain "at large" for long, however. When he arrived in Moscow seeking to have his party membership restored (and disregarding Mikoyan's advice to go south and stay at a sanatorium), he was arrested in the very building of the Party Control Commission where he had just had a meeting with Matvei Shkiryatov, a friend of Beria.

[No. 37, October 1967]

The foremost butcher of 1937 and 1938, Nikolai Ivanovich Yezhov, came from a working-class background. Before the revolution, when he was still a young boy, he lived for a time with the Shlyapnikovs, helping with the housework. It was through [the Old Bolshevik] Aleksandr Shlyapnikov apparently that Yezhov joined the Communist Party. When Shlyapnikov was arrested in 1937 and no news of him was to be had, his wife, Aleksandra Gavrilovna, went to see Yezhov. The latter not only received her in his office but rose from his desk to greet her. "I can help you with any problem," he said, "getting an apartment, a pass, whatever. Just call me. Here's my number. But I cannot help you in any way with your husband's case." She left, and a week later was herself arrested.

Yezhov had a brother whom he once brought on a visit to the Boyarskys. After a few drinks, there was a squabble between the two brothers. "You're a bloodsucker," Yezhov's brother yelled at him. "You've drowned the country in blood." The host was terrified. A few days later, Yezhov's brother was arrested and was never seen again.

According to all accounts, Yezhov's wife, Zhenya, was an honest and very decent sort, and suffered terribly over the events of 1937. Her death was a suicide, although the papers reported that she died of influenza.

Long before Yezhov became commissar of internal affairs, he had a personal assistant named Volodya Sinko, who used to perform quite a few purely personal favors for Yezhov, especially after drinking bouts. Strong and solid, Sinko sometimes carried the short and slight Yezhov home in his arms. Later on, Sinko

---

8. Founder and head of the Cheka until his death in 1926.

himself became an alcoholic and was transferred to Chelyabinsk to supervise a shop in a factory. When the mass repression began, Sinko lost his job and returned to Moscow to seek help from Yezhov. He called Yezhov on the closed telephone circuit for high officials from the apartment of Maryasin, director of the State Bank. "I'd like to come see you," said Sinko. "Well, why not? Come along, come along," Yezhov answered and hung up. Sinko went to Yezhov's offices in the NKVD and never came back. What became of him remains unknown, although it is not hard to guess.

[No. 54, March 1969]

The issue of *Pravda* for November 29, 1935, published a joint decree of the Central Executive Committee and the Council of People's Commissars, dated November 26, on the awarding of titles of honor to the highest-ranking officials of the NKVD. From this, we learn the names of all the top leaders of that agency, as of late 1935.

All of these top NKVD leaders were eliminated. Most of them were arrested and shot after the downfall of Genrikh Yagoda [in 1936]. But Yezhov did keep several of these men on his "team," and they were annihilated only two years later, together with the new "general commissar of state security" and a multitude of new commissars of state security, first and second class. Having carried out the dirty work to which they were assigned, these men were no longer of any use to Stalin, and he dealt with them savagely, using the machinery of annihilation they had created. The sole figure who survived long enough to be shot after Beria was Goglidze.

[No. 54, March 1969]

During the making of the film *Lenin in 1918*, the director, Mikhail Romm, and his assistants needed to look at Lenin's quarters in the Kremlin. Nadezhda Krupskaya [Lenin's widow] accompanied Romm and the others of the film crew. While showing the rooms, Krupskaya called attention to the soldier on sentry duty there. "In the old days," she said, "Red Army men weren't like that, of course. Can you call him a soldier of the revolutionary army? What do you see written all over his face? 'Yessir, right away, sir.' " All this was said right in front of the guard, who stood like a statue the whole time, never moving a muscle.

Many rumors circulate about the cause of Krupskaya's death. Some say she was poisoned soon after her seventieth birthday. They say this was done on Stalin's orders and that the poison was in a cake baked especially for her. However, P. V. R—v considers these rumors totally unfounded.

[No. 11, August 1965]

The tragic fate of Marshal Semyon Budyonny's second wife, the singer Mikhailova, is told as follows. She was arrested in 1937 by order of Budyonny himself. She was having an affair with the singer Alekseyev (who was singing the part of Lensky to her Olga in *Eugene Onegin*). Mikhailova announced to Budyonny that she wanted to leave him. He replied that she would be leaving all right —not for Alekseyev but for prison.

After arresting Mikhailova, the NKVD authorities accused her of giving information to the Japanese ambassador on the number of horses in the USSR. (This she told her cell mate in Lubyanka Prison.) Mikhailova survived prison and was rehabilitated. However, Budyonny refused to have anything to do with her. By the time she was freed, she was nearly half-senile, and she worked for a time as a cleaning woman in a school somewhere in the Soviet Far East. The schoolboys would tease her, "Hey you! Budyonny's wife!" And she would chase after them with her mop. Only recently was she moved to Moscow and given a room. On its door is the nameplate "Budyonnaya."

[No. 11, August 1965]

Aleksandr Poskrebyshev's wife was the full sister of Sedov's wife, and Sedov was one of Trotsky's sons. It is said that Poskrebyshev [head of Stalin's personal secretariat] himself had to submit the order for his wife's arrest to Stalin for his signature. In doing so, he tried to come to her defense. "Since the organs of the NKVD consider the arrest of your wife necessary," Stalin said, "that's how it must be." And he signed the order. Seeing the look on Poskrebyshev's face, Stalin laughed, "What's the matter? You want a broad? We'll find you one." And sure enough, a young woman soon came to Poskrebyshev's apartment and said that she had been assigned to keep house for him.

[No. 5, June 1965]

In 1947, Marshal Konstantin Rokossovsky, who was vacationing at his dacha, received a phone call from Stalin's staff inviting him for lunch with "the boss." With his wife and daughter, Rokossovsky went to Stalin's dacha. The dinner proceeded in a relaxed atmosphere, with everyone eating and drinking their fill. Occasionally Stalin rose from the table and walked around the room. At one point, he suddenly came over to Rokossovsky and said, "I heard you were sent up once, Konstantin Konstantinovich."

Rokossovsky replied unexpectedly, "Yes, Comrade Stalin. I was in prison. And, you see, they looked into my case and cleared it up and I was released. But how many good people, remarkable people, died there!"

"Yes," Stalin said slowly, "We have a lot of good people, remarkable people." He turned quickly, left Rokossovsky, and went out of the room into the garden.

Someone kicked Rokossovsky under the table. "What have you said to Stalin," Malenkov hissed in quiet anger. "Why?"

There was total silence. After a few minutes Stalin came back. He had three bouquets of roses. One he presented to Rokossovsky's wife, one to his daughter, and one to the marshal himself. Rokossovsky, who had expected the very worst, was stunned. He never spoke to Stalin again about his prison mates who had died.

[No. 11, August 1965]

In the late 1940s, mass arrests were carried out among the Jewish intelligentsia in Moscow. The famous Jewish writer Itsik Feffer was one of those arrested. He was held in Butyrka Prison. Soviet writers who traveled abroad, however, were under instructions to deny any facts connected with the arrests of Jewish writers. When Paul Robeson, the well-known American Negro singer, friend of the USSR, and fighter for peace, arrived in Moscow in 1949, he told Aleksandr Fadeyev [head of the Writers' Union] that he wanted to see Feffer; there were rumors in the West that Itsik had been arrested, and he personally wanted assurance that it was not so. Fadeyev promised to arrange a meeting, but in the meantime Robeson was persuaded to go to a resort for creative writers in Yalta. Robeson did not drop his request, however, and continued to insist on a meeting with Feffer, whom he knew well.

When Robeson returned to Moscow, Fadeyev invited him for dinner at the Metropol restaurant. The table was covered with hors d'oeuvres and bottles of wine. Suddenly, in the company of an unknown individual, Itsik Feffer came up to the table. He was pale and thin, but was quite well dressed and seemed in good spirits. They visited for several hours in an atmosphere free of restraint. At the end, Feffer asked Robeson to pass on his greetings to his friends in the United States. Then they went their separate ways: Robeson back to his hotel room, Fadeyev to his home, and Feffer, escorted by the MGB agent in a passenger car, back to his cell in Butyrka Prison. As we know, Feffer died in prison, and Fadeyev committed suicide after the Twentieth Congress, in 1956.

[No. 54, March 1969]

Our Fate

BY IRINA KAKHOVSKAYA

Stalin's assault on the Old Bolshevik Party sometimes obscured the much larger dimensions of the great terror. Millions of ordinary citizens fell victim, as did former members of Russia's other political parties, which had long since disbanded inside the Soviet Union. The Left SRs were a radical faction of the Socialist Revolutionary Party, whose traditions went back to nineteenth-century Russian populist or propeasant thought, and which remained the largest political movement in Russia as late as 1917. The Left SRs broke away in 1917 and formed a separate party. They supported the Bolshevik takeover in October and helped form a coalition Soviet government that lasted until they withdrew and organized an abortive uprising in July 1918. By the 1920s, most former Left SR leaders had been exiled to provincial towns. Retired from politics, they worked loyally in various Soviet administrative institutions. The terror caught up to them in 1937–38. Irina Kakhovskaya (1888–196?) was one of the very few who survived. After almost seventeen years in prisons and forced-labor camps, she was freed in 1954, aged and in poor health. She settled in the district of Kaluga, not far from Moscow, and began writing her memoirs.[9] After the anti-Stalinist Party Congress in 1961, Kakhovskaya sent a lengthy memoir-account of the fate of her exile circle of Left SRs and their families to the Soviet Central Committee, Council of Ministers, and Procuracy. Her account, which is abridged slightly here, is valuable not only for the details of arrest and "interrogation" but also for the last years of Maria Spiridonova, the famous antitsarist revolutionary. Kakhovskaya's own fate, while common, was not entirely typical; as she remarks, "there were even worse things that year."

Early on the morning of February 8, 1937, a large group of men appeared at the door of our quiet apartment in Ufa. We were shown a search warrant and warrants for our arrest. The search was carried out in violent, pogromlike fashion and lasted all day. Books went pouring down from the shelves; letters and papers, out of boxes. They tapped on the walls and, when they encountered hollow spots, removed the bricks. Everything was covered with dust and pieces of brick.

At the height of the search, a terrified, crying boy ran in, the son of Anton Makovsky. The boy's mother had sent him to tell us that Makovsky had been arrested and that some packages of rat poison had been found in the search. (The

---

9. A fragment about Maxim Gorky appeared in *Novy mir*, no. 3, 1959, pp. 218–21.

macaroni factory, where Makovsky worked, had many rats, and the Makovskys' apartment adjoined the factory.) They detained the boy at our place.

Toward evening they finished. They led us away, leaving Mayorov's weeping legless old father behind, together with Mayorov's son Lyova, to whom we four [Ilya Mayorov, Maria Spiridonova, Aleksandra Izmailovich, and I] had given instructions pertaining to our jobs, including the keys to our desks at our various places of work (the State Bank, the Milling Works, and the Timber Enterprise). At that point, we suspected nothing unusual. Many times we had been searched, taken away, and a few months later delivered to another city. But Mayorov's father wasn't well, and the boy was about to take his final school exams. All this made the situation more unpleasant than usual.

We went off without saying good-bye to one another, taking nothing along but soap and towels, leaving all our money with Lyova and his grandfather, and hoping to be reunited with them soon in some other city. We never saw them again. They, too, were soon arrested, and I know of their subsequent fates only from unverified rumors.

In addition to the Left SRs, all the other political exiles in Ufa were rounded up the same night—Right SRs, Mensheviks, Anarchists, Zionists, and so on. An investigation began that was shattering, unheard-of, and implausible. It lasted eleven months.

The other arrested exiles were placed in the isolation-cell building, which was jammed to the full with fourteen to twenty prisoners in each "solitary" cell. For the most part, the Left SRs were put in Isolation Prison No. 1. That was the name for the death house, where there were only nineteen tiny solitary cells (four of them holding ordinary criminals whose death sentences had been reprieved).

I have seen a lot of prisons in my long experience, but I never came across cells like these before or since, or experienced such horrendous prison conditions. Here everything was aimed at breaking prisoners' spirits immediately, intimidating and stupefying them, making them feel that they were no longer human, but "enemies of the people" against whom everything was permitted. It was not only that, however. All elementary human needs were disregarded (light, air, food, rest, medical care, warmth, toilet facilities). The entire behavior of the guards was extremely harsh, rude, unceremonious, and pointedly contemptuous.

In the tiny, damp, cold, half-lit cell were a bunk and a half bunk. The bunk was for the prisoner under investigation to sleep on, and on the half bunk, their legs drawn up, the voluntary victims, the informers from among the common criminals, huddled together. Their duty was never to let their neighbor out of their sight, never to let the politicals communicate with one another by tapping on the walls, to find out what they could, and above all to prevent the politicals from committing suicide. This noble mission was undertaken by several individuals of both sexes in the hope of improving their own lot.

The window was barred on both sides of the glass and was covered on the outside by an airtight piece of metal sheeting. The inside was further protected by a fine wire screen, to keep the prisoners from getting broken glass to cut their wrists with. There was no daylight. Around the clock, a small dust-covered bulb burned high up close to the ceiling. The air was fouled by the huge wooden latrine bucket, which stank to high heaven and barely fit between the bunks and the corner of the unlit heating stove. No books were allowed, and if the prisoners were in their cells, rather than being questioned, they had to sit on the bunk facing the guard's peephole in the cell door, so that the authorities could be sure the "enemies of the people" never slumbered or dozed.

The interrogation began on the very first night. The entire ground floor of the huge building had been adapted for interrogation. Shouts, and the indignant voices of those being questioned, could be heard through the doors of the solitary cells. The interrogators at first tested the ground and got to know the particulars about each prisoner. Using threats, endearments, promises, and enigmatic hints, they tried to confuse, wear down, frighten, and break the will of each individual, who was kept totally isolated from his or her comrades. The prisoners saw only their investigators and could rely only on themselves, their own stoutness, their sense of morality and honor, their revolutionary consciousness. There was no support from others, no way to avoid or counteract provocations. Your name could be misused as they wished. Fabricated testimony attributed to you could be shown to others with the aim of undermining their determination and making them distrust their closest friends.

"No one's going to know that you stuck firm. You're going to die unknown and be left on the rubbish heap of history. No one will bring flowers to your grave," the investigator would sneer. "We have many ways of making you say what we want. No one yet has left this chair without confessing. We have great need for people like you; confess, and Soviet power will forgive you all your crimes; you'll be able to live and work as an honest Soviet citizen."

The investigators operated with methods like that to begin with. They felt out the weak people, seeking their most vulnerable places.

But these attempts to break people down lasted no more than a couple of weeks. The material proved intractable. No one wanted to slander anyone else. The interrogation technique changed abruptly from psychological to physical pressure. Insults and shouts began, and ugly threats to resort to measures of a kind no one could withstand. The chairs on which the person being interrogated sat were replaced by high stools from which one's feet would not reach the floor, and severe pain in the thighs resulted. Later the stools were also removed, and the victim had to simply stand for hours on end. Now cries could be heard from every cell: "Hangmen! Gendarmes! Murderers! Sadists!" Then violent cursing by the interrogators, blows, the sounds of bodies falling.

I had to pass the whole length of the corridor, because my investigator Lobanov had positioned himself at the end of the corridor right next to the lunchroom where the investigators refreshed their energies. I heard familiar voices. Across from my cell they were working on Spiridonova. Her investigator

(Mikhailov or Petrov) kept running from her to me, back and forth. One minute he would claim that Spiridonova had already confessed, the next he'd shout that none of the women would talk; the men were easier. To that Lobanov would reply reasonably that the men were "high principled" too, obviously implying that "principles" were something deplorable. Now the questioning went on for two or three days and nights in a row, without a break. One investigator would replace another, but the prisoner remained there, night and day, whether sitting or standing, and was taken to the limit of endurance.

Two men, however, did cave in and became obedient tools of the authorities for the remaining course of the investigation. They said monstrous things against innocent people at the bidding of the investigator. They were Makovsky and Leonid Dravert.

How Makovsky was caught I heard with my own ears:

On one occasion toward morning, my tired interrogator couldn't control his drowsiness and began to snore softly, leaning on his elbows at the desk. The other interrogation cells gradually emptied out, and the prisoners were taken back to their own cells to relieve themselves. I could hear quite plainly what was going on in a neighboring cell:

"Get up! Sit down! Get up! Sit down!" Then the crying of a child. The door opened. "Take him to number 104," yelled the interrogator to the guard. "How do you get there? Follow the floorboards. You're not with your mother in the nursery." Once again a child's tears. They were working over Makovsky's son while his father looked on.

Then I heard: "And if I sign will you let him go?"

"Word of honor. He'll be home today."

And that's how Makovsky came to sign the false testimony that served as the cornerstone for the edifice of lies they were building. The story was, as it turned out, that he had left the chandeliers in Government House insecurely fastened on the orders of the "foursome" (us), so that the chandeliers would fall on the heads of the Soviet Bashkir government leaders and kill them.

Later on, so his story went, a decision was made at a conference of Left SRs in our apartment to kill all the members of the Bashkir government with bombs as they left work. Certain tasks were set and assigned to each of the terrorists. Makovsky, who just happened to drop by, was given the task of tracking down the secretary of the Party organization. "I accepted this proposal, which I deeply regret and for which I repent wholeheartedly." With that sentence he completed his tale.

It is superfluous to point out that this whole fable was concocted by the investigator and signed by Makovsky out of fear of reprisals against his family.

With every day, a new strand of this sticky spiderweb was spun. For a long time, I couldn't understand what exactly I was being accused of: there were generalities about organizing peasant revolts, terrorism, and the establishment of some vast, counterrevolutionary central organization. To all my requests to make the charges more specific, I received the same reply. "Why don't you tell us about that yourself; go ahead, tell us, tell us." I knew only that all of the Left SRs were being charged under Article 58, Clauses 8, 10, and 11.

At last, something definite crystallized out of the vast chaos of accusations and denunciations. The charges were formulated and the testimony fabricated along two lines: first, the establishment of a central organization, embracing all opposition parties and groups; second, preparations for acts of terrorism against the leaders of the Bashkir government. Since both charges were being brought against one and the same individuals, there were a great many flagrant contradictions.

At first, it seemed that the whole thing was a tremendous and terrible misunderstanding, that it was our duty to clear it up not only to save ourselves but also to keep the legal authorities from being misled. But it soon became quite obvious that what was involved was deliberate ill will and the most cynical possible approach to the truth. The most elementary requirements for a genuine investigation were trampled under foot, facts were juggled around, the meaning of certain simple words and phrases was distorted, the most obvious alibis were disregarded, and people who were known to have never left Ufa were said to have taken long trips to various parts of the Soviet Union. A person named Zhan Krestov, whom no one had every heard of, made his way into the case. He had signed testimony with his own hand giving incriminatory evidence against several of the defendants. Later it turned out that this was the main character in Romain Rolland's novel *Jean Christophe*. A huge trial was planned—an "amalgam" in which a dreadful conspiracy extending throughout the country would be revealed. But since no compromising correspondence, no documents, no weapons, had been found, and since there was nothing to prove any tie between us and other party organizations or individuals, it became necessary to make things up—caches of arms in Moscow, which Boris Belostotsky allegedly arranged on my orders; a bomb in Ufa; and trips to all parts of the Soviet Union to establish connections, trips that never happened. "We'll put you on trial in public, in front of all the people, and there you'll have to talk," the investigators threatened us.

This was some sort of illiterate detective story with the Left SRs as the chief villains, as people who thirsted for blood, blood, and more blood, but who were exposed by their own repentant comrades. In the interrogation sessions, I now had several investigators in a row, and the "conveyor belt" questioning would go on for six days and nights on end.

In the dark morning hours of Sunday, they sent me back to my cell to sleep. "So you can get recharged for the week," my investigator Lobanov told me. But the corridor guards took a hand in the matter. Pretending to test the locks, the guards who kept watch on the doors deliberately kept up a clanking sound that prevented me from sleeping. In the middle of the night a guard would suddenly pull the covers off you because they had accidentally covered your face, blocking off the light: "We got you alive and we'll deliver you alive to the next shift."

Exhaustion reached the ultimate limit. The brain, inadequately supplied with blood, began to misfunction. I suddenly forgot the names of all the people I had worked with and the names of the enterprises I had helped to plan for a period of five years. "Sign! We won't bother you any more. We'll give you a quiet cell and a pillow, and you can sleep and sleep and sleep. We'll put all four of you in together. You can talk to your heart's content." That was how the investigator would try to bribe a person who was completely debilitated and stupefied from lack of sleep.

In the solitary cell where far too many cigarettes had been smoked, to the sound of curses, ridicule, shouts, and threats, days stretched out into weeks. The sun rose and the sun set, your tormentors kept changing at the desk in front of you, and there you sat, half-alive, fearing one thing above all else—hypnosis. Ever so gently you touch your cheek with a piece of broken glass you found during a walk and held on to like a treasure: If they start to hypnotize you, chew and swallow the glass and then the pain will prevent hypnosis. Who's sitting in front of you: A Soviet investigator or a spy and a fascist who has snuck into our country? Why, these people know very well that we're not guilty of anything, but they don't care about the truth; they want us to slander ourselves and others. Why? What is this? Whose needs are served by this totally criminal operation? This doesn't fit the definition of "vigilance" or "showing no mercy to the enemy."

And then I was handed a letter to read, from Mayorov to Spiridonova, typed on onionskin paper, in which he tried to persuade her to "confess her counter-revolutionary activity." Later they showed me several excerpts from his confession—a monstrously false accumulation of every possible fantasy. Nothing in them, neither the phrasing nor the meaning, was consistent with the kind of thing Mayorov would say or the way he would say it. He was a sturdy and honest person who had gone through many hard experiences under the tsarist regime. The style was that of Makovsky's confession, but the signature I knew very well was Mayorov's.

Later, when I thought back over this letter and with a shudder tried to imagine what torments had forced Mayorov to give this false testimony, which could bring the most severe punishment down on people who were close and very dear to him and could bring his own ruin, how he could have handed over to the court such material distorting the truth and deliberately misleading the Soviet judiciary, I came to two possibilities: it was either done by hypnosis applied to a person whose will had been weakened by lack of sleep, or it was done by frightening the person with rats, a form of torture widely used in prisons under all kinds of different political systems. Strange as it may seem, Mayorov had an absolutely pathological fear of mice and rats, and even at home when he saw a rat he would shriek wildly and lose his self-control. All of our comrades knew this well. "Hey, but your Mayorov is really afraid of rats," the informer in my cell said to me once with a snort and then stopped short, realizing that she had spilled the beans.

Mayorov's confession gave the investigation a solid basis to work from. After all, he was a serious and responsible person. I asked for a face-to-face meeting with Mayorov. "Oh no, you'll undermine him right off. You won't get to see him." Finally, after two consecutive "conveyor belt" sessions, each lasting nine days and nights, from which I was dragged by the arms, I came down with dysentery, a disease that was raging in the prison and had carried off quite a few people.

I lay flat out in the cell without any medical assistance for a long time, because the investigator refused to allow me to be sent to the hospital (that would break my isolation). Only on the fourteenth day was I carried off on a stretcher. The conditions in the prison hospital would require separate description, if it were not that they have faded irrevocably into the past. I gradually got better there and eventually was released, still half-sick and extremely weak.

After the hospital, I was put in a totally dark cell next to the latrine with damp walls and a penetrating stench. When the chief guard asked in checking my papers why I was being put in this cell, the woman guard in charge of me replied, "Her investigators' orders."

Late at night, I was taken out into a courtyard and led into a small wooden structure, a former hospital laundry that was apparently being used now to store rubbish. In it were an old unpainted table and two benches, and several men in uniform sitting on them. A tiny kerosene lamp was burning. On a stool by the wall, I made out the features of Dravert. For some reason, he had on only his underwear. There were two glasses of sour cream on the windowsill and a pack of cigarettes. They seated me at one end of a bench.

After a few of the questions usual in such cases, Dravert assumed the pose of an orator and began to shout out his denunciations in a hysterical tone. There wasn't a single word of truth in his whole tirade; it was more like incoherent raving that the investigator tried to steer down a certain course with his prompting and leading questions. When Dravert finally fell silent, he was given the sour cream. Greedily and in great haste he devoured it and then continued. I wasn't allowed to say a word. "Confess! Because of you, they won't let me smoke!" he finally shrieked and sank down on the stool, exhausted. They shoved a lit cigarette in his mouth. They gave me the record of this confrontation to sign, and I wrote down, "All 100 percent lies." My words were erased, and I was cursed in gutter language.

The whole scene had been accompanied by the coarsest kind of insults, hooting, and laughter from the young toughs sitting there. I returned to my cell totally shaken. This was the first time in my life I had seen anything like it. It is understandable when a person deprived of a conscious will is brought to the point of signing whatever is desired. But the kind of ardor Dravert showed, such self-assurance and shamelessness in the midst of lies—where did that come from? And they were the kind of lies that could cost many people their lives. Yet he was not an evil person; just a very weak, burnt-out individual.

Of course, such things don't seem strange to anyone now, and there were even worse things that year. But, at the time, each of us thought that the experience was unique, something unprecedented, and we were greatly confounded and tormented in our efforts to understand how it could happen.

I was given a second confrontation with my accuser Makovsky—right in the office of the investigator in the inner prison. Here there were bright lights and correct procedures. Makovsky was pale, his pupils looked enlarged, and out of his mouth came an endless stream—to the prompting of the investigator—of every kind of cock-and-bull story, and his tone was one of hatred, poison, and malice, the only grounds for which seemed to be his personal resentment toward us for always avoiding his company. But that is small reason to send people to their deaths.

The interrogations continued with the same results. My physical strength was running out from lack of sleep, the terrible food, the illness I had suffered, and above all the inhuman nervous strain lasting for many months—all this was becoming unbearable, and there was no end in sight. They still didn't have enough material.

Each of us fought alone to keep an honest name and save the honor of our friends, although it would have been far easier to die than to endure this hell month after month. Nevertheless, the accused remained strong in spirit and, apart from the unfortunate Mayorov, not one real revolutionary did they manage to break.

Then, in the world outside the prison, a new event occurred. All the commissars of Bashkiria, as well as the Party Committee and its secretary, were arrested. These were the people against whom we were supposedly preparing acts of terrorism. Our solitary cells were now needed for them, and they had to transfer us to the big isolation-prison building, which hummed like a beehive. Each solitary cell held fourteen to twenty people. After that house of the dead, Isolation Prison No. 1, things here seemed noisy and freewheeling. The extreme isolation was over, and I tried to find out at least a little something about my comrades—but without success. They kept bringing in new people, and since the investigation was obviously coming to a close, some of us ended up in the same cell. Here I met Lydia Arbuzova and Dravert's wife, Khava, who was brought there with her two-year-old child. I learned what had been done to them. Arbuzova had been extremely sick, delirious at night. In a cell for nine, there were at first forty-five; later the number reached fifty. People took turns sitting against the wall while the rest stood. Soon the wives of the Bashkir commissars also showed up here.

Nothing ever came of the grand project for holding a major public trial. "You will be judged by a military collegium. They work fast. One, two, and they're done."

On December 25, 1937, I was tried by a court of the Military Collegium of the Supreme Court. The prosecutor read off the indictment in a singsong voice. It said that I had prepared an attempt on Voroshilov's life, had led peasant revolts, and some other things. I said that it was all lies. I was taken out for a minute, then brought back. They read off the sentence: ten years in prison and five years loss of rights. The entire procedure took seven minutes in all. I was surprised by the mildness of the sentence, since the nature of the charges and the tone of the investigation led me to expect much more. Izmailovich, Lyubytsyna, and Galina Zatmilova were given the same sentence. Yelena Novikova, who had never been arrested and was in Ufa only because of her exiled husband, expected to be cleared entirely and immediately freed. No charges were brought against her during the investigation. The only thing they asked her about was her relations with me and my friends. She returned from the courtroom with her eyes wide open: the same ten years and five years loss of rights.

After the trial, we were still held in prison as persons under investigation and I was called out for questioning many times. They asked me about newly arrested Left SRs in various cities and about people entirely unknown to me that they were trying to link to us. "We'll interrogate you for seventeen months; it's nothing to us!" said the investigator angrily.

In the summer, Izmailovich and I were sent to Yaroslavl isolation prison and there separated forever. The others had been taken away earlier, except for Novikova, whom we left behind quite ill in the Ufa prison. Later she was taken away and soon died in Kolyma. The other three women—Zatmilova, Lyubytsyna, and Novikova—had been arrested only because of their husbands and had never participated in political activity. They were given these dreadful sentences only because they had withstood all the burdens of the investigation and had not soiled their consciences by slandering others. The harshest sentences had been given to Spiridonova and Mayorov: twenty-five years imprisonment (prison terms of that length had been introduced on Stalin's orders shortly before).

I was unable to make contact with my two comrades Mayorov and Spiridonova throughout the investigation. After about two or three months, Spiridonova had announced a hunger strike demanding that the inhuman prison system be changed and our case be transferred to Moscow. (It seemed to us that such unheard-of goings-on could happen only far from the capital.) Spiridonova had already suffered from tuberculosis and scurvy in the tsarist hard-labor camps, and therefore both diseases broke out again with renewed intensity. In an effort to keep her alive for the investigation, she was transferred to another building, where she was treated and given promises that she would be transferred to Moscow. They would torment her with the same promises during the questioning. . . . Spiridonova's hearing was bad (because the tsarist gendarmes had damaged it when they beat her), and so the investigators spoke very loudly. I always knew which cell they were tormenting her in and what they were using to try to wear her down. Later on she was actually transferred to Moscow but found no justice there either.

After her sentencing, Spiridonova was sent to the Yaroslavl isolation prison, from there to Vladimir Prison, and then to Oryol. I saw her once in a railroad car as we were being transferred from Yaroslavl to Vladimir. She was going down the hallway of a Stolypin car, gray, thin, holding on to the wall. When she saw me behind the bars of the next compartment, she called out what sentence she had gotten, pointed to her ears, and said, "I can't hear anything."

When Oryol was evacuated during the war, Spiridonova, Izmailovich, and Mayorov were in the Oryol isolation prison. They were not removed along with the other prisoners. Rumor has it they were shot there, but I don't know whether that is true.

From the Vladimir isolation prison, I was sent off in December 1939 to the NKVD's Kraslag labor camp in Krasnoyarsk region as a person "physically able to work," and there I spent seven years doing nothing but heavy general work —felling trees and agricultural work.

That, very briefly, is the story of how we were destroyed—people guilty of nothing, who were linked by all our thoughts and feelings with the revolution and who had served it in our day to the full extent of our abilities and powers.

[No. 67, April 1970]

Days of Shame and Sorrow
BY OLGA BERGGOLTS

This poem, originally untitled, is an example of literature about the terror years that has become popular while remaining unpublished in the Soviet Union. Written in 1956,[10] the poem has circulated widely and is often recited movingly, from memory, by Soviet citizens. A well-known lyrical poet whose writing evoked the special agonies of her native Leningrad during the Stalin years, Olga Berggolts (1910–1975) survived an unusually brief, though traumatic, encounter with the terror. Her first husband, the poet Boris Kornilov, was arrested in 1936 and later shot as an "enemy of the people." Berggolts was herself arrested in December 1938 and jailed for almost six months. After her release, she won popularity and official favor, including a Stalin Prize in 1950, as a poet of the war years. The intensely personal and melancholy quality of Berggolts's poetry and prose caused her occasional conflicts with Soviet literary authorities in the post-Stalin era, but she continued to publish and her reputation grew. Berggolts clearly felt a lasting tie to less fortunate victims of 1937–38. In 1955, as survivors of the labor camps were being freed after "seventeen years—always seventeen years," she wrote of "that year when from the bottom of the sea, from the canals, friends began to return."[11]

No, not from our meager books,
Resembling a pauper's sack,
Shall you find out how life for us
Was hard, unbearable,
How we had loved with anguish,
How, loving, we deceived ourselves,
And, with clenched teeth,
Renounced our faith, our persons
When they interrogated us.

We tried to find a reason
For our mother to bestow
Senseless torment
On the best among her sons.

10. E. Etkind, "Bezumstvo predannosti: o dnevnikakh Ol'gi Berggol'ts," *Vremia i my,* no. 57 (1980), p. 271.

11. "Tot god," *Novyi mir,* no. 8, 1956, p. 28.

And in the silence of sleepless cells
Days and nights on end,
Without tears, with bleeding lips,
We whispered: Motherland . . . the people.

Days of shame and sorrow!
Yet could it be that even we
Had not drained all the grief
Out of the secret mines of Kolyma?

Those who were saved by chance
Stand sentenced more severely
To cowardly silence,
To the distrust of friends.

And daily, hourly while working,
We feared the prison once more.
But no one was more fearless
And more patient than were we.

We crossed Mongolian sands
And fell upon the Finnish snow
For her, evasive and beloved,
And treacherous to the end.

She did not let us sing
Of our chains, of our shackles.
And our books are empty now.
And praise in them is triply false.

Should you, then, suddenly, somehow
Stumble over these lines
Written in contorted pain, as if
A dead circle left around the fire,

Should our scorching legend
Reach you now if only as cold smoke,
Well, then, honor us with silence
As we keep silent in front of you.

[No. 28, January 1967]
Translated by Vera Dunham

Kolyma *and a Letter to Friends*
by Yelena Vladimirova

Yelena Vladimirova (1903–1965?) was among those who returned after sev-
enteen years of prison and camps. As she explains in the letter below, her
narrative poem Kolyma, *or* A Northern Story, *about that remote and dread Gulag*
region, was actually "written" in camp in 1948–49. A Leningrad Communist,
veteran of the civil war, and Party journalist in the 1920s and 1930s, the young
Vladimirova was remembered by a friend as having been like a girl from a
Turgenev novel—bold, mocking, and beautiful.[12] *She and her husband, Leonid*
Syrkin, a prominent Communist editor, were arrested in 1937. He perished.
Vladimirova began writing poetry in her cell in 1937 and continued throughout
her years of imprisonment. Even though she was fully exonerated and rejoined
the Party after her return to Leningrad, Vladimirova's prison-camp writing was
never published. Instead, her poems circulated in manuscript among other Com-
munist survivors of the terror. Kolyma, *two sections of which are printed below,*
became especially popular in these circles.

Friends:
    Since our discussion has turned to *A Northern Story,* I will tell you how it
was created. This is also a complete story in its own right, and even you, Alya,
don't know it.
    When the orders for my execution were changed to hard labor, I ended up
in a godforsaken mountainous region, in a small valley cut off from the world.
There was such hopelessness about everything there that I began to think: How
should I spend my remaining strength and time? Doing what? My capacity for
mental work, I realize only now, was exceptional. In my head, I could do everything I wanted, under any circumstances. And I decided I would write a story
that would capture everything I had seen, a cross-section of the most important
things. Of course, writing was forbidden. But "writing" is a relative concept. I
began to write in my head. However, I understood that I had to preserve the
product in some way, and I did not count on my own survival. A thought came
to me that seemed unrealizable, but in life, when you put your mind to it, many
impossible things may be accomplished.
    I decided to find a young person who would undertake to *preserve* what I
"wrote." To do this, *every word* would have to be learned by heart. Such a person
was found, and we began our project.

12. Yelizaveta Drabkina, "Vernost'," *Izvestiia,* September 15, 1966.

After work, that is, after a day of felling trees (my work was easier than hers, but still not easy), we would sit down somewhere in the courtyard and, pretending casual conversation, get busy with the job. One word overheard by an outsider could bring with it the most terrible consequences.

But we were separated. I went off to the "continent" [Kolyma], and the work was interrupted for over a year. Then I took myself in hand and, at a fairly rapid rate, finished it all. I resorted to paper only in order temporarily to fix bits and pieces as they were born (by the first letter of each line); later I threw the paper away. But sometimes I managed without using paper at all. At last, the work was done. The result was quite sizable—roughly four thousand lines. And then I found that I was dissatisfied with a lot of it.

Can such things be revised in the mind? I didn't think it was possible, but I began trying, and I did it! It was even harder than "writing"! But possible! A very flexible thing—the human mind. But after I completed this, I faced another task which was probably the hardest of all; in any case, it was infinitely dangerous. The thing had to be drawn out of my head and made material. I decided to begin writing it on cigarette papers, and then bury or conceal them somewhere. Of course, as I now know, I was doing useless work, but I carried it through to the end. It was useless because, through inexperience or thoughtlessness, I stuck it all in a tin can. It has probably all rusted and rotted away, although that makes no difference now.

I remember certain episodes in the work. In the first place, the writing absolutely had to be done in the open, without any secrecy, because otherwise everything would be lost at one blow. This openness also meant that everything had to be done under the very noses of the authorities, in the view of everyone, but in a way they wouldn't notice. I would take a needle and some mending, as well as a pencil stub and some paper, and do the two things at once. I usually sat close to water—just in case—so that I could drown the "paperwork" in a puddle, a well, a bucket, a pitcher, and thus limit the consequences to nothing more than the punishment cell.

I remember one incident. I was sitting by our "club" in the early spring, writing. About twenty steps behind me was a large puddle from melting snow. Suddenly the duty officer came running from his office, straight at me! I said to myself, "Hold on! Don't run till the last minute!" And then I noticed (with my heart in my throat) that he was looking over my head. That meant I should remain sitting, that it wasn't me he was after. Someone, it seems, had sacrilegiously hung underwear out to dry on the barbs of the clubhouse roof. The officer had seen it from his window and was running to tear it down.

What this was like can be understood only by those who know what a threat my work was for someone like myself who had already been given a death sentence for the same "offense." And he was so enraged he tore the underclothes to pieces.

All this filled my days completely. At last, everything was finished. I had written about twenty verses for each piece of paper. This meant I was carrying two hundred papers in a little gauze bag around my neck, always having to take care not to crush or crumple them. And then I hid them in that tin can, which by now has surely rotted, and I hid it away.

There was one friend, a very great friend indeed, who always stood by me, who risked sharing my fate for no good reason. I will never forget her. She will never be a stranger to me. I have tremendous confidence in her—in her friendship, courage, tenacity, and her capacity for silence. She did not share my views, but she never—and this has been tested by the years—took advantage of my confidence in her to further some different aim. I do not write about this casually, as I'm sure you understand.

And so. You all know the second variant I used to preserve the work, and the "technology" that it involved. But the main "technology," the main prop, the main luggage rack, was my head. That was what enabled me to recreate everything here in Leningrad, and to send it where we Communists cannot fail to send our thoughts and our experiences.

Well, that's it, in a nutshell!

Lena (Yelena Lvovna Vladimirova)
[No. 9, June 1965]

From Yelena Vladimirova's Kolyma

The Halt

Hands tucked into their sleeves,
Necks bent against the wind,
They shuffled slowly on and on,
Taking distance yard by yard.
Not hearing the shouting guards,
Barely feeling their own bodies,
Weak legs slipping on ice,
These people went on—if
It is possible at all
To call them people.
They got up and they fell again,
Got up and marched.
Should one of them have died,
No one would have picked him up,
No one would have stopped near him.
Each and every person
Had strength enough
Only for himself.
Reaching relay stations,

They clutched the heart side
Of their chest
And fell pell-mell upon
The icy snow crust.
And even the blizzard
Would yield
In its icy rage in front
Of the fearsome spectacle
Of the halt
Of half-unconscious people.

The Lower Camp

. . . Again we part: Today
Ivanych has been sent away.
Those who are sick, no good,
Too weak for mining
Are lowered down, sent
To the camp below
To fell the trees of Kolyma.
It's very simple when
Written down on paper.
But I cannot forget
The chain of sleds upon the snow
And people, harnessed.
Straining their sunken chests,
They pull the cartage . . .
They either stop to rest
Or falter on steep slopes.
The heavy weight rolls down
And any moment
It will trip them, break them down . . .
These poor bodies are now taut,
The veins blown up
On emaciated necks . . .
Who has not seen a horse
That stumbles?
But we, we have seen people
In a harness.
Dreadful
Is this novel winter transport.
It ferries lumber from the valley
Through the taiga, white
In all directions;
It moves through icy space

Which has no roads.
You cannot cross it.
You cannot make a step.
He who has seen the cartage
May have turned blind.
But not forgetful.

[No. 9, June 1965]
Translated by Vera Dunham

Rebellion in the Northern Camps
by Mikhail Baitalsky

After three arrests and many years in prison camps, Mikhail Baitalsky (1903–1978) emerged, late in life, as one of the most remarkable samizdat writers of the 1960s and 1970s. Writing mostly under various pseudonyms (M.D., D. Seter, I. Domalsky, A. Krasikov, Aronovich, and Ilsky), he produced a wide range of books, scholarly essays, reviews, and poetry. They included important studies of Russian anti-Semitism, a famous article on Soviet vodka consumption ("Commodity No. 1"), poetry on Jewish themes, and his memoirs This Was Our School: Notebooks to My Grandchildren. Baitalsky began political life in the 1920s as a Young Communist and Trotskyist in Odessa. After a brief arrest for Trotskyist activities in 1927, he worked on Kharkov, Leningrad, and Moscow newspapers as a journalist until 1934, when he, like many former Party oppositionists, lost his job in the first repressions that followed the Kirov assassination. Thereafter, Baitalsky worked, whether as a free man or in camp, at hard labor. He was arrested again in 1936. Apart from a few years in the 1940s, when he fought in the Red Army all the way to Berlin, Baitalsky remained in forced-labor camps, including the infamous Vorkuta, until 1956. During this period, he turned to the Jewish faith and began to write poetry. After official rehabilitation in 1957, he moved to a town in the Northern Caucasus and later to Moscow, where his writings brought him again to the attention of the KGB. This section from Baitalsky's memoirs is a firsthand account of the events in 1953–55 that attended the decision to liberate most of the inmates of Stalin's archipelago of forced-labor camps.

Soon after Stalin's death, a broad amnesty was proclaimed. It was called the "Voroshilov Amnesty," after the Party leader who signed the proclamation and who was then Chairman of the Presidium of the Supreme Soviet. The amnesty affected only criminals, that is, nonpolitical prisoners. The politicals remained in the camps, waiting for a review of their cases.

A prisoner transport of many thousands was brought from the Karaganda camps to Vorkuta. The new arrivals were dispersed among the various mines. Before their departure from Karaganda, they had been promised, "As soon as you arrive in Vorkuta, the review of your cases will begin." But no steps were taken to carry out this promise.

The prisoners from Karaganda then agreed among themselves to go on strike. They decided to strike with the slogan "You gave your word—keep it." On the appointed day, the prisoners from Karaganda refused to come out for work and raised a red flag over their mine. Other prisoners not from Karaganda joined the strikers, and two mines were shut down. Then the boss of the camp subsection of Mine Administration No. 2 seized several people and put them in the BUR [severe-punishment barracks]. According to the standard practice, he pronounced them the ringleaders and was planning to take reprisals against them in order to intimidate the rest. They were sitting in the BUR when the doors were opened for delivery of the usual pails of gruel. Knocking the wardens aside, the prisoners rushed out. But they weren't trying to escape; they ran into the camp, heading for the barracks. The chief of the prison administration was nearby. He drew his pistol and emptied it at the fugitives. Hearing these shots, the soldiers in the towers also opened fire. They fired in panic, without knowing who they were shooting at and without any orders to open fire or cease fire. Two prisoners were killed. One by the chief and the other by a stray bullet from a tower.

The strike at the two mines continued for ten days. The compound was ringed by troops, and there were machine guns at the four corners of the rectangular compound. The authorities dickered with the prisoners over every concession. The only concessions had to do with camp regulations. They did not involve the main demand of the strikers—the review of their cases. That they would not grant. They would not even announce that those guilty of the shootings would be punished. On the other hand, they did allow the prisoners themselves to bury the two who had been killed.

The death of these innocents united everyone in one great burst of passion —Banderovtsy [collaborators with the Germans] and former prisoners of war, both Russian and German; Jews and former Nazi collaborators. Everyone put on black arm bands. The dead were carried to the beat of a funeral march—the subsection having its own amateur orchestra. Two red coffins were raised on high; the dead mens' faces were turned to the mute and indifferent heavens above Vorkuta, where thunder was never heard. The subsection authorities gathered and stood at a distance. In solemn silence, the prisoners passed before the red coffins, having removed their flap-eared caps. Each paused for a moment before the coffins. Some simply stood there; others bowed to the ground or kissed the foreheads of the dead; others kneeled and whispered a prayer. The camp bosses kept their distance and remained silent. The ceremony lasted almost all day. Then a small group chosen by the prisoners themselves went off under guard to bury the dead. Those were the first *zeks* [prisoners] at Vorkuta to be buried by daylight.

There was also shooting at Mine No. 29. What happened there was no joke. Work had already resumed at No. 2 when No. 29 went on strike. It was located not far away, and the movement spread there quickly. No. 40 also went on strike. Many were killed there, but no one knew the exact count.

In the summer of 1955, unexpectedly and quite spontaneously, a strike broke out in our mine, too. A convoy guard provoked it when he shot down an old prisoner for no reason at all, only because the man had sat down on the ground. But he picked the wrong year for shooting people. The prisoners began to shout; the convoy guards got scared and raised their weapons. Then someone shouted, "We won't march with a convoy like this." Everyone rushed back through the gates, and the convoy guards were left to themselves. All night long the prisoners sat in the mine yard and waited. When the evening shift came up from the pit faces, they joined the others. The night shift was not brought in. They, too, had refused to move. On the next day, the hungry and exhausted prisoners agreed to leave the mine. They had been promised that the problem would be discussed "at home" in the camp compound. Ringed by guards, they made their way "home." The mine was shut down. The *zeks* raised one demand, "We will wait for a representative of the central procuracy office. We don't trust you local people any more." A representative flew in, had discussions, and took a great many statements. A general meeting of prisoners was permitted, and many spoke. A former Soviet army pilot by the name of Dobroshtan, who had spent twenty-five years at hard labor, spoke the most daringly and effectively. He was taken off to Moscow and after a little while returned rehabilitated. He was the first swallow of spring in our subsection. He took a job at Mine No. 40 because the woman he loved was there and he couldn't leave her.

The Twentieth Congress of 1956 had not yet delivered its message, but the winds of change were blowing stronger. General Maslennikov, who was in charge when some new shootings occurred, committed suicide, taking all the responsibility upon himself. Once he was gone, there was no one to complain to or ask why it had happened.

Then it was announced that wives would be allowed to come to the camps for personal visits. Autumn was nearly over and winter coming. In honor of the thirty-eighth anniversary of October, I received the long-awaited permit, which we *zeks* called our passport. This gave us the right to enter Vorkuta, the Arctic city we had built, and to live there with our wives—not forgetting, of course, about the camp guardhouse, where we had to check in every day and to which we could be called at any moment to have our permits revoked and be locked up in the camp compound once again. "Be ready for the unexpected," the long life I had lived told me. And in reply I answered with the oath of the Young Pioneers—"Always ready!"

[No. 37, October 1967]

Fisherman
BY AN ANONYMOUS POET

Mass liberation of the prison camps finally got underway in 1956, three full years after Stalin's death. Perhaps seven to eight million survivors of the terror were set free. Their fates after camp or exile varied greatly. Some former prisoners managed to salvage at least part of their shattered lives. They reunited with their families or found new ones; they resumed their careers or received livable pensions. A significant number of returnees went on to make a mark on official or dissident Soviet life, including a few who appear in this book—Kopelev, Yakir, Kakhovskaya, Vladimirova, Baitalsky, Shabalkin, Gen. Aleksandr Todorsky, Pavel, Solzhenitsyn, and Boris Dyakov. But many survivors of the terror had already lost everything—career, family, health, pension, and purpose. Abandoned and forgotten, they were the flotsam of the nearly emptied Gulag, a living reproach to the crimes of the past and a Soviet state that still "does not accept the blame." The following poem, which circulated anonymously in typescript in Moscow in the 1960s, tells one such story.

In a village on the upper Volga
Where seagulls make noise,
There lives a quiet old man.
He has a smart sharp-faced dog.

He spreads his simple tackle
And sits through the dawn.
Comes frost, he cracks the ice
Over fish runs for luck.

And the catch, so hard to get,
Bream, roach, and pike,
He takes in a frozen tub
To a market in Moscow.

Ladies with monarchical grandeur
And Muscovite gloss and chic
Call him "pops" as they cast
Furtive glances at the scale.

How can they possibly know that
In a still Arbat lane long ago
An engineer with gray hair was seized
According to order prescribed.

And that he was tortured, abused
In sleepless cellar captivity
And that another woman was added
To the bitter list of straw widows.

In the mine, in the shifty peat bog,
Month followed month.
And then they proclaimed as error
The stolen seventeen years.

He came out awkward, nameless,
Having fully received his due.
He learned that his wife serves
Her term in the heavenly kingdom.

He learned that in this prudent,
Cold world of lackey hearts,
He was no more needed than
A lodger forgotten long since.

And again the titled grandees
Do not let him go on.
And again my State
Does not accept the blame.

Let the fisherman's hut, let
The river sustain his pride . . .
I can think of him, comrade,
Only with clenched teeth

And of all those left to rot
In hidden cement coffins . . .
The Volga rises in storm . . .
The fisherman hoists his sail.

He is old. He is what he is.
He can't bear his head to bow low.
I wish you luck and good catch
And good wind, old man!

[No. 28, January 1967]
Translated by Vera Dunham

2

Guilt and Responsibility

J UST AS PROLONGED MASS CRIMES require a great many accomplices, public exposures of such crimes raise large questions of political responsibility, personal guilt, and punishment. In the case of the crimes of the Stalin era, these questions were potentially explosive because so many culprits remained in positions of authority, high and low, throughout the Soviet system. The fact that issues of responsibility and criminal guilt were discussed only occasionally, and guardedly, in the Soviet press should not be misconstrued. Behind the scenes, they were the source of intense controversy and great alarm almost from the moment of Stalin's death in 1953.

Such questions were raised officially on three important occasions, though for the most part ineffectually. The first was in 1953, when the new post-Stalin government announced that Beria had been arrested (and subsequently, along with several other high policemen, executed) for certain "criminal activities." The point was to limit all responsibility to "Beria's clique," but the idea of Stalinist crimes and present-day punishment had been officially established; it sent shock waves through security forces all the way to the furthest islands of the Gulag.[1] The second occasion was the Twentieth Party Congress in 1956. Even though Khrushchev's speech extended the criminal indictment only upward to

1. See, for example, Aleksandr Solzhenitsyn, *The Gulag Archipelago* (New York, 1978), III, 280–81.

Stalin, it, too, caused panic among police officials and others implicated in the terror; many of them immediately suffered "mental breakdowns from their fears of being made to answer for their crimes."[2] The third occasion was the Twenty-second Congress in 1961, when Khrushchev's public revelations not only implicated Molotov, Kaganovich, Malenkov, and Voroshilov, but set off a short-lived public discussion about mass accomplices in the terror.

Little came of these official half steps. No more than a few thousand people were ever punished in any way, most of them being merely demoted or prematurely retired. And even elliptical references to the problem were largely banished from official Soviet publications by the mid-1960s. General and specific questions of criminal responsibility for the Stalinist past were thus left to fester behind the scenes until they emerged openly in samizdat in the form of detailed accusations as well as discussions of the general problem.

Germany was the analogy suggested most often in these discussions. The Soviet Union had been a prosecuting party at the Nuremberg trials and a signatory to the judgments on "crimes against humanity." (Indeed, Khrushchev's attorney general, Roman Rudenko, had been a chief prosecutor at Nuremberg.) Anti-Stalinists argued, even in the official press, that the Nuremberg principle should be applied to crimes of the Stalin years as well.[3] (Nothing like even the modest program of German denazification had occurred in the Soviet Union.)

These and related issues began to appear in Political Diary from its beginning. While the individual guilt of various high officials was often easy to document, larger issues were more complex. As Roy Medvedev observed, "The question of responsibility for past crimes cannot be separated from the question of what a person could have done to prevent them. And of course that is no simple question. The answer necessarily depends on the circumstances."[4]

2. *Politicheskii dnevnik*, II, 123.
3. See the excerpts from official publications in ibid., pp. 109–22.
4. Ibid., p. 123.

Recriminations
PARTY WRITERS DISCUSS THE PAST

Khrushchev's dramatic revelations about Stalin at the Twentieth Party Congress on the night of February 24–25, 1956, soon became widely known. Copies of his text were closely guarded, but it was read to many groups across the country, and special meetings were called to discuss its contents. The impact was profoundly traumatic and divisive, especially in official circles, as is clear from the following record of one such meeting. Evidently the only uncensored document of this kind ever to become public, it is a partial transcript ("excerpts from the protocol") of a discussion by Party members of the Soviet Writers' Union, held in Moscow in March 1956, on the "results of the Twentieth Party Congress." The meeting took place in the charged political atmosphere just after Khrushchev's speech and as survivors of the camps, including writers, were returning to Moscow and other cities. The nature of the sometimes elliptic document—it is an amalgam of verbatim stenograph, summary, and an observer's commentary—has required more than the usual number of bracketed editorial insertions. Otherwise, this remarkable document, published here with only a small deletion, speaks for itself. Most of the speakers at the meeting, which must have been sizable, were well-known authors and literary critics. Some were accomplices of the terror, others victims. Thus, the discussion turned quickly and inexorably to the subject of guilt and responsibility for the crimes of the past.

Summary of Aleksei Surkov's Report : [Surkov said,] the foul hangmen's work of Yezhov and Beria also left its mark on the work of Soviet writers: as more and more people disappeared, the range of problems that could be dealt with grew narrower. Surkov objected sharply to Mikhail Sholokhov's remarks at the Twentieth Congress, that the Writers's Union had become a Union of Dead Souls. (Applause.) He criticized Vera Panova's *Seryozha*, arguing that her range of vision had narrowed. (Shouts of "Not true!") I am not assuming the right to judge, he continued, but I too can express my view. . . . This process in literature explains why readers are more and more annoyed by our books. (Shouts from the audience: "It's not Panova that annoys readers" and "What annoys readers is the lack of truth.") At one writers' meeting there were even remarks to the effect that perhaps Marxism is not obligatory for writers, that free people are allowed to think as they wish. (Shouts: "Correct!") But I think that is incorrect. I think the fact that someone belongs to the Party means that certain things become obligations for Party members, based on a voluntary mutual understanding.

Nadezhda Chertova: The Twentieth Congress was a veritable ocean of ozone. We have learned how much the people's great love was abused and how false were the words that our most valuable capital is man—words spoken at a time when thousands of honest people were in prison. When we were in the countryside, only one form of literature remained for us—reports to the Central Committee. The worst production of the last few years was the [Stalin cult] film *The Vow.* It is proof that the circumstances affected even such a talented person as [the late] Pyotr Pavlenko. He would be sick at heart if he were sitting in this hall. There are officials who are accustomed only to carrying out orders. Such people will now be removed and new ones appointed. But it is impossible to dismiss writers. They themselves must change.

Aleksandr Avdeyenko: I warmly and sincerely loved Stalin. And then, as screenwriter for the film *Law of Life,* I was called in to see Stalin, who was in a rage. It was an investigation and trial combined, and lasted for five hours. Stalin behaved like the investigator in the [film] *The Rumyantsev Affair.* I was shocked. Stalin was the only one to speak. He didn't speak so much as pass sentence on me, and the sentence was to be carried out immediately. I was banished from every place. I was not trusted even to fight in the war. But I continued to believe and to love him. I often stopped believing in myself. I am recalling this, not in order to settle a score: my example just shows how complicated and difficult it all was. You know from the materials of the Twentieth Congress that Molotov, Mikoyan, Khrushchev, and Bulganin also continued to believe in Stalin. By the time they realized the truth, it was probably too late. Stalin the godlike betrayed our love. Thousands and thousands of Communists suffered the torments of prisons and camps, perishing from hunger, cold, and despair. We remember the tragic fate of the Kalmyks. We remember the armies abandoned to Hitler's mercies. Flagrant contradictions were embodied in this individual [Stalin]. The brand of shame must be placed on all informers. Nor can those who encouraged slanderers be forgiven. We ourselves are not blameless; we remained silent when honest Communists were taken away, and we did not help their families.

Avdeyenko went on to praise the Central Committee, arguing that it had never diverged from the Leninist line, that the Party had grown year after year, and so on. Shouts began to come from the audience: "Enough hypocrisy!" and "Timeserver!"

Pavel Blyakhin (author of the scenario for *The Red Devil Cubs*): I don't agree with Mikoyan. No, Leninist norms and Leninist principles have not yet been restored. We should not confuse what we want with what actually exists. The way things were has left very deep traces on the people's consciousness, on the Party, and on the government apparatus. Lenin dreamed of creating a socialist apparatus not just in words but in reality. How has Lenin's sacred trust been fulfilled? Instead of a socialist apparatus, a bureaucratic apparatus has been built and trained in the spirit of the worship of rank, mindless careerism, and the pursuit of the soft job. An apparatus that has lost all sense of responsibility. Stalin held the place of the tsar, and his power rested on this apparatus. There was a disparity in material standards of living that is inadmissible for a Soviet society. Among other things, this led to such loathsome developments as the Aleksandrov affair, in which [G. F. Aleksandrov,] a member of the Central Committee, a doctor of philosophy, the minister of culture, and the head of the Central Committee's department of propaganda, turned out to be the key figure in a den of debauchery, a dacha where orgies were held. The Stalin era jeopardized the foundations of [the Soviet] constitution, the brotherhood of the Soviet nationalities, and socialist legality itself. The Kalmyks have already been discussed here. But what should be said about the sufferings of the Jewish people? The Beilis case discredited the tsarist autocracy in the eyes of the whole world. [Similarly] the disgraceful "Doctors' Plot" [an anti-Semitic frame-up in 1951–53] has left a stain on the Party and above all on us, Russian Party members. People were fired on account of nationality; obstacles were created for Jews when applying for jobs; attempts were made secretly to reestablish the Jewish Pale. All this has left its ugly mark on us, the Russian members of the Party. (Loud applause.)

Can it be said that no trace of all this remains? Are there really no hidden anti-Semites now? There are people who, on the sly, are trying to slow down every change and even to prevent rehabilitations. So far, only seven to eight thousand people have been rehabilitated. Khrushchev's remarks at the congress on the number of prisoners made a painful impression. How long will innocent people still have to languish in prison? A series of measures must be undertaken to bring about mass rehabilitation. The only guarantee against a repetition of what happened under Stalin is Leninist democracy in the Party and the Soviets.

Nikolai Rodionov (who spoke about Leonid Zorin's play *Guests*): The minor defects in this play have been exaggerated. It is a weak play and not up to snuff ideologically, but in order to make this point, was it really necessary to hold a special session of the Ministry of Culture, which the newspaper *Sovetskaya kultura* publicized, with bootlicking eagerness? After all this working over, the author was taken seriously ill.

Yelizar Maltsev: Putting the changes into practice will be difficult. From top to bottom, cadres have been trained in the old style of leadership. In Ryazan province, just as before, the collective-farm chairman is all-powerful, and the secretary of the Party's province committee pounds the desk with his fist. And at the Party Congress many behaved in a cowardly fashion. Many of the speeches, stereotyped and uniform, were cause for alarm.

Dogmatism has reigned in our country. Life was checked against the quotations, and not vice versa. Fear prevailed. There was more faith in dogma than in people. How many times have we heard the [anti-Semitic] word *cosmopolitan* in this hall? The fate of the late Party member Shukin shows how tenacious demagogy still is. Vladimir Pomerantsev's article "On Sincerity in Literature" was a timid protest against hypocrisy. It was written with honest intentions. But what shouts rang out against it! And once again we frightened away a layer of non-Communist writers. Less harm was done by the article itself than by the reaction to it. Pomerantsev was proclaimed to be an ideological enemy. At the same time, Fyodor Abramov's article appeared in *Novy mir*—the first timid step in a serious discussion of our agricultural problems. The label "nihilism" was pasted on it. Abramov's mouth was stopped. Mark Shcheglov's article on Leonov's *Russian Forest* has a very thought-provoking article paragraph about [the character] Gratsiansky. This article, too, was declared to be of the enemy.

Surkov should have said that it is ridiculous, to say the least, to accuse criticism of every crime. There is no need to hunt for bourgeois ideology where it does not exist. Rather, the Central Committee should look into all the unseemly goings-on involved with the "special pay envelopes" for officials in responsible posts.

Even today the secretary of the Party Provincial Committee does not depend on the rank and file in any way. But fear has now been eliminated. As a writer, I would like to examine what kind of soil the personality cult arose from, what social causes produced it. After all, one cannot explain everything in terms of Stalin's individual peculiarities. The philosophers ought to give an explanation. Surkov's report is evidence that he hasn't understood a thing. Sholokhov hasn't understood anything either. His speech at the congress was shameful and very surprising. This was the reaction in the hall.

Vladimir Rudny: I am distressed by Surkov's report; it reeks of the inertia of the past. Again it turns out that those chiefly to blame for what happened in our country are the writers. Sholokhov, Surkov, and Fadeyev are linked together by their attitude toward us as "dead souls." Is it true that Surkov himself failed to consult with Party members about his speech at the Party Congress?

Nikolai Lesyuchevsky spoke here about the rehabilitation of dead writers. Of course, that must be done. But I want to speak about the rehabilitation of the living. A critical reappraisal of the literary policy of the last few years is needed. Why has Emmanuil Kazakevich's short novel *Two on the Steppe* been deleted from Soviet literature? Why does Pavel Nilin bear the burden of guilt to this day for the "errors" of the film *The Great Life*? We are asked, Why bring up the past? But the Central Committee was not afraid to bring up a past in comparison with which our literary concerns are a mere trifle. This is the first real Party meeting of writers. Why, then, are we afraid to speak of the Sofronov crowd? Not in order to cause a new 1937, but to make sure they don't escape our notice. After all, there were many who even believed in Anatoly Sofronov. They held the power in literary policy—Sofronov, Nikolai Gribachev, Aleksandr Chakovsky, Vasily Smirnov. It was they who brought suspiciousness into our midst. Even now, a muted campaign is being waged against Konstantin Paustovsky, Aleksandr Bek, and Kazakevich, and against the [new] anthology *Literaturnaya Moskva*. We have not forgotten the shameful case of Anatoly Surov, who is still being defended in all sorts of ways. We expelled him, but Sholokhov and Fadeyev signed a letter to the Central Committee saying that he does not drink. (Cries of "Shame!")

The Party Committee displayed a lack of principle. Gribachev and Sofronov decided they wanted to be dropped from the roster of the Party Committee of the Writers' Union, and that was permitted. But who was it who introduced the vicious use of parentheses? [That is, publishing people's Jewish last names after their adopted Russian names.] Sofronov! And why was it necessary to force people to vote for Sofronov?

To this day we have leadership by the phone-call method—some instructor from the Central Committee gives his opinion as though it were the opinion of the Central Committee. We ourselves are to blame. We turn every trifle into a directive. Khrushchev went to see the production of *Money*, and right away everyone began to praise it. Arkady Anastasyev was right to criticize it. The campaign against cosmopolitanism [in the late 1940s] was perverted. To this day, neither Grigory Brovman nor Lev Subotsky [Jewish writers] are asked to write articles. We are accomplices. We all bear the responsibility for what happened. The Politburo never supported demagogy. Here in this hall are people with varying degrees of talent, but what they all have in common is the same Party card.

Isaak Yermashev: This is very painful for all of us. But did everything really happen without any struggle? If that regime had not encountered resistance, who knows how far things might have gone? The wave of mass terror heightened the resistance. Silence is also a form of struggle. Not all books are false. Not everyone proved to be a toady and a hypocrite. Those who proved not to be were persecuted. If the vital forces of the Party, of Leninism, had not persisted, we would not be in this hall now. We must give a portrayal of this struggle, of the stages it went through. In the Party leadership, too, not everyone was the "stand at attention" type. There were heroes who were not intimidated.

Even now the struggle continues. It is not a thing of the past for us. The struggle is only beginning. There is a certain mechanism at work, aimed at sabotaging the decisions of the Twentieth Congress. I am not allowed to appear in print in defense of the congress decisions. I have written two books, fairly good ones, if I may say so myself, but they will not publish them.

Yermashev went on to polemicize against Bonifaty Kedrov, who had criticized Khrushchev's speech and said that, to be consistent with Marxism, one should investigate the social and economic soil out of which Stalin had grown. Yermashev tried to argue that in this case the personality of the individual himself was indeed the key to everything. How much had been falsified and lied about in the history of the party, [he said]. Khrushchev's speech was only a fraction of the truth. Where did this huge number of butchers come from? From what pit, what kingdom of darkness? Expunging Stalin from history isn't the method. Do we forget about the dukes de Guise [in the slaughter of the Huguenots] or about Ivan the Terrible? In our literature, Stalin should be treated as he deserves.

Olga Voitinskaya: When Pavel Komarov, [a deputy section head] at the Central Committee's offices, asked Communists who were being rehabilitated what had given them the strength to hold out during eighteen years of prison and internal exile, they answered, "Faith in the Party." Everything that happened was possible because there had been a retreat from the principles of Party democracy and proletarian democracy. A patron system of the Maecenas type was implanted in literature and art. The personal tastes of prominent Party officials decided everything. In elections, why do we have only one candidate for each workers' deputy in the Soviets? The apparatus has enormous power to this day. Trofim Lysenko's articles traveled around [scientific circles] on a visa from Stalin. Aleksandrovism and what was done in the literary world represented the same kind of thing— the pushing of people without talent, persecution of the talented, and reprisals against dissidents. It used to be considered indelicate to speak of anti-Semitism. How ashamed I was when my son asked me about it. I don't know where that feeling came from. In 1948 Ilya Ehrenburg announced that he would not publish anything more, because Jewish names were being dropped from the newspapers. Non-Party Russian intellectuals found this anti-Semitism a bitter experience. Aleksei Tolstoy and Sergei Obraztsov went to *Izvestia's* offices and asked to be allowed to speak out [on this question]. But they were not allowed to. There were people on the Central Committee who gave their blessing to the anti-Semites. They are still there. The so-called Point Five [requiring people of Jewish origin to state "Jew" as their nationality on official documents] is still in effect today. All this must be decisively changed. The personnel departments cannot be allowed to remain the sole guardians of the Party line.

Oleg Pisarzhevsky: I want to associate myself with the criticisms made by Maltsev, Voitinskaya, and others, expressing my warmest gratitude for their honesty and courage. Why do we hide so much from our own people in the special "white edition" of TASS [an uncensored news bulletin restricted to top officials]? We must be bolder about informing the people of our difficulties and the extremes of our backwardness. This is the only way to cultivate civic awareness. Self-respect must be restored. There are changes under way. But some very retrograde forces are trying to impede these changes. What can you expect from people trained in servility and the worship of rank? Who, if not writers, should fight to carry out the changes? But, thus far, we have only deleted a few words from our pamphlets. Under the Stalin regime, the term *the collective* lost its previous meaning. When a head stuck out, it was removed. The whole educational system was directed against the independent individual and toward the obedient "cog." The result was nothing but faceless nonentities. Panova's Seryozha is a young boy, but he already has a personality. That is why the novella drew hostile fire. Everyone must be a responsible person in his own sphere, not just someone who carries out orders—be like Lubentsov in Kazakevich's *The House on the Square*. In the recent past, writers did not need to know life well —it was enough to present the appearance that all was well and express the sentiments of a good and faithful subject. It was not from a sense of conviction that many people entered the literary profession; they have yet to pass the test proving they deserve the title of writer.

Yelena Usiyevich: For the first time, writers at a Party meeting are speaking warmly, honestly, passionately, not only about the situation in literature but the situation in the country, the condition of the people. When the special and precious link between literature and life is discussed, it is as though we do not live [by such a link]. Writers were sent out to learn the life of the country like convoys of prisoners. (Nikolai Shundik from the audience: "That's a slander.") No, it's the truth. [We were told,] If you are not linked with life, nothing will come of your efforts but a "blue fence" (a reference to an article in a Komsomol paper about the writer Nikolai Virta). But as for those whose hearts ached for the people, who had the temerity to speak out about those things—their statements were declared to be enemy attacks. No access was permitted to the truth. The real situation in the collective farms was known to all, but in literature lies prevailed.

Who created the cult? Stalin, but not only him. After all, we knew about Lenin's Testament [in 1922–23 calling for Stalin's removal as general secretary]. Why, then, did we vote for Stalin? When Trotsky came out against Leninism in 1924, we voted for the man who was for Leninism. It was after the Trotskyist demonstration in 1927 that we first began rising to our feet when Stalin's name was mentioned. The question is now being asked—In what social strata did the cult originate? Answers have already been given at this meeting—there was the big boss and a lot of little bosses. An entire apparatus was built and techniques developed suitable for the cult.

What Yermashev said here struck me as incorrect. His Stalin still has miraculous powers, only turned inside out. Yermashev has let loose the entire vocabulary of the Beria school against Stalin. The only thing omitted was calling him an agent of imperialism. Khrushchev's secret speech is the end of something [for all of us]; it is a tragic document. It brought those twenty years back to mind, and that was hard to bear. It's painful to think of those who perished, painful to think of those who've been brought back. But this is also a guide to action. Life will be rich and full, and literature too will be rich and full. . . . We forgot the art of persuasion that we had learned. And what's the result? Young people don't believe the Party press. Let's recall the meeting before the elections to the

Soviets: the Party fraction [caucus] was not allowed to discuss candidates. We knew that we were lying and lost all vestiges of moral authority.

I would like to say one more thing about the Aleksandrov affair. Even bourgeois morality does not permit what he did. Now he is in Minsk, teaching young people Marxism. Who will believe in the sanctity of ideas presented by such a person? We must get back to relying on our consciences rather than orders over the phone. How many times my conscience cried out, but Fadeyev would say, "They know best up there." Where is "up there"? In what other world? The people of [ancient] Novgorod always said yes, and they got by that way. But we can't get by being yes-men.

Raissa Orlova: The days we are now living through remind me of the days right after October—there is the same mass-meeting type of democracy. Everybody wants to speak. Those who have long held their tongues. And those who long spoke nothing but lies. And those who sincerely believed and who are now being told they believed in lies. People are coming to an accounting with their own consciences. It is as though everyone is answering the question, And where were you? I too ask myself, How could I have voted to expel decent people and honest Communists who were sitting in this very hall? But we can't allow ourselves the luxury of resting at this stage. We are not repentant nobles, but members of a militant party, responsible for the fate of our country.

The theme of the congress was the restoration of Leninist norms. In this connection, I would like to raise two questions. The Soviets were the great achievement of October. But in the work of the Soviets there is a great deal of window dressing; the deputies often feel no sense of responsibility toward their constituents. We need to have several candidates for each Soviet deputy, so that we will have elections and not just a hand-picked selection. We have a single party and a single program. But this program can be interpreted in various ways. Let the voters decide which of the candidates has greater personal merit. At present, the Soviet elections are just a ceremonial form.

My second question is about the personnel departments. This is the most undemocratic part of the apparatus. Actually, every leader selects his own personnel anyway—the special personnel departments only interfere.

One of the most burdensome legacies of the personality cult is "double bookkeeping." People said one thing and did something else. There was a vast gulf between the press and actual opinion. This has not been completely eliminated. The main thing about the Aleksandrov affair was not the debauchery but the hypocrisy. How did Aleksandrov and his kind dare to instruct writers in the true Party Spirit? Even today there are two sets of books for evaluating works of literature: one for the public and one for private consumption. Why was there not a word in the press about the three-day debate on the education of the young in which Nikolai Atarov, Pisarzhevsky, Frida Vigdorova, Lyubov Kabo, and Aleksandr Sharov participated? Why was nothing printed about the celebration of Ilya Ehrenburg's sixty-fifth birthday? Apparently they're waiting for his seventieth. Leonid Martynov's fiftieth birthday was in fact a celebration of that poet's rehabilitation. *Literaturnaya gazeta* carried only a tiny news item about it. There was silence on Panova's *Seryozha* and silence on Yaroslav Smelyakov's *Stern Love*. Why do they keep silent, if not because Smelyakov was in prison?

Aleksandr Isbakh: There is a past that we cannot amnesty in the name of the future. The concepts of love and friendship were trampled in the mud, while hypocrites and chameleons flourished. The most shameful pages in the history of our organization are linked with Gribachev's term as secretary. Why haven't Gribachev and Sofronov come to this meeting? They are young Communists. It would be good for them to hear from the Old Bolshevik Blyakhin. We had two forms of discipline. Surov and Semyon Babayevsky could get away with anything, but Aleksandr Mezhirov was nearly expelled from the Party because it was said he believed in life after death. Whoever occupied a high post might indulge all the seven sins. They were called weaknesses. But there was no honor in being an ordinary, decent person. How shameful it is to recall the terrible poverty in which Andrei Platonov died. At the same time, Sofronov and Gribachev had dachas and apartments with five or six rooms each. There is no need for repressive measures, but the Party must be relieved of people who do not want to live in a Party manner.

Leonid Makaryev: I ask myself, How were we able to maintain ourselves as Communists? Today there are many of us, so this is not simply a matter involving me personally. We know the situation in the Party was not normal. The war was an especially difficult time (the reference is to the situation of those in confinement, as Makaryev was). I remember that at the very beginning of the war two special trainloads, with 4,500 people, arrived [to join us] behind barbed wire. Sasha Milchakov [was there], and [former] delegates to the Seventeenth Party Congress. There were about four hundred people I knew, including writers. Our sense of comradeship helped to protect us. Not all came back, however. A fair number remained there. We lived under very tough conditions, not only physically but in every other respect as well. We were arrested by Communists, interrogated by Communists, guarded by Communists. We were considered fascists. [And all the while] we knew the country was fighting and building.

A large contingent of Soviet people was declared to be part of an enemy organization. There was no such organization. We are all equally to blame, from Khrushchev to me. Thanks to the Central Committee for the courage it showed in confronting this question. When I was asked what I placed my hopes in, I would answer, "The Party, and Stalin." We were all poisoned by a mass psychosis. Even someone as crystal pure as [Lenin's widow] Nadezhda Konstantinova [Krupskaya] gave in to this psychosis. The disease spread gradually—we failed to stop it at the beginning. The definitive answer to the why and wherefore of the Stalin cult can be given only by the collective reasoning of the Party. It cannot be regarded as just a body of fact having to do with Stalin personally. It was a negation of Leninism.

We must make it an object of ridicule and hound it out of existence. The atmosphere of the first several years of Soviet power must be restored in every respect, its simplicity and approachability. There will be no [more] personality cult. The entire Party and the Central Committee have risen up against it. There is no need for a cult of Khrushchev, Bulganin, and the others. Nor for a cult of Lenin either. He was too simple and approachable for that.

[Makaryev then] read an excerpt from Mayakovsky's long poem *Lenin.* The names of those who will never return should be mentioned here; in fact, Surkov should have done so—Bruno Yasensky, Vladimir Kirshon, Aleksei Selivanovsky, Artyom Vesyoly. May all the other names be named as well. (All rise from their seats.)

Rudolf Bershadsky: When the interrogator in Lubyanka Prison showed me the charges against me, the dossier included a statement by Tamara Trifonova asserting that I was a bourgeois nationalist. Today, this woman and others like her want to dump all the blame on Stalin. I am certain that when we have completely exposed all the causes [of the cult], no repetition will be possible. We must not be afraid to dig up the past. That is the only thing that will teach us how to conduct ourselves in the future. I will never forgive myself for having raised my hand in favor of the expulsion of Johann Altman. Yermashev said here that silence is also a form of resistance. But we have no need for heroes of silence. It is no accident that many of the people at this meeting are holding their tongues. What is that? A form of resistance to the Twentieth Congress? I want to ask [Daniel?] Romanenko, who is present here, a question: At a meeting in 1949 you accused Altman of nepotism. This nepotism consisted in the fact that he had his eighteen-year-old son join his unit at the battlefront, where his son died in combat. Romanenko's is the kind of voluntary butcher's work, vileness, and baseness that we must never forget. A short memory is no adornment for a Bolshevik. It is true that there was no particular social class on which Stalin could base himself. On whom did he base himself, then? It was a specially created and costly apparatus. It had only minimal ties with the people. To make up for that, every lower level of the hierarchy was controlled by three-dozen higher bodies. We must remember the Rabkrin [and early Soviet agency intended to combat bureaucracy]. We must carry through a purge of the apparatus and a purge of the Party. (Commotion in the hall; shouts of "Who will carry out the purge?") The personality cult still exists in regard to the Presidium [or Politburo] of the Central Committee. The practice of [special pay] "blue envelopes" must be brought to an abrupt halt.

The writers' meeting continued for three days and ended with the singing of the "Internationale."

[No. 30, March 1967]

Fadeyev's Suicide

There were other politically motivated suicides after Stalin's death, but Aleksandr Fadeyev's was the most notable. (Unless it is true, as wide-spread rumors insisted, that Andrei Vyshinsky, Stalin's procurator and prosecutor in the Moscow Purge Trials of the 1930s, killed himself in 1954.) By the time Fadeyev (1901–1956) shot himself to death in the artist colony Peredelkino on May 13, 1956, he had the reputation of a once gifted novelist who had delivered his talent and soul to Stalinism. The only dispute was whether he had served Stalin out of conviction or cynicism. The Rout (1927) established Fadeyev's literary reputation; The Young Guard (1945), a novel about the war, won him great fame and a Stalin Prize. From 1946 to 1953, one of the most repressive periods in Soviet cultural history, he served as general secretary of the Writers' Union in an imperious way that made him known in literary circles as "the marshal." Neither bureaucratic power nor membership on the Party Central Committee could protect even Fadeyev from Stalin's occasional caprice; Stalin ordered The Young Guard withdrawn from circulation and rewritten. Nonetheless, Fadeyev served the despot faithfully to the end. A longtime alcoholic, Fadeyev evidently spent his last three months after the Twentieth Congress in a tortured haze of guilt-ridden conversations, encounters with camp returnees, and efforts to make amends.[5] Nothing helped. According to rumors, Fadeyev's suicide letter to the Central Committee consisted of only one sentence: "The bullet fired was meant for Stalin's policies, for Zhdanov's aesthetics, for Lysenko's genetics."[6]

Having returned to Moscow after [years in the camps], I—v, an old Party member, renewed his friendship with Aleksandr Fadeyev. In their youth, they had fought side by side in the civil war in the Far East. I—v had been the commander of a guerrilla unit and Fadeyev the political commissar.

On the eve of Fadeyev's suicide, I—v was a guest at Fadeyev's house for a day and a half. They talked about the past. During one of these conversations, Fadeyev asked his comrade whether he would be able to go on living if he learned that many honest, decent people had been killed as a result of his own complicity. I—v answered that he probably would not be able to live with that. Fadeyev then told I—v that in 1937 the Politburo had passed a resolution that the arrests of people working in one or another institution had to be sanctioned by the head of that body. As the head of the Writers' Union, Fadeyev therefore frequently had to authorize the arrests of writers.

5. See, for example, *Novyi mir,* no. 12, 1961, p. 195, for his effort, in March 1956, on behalf of the imprisoned son of Anna Akhmatova.

6. Quoted in Abraham Rothberg, *The Heirs of Stalin* (Ithaca, 1972), p. 178. The references are to Andrei Zhdanov's tyranny over cultural life and Trofim Lysenko's over science.

Fadeyev spoke also about several of his meetings with Stalin. It was Stalin who urged Fadeyev to write the novel *Ferrous Metallurgy*. This happened during a dinner at Stalin's apartment in the Kremlin. Stalin told Fadeyev about the discovery of a "wreckers' plot" in the ferrous-metals industry and asked him to write a novel about it. Stalin told him he could obtain the factual material on the "plot" from Ivan Tevosyan [the minister of metallurgy]. Fadeyev was given the material he needed, and he began writing the novel. A substantial part had been written by the time of Stalin's death, when Fadeyev learned that the whole affair was the usual type of NKVD fabrication of that time. The metallurgists arrested as "wreckers," most of whom had died, were rehabilitated. Fadeyev realized that Stalin had used him for his own vile purposes. Almost all the writers arrested on Fadeyev's authorization were also rehabilitated after Stalin's death.

I—v thinks that Stalin actually had bought Fadeyev, as he bought so many others, by surrounding him with material wealth and honors. Fadeyev told I—v that Stalin had treated him like a loving father and advised him on many matters. Fadeyev said also that he was always given much more money than he needed.

Fadeyev shot himself several hours after his last talk with I—v. In the morning, Fadeyev did not show up for breakfast, and after a long time his sister sent his son to find out why the father wasn't coming down for tea. The son went upstairs and found his father covered with blood. Fadeyev had covered the gun with a pillow to muffle the sound. Fadeyev's sister immediately called the Central Committee. Under the pillow was a letter, sixty pages long; the contents remain unknown except to the Central Committee, to whom it was given. I—v asserts that Fadeyev had stopped drinking in his last days. His conscience was gnawing at him, and that was the reason for his suicide, not the alcoholism mentioned in the official announcement of his death.

[No. 28, January 1967]

Where Are Stalin's Accomplices Today?
BY GEN. ALEKSANDR TODORSKY

Some of the discussion of mass complicity in Stalin's terror, which appeared in official publications for a short time after the Twenty-second Congress in 1961, took place in novels, short stories, and plays. One example was the unproduced play Loyalty *by the older establishment playwright Nikolai Pogodin. The short essay below is extracted from an unpublished review of Pogodin's play. It was written by Gen. Aleksandr Todorsky (1894–1965), who objected to Pogodin's implication that the issue of guilt was only a historical question. Todorsky, a Party member since 1918, had a strong personal interest in the question. Then a corps commander, head of the Air Force Academy, and director of the higher educational system of the Commissariat of Defense, he had been arrested in 1938 and spent fifteen years in prison camps. One of the few high-ranking officers to have survived the military purge, Todorsky was freed in 1953 and eventually promoted to lieutenant general. He was a determined anti-Stalinist, military historian, and friend of future dissident historians such as Roy Medvedev in the early 1960s. It was Todorsky who compiled official statistics showing that Stalin's terror had destroyed virtually the entire Soviet officer corps from top to middle rank.*

By now, of course, through the operation of the laws of nature, many who took part in the tragedy of 1937–38 have died. There were undoubtedly cases in which members of the punitive agencies died as a result of the mortal blow dealt by the abrupt change of political climate. For example, in 1956 an old member of the military tribunal of the Moscow military district died virtually before my eyes when he was visited at his ward in the general hospital on Serebriany Lane by Nikolai Vasilyevich Lisovsky, whom he had previously convicted and sentenced. Lisovsky, too, died several days later at a branch of the hospital in Bolshevo. On another occasion, I was present when a victim confronted his accuser. The victim was Aleksandr A. Turkhansky, an air force major general, and the informer was a Colonel Kovalev, formerly an instructor at the Air Academy. They met at a ward in Lefortovo Hospital. And Kovalev turned as white as a sheet.

But I must say frankly that many former false witnesses—or more precisely, the overwhelming majority—will never have the occasion to meet their victims, of whom not a trace remains. A great many informers got off with only an initial slight scare in 1955–56, and since then they have lived quiet lives like everyone else.

In general, such people are not troubled by their consciences. They understand a good hard stick or a horsewhip much better. But there was no decision
to beat or whip them; if so, mass floggings on a huge scale would have had to
be organized. Instead, these people were just left to their own devices.

Just the other day, a Moscow physician, Isaac Porfos, visited me. (We knew
each other from an East Siberian prison camp.) He had been jailed as a result
of a denunciation by his wife's sister's husband. There had been nothing subtle
about the whole business. The two couples—Porfos and his wife; the wife's sister
and her husband—all Jews, had celebrated some family occasion. The conversation naturally turned to such matters as the obvious restrictions on the admission
of Jews to the universities. Two days later, Porfos was arrested, and the evidence
against him was this conversation over a family dinner table. Porfos was jailed,
but his sister-in-law's husband thrived in freedom. I asked Porfos what kind of
life the man who betrayed him was leading now. He is just as prosperous as ever,
climbing the ladder in the world of science, without a care in the world.

In fact, things are even worse than this. Many of the genuine butchers of
Stalin's time—and I'm using that term for the thugs and interrogators who
worked under Yezhov and Beria—are enjoying their freedom and living far better
than ordinary mortals. It's true that after 1956 many of them were brought to
trial and some shot or sentenced to prison, expelled from the party, stripped of
their pensions, and so on. But there were so many of them that it was apparently
impossible to organize mass trials, and a number of them undeniably got off with
just a slight scare. It would be wrong, then, to say symbolically that the "crag-
faced killers" are now extinct. Many of them are still alive and nursing their
hatred for the Party's policy of combating the Stalin personality cult.

[No. 31, April 1967]

Sverdlov's Son

BY ROY MEDVEDEV

It was clear by the mid-1960s that even people deeply implicated in Stalin's terror would escape any official punishment. Most of them now felt secure, as Todorsky reports, and many confidently went on to other work or to large pensions. Their past criminal activities and present positions therefore were a special subject of samizdat in the late 1960s. The underground newspaper Chronicle of Current Events, for example, often published the current occupation, address, and telephone number of these "hangmen"; and a special samizdat bulletin, Crime and Punishment, devoted exclusively to this subject, began to appear in 1969. Originally titled "The Unusual Fate of the Sverdlov Family," the following case study is an example of this kind of samizdat investigation and indictment. It was written by Roy Medvedev in April 1969 under the pseudonymous initials "Al. M-ii." Yakov Sverdlov was a Soviet founding father and the Party's chief organizer in 1917–19. He has been an illustrious figure in official history ever since his death in 1919. Medvedev's report on Sverdlov's son, published here in abridged form, therefore is doubly interesting. It shows, among other things, that Stalin's terror against the Old Bolsheviks found a few eager accomplices even in those decimated circles.

The lives of many members of Yakov Sverdlov's immediate family turned out to be highly unusual.

Sverdlov himself was one of the most prominent organizers in our party, one of the leaders of the October Revolution and Soviet government. He died of Spanish flu in March 1919 while serving as chairman of the All-Russian Central Executive Committee of the Soviets. The general opinion is that Sverdlov was the second-most important person in the Party and Soviet government apparatus at that time.

The fate of Yakov Sverdlov's younger brother, Zinovy, took quite a different course. The Sverdlov family had close ties with Maxim Gorky, who also lived in Nizhny Novgorod. Gorky adopted Zinovy with the aim of helping this capable young Jewish boy gain admission to a gymnasium [high school]. Under the name Peshkov [Gorky's real name], Zinovy was admitted and graduated; he then went abroad, where he remained. After the October Revolution, he lived in France, choosing a military career, first as a soldier, then an officer in the French Foreign Legion. At the beginning of World War II, he held the rank of general in the French army. He was a firm anti-Communist and refused to see Soviet citizens visiting France who sought him out. This French general died only a few years ago.

Sverdlov's second oldest brother, Veniamin, was well known in the 1930s as an economics specialist and government official; he was a member of the board of the Commissariat of Railways. In 1937, he was arrested, held for a time in a group cell in Lubyanka Prison, then was sent to one of the northern camps, where he died or was shot as an "enemy of the people." He has now been fully rehabilitated.

Sverdlov's third brother, German, was never arrested. He had a notable, though not brilliant career as a propagandist. For many years, he was very popular as a lecturer on international affairs; only after the Twenty-second Party Congress did his popularity begin to decline. German was twenty years younger than Yakov, and in the late 1930s bore a striking resemblance to his older brother. When the film *Lenin in 1918* was being made, German was asked to be a consultant for the many scenes in which Yakov Sverdlov was to appear. As it turned out, the actor playing Yakov's role was obviously unable to handle several of these scenes. At that point, the director unexpectedly suggested that German try playing the part. German agreed and in fact gave an excellent portrayal of his brother. At the first viewing of the film in the Kremlin, everyone was pleased. But in reading the credits, Stalin noticed German's name. In reply to Stalin's inquiries, he was told that this was Yakov Sverdlov's own brother, a propagandist and lecturer. "It's no good," said Stalin, "a propagandist appearing as an actor. And no one will understand this business of 'Yakov Sverdlov is played by German Sverdlov.' It can't stay that way. Take it out." All the scenes with Sverdlov had to be cut and reshot, and the sets of the Kremlin had to be reconstructed. Several scenes were dropped altogether, because the professional actor still could not bring them off effectively. After this episode, German refused any further duties, even as consultant, and lived in fear that he would be arrested.

Yakov Sverdlov's only son, Andrei, began to work for the NKVD as a very young man (not much older than twenty). Here he won rapid promotion owing to his pathological cruelty, rudeness, and crudeness. At the beginning, when he was not sufficiently experienced in this work, he was assigned mainly to cases involving "the children," that is, the sons and daughters of prominent Party and government figures who had been arrested. Not long before that, Andrei had been their fellow student at the Kremlin secondary school, having known them since the days when they had played together as children. At first Andrei got conversations going among the arrested children, acting as an agent provocateur, then he wrote denunciations of them and directed the investigation. These young people, who had barely reached legal age, were accused of forming a "counter-revolutionary organization."

Hanna Hanecka, the daughter of Lenin's close associate Jakob Hanecki, had refused for a long time after her arrest to make a "confession." When she saw Andrei Sverdlov enter the interrogation room, she rushed over to him, crying

"Adik" [a familiar form of Andrei]. "I'm no Adik to you, you swine!" he shouted in reply.

As recently as a few years ago, there were still seven Communists living in Moscow whom Andrei Sverdlov had personally interrogated, using torture and brutality. He also took part in the investigation of Yelizaveta Drabkina, now a well-known Communist writer. Daughter of one of Lenin's closest collaborators (S. I. Gusev), Drabkina had been Yakov Sverdlov's secretary in 1918–19. Several hours before Yakov died, she had taken his children from the apartment where he lay–the son Andrei and the daughter Vera. Andrei Sverdlov knew very well that Drabkina had not committed the crimes charged against her. Nevertheless he obtained her "confession" and "recantation."

Similarly, Andrei Sverdlov personally interrogated and directed the investigation of the well-known Bolshevik Pyotr Petrovsky, son of the prominent Party leader Grigory Petrovsky. Along with a group of NKVD interrogators, Andrei Sverdlov used torture on Petrovsky, who had been one of the leaders of the heroic defense of Uralsk in 1919 and had later helped organize the Komsomol and the Young Communist International, then held a responsible position in the Party's Leningrad regional committee. (Pyotr Petrovsky has now been fully rehabilitated.)

There are reports that Andrei Sverdlov was one of those in charge of the "case" of an outstanding Soviet poet, Pavel Vasilyev. Literary historians now refer to Vasilyev's work as "classic" in Soviet poetry. He was arrested and died in confinement, not without the complicity of Andrei Sverdlov.

It is true that there was a time when Andrei Sverdlov himself was behind bars. But this was a fictitious arrest, only for show, a "trick of the trade." As Sverdlov himself told his cronies, the accounting department of the NKVD regularly continued to pay his salary as an NKVD operative during his confinement. From this, one may safely assume that he played the role of an informer, taking advantage of the confidence his name inspired among the other prisoners.

The practice in the NKVD was to eliminate most informers sooner or later, and the same held for their bosses. But Andrei Sverdlov survived Yagoda and Yezhov and Beria. When Sverdlov's role as a secret informer was discovered by many prisoners, he was "recalled" and openly reappeared in his NKVD uniform. After Yezhov was shot, Sverdlov, holding the rank of colonel in the NKVD-MGB, became one of the prominent members of Beria's entourage. Evidently Beria and Stalin found it gratifying to have as a lackey the actual son of Yakov Sverdlov, whom Stalin had hated since the time of their exile together in Turukhanka.

After the war, Andrei again directed many "investigations." One case he took charge of, personally interrogating the victim, involved the Soviet army colonel Mikhail Meshcheryakov, who had written Stalin a letter about the way several aspects of the history of the Nazi-Soviet war were treated. During the "interrogation," Sverdlov himself knocked out six of Meshcheryakov's teeth.

After Stalin's death, Sverdlov took off his NKVD uniform and turned to "scholarly work" at the Institute of Marxism-Leninism. In 1955, he even defended a dissertation for the candidate's degree at the institute on the topic "Anglo-American Contradictions in Latin America in the Age of the General Crisis of Capitalism." When the Twentieth Congress was held and Sverdlov heard of its decisions, he was seized by panic. He was immediately "taken ill," stricken by a peculiar facial twitch. The diagnosis was that he was "psychologically disturbed," and a rest cure was arranged for him for nearly a year at the Kremlin hospital, in a special wing for mental patients. After the difficult times for former members of the Yezhov-Beria apparatus passed (and they passed very quickly), Sverdlov returned to his "scholarly" work. However, he has actually done very little such work; in the last fifteen years, the only works he published that could nominally be called "scholarly" were a few short articles and one pamphlet (coauthored with another writer). On the other hand, he has been quite active in literary work. It is a known fact at the Institute of Marxism-Leninism that he helped his mother prepare her reminiscences of Yakov Sverdlov for publication. He assisted in the compilation of a biography of Sergo Ordzhonikidze and helped Pavel Malkov, the former commandant of the Kremlin, in preparing his memoirs. However, hardly anyone at the institute knows that in recent years Sverdlov has been busy producing detective stories for children under the pseudonym A. Ya. Yakovlev. Just in the last few years, two such stories by this author have appeared, *The Thin Thread* and *The Two-Faced Janus*. The main theme of these "bestsellers," in which Sverdlov draws extensively on his experience as an NKVD agent in the days of Yezhov and Beria, is the "struggle of the Chekists against the espionage of the imperialist intelligence agencies."

We do not know whether Andrei Sverdlov pays his Party dues from the proceeds of his literary work. But we do know for certain that he still works as an informer on the side. He pores through many different magazines and newspapers, seeking out "Trotskyist" errors. When he finds them, he "sounds the alarm" and writes rude letters to editors demanding that steps be taken and the "guilty" be punished. He was the first to raise a hue and cry over the discussion of Aleksandr Nekrich's book [which was highly critical of Stalin's preparation for war in 1941] at the Institute of Marxism-Leninism. On the very day it was held (although he did not have the nerve to join in the discussion openly himself), Sverdlov sent a denunciation of the [pro-Nekrich] organizers and participants to the Party Committee at the institute and to the Party Control Commission of the Central Committee, slanderously charging that "anti-Soviet" statements had been made during the discussion.

Andrei Sverdlov has more than ten government decorations to his name. He was awarded almost all these orders and medals while serving as "senior investigator for especially important cases" in the central apparatus of the NKVD-MGB.

While hundreds of his innocent victims lie in mass graves at [the camps of] Kolyma, Norilsk, Ukhta, and outside Karaganda, Andrei Sverdlov lives in Moscow, in a large and elegantly furnished apartment in the so-called Government House at No. 2 Serafimovich Street, apartment 319. His home telephone number is 231-94-97. His number at work is 181-23-25. He does not intend to retire to a [more modest] pension. In recent years, he has hardly ever felt the pangs of fear. He even has hopes that better times will come. After all, it is only for *fascist* murderers that the statute of limitations has been cancelled.

[Editor's postscript: Andrei Sverdlov died in November 1969, a few months after this article began circulating in samizdat. The official obituary praised his service in the NKVD-MGB.[7]]

[No. 55, April 1969]

7. *Sovetskaia Rossiia*, November 25, 1969.

I Accuse

BY PAVEL SHABALKIN

Petitions for justice were an important behind-the-scenes aspect of the politics of de-Stalinization. Between 1953 and 1956, written appeals by victims of the terror still in camp or exile, and by their relatives, swamped Party and state judiciary agencies. The outpouring contributed to the decision in 1956 that only a policy of mass liberation, rather than the initial practice of reopening individual cases, could solve the camp problem. Many returnees then began to demand official actions against people who had contributed to their misfortune. This, too, often took the form of petitions to relevant institutions or to Soviet leaders. Understandably, many were addressed to Khrushchev, such as the one below from Pavel Shabalkin (1904–1964). Shabalkin's two letters, abridged somewhat here, and the other documents, including Medvedev's explanation, appeared in Political Diary *under the title "Responsibility for the Repressions in Philosophy." The protestations of innocence by those who had victimized Shabalkin were characteristic, as was the official silence and inaction that finally resulted. Charges of criminal complicity against prominent officials, even of the second rank, were potentially too threatening to people higher up, including Khrushchev himself.*

Preface by Roy Medvedev

It is generally known that in the mid-1930s nearly all the most capable Soviet Marxist philosophers, no matter of which trend, fell victim to political repression. Most of them died. Among the isolated few who returned from the camps was Pavel Ivanovich Shabalkin, who had been arrested in April 1936 in the Far East and spent twenty years in prisons and camps. In the early 1930s, Shabalkin had been a promising young philosopher and had written a number of books on historical materialsm.

After his return to Moscow, Shabalkin was reinstated in the Party and given an apartment in Moscow and a job as philosophy instructor at a higher technical school there. In 1961, soon after the Twenty-second Congress, Shabalkin addressed a letter to Nikita Khrushchev asking that four [very eminent official] philosophers be brought to account before the Party. Their names were Mark Mitin, Pavel Yudin, Fyodor Konstantinov, and Vladimir Berestnev, and they were responsible for the deaths of dozens of Soviet philosophers.

After Shabalkin's letter was received, Mitin, Yudin, Konstantinov, and Berestnev were called in by an official of the Central Committee apparatus. They were shown Shabalkin's letter and allowed to read it. Then, in violation of the elementary rules for any investigation, all four were placed in one room and asked to write a *joint* explanatory memorandum. (Of course, each should have been asked to write an explanation separately.)

A few days later, Shabalkin himself was called to the Central Committee. He was presented with the explanation by Mitin and the others, and an attempt was made to persuade him to drop the matter. He was told the Party did not consider it correct to organize a St. Bartholomew's massacre, to take vengeance for what was past and gone, and so on. However, Shabalkin was not satisfied with the explanation by Mitin et al. or the arguments of the Central Committee official. He sent a new letter to the Central Committee. It, too, remained unanswered. None of those mentioned in the letter were punished, even on a Party level. They all remained in their posts—e.g., Mitin as editor in chief of the [official] magazine *Problems of Philosophy,* Konstantinov as director of the Philosophy Institute of the Soviet Academy of Sciences, and Yudin as head of a division at that institute. All three became academicians, Konstantinov having just been elected this year (1964). Articles by these "academicians" regularly appear in the press, including articles on Communist morality. These men have their disputes among themselves, especially Yudin and Konstantinov, but they are united when it comes to the events of the 1930s.

Shabalkin recently died, the ailments and burdens of his time in the camps having taken their toll. Before his death, he entrusted to me his correspondence with the Central Committee on Mitin and the others.

[Editor's postscript: Shabalkin also contributed essays to samizdat before he died, including one advocating multicandidate elections in the Soviet Union. Mitin and Yudin, once described as "the best philosopher among the NKVD men and the best NKVD man among the philosophers," continued to prosper, despite other serious charges against them. Yudin's obituary in 1968, signed by Brezhnev and other Soviet leaders, praised his "long and glorious career."[8]]

Shabalkin's First Letter to Khrushchev

Dear Nikita Sergeyevich:

Because of a long and serious illness, I was not able to address this letter to you earlier. In April 1936, when I was thirty-two, I was arrested by the NKVD and, though guilty of nothing, spent twenty years and eight months in prisons, camps, and exile. After my complete rehabilitation, both in civil and Party respects, I returned to my former permanent place of residence in February 1957,

8. The characterization of Yudin is from Vladimir Dedijer, *Tito* (New York, 1953), p. 297. See also Nekrich, *Otreshis' ot strakha,* p. 179; and *Pravda,* April 12, 1968.

a sick and crippled man, a Class Two invalid. Those who bear immediate and particular guilt for all the ill that befell me are M. B. Mitin and P. F. Yudin (now academicians) and Professors F. V. Konstantinov and V. Berestnev.

I accuse all these men of slander, which served as the pretext for my arrest by the NKVD and became the basis for all the subsequent monstrous accusations. Allow me to briefly relate the key facts.

From 1929 to 1932, I studied at the Institute of Red Professors in the same group with Yudin and Konstantinov; you might even say we shared the same desk. During the years of our studies, especially during the well-known philosophical discussion of 1930–31, I had occasion to make sharp criticisms of shortcomings in the work of the bureau of the Party organization at the institute, the secretary of which was Yudin; Mitin and Konstantinov were members of the bureau. My criticisms had to do with their incorrect position in the discussion, which they tried to turn into a narrow theoretical and scholastic dispute over terms and quotations from Hegel, Kant, Plekhanov, and other thinkers, avoiding a serious and forthright confrontation of the issues—the relation between philosophy and politics and the unity of theory and practice.

Many other Communists expressed the same criticisms I did. Sensing that the Party organization at the Institute had lost confidence in them and was about to vote in a new Party bureau (which it did), Mitin and Yudin turned to Lazar Kaganovich for help. Kaganovich ordered the Frunze District Committee of the Party to interfere in the affairs of our Party unit and render assistance to Mitin and Yudin. Using this advantage, Yudin and the others branded all who had criticized them "members of the Shabalkin group," began to drag these people in front of Party control commissions, to give them a going-over, and so forth.

After graduating in philosophy from the institute, I was sent by the Central Committee to the Far East, where I did Party work from 1932 to 1936 (until my arrest). I was in charge of cultural and propaganda work, at first for the Party Committee of the Maritime Region and then for the Party Committee of the Far East Territory. At the same time, I did scholarly work, taught at higher educational institutions, and edited the magazine *Party Education.*

In the strenuous practical work in the Far East, which engaged me totally, I forgot about Mitin, Yudin, and Konstantinov. But they did not forget about me; I was still in their thoughts years after graduating from the institute. Using the monopoly that they effectively held on the editorial board of the [central philosophical] magazine *Under the Banner of Marxism*, they turned it into a vehicle for slander and insinuation against those not in their favor.

In early 1936, articles filled with the spirit of the pogroms began to appear, hurling accusations "right and left" at numerous Communists, branding them Trotskyists, semi-Trotskyists, demi-Trotskyists, Right Opportunists, or simply "unreliable."

Soon after, the arrests began. Almost all the Communists listed in these articles were arrested. I was arrested as the head of the so-called Shabalkin group, which had never existed. Among others arrested were Professors Dmitriev, Furshchik, and Kolokolkin and a number of young Communist philosophers who had just graduated from the Red Professors Institute of Philosophy and Natural Science: Adamyan, Lepeshev, Tokarev, Leonov, Tashchilin, Bazilevsky, Yevstafyev, Novik, Pichugin, and many others.

There were two men who did especially vicious jobs of slander in articles in this magazine: V. Berestnev (who now works at the Research Institute of Philosophy) and F. V. Konstantinov (now an editor of the magazine *Kommunist*). These exceptionally slick slander artists dreamed up the most grotesque accusations [that Shabalkin and others were "enemies of the people and counterrevolutionary terrorists"] and clothed them in pseudoscientific form and "philosophical" terminology, without a care for facts or evidence. . . . And the tone for such slander was set by the editors of the magazine, headed by Mitin and Yudin. . . .

I cannot reproduce here everything that was written by these "complex" philosophers. Judge for yourself who indulged in vulgarization, oversimplification, and demagogy. This kind of "complexity" you yourself exposed at the Twentieth Congress.

These people equated their own errors and their low philosophical level with the Party line on questions of philosophy and went on to make a profession out of slander. They did not complicate their despicable labors with facts or evidence, especially since there was none to be had. Instead, they slandered and lied, lied and slandered without ever feeling the nag of conscience. Let them now introduce just one fact as evidence of their monstrous charges of treason, terrorism, and betrayal of the motherland, or the charge that I opposed the Party's line on philosophical questions. Let them cite the foul sources from which they dredged this muck for smearing honest and decent Communists. Let them explain to what purpose they transformed a serious philosophical journal into an organ of slander and savage baiting of their own fellow Party members, why they organized this witches' Sabbath, for what and for whom they organized this slander.

These people fashioned a happy life and made careers for themselves out of the blood, tears, and tragic sufferings of their Party comrades. Terrible were the results of their "prolific" labors. I have every justification for asserting that Yudin, Mitin, and Konstantinov deliberately and consciously lied. No one led them astray, and they cannot hide behind those who are now dead—the vicious enemies of the people Yezhov and Beria.

The investigative agencies, as I now learn, read the magazine and brought charges against me on the basis of the slander contained there. I was indicted at first under Article 58, Points 10 and 11, i.e., counterrevolutionary agitation and organization. After the appearance of further articles in the magazine, in addition to the initial charges, I was cited under Points 7 and 8 of Article 58, i.e., terrorism and "wrecking." I was convicted on all these charges.

There is no reason to suppose that Yudin, Mitin, Konstantinov, and Berestnev have repented of the evil they did. At least, they have not appeared in the press with any criticism of their own "errors" (putting it mildly). Like all slander-ers, they portray themselves at one moment as poor fools who didn't know what was going on, the next as "fighters for the Party line," correct and infallible in all things, and the next as innocent lambs who were deceived and led astray. How can such unprincipled people, ready to serve any master, be trusted to "develop and carry further" Marxist-Leninist philosophy, to bring the lofty ideas of Com-munism to the masses, to preach the most exalted, just, and humane of morali-ties?

I request (1) that Mitin, Yudin, Konstantinov, and Berestnev be compelled to exonerate me officially in the press, along with all the others whom they slandered, and to acknowledge openly and honestly their "errors"; and (2) that they be brought up on charges before the Party for lies and slander.

P. I. Shabalkin, Party Member

Explanatory Memorandum of Mitin, Yudin, Konstantinov, and Berestnev to the Party Central Committee

Having acquainted ourselves with Comrade Shabalkin's statement of October 1961, we consider it our duty to state the following:

After the resolution of the Party Central Committee on the magazine *Under the Banner of Marxism* in early 1931, which defined the tasks we then faced in the field of philosophical science and in the struggle on the philosophical front, the philosophical discussion developed on a broad scale. The ideological struggle of the Party organization at the Red Professors Institute of Philosophy and Natural Science at that time was directed both against those who sought to defend old traditions (represented by the so-called Deborin group) and against a number of students at the institute, Comrade Shabalkin among them. The latter accused the Party unit of not fighting energetically enough against the Menshevizing idealists of the Deborin group and even of being conciliatory toward that group.

At the same time, they took the liberty of attacking the leadership of the Party unit in various ways on the grounds that, in their opinion, it was not carrying out with sufficient energy and zeal the instructions of J. V. Stalin, given during a discussion with the bureau of the Party organization at the institute. The Party organization took action against these students, who were pushing it in the direction of criticism in regard to the conclusions of the Central Committee and diverting it from consistently carrying out the tasks set by the Central Committee for the philosophical sciences, the critique of mechanism and Menshevizing idealism, and reorganization of the effort to produce well-trained people in philosophy.

The Party unit at the institute was obliged to criticize some of the views of Comrade Shabalkin and other comrades who made the same theoretical errors as he, falling into confusion on the question of the relation between philosophy and politics, the role of Plekhanov in philosophy, and questions of dialectical materialism. The essence of these errors was to equate philosophy and politics directly and to deny the value of Plekhanov's philosophic work; therefore the Party unit at the institute could not do otherwise than to respond with criticism.

Comrade Shabalkin writes that we conducted ourselves improperly in regard to him. But after his graduation from the institute in 1932, the leadership and the Party organization gave positive recommendations to him and the other comrades who shared his views. This is evidence of our attitude toward him and the other comrades at that time. It is also known that Comrade Shabalkin was assigned to leading work in the Party in the Far East, where he held the post of director of the cultural and propaganda division of the territorial committee of the Party. At the institute from 1932 to 1936, we gave practically no thought to the so-called Shabalkin group, assuming that the discussions about it had ended in 1932.

But in 1936, four years after his graduation from the institute and after he had been working in the Far East, we were informed of Comrade Shabalkin's arrest. Moreover, we were informed that Comrade Shabalkin and several other students of the institute had been arrested as "enemies of the people." After that, articles against Comrade Shabalkin and a number of other comrades who had taken the same position as he on philosophical questions were published. We were naturally shocked and indignant toward them at that time, because we sincerely thought that if the security agencies had arrested them, they must have committed serious crimes against the Soviet Motherland. In view of the fact that we, like the absolute majority of Party members, had faith in the security agencies and regarded their activity at the time as correct and necessary, it becomes comprehensible why we took the attitude and position we did toward those who were arrested as "enemies of the people." It was this situation, and the fact of the arrests, that explains the nature and tone of our statements and articles.

After the personality cult was liquidated, when the causes and the real nature of the mass repressions against honest Communists became known and comprehensible, the tragedy which many honest Communists were forced to undergo, among them Comrade Shabalkin, also became comprehensible.

These are the facts and circumstances.

> June 15, 1962
> Mitin, Yudin, Konstantinov, Berestnev

Shabalkin's Second Letter

To the Central Committee:

Having read the "explanation" of June 15, 1962, which Academicians Mitin and Yudin and Professors Konstantinov and Berestnev gave to the Central Committee in response to my statement, I must conclude that these men have not understood, and do not wish to understand, the spirit of the decisions of the

Twentieth and Twenty-second congresses, that they are completely hardened liars, having lost all sense of Party honor and conscience, and that in violation of Party rules, they have taken the course of lying and trying to deceive the Central Committee in a flagrant and ignominious way.

1. They write in their "explanation" that it was only after the arrests that "articles against Comrade Shabalkin and a number of other comrades who had taken the same position as he on philosophical questions were published" and that it was that situation, their faith in the security agencies and the fact of the arrests, that explains the nature and tone of their statements and articles.

This is a blatant lie. I was arrested on April 1, 1936. But here is what they wrote in the name of the administration of the Institute of Philosophy in January 1936. They were faced, they said, with the "necessity of unmasking the maneuvers of the class enemy [the Shabalkin group] in specific realms of theory, taking the most subtle and convoluted forms . . ." (see *Under the Banner of Marxism*, 1936, no. 1, p. 166).

And that is not all. A majority of the comrades to whom they imputed membership in the "counterrevolutionary, Trotskyist, terrorist Shabalkin group" were arrested quite a while after the appearance of issue number 4, in which the slander assumed its most intense expression. This issue appeared in April or early May 1936, but Comrade Yevstafyev was not arrested until early 1937, Comrade Bazilevsky in December 1936, and Comrades Kolokolkin, Furshchik, Tashchilin, Novik, and others even later.

But let us grant for the moment that they slandered Shabalkin because, as they put it, the security agencies had arrested him and they believed blindly in those agencies (although, as I have shown, they are lying on this point). Does that mean that once he was arrested, everything was permissible—"slander to your heart's content"? And what about those who had not yet been arrested? Here you can't just shift the blame onto the security agencies. What criterion did these "philosophers" follow? And why did they say nothing about such a criterion in their "explanation" to the Central Committee?

Moreover, no one could have informed Mitin and the others in the first half of 1936 that "Shabalkin was a terrorist." Initially, no such charge was brought against me. At first, I was accused under Article 58, Points 10 and 11, of "counterrevolutionary agitation" and "counterrevolutionary organization," which was consistent with what had been written in the January issue of the magazine. On these charges, I was given five years in a corrective labor camp by a special board of the NKVD. I was sent to Solovki. Then suddenly, in the second half of 1936, I was taken from my cell for further investigation. New charges, based on the new slander that appeared in the magazine, were brought against me—Article 58, Points 7 and 8, "wrecking" and "terrorism." The earlier sentence was annulled as being "too mild," and the Military Collegium of the Supreme Court gave me fifteen years imprisonment and five years deprivation of civil rights.

I demand to know: What grounds and what facts did these academicians and professors have to assert in the pages of their magazine in 1936 that Shabalkin was a "Trotskyist, terrorist, and traitor"? Incidentally, I never was a Trotskyist, still less a terrorist or traitor, and unlike some of the authors of the "explanation," I never deviated from the Party line in all my years in the Party.

2. In their "explanation," these academicians and professors maneuver skillfully. When it is a matter of the differences on philosophical questions, they hide behind the Party organization at the institute. When it is a matter of their own slanderous writings, they hide behind the Party as a whole. "We, like the absolute majority of Party members, had faith in the security agencies," and that "explains the nature and tone" of their statements. As if it were a matter of tone and not of the slanderous content of their articles and statements! That is what we are talking about. An honest Communist should never under any circumstance engage in slander. That is an axiom of Leninist justice and elementary Party decency.

It is true that "an absolute majority of Party members" at that time had faith in the security agencies, but they did not slander. Only a tiny minority of careerists and scoundrels "wanted to believe" and indulged in slander.

The entire "explanation," despite the authors' intent, exposes the real reasons behind their vicious slandering of myself and other comrades who dared to criticize the "infallible" leadership of the Party organization at the institute in 1930–32. The truth is that Mitin and Yudin wished to be free of any and all criticism.

3. I categorically reject the lying assertion by the authors of the "explanation" that, while a student at the institute, during the philosophical discussion of 1930–32, I spoke against "the Party organization," behind whose name the academicians and professors now wish to hide, although they have no right to.

There is no harm in reminding them that the majority of members of the Party organization at the institute subsequently found themselves behind bars, thanks to the connivance and complicity of all the Mitins and Yudins.

4. The authors of the "explanation" even lie in small things. They wriggle about in as scoundrelly a way as Gogol's Nozdrev. They write that after my graduation from the institute they gave me a favorable recommendation and imply that they assisted in my appointment as director of the cultural and propaganda division of the territorial committee of the Party. First of all, it would have been illogical and incorrect to give a favorable recommendation to a person who, as they claim, was fighting against the Party organization. Second, I was sent to the Far East to work as a rank-and-file instructor. While there, I was promoted from the ranks, first to become a member of the bureau and later the director of the cultural and propaganda division of the Party Committee of the Maritime Region in Vladivostok and later of the Party Territorial Committee in Khabarovsk.

The authors of the "explanation" write that Shabalkin and others criticized the leadership of the Party organization at the institute because "in their opinion, it was not carrying out with sufficient energy and zeal the instructions of J. V. Stalin," given by him at a discussion on philosophical questions in December 1930 (see the explanation).

But this is what they wrote in *Under the Banner of Marxism* (no. 8, 1936). The Shabalkin group, they said, conducted a struggle "against putting into effect the instructions that Comrade Stalin had given in his historic meeting on philosophical questions in December 1930." One must ask, When are the authors lying and when are they telling the truth?

One thing is clear: The lie is always suited to the moment and aimed at demolishing Shabalkin. Everyone knows what became of people accused of struggling against Stalin's instructions. In their present lie, they seek to effect a different aim: "Look, he was a bigger Stalinist than we poor sinners were!"

. . .

During the more than thirty years of their work as leaders in the field of philosophy, Mitin, Yudin, and Konstantinov, because of their dogmatism and their toadying to the Stalin cult, as everyone knows, never succeeded in truly linking philosophical science with the life and struggle of the Soviet people. This is what they were justifiably criticized for in 1930–32. They were divorced from real life and had no knowledge of it.

5. There is no room here to go into all the philosophical and political errors made by these academicians and professors over the years, but their attempt to divert this whole question into the realm of abstract theoretical and philosophical debate must be emphatically rejected.

There is a specific matter under discussion—their *slander* against honest Communists, including myself, in 1936. *Slander,* which served as the basis and justification for the arrest, conviction, and subsequently the death of a whole array of young philosopher-Communists, loyal sons of the Party and the motherland.

For this crime, Academicians Mitin and Yudin and Professors Konstantinov and Berestnev should receive the punishment they deserve.

July 1, 1962
P. I. Shabalkin, Party Member
[No. 3, December 1964]

Conscience

BY P. LEONIDOV

Face-to-face confrontations between former victims and victimizers were another dramatic feature of the post-Stalin years. Stories of such encounters can be heard even today. Sometimes both parties were too stunned or frightened to react. But there also were meetings that led to harsh words, fistfights, and even suicides—by former victims as well as their tormentors. A few encounters had comic aspects; the elderly widow of a purged Old Bolshevik once chased Molotov down a Moscow street, swinging her handbag at the old pensioner's head. But most of these confrontations were traumatic, especially when victims actually met people who had physically tortured them or had been responsible for the execution of their relatives, as in the following memoir-story by P. Leonidov. Leonidov (a pseudonym) comments at the end on two topics of private discussion shortly after Khrushchev's fall in 1964. One was the argument that "conscience" was punishment enough for people responsible for crimes of the past. The other was the gradual but perceptible rehabilitation of Stalin's reputation in official circles.

February 23 is the birthday of the Red Army. Those who took part in the civil war and the Great Patriotic War have a thing or two to remember and to talk about on that day. On February 23 in 1963, I was returning from a business trip. And I was waiting impatiently to board my plane, because that day there was to be a celebration in the recreation room at work. Those who had fought were going to give their reminiscences of those bygone days. Quite a crowd of passengers had gathered at the airport. I sat and watched them, trying to imagine what each one was like, where they were hurrying to and why.

Time passed slowly. There were thunderstorms somewhere off in the distance. Because of this, the departure time for my flight kept being postponed.

I tried to draw my neighbor into conversation, to kill time. But he turned his chair away sharply, to face the wall. Apparently he was tired and in no mood. He wanted to be home.

Just then, a person I didn't know came over, a man with a puffy face, whose most prominent features were a lumpy, heavily veined nose, and a receding chin.

Looking closely at me, he asked, not at all surely, "Excuse me, aren't you Kistov?"

"No."

But something tugged fiercely at my memory. Somewhere I had encountered those dull eyes, which had something bestial lurking in their depths.

"I beg your pardon," he continued. "You see, I'm in legal work, and I've run out of money on the road. Just like that. Here I am without a penny left. Well, it occurred to me that I might borrow some. I thought you were someone I knew . . ."

He stood alongside me in a gray suit that was almost new but already had an untidy look. There was a foul smell of wine on his breath; his face was purplish, and his chin had a scrape on it. And I kept thinking, trying to remember . . .

"Maybe we should have a drink to get to know each other. I saw some terrific cognac over there."

"Of course, it's him!" In an instant everything connected with this dreadful person came flooding back. Everything—the stinking, crowded-to-overflowing cell; and the interrogations. Endless interrogations—day and night; in the evening, in the dead of night, when you no longer have any idea what's going on.

And those same eyes, where not a grain of humanity was to be found. Staring at me. And the same hoarse voice demanding, "Tell me about your ties with Kutyakov. Tell me. You rotten piece of flesh. I'll make you tell me. Read the poetry you dedicated to this enemy of the people."

I was a little over seventeen. I had never written any poetry, never dedicated any to anyone. But I didn't know how to prove that. I knew Kutyakov as a hero of the civil war, the comrade-in-arms of [Red Army hero] Chapayev.

"Speak! Read!"

And I recited some lines by Peter Oreshin that had stuck in my memory:

> And the soldiers went charging again
> From our lines to the enemy lines
> And commanding them went Kutyakov
> The man whom Chapayev loved."

"Swine! Making fun of an interrogator!

The sharp blow knocked me to the cement floor. Kornin (I remembered the man's name now) could really deliver punches with no warning, and in the most painful places . . .

"I know you, lawyer."

He gave a start, looked around furtively, and drew in his head. But in a moment he regained control. It seemed that he recognized me too. But the urge to drink was stronger than everything else. And with an insolent smile, taking my elbow, he said, "Then how about two hundred grams in honor of meeting again? You treat. We'll talk a little, remember old times."

"Perhaps they are better not remembered!" I took out my glass eye and held it out to Kornin on my palm. "You recognize whose work this is?"

"Hey, that was twenty years ago, plus. And do you think I was the only one doing investigations? Everyone was looking for enemies in those days. Come on, now . . ." He watched to see what I would do, and moved back discreetly. Suddenly, unexpectedly, in a different tone he asked again, "How about enough for just a hundred grams?"

I understood that this was a lost man. I gave him everything I had left from my trip, and it was a lot. I gave it to him so that he would leave quickly. I was afraid I wouldn't hold out. I felt an overpowering desire to let loose my hatred, pent up for so long, against him and his kind.

The impudent fellow knew quite well that those times when fear had become an inseparable part of you were gone forever. That no matter what he had been, the fate of those who were turned into prison-camp dust would never befall him. His teeth would not be kicked out; he would continue to look at the world with two eyes, unlike me. No matter what might happen to him, his family would never be sent to Kolyma. No prison supervisor would come up to his wife and knee her in the stomach. His father would never be thrown into the central prison for nothing . . .

It was quiet in the recreation room. I listened to the speakers' voices. Their emotions were stirred as they spoke of those unforgotten fighting days. The open face of the metalworker Safonov—he had helped to take Berlin; the rapt, thoughtful face of the lathe operator Stolyarov—he had fought to defend Leningrad; the energetic face of his comrade Kudinov, also a lathe operator—he had blocked the enemy's road to Moscow . . .

These were the ones who had defended the motherland. It was these simple Soviet lads who had freed the nations of Europe from the fascist yoke. Such people never hid behind their comrades. Such people never betrayed their friends. They never confirmed unfounded accusations for any reason.

I was the last to leave this ceremony dedicated to the forty-fifth anniversary of the Soviet armed forces. I didn't realize immediately that the person leaving in front of me was Timofeikin. Suddenly he turned. I was looking him straight in the eyes.

Shame, burning shame, not fear, brought beads of sweat out on his forehead. As part of the investigation, in a confrontation between accuser and accused, on June 8, 1938, in the presence of the man he had slandered, Timofeikin had confirmed his lies, his unfounded accusations. In the dossier on the case is a copy of a written entry. It was made immediately after this confrontation by the investigator for especially important cases. The entry was brief: "To be shot." And my father was shot.

"Why is he here?" I also remembered that Timofeikin had managed to slip off to Tashkent, far from the front. I looked at his graying face and began to understand why for years he had not been able to look anyone in the eye. He turned away from me, swayed a bit, and for a long time tried to open the door in the wrong direction. I had the impression he was crying. And I understood that sometimes there is nothing worse, nothing more terrible for a person, than the pangs of conscience.

I was badly mistaken. In early November 1966, I ran into both of them again. It was at a city Party committee meeting. On the presiding committee, next to Timofeikin, I recognized Kornin. He sat in the center, stroking his receding chin. His bestial eyes scoured the auditorium. Every now and then, Timofeikin would lean over and ingratiatingly whisper something in Kornin's ear. During the intermission, I saw them in the hallway. They were discussing something loudly and gesticulating next to the glass case in which the day's issue of *Pravda* was displayed. After they moved away, I went over to the newspaper and read the part Timofeikin had been pointing at for Kornin to see. Under the headline "Order of Lenin Awarded to Georgia," a little way down, following the name "Joseph Stalin," stood a word in bold face: APPLAUSE.

[No. 34, July 1967]

A Critical Review of a Victim's Memoirs
BY A NKVD OFFICIAL

We must now listen more fully to the self-defense of people and institutions accused of direct complicity in Stalin's mass terror. Just as the question of political responsibility involved different levels of authority—from Politburo leaders, police and judicial officials, and other high functionaries, to ordinary prison camp guards—various kinds of reasoning were used to deny any guilt. They ranged from sophisticated arguments about historical necessity and necessary excesses, and bureaucratic explanations of having only "carried out the orders that came down from above," to flat assertions that no crimes had taken place because the alleged victims actually were guilty. The following defense of the Soviet secret (or political) police is less crude than many. While acknowledging mass injustices, it combines historical justifications, extenuating circumstances, and factually true and false statements to exonerate the NKVD (though not the Communist Party) as an institution. The anonymous author, a retired high official in the NKVD-MGB, was reviewing (possibly for a censorship office) the first volume of Evgenia Ginzburg's memoirs, which were then circulating in manuscript and have since been published in many countries (Journey into the Whirlwind. New York, 1967). Ginzburg was a Party member, the wife of an important Bolshevik mayor, Pavel Aksyonov, and the mother of Vasily Aksyonov, the popular Soviet writer of the 1960s who now lives in the United States. She was arrested in 1937 and suffered eighteen years of jail, camp, and exile. Her memoirs of this ordeal remain the most powerful, informative, and persuasive testimony by a Communist victim of the great purge of 1936–39. (A second volume, Within the Whirlwind, was published posthumously in 1981.)

The documentary novel *Journey into the Whirlwind* was written from the heart, with passion, acuity, and insight. Its effect on the reader is overpowering. Leaving aside the young and inexperienced Soviet readers who know our "year of darkness and evil" only by hearsay, even old and "unbroken" Chekists are made downcast and depressed by reading it.

The author depicts the tragic and gloomy events of the Yezhov-Beria period in a powerful and truthful way but somewhat one-sidedly, as though she had only dark colors at her disposal. The mass psychosis, the spy mania, the universal suspicion, repression, and slaughter of the best Party, scientific, military, and other cadres of the Soviet intelligentsia, have shrouded from her view the heroic deeds of the Soviet people and the Party during that same period (industrialization of the country, the revolution in agriculture, the exploits of Soviet fighters in the revolutionary battles in Spain). She does not reveal and analyze with sufficient depth or objectivity, in our opinion, the roots and sources of the Stalin cult, in whose madness Soviet society of that time was caught up.

The book lacks a dialectical approach in evaluating the events of the 1930s. Until December 1934, it would seem from the book, Soviet society developed normally and in accordance with the basic tenets of Marxism-Leninism, and then in 1935 there suddenly came a time of unbridled Stalinist lawlessness, spy scares, and every kind of mania, resulting in mass repression and the annihilation of hundreds of thousands of Communists and Soviet intellectuals and the degeneration of the Party and state. The book does not have a single reference to the presence of truly dangerous political prisoners in the jails and camps (spies, counterrevolutionaries, and so on). But it is common knowledge that from the very first day of its existence the Soviet government faced a life-and-death battle not only against its open enemies but also against numerous counterrevolutionary conspiracies and foreign intelligence agencies of every stripe. After fascism came to power in Germany, subversion and espionage directed against the USSR increased many times over. By then, the Trotskyist, Zinovievist, and Bukharinist oppositions had completely degenerated into anti-Soviet underground organizations, using the methods characteristic of such organizations (the dissemination of leaflets and opposition platforms, underground printing presses, demonstrations, agents sent by [Trotsky's son] Leon Sedov and others into the USSR through the *cordon sanitaire,* preparations for the overthrow of the government, and so on).

These were the preconditions which, in the wake of the Kirov assassination, resulted in the ugly Yezhov-Beria period, based on universal suspicion, distrust, and persecution mania. To this, one should add that the foreign intelligence agencies, especially the fascists, sought in every way to exacerbate the mass psychosis and atmosphere of suspicion reigning in the USSR by sending in special materials discrediting prominent Soviet Party and military leaders (in particular, the "case" of Tukhachevsky, Yakir, and others was inspired in this way). If the author were to take a more objective approach in her recollections of the political prisoners she met in that period, she would undoubtedly corroborate our assertion that these prisoners were an extremely variegated lot, a regular Noah's Ark, ranging from actual or hidden opponents of Soviet power to the large number of honest Soviet patriots who fell victim to slander and lawlessness on a vast scale.

Now a word on the Chekists of that time and the agonies they were subjected to. It is quite understandable that the author, having passed through all the stages of the Yezhov-Beria hell, cannot view the Chekist functionaries of that inquisitorial system as anything but vicious butchers, sadists, and fiends. But what were they like in reality? In their vast majority, the Chekists of that time (as those of subsequent times) were active Party and Komsomol members mobilized for this work. Among them, a chance careerist or amoral type might have cropped up here or there of whom it could be said that power went to his head. But the majority were honest and decent Communists.

How could they have degenerated into butchers and sadists? We must declare with full responsibility for our words that only individual, morally unstable, and unprincipled Chekists went so far as to use physical torture and other means of inflicting suffering. For which they were shot in 1939 after the November 1938 letter of the Politburo on "excesses in investigative procedures." The atmosphere of psychosis permeated the leading bodies of the Party first and foremost. They in turn exerted heavy pressure on the NKVD—for example, forcing it to arrest without exception all those expelled from the Party as "enemies of the people." The NKVD itself exerted heavy pressure on the institutions of the judiciary and procuracy. There developed a chain reaction. In addition, Chekists themselves were arrested on an equivalent scale—for "liberalism," "complicity with the enemy," and so on. We were dealt with even more harshly, as "doubly dangerous" enemies. Attempts to signal Stalin that a frame-up was going on ended tragically for the Chekists who tried.

Despite the urgency of the topic and the literary merits of this work, it should not be published in its present form, because it would have a harmful influence on young people, promoting pessimism and demoralization among them, and because the press in the imperialist countries would add this to their arsenal and use it against us. The second part could be published with some reworking.

Comment by Roy Medvedev

What can we say about this commentary? Of course, the complaints against Ginzburg for not having written about the heroic deeds of the Soviet people in the 1930s are absurd. One's memoirs discuss what one has lived through. It is also wrong to continue today to accuse the former oppositionists of planning a counterrevolutionary overthrow of the government, and so forth. As for actual spies and saboteurs, there were hardly any in the prisons and camps of that time. Many inmates of the camps never encountered such people at all. Moreover, no one today will believe that only a few interrogators used physical means of inflicting punishment, i.e., torture, or that there were only some "excesses." Torture was practiced on a mass scale, and such methods persisted after 1938. It is true that the top bodies of the Party bear great responsibility for the repression. Nevertheless, the NKVD did have a leading role. And, of course, we must refer not to the "Yezhov-Beria" period but the *Stalin* era.

[No. 12, September 1965]

The Defense of a Prison-Camp Official
BY ANNA ZAKHAROVA

A different kind of self-defense, less complex and more indignant, is presented
here by a person who worked at the bottom, or receiving end, of the terror
apparatus—a former Stalinist camp official still on active duty in the 1960s. Her
letter to the government newspaper Izvestia, which went unpublished, is
abridged here. It was provoked by the official publication, first in popular journals
and then in book form, of two firsthand accounts of prison camp life: Solzhenitsyn's novella One Day in the Life of Ivan Denisovich (Novy mir, no. 11, 1962)
and Boris Dyakov's memoir A Tale of Survival (Okyatbr, no. 7, 1964). Solzhenitsyn and Dyakov were dissimilar in important ways; in particular, Dyakov remained a loyal Communist who wanted to exonerate and glorify the Party. But
both authors depicted a Stalinist camp regime that utterly tyrannized and brutal-
ized millions of political prisoners; indeed, both understated the bestiality of
camp life in order to get their publications through the censorship. Roy Medvedev's introduction places Anna Zakharova's effort to refute Solzhenitsyn and
Dyakov in the larger context of the problem of responsibility. It is also worth
noting that her self-defense contains two anomalies: she portrays herself as a
small, ordinary person in the scheme of things, but her husband is a major in the
prison camp service; and she cites repeatedly the more lenient camp regime of
the Khrushchev years, but her purpose is to defend the regime under Stalin.

ROY MEDVEDEV • *The Responsibility of Stalinist Camp Officials*

The dread conveyor-belt system designed by Stalin and his closest associates
for the destruction of millions of people they found objectionable was made up
not only of informers, investigators, judges, and prosecutors. The entire government and Party apparatus was involved to one degree or another, with one layer
or group of officials taking part in the destruction of another such layer or group.
The conveyor belt ended, as a rule, in the "corrective-labor camps"—leaving
aside, of course, those hundreds of thousands who were shot immediately after
being sentenced.

We must make a differentiation in approaching the question of the responsibility of camp officials, great and small, and of those who "tended" the machinery
of destruction. Many soldiers, after being drafted, were assigned to guard duty
in the camps. They spent their time on duty in the watchtowers and had virtually

no communication with the prisoners. These soldiers might have thought, and most of them actually did think, they were guarding "enemies of the people," dangerous "spies and saboteurs." In the case of the camp administration and the camp garrison, it was a different matter. These people were not only diligent in carrying out criminal orders and instructions (and the treatment of prisoners in the Stalin camps was criminal, regardless of whether real lawbreakers or totally innocent people were affected). In practice, the administration had unlimited power over the prisoners, and many camp officials (although of course not all) mocked them, robbed them, beat them, and from 1938 to 1945 frequently had them killed by the thousands. When a guard beats a person in weakened condition who has had to do work beyond his powers and ends up killing that person, it does not matter whether that guard believes he is killing a real enemy of the people or not; he has committed a crime in either case. Even an order from a commander does not justify this guard, because he has followed an obviously criminal directive.

The only "mitigating circumstance" for the camp administration is the fact that officials were apparently selected (or possibly this was the result of a peculiar kind of self-selection) from among semiliterate people and those of quite limited mentality, people who were extremely undeveloped in both the intellectual and the moral sense. Many of them were convinced they were doing something useful for the country. Often they themselves found life in the camps not particularly pleasant. And, of course, they do not like to think now that it was all to no good end, that it actually did harm to the country and society, and that they themselves were accomplices in crimes of extreme gravity. There is a certain tragic aspect to all this, because no one wants to think he has lived his life in vain. All of the present and former members of prison-camp administrations have responded in an extremely hostile way to the works of Solzhenitsyn, Dyakov, and several others.

To the Editor in Chief of *Izvestia:*

I, Anna Filippovna Zakharova, have worked for the Ministry for the Preservation of Public Order [Russian initials, MOOP] since 1950. I was a member of the Komsomol and have been a Communist since 1956. Having read *One Day in the Life of Ivan Denisovich* by Aleksandr Solzhenitsyn, I was angered to the depths of my soul, as I am sure all MOOP employees who read the book also were. I intended to write immediately to the publisher but somehow never had the free time. But now that I have read another work of the same kind, *A Tale of Survival* by Boris Dyakov, I decided to write even though time is precious. In discussing this article, or rather these works, with MOOP employees who had read them, what I heard universally was anger, rage, and indignation.

Please try to understand our question. What were the officers and guards guilty of, these people who are painted in such dark colors by the former prisoners (although granted they were unjustly condemned)? Are they to blame because the Party and the people called on them to shoulder the most difficult burden of our time—working with the criminal world? We practical workers, who lived in the outlying areas, were deprived of the most elementary conditions for a human existence, unlike the inhabitants of cities and urban districts. Sometimes there was not enough food or housing for us, not to mention apartments with all the modern conveniences. Or real schools and libraries. And there's no need to even go into the question of the theater or various sports facilities. For us those were luxuries.

We work with what actually are the dregs of society—criminals. Just imagine. A person is working as part of the collective at one place or other. He gets drunk, he is a debaucher and a thief, he steals, he kills, and so on. The collective goes to great pains over this person, worries about him, and finally hands him over to the courts as the very worst of the worst, who prevents others from living and working normally. And here we have this "cream of society" all together in a camp. Can you imagine what it's like to work with them? But we have to. And what are we? Aren't we also Soviet citizens who should be able to live and work normally? Are we people of such a kind that we should not be able to enjoy the gains achieved by our fathers and children? We, too, wish to live quiet and pleasant lives in normal conditions among normal Soviet citizens. But the Party and the people have called upon us and have entrusted us with the most difficult lot in life, and we shoulder this burden for the good of all the people, for the sake of their tranquillity. So why are we blackened and discredited? And why do our organs of the press allow MOOP workers to be made fun of, and all the services they rendered be trampled into the mud? It's disgraceful! Among us there are many officers who are veteran Communists, who served their time and have retired on pensions as invalids because of the terrible and difficult work. And here this noble work is being mocked at, work in which a person's health has been ruined and in which some people even laid down their lives, and for what?

And what do the camp guards have to do with it all anyway, may we ask? They were only carrying out what was required of them by the regulations, orders, instructions, and so on, as people do in any office, factory, or plant. They didn't make up things on their own on the spot, taking advantage of the absence of control over them, or the personality cult. It's not our fault that such policies were followed. That's not the fault of the rank-and-file guards, the camp officers, Communists, and so on. So why abuse and insult them? Because every year it was harder for us to work with this criminal element? [Nowadays] the prisoners, taking advantage of the humanness of our policies, try in every way to taunt and mock the prison staff in the camps and labor colonies. At any time, they can insult any employee, and right to their face in front of everyone. And nothing will be done to them for that, except that certain possibilities, not very large, are available to the chief of a prison unit. The prisoners can call any of us Beria-ites freely, and say this to Communists, and this can't be reported. And no measures are taken against them. We have to operate by methods of explanation and clarification. And their errors are explained to them. But is a hardened criminal going to listen? Of course, there are some among the convicts who conduct themselves in a model fashion. But, for the most part, they are all hostilely disposed.

In this letter, I can't tell everything about how difficult it is for us to work with them. And we get no thanks. On the contrary, one of the prisoners will write a letter and make up such things against the administration and put in such details about this or that incident that the higher authorities take it as absolutely true. They send commissions, representatives from the procurator's office, and so forth. This makes the staff members nervous, and after things have been investigated, it turns out that the facts were not confirmed. Imagine. How can you work normally here? There are a lot of letter writers like that. And so we have to work in this kind of feverish atmosphere almost all the time. Is it possible, do you think, to describe and explain everything?

For thirteen and a half years, I have been working with these prisoners, as has my husband, Major Zakharov. His health has already been ruined working with the criminal world, because all the work here wears on your nerves. We would be happy to move on, because my husband has already served his time, but they won't let him go. He is a Communist and an officer, and he is bound by the duty of his position. But don't we have the right to live and work among positively oriented Soviet people? Don't we have the right to give our children a good education, since we have known no such thing? But here we are being blackened for all the misfortunes we have known, and the possibility of working any more is taken out of our hands. How unjust this is!

Let me go directly now to Solzhenitsyn's story.

Solzhenitsyn calls the security officer a "godfather." What does that mean? Who gave him the right to heap insults upon an official position that was established under the regulations of the MOOP of the Russian Republic? Or is that the customary practice among writers, to distort things? A person in this position has to be an officer and usually is a Communist. And they are at the present time also. And in regard to this "godfather," he certainly does use foul language; the writer says so himself. Also, according to Solzhenitsyn, if one of the prisoners is more conscientious, realizes his duty to the motherland, and does what his conscience calls upon him to do—that is, tells the security officer that one of the criminals is planning a murder or an escape or some other crime—Solzhenitsyn says that this is "self-preservation at someone else's expense." Some patriot, I must say.

I myself worked with a contingent of Article 58 [counterrevolutionary] prisoners, and there was nothing like what Solzhenitsyn writes about. The only thing was that some prisoners, as I have written, were more conscientious and revealed to the security officer a number of additional crimes against the motherland—committed by murderers, traitors, German collaborators, and the like. And for this, the Soviet people should only say thank you to these prisoners who came to a proper understanding. But Solzhenitsyn isn't pleased with this, you see.

Now about reveille and bedtime. This is part of the daily routine. You can't do without this in a camp. If there's no daily routine, there'll be no order in the camp. There are, in fact, particular regulations providing for such routine, and this continues to be the case now as it was before. There isn't any other way. But apparently Solzhenitsyn would like to have chaos in the camp and to have no order at all. But that cannot be.

And how Solzhenitsyn carries on about the guards. "Having stripped to their grubby tunics." One might think that they weren't wearing uniforms provided for in the MOOP regulations, but that these were tramps of some sort living on an uninhabited island without any higher ranking leadership, commanding officers, and so on.

And what is the implication, that the guards are fools? They are doing their duty, and they are obliged to carry out what is required of them.

And what does the hero of this story represent? One can guess right away what he was. When he had washed the floor in the camp supervisor's office, he tossed the unsqueezed cloth behind the stove and poured the dirty water out onto the path, the very one the authorities used. This shows how much he respects Soviet people—Communists—and how he takes care of socialist property. If every prisoner sloshed water around in the barracks the way he did, what would be left of them after five years? Everything would rot away, and the state would have to build again and the people would have to pay. But that's all right with Solzhenitsyn.

We can see why the hero of this story, having such an attitude toward the Soviet people, hopes for nothing but the sick bay in order somehow to get out of redeeming his guilt, the wrong he did to his motherland, through toil. After all, he is in a corrective-labor camp, even if he is innocent, and so he ought to set an example for the others, as a real Soviet citizen, as a Communist, to inspire others and not to get demoralized and demoralize others. And why exactly should a person try to avoid physical labor and show scorn for it? After all, for us labor is the foundation of the Soviet system, and it is only in labor that man becomes cognizant of his true powers. But here, as we see, the heroes of these stories are afraid of work, have a fearful attitude toward it; they seem to be afraid to go out felling timber. Millions of our Soviet people, however, fell timber for a living and praise this kind of work, and they don't march out to work at rifle point; they undertake this difficult and noble labor following the dictates of the heart.

Now, as for the "frisking"—or the body searches, to use the proper expression —they still exist today; there is no other way. The prisoners, you know, try to take anything they can outside the camp and sell it or exchange it for tea, vodka, and so on. There are free workers of all kinds around us, most often former prisoners of the same type, and they try by any means possible to interfere with the camp administration's attempt to organize the workings of the camp in a proper way. That is why the prisoners try to carry off camp property—and it is state property—and they try to smuggle out various letters of a slanderous nature against the Communist Party and Soviet government, and to engage in various kinds of criminal contacts, and so on. The administration is obliged to protect itself against this; otherwise, it cannot fulfill its mission and cannot follow the instructions outlined in the regulations on operating procedures and treatment of prisoners. If this kind of thing were permitted, if searches were not carried out, the prisoners would commit such crimes that the people would long remember their mistake in allowing prisoners to do just anything they wanted. These authors themselves write that there were real criminals in the camps—robbers, killers, counterrevolutionaries—as well as innocent people, and how is the administration to distinguish between who is guilty and who is not?

Solzhenitsyn describes the workings of the camp in his story as if there were no leadership by the Party there. But the fact is that there were Party organizations previously, just like now, and they directed all the work as conscience required. Nobody knew that a wrong policy was being carried out by Stalin. This was reflected only in the trials where people were unjustly condemned under Article 58 and in the conditions under which prisoners were held: with bars on the windows, locked barracks, and numbers on the prisoners' clothes. But what did the members of the prison-camp staffs have to do with this? The same people who worked there then for the most part work there now; maybe 10 percent are new. And they have been given incentive pay more than once for their good work. They have good records as hard workers. Let's take Comrade Likhosherstov as an example, the man of whom the author of *A Tale of Survival* writes. At present, Comrade Likhosherstov is a captain, the secretary of his Party organization, and is working in agriculture, where he has carried out measures called for by the Party for sharply increasing agricultural production. And imagine how hard it is for him to work when they write these kind of things about him.

They are now saying, for example, that Likhosherstov is going to be investigated and has barely avoided being taken to court. But for what? If this is only talk, that's fine, but the possibility isn't excluded that they'll decide to go that far. This is creating a real uproar among MOOP personnel, if we may put it that way. Investigate him for what—for carrying out the orders that came down from above? And is he supposed to answer now for those who gave those orders? That's a fine thing! It's like in the proverb, "The one at the bottom is always guilty."

And what nonsense Solzhenitsyn writes, that the disciplinary officer carried a whip to beat the prisoners with. I don't know where such a thing could have happened. From 1950 to 1954 I worked with political prisoners, and our relations with them were quite humane, not like that at all. If someone from the administration even tried to say something rude to them, he'd be dismissed from his post right away, let alone for corporal punishment. After all, we know very well that corporal punishment was abolished in our country with the advent of Soviet power, but Solzhenitsyn makes out as though there was such lawlessness and rudeness in the camps that it would seem they weren't even being run by Soviet people. We must realize that he is deliberately inciting the people against the organs of the MOOP just because he personally is embittered against them.

And he calls the soldiers "screws." What does that mean? A Soviet soldier and a "screw." What kind of mockery is this? They were drafted into the Soviet army. Some were sent into the air force, others into the navy, and some into the guards. Not on the basis of their personal wishes or desires. The service regulations were read out to them, and as military personnel they were obliged to abide by those regulations, no matter where they were. But Solzhenitsyn makes fun of them. And you know convoy troops still exist and still do their military service guarding criminals. So it seems the soldiers are to blame for being assigned to camps when the tasks are given out? No matter what, someone has to be assigned to this. And it seems to me it's not a shameful thing to protect the peaceful labors of the Soviet people. But according to Solzhenitsyn, it seems, nothing could be more shameful.

There's one other aspect of Solzhenitsyn's story I would like to comment on. The way he talks about the prisoners' food. "You can't dig food out of the earth; you get no more than the chief assigns you." He writes as though the camp commandant had control of this. But, in fact, there is one standard prison ration throughout the Soviet Union, and the camp commandant has nothing to do with it; a certain amount is assigned to him per prisoner and that is all he receives. If a ration double the standard one is assigned, the camp commandment in turn assigns a double ration. Do I need to repeat again that one must have a very crafty mind to think up things like this?

It's simply amazing how much bile against the camp administration, how much ridicule, mockery, and insult there is in this story. A few words more on this same point. "They steal here, and earlier in the warehouse they stole." It is as though the freely employed Soviet citizens working in the camps were all thieves, as though there was no control, no honest people, and so on. The truth is the opposite. Everyone who works here knows who they are dealing with and would never do such things, because they would be sure to end up there themselves. Perhaps thieving occurred in some places—there may have been such cases in our country—but I know that at Ozerlag there was none, or else those officials themselves would have been behind the barbed wire long ago. But Solzhenitsyn slings mud at everyone without exception and calls them all thieves.

In this letter, I can't cover everything negative in Solzhenitsyn's and Dyakov's stories. And almost everything in Solzhenitsyn's is negative. These stories are full of concealed hatred and malice toward the Communist prison officials. This is especially true, I repeat once again, in Solzhenitsyn's case. Every line of his story is full of such bile that it hits you right in the eye how aggressively prejudiced he is against the entire order and system in the camps. I had to sit down and go over his story for a long time in order to express my opinion. I have been working on this letter for about two months, snatching half an hour a day, sometimes through great exertion an hour a day, but sometimes only an hour a week. In spite of this, I wanted to write and express my opinion, although I can't do it the way a writer can, for example—smoothly and beautifully. But I feel this injustice in my heart and I am indignant, although I can't express it on paper in a very concise and elegant way. Even in this long letter, I have not expressed one-thousandth part of what I would like to say.

My understanding of things is this: it is necessary and indispensable to criticize the personality cult, and we all are doing that now; but it is not necessary to drag in people who had absolutely nothing to do with it. All Soviet citizens experienced this period the same way, so why should a certain section of the people be blamed for it? It's quite clear that this period was the result of the policies of a certain category of people and not of all the people, and so there's no reason to let such writers as Solzhenitsyn and Dyakov discredit and smear the MOOP.

I somehow feel certain that all employees of MOOP feel the same way I do; I am convinced of this from my conversations with a great many of them. And all of them that I have had a chance to talk with are of the same opinion—the authority of MOOP has been undermined decisively in the eyes of the people and cannot now be restored.

[No. 3, December 1964]

Open Letter to Konstantin Fedin
BY VENIAMIN KAVERIN

We end this chapter with a melancholy literary document that brings the question of responsibility squarely into the present and serves as a prelude to the next chapter. A number of older Soviet writers came to feel in the 1950s and 1960s that their collective failure to speak out in the past had contributed to the crimes of the Stalin years. Determined to revive the Russian tradition of an outspoken intelligentsia, they resolved to end their submissive silence: "May muteness perish—it always supports despotism."[9] This sense of historical guilt was a political factor in the second half of the 1960s, when the post-Khrushchev government began to rehabilitate the Stalinist past and repress anti-Stalinist authors. Many Soviet writers, of course, had participated or acquiesced in Khrushchev's own scurrilous campaign against Boris Pasternak in 1958, when his Doctor Zhivago was awarded the Nobel Prize while under a ban in the Soviet Union. But when state censorship and persecution turned against Solzhenitsyn in 1967–68, several establishment writers were ready to speak out. Veniamin Kaverin (born 1902) and Konstantin Fedin (1892–1977) were venerable novelists with eminent literary careers going back to the 1920s. Both had survived the Stalin years with their literary reputations and personal honor more or less intact. Their paths then diverged. Kaverin became one of the most respected liberals of the post-Stalin period. Fedin became the country's chief literary bureaucrat, First Secretary of the Writer's Union, in 1959. Kaverin's letter was precipitated by the ban on Solzhenitsyn's great novel about the Stalin years, Cancer Ward. *The novel helped Solzhenitsyn win the Nobel Prize in 1970; it remains unpublished in the Soviet Union.*

January 25, 1968

To Konstantin Fedin:

We have known each other forty-eight years, Kostya. We were childhood friends. We have the right to judge one another. It is more than a right, it is an obligation. Your former friends have pondered more than once what motives could have prompted your behavior in these unforgettable events in our literary life that strengthened some of us but transformed others into obedient bureaucrats far removed from genuine art.

---

9. From Lydia Chukovskaya's samizdat credo of 1968, in Abraham Brumberg, ed., *In Quest of Justice* (New York, 1970), pp. 313–18.

Who doesn't remember, for example, the senseless and tragic history of Pasternak's novel, which did a great deal of damage to our country? Your involvement in that affair went so deep that you were forced to pretend that you didn't know of the death of the poet who had been your friend and had lived alongside you for twenty-three years. Perhaps the crowd of thousands that accompanied him, that carried him on outstretched arms past your house, was not visible from your window. How did it happen that you not only did not support *Literaturnaya Moskva* [in 1956–57], an anthology that was indispensable to our literature, but crushed it? After all, on the eve of the meeting of 1,500 writers in the cinema actors' building, you supported its publication. With an already prepared and dangerously treacherous speech in your pocket, you praised our work without finding even a trace of anything politically undesirable in it.

This is far from everything, but I do not propose in this letter to summarize your public activities, which are widely known in writers' circles. Not without reason, on the seventy-fifth birthday of Konstantin Paustovsky, [the mention of] your name was greeted with complete silence. After the banning of Solzhenitsyn's novel *Cancer Ward*, which had already been set in type by *Novy mir*, it will not surprise me if your very next appearance before a wide audience of writers is received with whistles and foot stamping.

Of course, your position in literature should have prepared us to some degree for this staggering fact. One must go very far back to discover the very first point at which the process of spiritual deformation and irreversible change began. For years and years, it went on beneath the surface and did not come into any striking contradiction to your position—a position that at times, although one could not exactly approve of it, could somehow be explained in historical terms. But what is pushing you along that path *now,* with the result that once again our literature will suffer gravely? Don't you understand that the mere act of publishing *Cancer Ward* would relieve the unprecedented tension in the literary world, break down the undeserved distrust of writers, and open the way for other books that would enrich our literature? Aleksandr Bek's superb novel [*The New Appointment*], which was first authorized and then forbidden, although unconditionally approved by the best writers in the country, just lies there in manuscript form. So do the war diaries of Konstantin Simonov. One could scarcely find a single serious writer who does not have in his desk a manuscript that has been submitted, deliberated upon, and prohibited for unclear reasons that exceed the bounds of common sense. Thus, behind the scenes of the imaginary well-being proclaimed by the leadership, a strong, original literature is growing—the spiritual treasure of the country that it (the country) urgently and keenly needs. Don't you see that our tremendous historical experience demands its own embodiment (in literature) and that you are joining forces with those who, for the sake of their own well-being, are trying to halt this inevitable process?

But let's return to Solzhenitsyn's novel. There is now no editorial board or literary organization where it is not being said that Georgy Markov and Konstantin Voronkov were for the publication of the novel and that the typesetting was broken up only because you spoke out decisively against it. This means that the novel will remain in thousands of separate pages, passing from hand to hand and selling, it is said, for a good sum of money. It also means that it will be published abroad. We will be giving it away to the reading public of Italy, France, England, and West Germany; that is to say, the very thing that Solzhenitsyn himself repeatedly and energetically protested against will occur.

Perhaps there can be found in the leadership of the Writers' Union people who think that they will be punishing the author by giving his book away to foreign publishers. They will punish him by [giving him] a worldwide notoriety that our opponents will use for political ends. Or do they think that Solzhenitsyn will "mend his ways" and begin to write in another way? This is ridiculous in reference to an artist who is a rare example, who persistently reminds us that we are working in the literary tradition of Chekhov and Tolstoy.

But your path has still another meaning. You are taking upon yourself a responsibility, apparently without recognizing its immensity and significance. A writer who puts a noose around the neck of another writer is one whose place in the history of literature will be determined not by what he himself may have written but by what was written by his victim. Perhaps, without even suspecting it yourself, you will become the focus of hostility, indignation, and resentment in literary circles.

This can be altered only if you find in yourself the strength and courage to repudiate your decision.

You undoubtedly understand how difficult it is for me to write you this letter. But I do not have the right to keep silent.

V. Kaverin
[No. 40, January 1968]

3

Neo-Stalinism

Neo-stalinism is a complex phenomenon in the Soviet Union. It exists in official circles but also among right-wing dissidents. It is a kind of policy advocacy as well as diffuse popular sentiments. Its emotional ingredients range from grumbling dissatisfaction with everyday life and simple nostalgia for the past to fascist-like cults of Russian nationalism. Its adherents are educated and uneducated. They can be found in every adult age group and occupation.

The resurgence of official Stalinist attitudes that followed Khrushchev's overthrow at a Central Committee meeting in October 1964 was the product of two political factors. First, the growing conservatism of the new Brezhnev government required an ideological counterpoint to Khrushchev's anti-Stalinist reformism. Second, this backward drift in leadership politics was abetted by a reinvigorated Stalinist lobby inside the Party, whose strongholds included influential segments of the ideological apparatus, the Political Administration of the Armed Forces, the central Komsomol organization, and the Party leadership of Stalin's native Georgia. The result was a number of inconclusive but significant neo-Stalinist victories in 1965–66—a resumption of tighter censorship of literature about the Stalinist past along with statements favorable to Stalin in the official press, a growing campaign against Party strongholds of anti-Stalinism, including the influential journal Novy mir, and an evolving pattern of repression against writers, most notably the trial of Andrei Sinyavsky and Yuli Daniel in February 1966.

All of these developments greatly alarmed anti-Stalinist intellectuals inside and outside the Party. They saw neo-Stalinism as a grave menace in Soviet and in international politics. (An analogue was already underway, they thought, in Mao's China.) As Party anti-Stalinists suffered successive defeats over the next few years, dramatized by the significant official rehabilitation of Stalin's reputa-

tion on the ninetieth anniversary of his birth in 1969, public protests grew steadily
into the dissident movement of the late 1960s and 1970s.

Political Diary provides a rich chronicle of this turning point in modern
Soviet politics. Its monthly issues documented the struggle between anti-Stalinism and neo-Stalinism in many official and samizdat materials. Created in
October 1964, in response to the first omens of a Stalinist revival, Political Diary
was, in this respect, an uncensored samizdat counterpart of Novy mir. The two
journals shared a Party-oriented anti-Stalinism and, as Novy mir was diminished
increasingly by censorship, authors and manuscripts. Indeed, Roy Medvedev's
analysis of the neo-Stalinist danger in 1966, which opens this chapter, was an
uncensored statement of warnings that were appearing more guardedly in Novy
mir at about the same time.

The Danger of a Revival of Stalinism
BY ROY MEDVEDEV

Many people in the Soviet Union and outside it are now asking, Is it possible that a revival of the Stalin cult, and the reversal of the resolutions on that question passed at the Twentieth and Twenty-second congresses, could occur in the Soviet Union? An even more essential question is, Is it possible that the restoration of Stalinism as a terrorist system of rule could occur without the formal revival of the Stalin cult? What guarantees are there against arbitrariness and violations of Soviet legality on a massive scale?

The question of legal guarantees, of the creation of social and governmental mechanisms capable of preventing mass coercion, is a most important question for socialist theory and practice. This problem cannot be dismissed with stale jokes, as Pyotr Demichev, a secretary of the Party Central Committee, tried to do with his comment at a conference that "only watchmakers give guarantees."

Unfortunately, in the most general terms there can only be an affirmative answer to the questions raised here. Yes, a revival of Stalinism in our country is possible, either in conjunction with some sort of rehabilitation of the Stalin cult or even without a formal reversal of the resolutions passed at the Twentieth and Twenty-second congresses. How likely is such a development however?

To answer this question, we must look at several of the factors that contribute to or, alternatively, act as an obstacle to neo-Stalinist trends.

1. First of all, we must note that Stalinism per se never *fully* disappeared from Soviet social and political life. After the Twentieth and Twenty-second congresses, we were freed from the most extreme forms of authoritarian rule. In the process, the Party and people were told only part (and not a very large part) of the truth about the crimes of Stalin and the Stalinists. The overwhelming majority of those who took an active part in those crimes have not been brought to justice. Many continued to hold important posts in the government, Party, and economic apparatus. Some still do. Those who have been rehabilitated do not include all of the most important figures in our Party, active leaders of and participants in the October Revolution, civil war, and early years of Soviet construction, who fell victim to Stalinist arbitrariness. Far from it. Moreover, hardly any of those who were rehabilitated and returned to their families have been allowed to resume normal participation in public political life. Additional facts of this kind could be listed.

2. After the Twentieth and Twenty-second congresses, there were many instances of arbitrary policy in the economic, cultural, and diplomatic spheres. In those years, there were quite a few illegal acts of repression on the administrative, judicial, and intra-Party levels. From 1961 to 1964, a system of rule by a single dominant personality was reestablished, and "enormous power" [the phrase

used by Lenin in his famous Testament calling for the removal of Stalin], hardly limited in any way, was concentrated in the hands of Khrushchev. The inordinate glorification of Khrushchev, which began at the Twenty-second Congress itself, became a routine occurrence and was encouraged in every way, essentially taking the form of a new personality cult. After the October plenum of the Central Committee, which condemned "voluntarism" and relieved Khrushchev of his responsibilities, the situation changed. However, many economic difficulties persisted. Cases of illegal repression on the judicial and Party levels also persisted and in some respects became more frequent. Press censorship was intensified. And there were increasingly stubborn and determined efforts to rehabilitate Stalin on the part of highly influential military and Party leaders.

3. As in the past, the majority of the Party, the people, and the intelligentsia are politically passive. On the other hand, extreme centralization persists in the economy and in political life. We do not have the right to engage in opposition activity, and no democratic mechanisms exist for control by the ranks over the actions of the leaders. The "top brass" are still too much removed from the "rank and file." There is also a dangerous gap between the ruling *nomenklatura* [appointed from above] apparatus in the Party and government, and the intelligentsia.

4. A substantial number of Party and government officials, as well as officials in the economic, military, and other apparatuses, favor a "stronger" leadership. Even today, these people long for the "firm hand" of old. They seek a way out of the present difficulties not through greater democratization or rejuvenation of the apparatus, but through greater centralization, fiercer repression, administrative and judicial, against dissenters, tighter censorship, and so on.

5. In recent years, the influence of top military leaders—most of whom are overtly opposed to democratization and favor the reestablishment of Stalin's military and political "reputation"—has increased in the upper layers of our society. The influence of the military in foreign policy has also increased. In the last two years, the state security agencies have gained increased influence over domestic policy. Once again the staffs of the security forces are expanding (as are the "informant" staffs).

6. The neo-Stalinists have skillfully tried to exploit for their own ends certain nationalist, anarchist, and antisocialist (or anti-Marxist and anti-Leninist) moods that have become evident among a small number of young people and intellectuals and that represent the reaction of politically immature people to the monstrous crimes of Stalin and Stalinism. These moods do not constitute a threat to our society. They can be overcome by ideological means if socialist democracy is encouraged. On the other hand, such moods will increase with any revival of Stalinism.

7. Recently, for various reasons, the Soviet Union has become more isolated internationally. A policy of democratization could help reverse this trend and win new friends abroad for our country. However, some people advocate the opposite —that moods such as existed among the people in the 1930s be revived, that is,

the besieged-fortress mentality. And attitudes of intolerance are being encouraged accordingly. Disagreement with any aspect of the domestic or foreign policy of the Soviet government is adjudged to be hostile, anti-Soviet, and antisocialist.

Other factors working in the same direction can be specified. We cannot fail to assign the proper importance to all these factors, and it is not excluded that they will indeed play the central role in our domestic and foreign policies.

But we do not believe that the shift in the direction of neo-Stalinism can be long lasting. For there are other fundamental factors pressing in the other direction. We shall list only a few of them below.

1. The scientific and technical revolution, which is inevitable in the USSR, just as it is elsewhere in the world, will bring about changes in the social structure and in its economic base that will prove incompatible with the system of unlimited rule by a single individual (or by a small group). Extreme centralization and lack of democracy in politics, economics, and culture; the absence of any mechanisms allowing the advancement of the most able and gifted; the absence of the free exchange of ideas and information—all of this becomes an enormous impediment to the development of the productive forces. The intelligentsia is growing rapidly in numbers, and it cannot function efficiently without free discussion and freedom of information, at least in narrow professional respects. The structure of the economy is becoming more and more complex and, consequently, more sensitive to incompetent interference of any kind. It is no longer possible to arrest tens of thousands of engineers, plant managers, and heads of shops and institutes within one year [as in the 1930s] and replace them with Stakhanovite [or shock] workers. Not only might mass repression among the scientific and technical intelligentsia act as a brake upon our economic development; it could also bring about the total collapse of our economy.

2. The arms race is becoming an increasingly onerous burden. It is slowing down our rate of growth and maintaining the gap between the Soviet economy and the more powerful U.S. economy, as well as our lag behind the Western European countries and Japan, which do not spend so much for military purposes. Thus, the objective necessity for a new foreign policy becomes evident—a policy that would be hard to implement without changes in domestic policy.

3. The scientific and technical revolution is inseparably linked with the rising cultural and educational level of the masses. This in turn contributes to greater political interest and activity in the population as a whole.

4. Given the present state of public awareness (after the denunciation of both Stalin and Khrushchev), it would be rather difficult for the cult of some new "personality" to arise. Of course, it is possible for the apparatus to indulge in new outpourings of official praise and to heap excessive honors upon some new "personality." But it is hard to imagine that such propaganda would have any success among the masses or the intelligentsia. It is a known fact that the immoderate glorification of Khrushchev evoked no real response among the masses and was often greeted with mockery. In this regard, the country has developed a rather

strong "immunity," which cannot be overcome through propaganda, still less through repression.

5. On the present Politburo, there are no individuals who enjoy any special popularity among the people, who have any outstanding revolutionary service records, exceptional intelligence, unusual oratorical abilities, or the like. Therefore, in spite of mutual hard feelings or even animosities among them, these people cannot—it seems to me—indulge in any serious internal dispute of the kind that usually occurs as part of the creation of a new "personality cult." On the other hand, without such a "cult" it is hard to move toward repression of dissenters in any substantial way.

6. In many respects, neo-Stalinism is worse off than the original Stalinism was, because it is not in a position to attract a significant number of people to its banner. Stalin, by coming forward as the heir of Lenin, was able to exploit the political enthusiasm present in the Party in the wake of the Soviet victory in the civil war. The Stalinist system was able to deceive and attract not only the worst people but also a layer of talented and capable people devoted to the ideals of socialism. Of course, they too were corrupted by Stalinism, but not all of them changed their behavior and thinking irreversibly. The Stalinist system was not only based on mass terror; it also contained a measure of social demagogy, which worked rather effectively in the 1930s, during the war, and in the postwar period. For this reason, it managed to win over not only a large part of the new intelligentsia but a large part of the younger generation as well. For these people, Stalin was truly the highest authority and an infallible leader. After the denunciation of Stalin, however, all the most intelligent and capable people in the country turned away from Stalin and Stalinism. Today the Stalinists are represented in cultural fields by such figures [whom we will meet below] as Trapeznikov, Kochetov, and Gribachev and in politics by the likes of General Yepishev and Sturua. They have practically no talented or able people on their side. They are led by morally and intellectually inferior individuals. Their demagogy does not stir anyone; it has little effect on the intelligentsia or the youth. Therefore, it is hard to conceive the possibility of their political success.

7. While the majority of top Party officials lack what is usually called popularity among the masses (in general the masses and even the intelligentsia know nothing about them but their names), many prominent intellectual figures, e.g., writers and scientists, do have such popularity and moral authority. Among the intelligentsia and the people as a whole, a system of values and a way of judging people has grown up that is different from the past in many respects. In fact, the influence and authority of some of the most outstanding scientists, writers, and artists is increasing. The Party apparatus instinctively reacts against this, surrounding the most prominent scientists with secrecy, although this is not at all necessary for considerations of security. (Of course, even the most popular intellectuals have no power. Nevertheless, their views, opinions, and objections must be taken into account by any present-day politician, as was shown by the unofficial precongress discussion on the question of Stalin. Sergei Trapeznikov, as head of

the science section of the Central Committee, unquestionably has more power than [the famous physicist] Pyotr Kapitsa. But, for most academicians in the natural sciences, even a political argument between Trapeznikov and Kapitsa would go in Kapitsa's favor, we are sure—if a secret ballot were held on this question.) What is usually called "public opinion" is beginning to emerge in our country in spite of everything—numerous unofficial centers of intellectual influence that will continue to have a greater and greater effect on the thinking of our society.

8. The scientific and technical revolution is intensifying the international division of labor and increasing the dependence of our economic system on the economies of other countries, including capitalist countries. The Soviet Union cannot long remain in a state of de facto economic isolation from the developed capitalist countries. We have a greater and greater need for expanded economic, cultural, and scientific contacts with these countries. And we therefore cannot disregard international public opinion today, since the effectiveness of these contacts depends on it to a large extent.

9. The position of the Soviet Communist Party in the world Communist movement has also changed. Even Communist parties that continue to recognize the *leading* role of the Soviet Party in the world movement are no longer inclined to give blind support to everything that happens in the USSR. The Sinyavsky-Daniel case brought with it considerable criticism detrimental to the Soviet Communist Party from much of the Western Communist press. Increased repression in the USSR would provoke even more emphatic protest by Communist parties in many other countries, and our leaders can no longer simply ignore that fact.

10. A worldwide system of mass communication is coming into existence at present, and within fifteen to twenty years no country will be able effectively to prevent the flow of information from other countries. It will be necessary more and more to counter ideas, not with force but with other ideas. The Soviet Union will be no exception. Technological change brings with it increased possibilities for the growth of public discussion outside the control of the censors. Typewriters will be replaced by more refined and efficient duplicating devices, the use of which will be hard to restrict. With technical progress, freedom of speech can become a reality; it can arise "without prior arrangement" and will undeniably limit the possibilities for arbitrary action.

Peace on earth is threatened by many forces. We must combat the revival of fascism and other manifestations of political reaction such as *revanchisme*, imperialism, neocolonialism, and McCarthyism. But the best contribution Soviet citizens can make to the struggle between the forces of progress and those of reaction is to combat the Stalinist and neo-Stalinist tendencies in our own country. For the victory of Stalinism in the USSR would inevitably strengthen the hands of reactionaries of every stripe in every other country of the world.

[No. 24, September 1966]

"I Am a Stalinist":
A Meeting of Party Officials

The Party's neo-Stalinist faction grew increasingly assertive in 1965–66, pro-moting its views more boldly and attacking anti-Stalinists more openly. The following document, which is abridged here, shows some of these high-ranking neo-Stalinists at work. Recorded secretly by an observer, it summarizes part of the closed proceedings of a nationwide "meeting-seminar" of Party ideological officials held in Moscow on October 12–17, 1966. About a thousand people attended, including ranking Party secretaries from around the country. Full-time ideological functionaries constitute a powerful lobby in the Party apparatus, from the center to outlying regions, which does much to shape the political climate inside the Soviet Union. This particular meeting seems to have been stage-managed by neo-Stalinists from the outset; a number of prominent anti-Stalinists were not invited. The conference discussed a variety of issues. But what stood out was, according to Political Diary, *the "unprecedented attempt by the repre-sentatives from Georgia to rehabilitate Stalin." The campaign was launched on the opening day by Devi Sturua, then secretary for ideology of the Georgian Communist Party. His bold declaration "I am a Stalinist" surprised less than did its favorable reception.*

[Sturua said roughly the following:] "We are sometimes called Stalinists, but we don't see anything to be ashamed of in that. I am a Stalinist because the name of Stalin is linked with the victories of our people in the years of collectivization and industrialization. I am a Stalinist because the name of Stalin is linked with the victories of our people in the Great Patriotic War. I am a Stalinist because the name of Stalin is linked with the victories of our people in the postwar reconstruction of our economy."

Sturua's remarks drew applause from approximately 70 percent of those at the conference. The rest either remained silent or protested. The speech by Shikhali Kurbanov, a secretary of the Azerbaijan Central Committee, gave support to Sturua's position.

Many of those who spoke at the conference were harshly critical of [the anti-Stalinist journals] *Novy mir* and *Yunost* (Youth) and the [anti-Stalinist] book by Aleksandr Nekrich. Sturua referred to Nekrich as "mister" [instead of as comrade]. General Aleksei Yepishev, head of the Chief Political Administration of the Soviet Army and Navy, announced to the conference that subscriptions to *Novy mir* and *Yunost* were banned in the military offices and units of the

Political Administration. Among those who expressed similar conservative views were Stanislav Pilotovich, secretary of the Byelorussian Central Committee; Sergei Trapeznikov, head of the Party Central Committee's department for science, schools, and higher educational institutions; Nikolai Mikhailov, chairman of the State Committee on the Press; Sergei Pavlov, First Secretary of the Komsomol Central Committee; and several others who gave reports or took the floor.

The speeches of all these figures apparently indicate that a faction of Stalinists has begun to take shape within the leading circles of our Party. There is no reason to doubt that some, even many, of these speeches were arranged in advance, in particular those of Sturua, Kurbanov, and Pilotovich. Evidence of this is the repeated stress in many of these speeches on criticism of the Politburo for allegedly failing to deal firmly enough with *Novy mir* and [its editor] Tvardovsky. One of the speakers (Pilotovich?) declared, "There should be a request that the Politburo summon Tvardovsky to the Central Committee and ask him what party line he is carrying out—ours or somebody else's?"

Pyotr Demichev, a secretary of the Party Central Committee, in his speech concluding the conference in behalf of the Central Committee, spoke out against the remarks by Sturua, Kurbanov, Pilotovich, and others, but Demichev's reproaches were rather mild. The factional statements by people like Sturua, which directly contradict the line of the Twentieth and Twenty-second congresses, were not condemned as they deserved to be. Demichev reiterated that the Central Committee resolution of June 30, 1956 [condemning the Stalin cult], should be seen as the Party's central statement of its position on Stalin.

Among the other speeches at the conference, the content of several should be mentioned.

Vladimir Stepakov [a high propaganda official] criticized the historians who in recent years had attempted to reassess the history of Soviet society, especially the period of collectivization and industrialization (an obvious reference to the Institute of History of the Soviet Academy of Sciences in Moscow and particularly to the work of the department on collectivization headed by Viktor Danilov).

According to Stepakov, the [then current] economic reform is not going smoothly in every respect. Labor turnover is very high in the new industrial regions, and the cultural level is low. Some of our economists exaggerate the law of value and propose that it be allowed free rein, to the detriment of planning. We still have inequality, but there are no good Marxist works that analyze and explain it. (Unfortunately, the conditions of scholarship in our country are not yet of the quality necessary for the creation of such works.) Social Democratic propaganda is trying to implant bourgeois values among us. Stepakov criticized the attempt to "deglorify" our history. (This term is replacing the old one, "the blackening of our reality.")

Stepakov said further that in many plants discipline has been shaken, and absenteeism and theft have increased. The Party Central Committee has adopted a special resolution on this. Our ideological work is being hurt by all sorts of rumors and political jokes. Democracy is not anarchy. There is no freedom without responsibility. Stepakov declared that a significant number of our young people are infected with skepticism and have shown instability in the face of Western propaganda. Military-patriotic propaganda must therefore be stepped up.

Vasily Shauro, the director of the Party Central Committee's cultural department, discussed the inadequacies of leadership in the fields of literature and art. In the West, there is a big outcry now about "the tightening of the screws" and a return to the times of the personality cult. Those times will not return, but one cannot help observing that in the last few years our literature and art have not only enjoyed success; there have also been instances of "the blackening of our reality," formalism, and epigonism. Foreign propagandists make much of every deviation from the correct line by our cultural figures. They favor a policy of "building bridges." A reevaluation of some writers is under way (e.g., of Andrei Platonov and Mikhail Bulgakov). At the same time, some writers are trying to argue that the October Revolution did not give the peasant anything. Literature about the war has gone through several stages. In the past, attention focused mainly on the heroism of the war; now some writers are fixing their sights on the darker aspects. Shauro referred to Sinyavsky and Daniel as "turncoats." Some young writers, he declared, have a lust for notoriety. All of us are against administrative measures, he continued, but we cannot disregard mistakes in the cultural arena.

Vladimir Semichastny, head of the KGB, who has spoken frequently before a wide variety of audiences recently, also gave a report to this conference. He said that American intelligence had intensified its drive against the USSR and that all the Western intelligence services were acting in concert. There had also been instances of sabotage—for example, equipment for export had been damaged. The American imperialists are trying in every way to exacerbate our conflict with China. U.S. intelligence takes an interest in everything in the USSR. The CIA obtains much intelligence information from tourists. Some scientists from the United States and other countries initiate discussions with our specialists for intelligence purposes. And there have been attempts to recruit or even kidnap Soviet personnel. The CIA is making extensive use of the latest technology. Approximately 2,000 fixed stations and 2,000 mobile units are located along Soviet borders for monitoring purposes.

Inside the USSR, Semichastny said, the situation is fine. However, there have been some crimes of a rather daring kind. The attitudes held by some young people should put us on our guard—for example, such [dissident] organizations as SMOG and the Izumisty. Organizations of a fascist character had also made their appearance. (It is said that at this point in his speech Semichastny was interrupted by Pavlov, who shouted that there was nothing surprising in this, since young people were reading all they wanted of *Yunost* and *Novy mir,* the sources of such attitudes. Semichastny is said to have replied that none of the young people who had been arrested were readers of *Yunost* or *Novy mir.*)

Semichastny continued that several letters on the fate of Sinyavsky and Daniel addressed to the Party Central Committee—for example, the letter from fourteen young poets and writers—reached the Voice of America before the Central Committee received them. Civic responsibility and vigilance must be heightened. The KGB will continue to take repressive measures only against genuine enemies.

[No. 25, October 1966]

Recensoring the Past:
Lydia Chukovskaya Sues a Soviet Publisher

A primary goal of neo-Stalinists, shortly before and after Khrushchev's overthrow, was a policy of what might be called anti–anti-Stalinism. They wanted to stop revelations about the past in official publications, including the "flood" of manuscripts about Stalin's terror that had come to Soviet publishers after the Twenty-second Party Congress in 1961, especially after the appearance of Solzhenitsyn's Ivan Denisovich in 1962, and to discredit anti-Stalinist works already published. The following document, a partial record of Lydia Chukovskaya's court case in April 1965 against the large publishing house that had reneged on a contract to publish her anti-Stalinist novella, shows how the neo-Stalinist campaign began and bore fruit. Chukovskaya (born 1907) is a well-known writer and revered figure among Soviet literary nonconformists and political dissidents. Her husband was arrested and shot in 1938, and she herself only barely escaped arrest during the terror. The adopted daughter of the famous writer Kornei Chukovsky, she is the author of fiction, literary criticism, celebrated memoirs about her friend Anna Akhmatova, and, since the mid-1960s, many samizdat protests. (Naturally, she was expelled, in 1974, from the Writers' Union.) Chukovskaya wrote Sofia Petrovna—the novella later was published abroad in Russian and English as The Deserted House *(New York, 1967), with the heroine's name changed to Olga Petrovna—in 1939–40. It tells the story of a loyal Soviet woman whose son is arrested on false charges in 1937, and who herself is then transformed, along with the society around her, by the sinister events of that era. To have written and preserved such a manuscript in those terror-ridden years required, as* Political Diary *observed, "great courage." Twenty-two years later, Chukovskaya submitted* Sofia Petrovna *for publication and received a contract in December 1962. It was abrogated in May 1963 by a secret order that gradually suspended, and eventually banned altogether, publication of works about the terror. Unlike most of the authors affected, Chukovskaya did not suffer her disappointment in silence. Her lawsuit is an example of early dissident efforts to find some support in the Soviet legal system. The court proceedings show that politics and censorship were still in flux as late as 1965, and indeed that the order suspending books already under contract created problems for publishers. But above all, the proceedings help to document the end of official anti-Stalinism in the Soviet Union.*

People's court of the Sverdlov district of Moscow. Judicial hearing of April 24, 1965.

A judge asks Chukovskaya to explain the reasons for her suit against the publisher Sovetsky Pisatel (Soviet Writer).

Chukovskaya: In September 1962, I submitted my short novel *Sofia Petrovna* to this publisher. It had been written back in 1940. In content, it was a protest against the mass repression of Soviet citizens that occurred in 1937–38. In December 1962, a contract was signed with me, in which the manuscript was designated as "accepted." In January 1963, I was paid 60 percent of the royalty. In March 1963, they showed me the format for the cover and the frontispiece. The manuscript progressed no further after that. I went to see Comrade Ivan Kozlov [at the publishing house]. He talked with me for a long time. He said that the novel could not be printed, because although it was a truthful work, it lacked any background depicting the life of the people as a whole. I reminded him that the manuscript had been accepted and that the publishing house had previously been pleased with it. Kozlov promised to discuss the question once again, but after that no one invited me back to the publishing house. After a long time, an editor, Comrade Valentina Karpova, informed me that the manuscript would not be printed. Then I turned to the Bureau for the Protection of Authors' Rights (Russian initials, VOAPP) and asked whether I had the right to the remaining 40 percent of the royalty. The answer was affirmative. With the help of the attorneys there, I prepared this suit against the publisher.

The judge gives the floor to the respondent—a representative of the publishing house.

The respondent asks whether Chukovskaya thinks the novel serves a useful purpose.

Chukovskaya: Yes, I consider it indispensable. Especially for young people, who have only the vaguest notion of the year 1937.

Respondent: Why, then, didn't you try to have your manuscript published in the period between 1953 and 1962?

Chukovskaya: Not only in the period 1953–62 but also in 1939–40, when the novel was written, it served a good purpose. But I no more attempted to publish it then than I did during the years 1953–62.

Respondent: In a formal sense the contract has been broken. But, after all, the novel was not written to earn money from the publishing house. As I understand it, the manuscript had been kept in the writer's personal archives [since 1940]. Before 1962, Chukovskaya did not want it published. There is in the novel a serious ideological distortion. It is true that the manuscript was praised at our publishing house. But since then the plenum of the Central Committee [that overthrew Khrushchev in October 1964] was held and the meetings between Party leaders and the intelligentsia took place. And a new look was taken at this work, with eyes that had been opened for the consultants and editors by these meetings and the plenum. I am not referring to all this in order to discredit Chukovskaya's work.

The respondent then quoted from a review by Kozlov (dated May 17, 1963) and one by Osip Reznik (dated April 7, 1965).

The respondent continues: Reznik analyzed the positive and negative aspects of the novel in a very profound and correct manner. This review is useful material for the author. Citizen judges, even if you have not read the novel, these contradictory reviews testify that there are both positive features and serious shortcomings in the novel. And the shortcomings predominate. Therefore, the novel is not useful at the present time. There is no analysis in the novel. It is a photograph, recording only the warped and misshapen phenomena of those times. At present, after the publication of Solzhenitsyn's short novel, which the publishing house is not planning to reprint, a flood of manuscripts on this same topic has reached our offices. These manuscripts are also being returned to their authors.

This was something we ourselves didn't understand. It was pointed out to us that there is absolutely no necessity for us as Communists to simply criticize this period. The important thing is that a useful purpose be served. Chukovskaya's work cannot come out, no matter what, because of its ideological bias. Chukovskaya is a respected writer, and people eagerly read her works. She should understand. Chukovskaya herself, in the book *The Editor's Laboratory*, cited [the writer] Vladimir Korolenko's words to the effect that the actions of a hero must be shown in such a way that, without any editorializing, they arouse the desired thoughts and feelings. And what feelings would *Sofia Petrovna* arouse? People would think, Where were we all? Feelings of hopelessness and despair would arise. There is no need to irritate old wounds and rub salt in them.

Article 512, to which the VOAPP attorney refers, has a second part—the contract may be dissolved if the publishing house cannot make use of the work because of circumstances depending on the author. In the present case, the circumstances depend directly on the author. The author, if we may speak in bookish language, has not done justice to her subject. This means that the publishing house is not to blame for breaking the contract. I am convinced that Chukovskaya is not interested in the money; the reason for her suit is her desire to see the novel in print. The book was delivered to our offices in ready-to-publish form; it was not subject to any legally binding terms. There can be no question of paying the 40 percent. In view of the unsuccessful ideological aspect of this work, I would think that the court would not want to set such a precedent. When certain members of the editorial staff, in the heat of the moment, without analyzing the matter, signed the contract, it was an error. There's no reason to throw away state money. The publishing house does not agree that this is a valid suit.

Judge: Will the publishing house continue to work with this author?

The respondent says that he is not authorized to answer that question.

Judge: You speak of the author being to blame. What circumstances depended on the author in this matter?

Respondent: The novel is unsatisfactory in ideological respects.

Judge: And when the contract was signed, was it adequate?

Respondent: At that time, there were two favorable reports by readers. I think that the guilty parties should take the punishment. Even then, they saw that the novel could not be printed. But they were influenced by the situation, by considerations of the moment, and signed the contract for those reasons. When it came to the official discussions, neither Karpova nor Kozlov nor Lesyuchevsky were able to say at that point that the novel should be published.

Judge: If publishing house employees were to blame, the publishing house has the right to file suit against them.

Respondent: Under Article 83 there is no one to sue.

An attorney from VOAPP: Who wrote the reports on the manuscript?

Respondent: Anatoly Moroz and Stepan Zlobin.

Attorney: Who signed the contract?

Respondent: Lesyuchevsky.

Judge: Is the director of the publishing house supposed to read the manuscript before the contract is signed?

Respondent: It's physically impossible for him to do that. He must rely on the opinions of the consultants who submit reports.

Chukovskaya: It's a good thing that you mentioned my book *The Editor's Laboratory.* In it, I urged editors to arrive at their own opinions and to defend them. The history of my manuscript is one more chapter for that book. Here the question has been asked, What was everyone doing in 1937? Where in the world was everyone when the evil was being done? Why was everyone silent? I tried to answer this question in my novel. Everyone was surrounded by lies. There were thousands of letters pouring in to the editors of various publications about slander and unjust legal procedures, but they could not be printed. The editors then were the same type as now; they measured off the permitted doses of truth. The readiness of the publishing house personnel, one day, to consider the novel good and, on the next, to say that it contained "ideological distortion"—that kind of thing is one of the reasons for what happened in 1937. Because the press lied, people did not know the truth. I wanted to show the helplessness of Soviet citizens, trapped in a prison of lies.

Several of the things that have been said here were absolutely outrageous. It's as though we were talking about some lower-ranking figures at the publishing house. My novel was accepted by Karpova and Lesyuchevsky, the heads of the publishing house. The respondent has expressed doubt as to whether I need the money. I'm not going to reply to that question. I was within my rights in filing this suit. But I wish to say that I have also been deeply offended by the position taken by the publishing house. If they had said to me, "Lydia Korneevna, the circumstances have changed. Our attitude toward your novel is the same as before. We want to publish it, but we can't. We don't have the option to do that now. Let's wait together for better times." Then I would, of course, have waited. But instead of that, the same people who earlier had praised the manuscript now discovered "ideological distortion" in it. This inability to arrive at and defend one's own opinion is repulsive to me.

It has been said here that the contract was signed in the heat of the moment. But isn't it also possible that they want to annul it in the heat of the moment?

Why are the events that followed the Twenty-second Congress considered the heat of the moment? You have said that Solzhenitsyn will not be published any more. I don't know in whose behalf you are speaking, but if that is true, it will be a great misfortune and a great injustice. Our readers need the truth spoken by Solzhenitsyn. As for the reviews, Reznik's review does not interest me. It was specially ordered for these proceedings to discredit the novel.

A certain note has been struck here several times, to the effect that the novel can be revised. That is not right. You can't replace the point of view of 1940, when the novel was written, with the point of view of 1965. This kind of substitution would be immoral, in my opinion, and even the publishing house is not trying to have work on the novel continue.

The attorney from VOAPP: I will not touch on the ideological aspect of the novel, although I fully agree with Chukovskaya's opinion. (He then proceeded to present the legal grounds for the suit.) In what way can Chukovskaya be called to blame? Since when is an author to blame for her work or her thoughts? I don't think it's necessary to speak of precedents. We are not in England. Our procedures are not based on precedent. It is not up to us here to decide the question of the publication of this work, although I personally think it should be published. Let us hope that the situation changes. But there are no legal grounds for rejecting this suit.

Respondent: I find it hard to add anything. As to the author's guilt, we cannot judge the author for her thoughts. If my remarks were taken that way, I apologize. But the publishing house has the right to select the kind of literature that, from its point of view, is beneficial to young people. We cannot wait for changes in the situation. For a number of years, the Party followed a particular ideological line. Specific individuals were to blame. And today a certain retreat is being made. Perhaps some steps are being retraced by the management of our publishing house also. But the decisions of the Twentieth and Twenty-second congresses remain the guiding principles. Basing itself on these, the publishing house came to the conclusion that the novel did not carry out the tasks that our people are now trying to accomplish. But as for principles, I concur with the concept of pride of authorship—not to change what one has written. When Chukovskaya publishes her collected works, she will include this novel (Chukovskaya: I certainly will [laughter in the room]), and readers will say, There, you see, she understood even then. As for the vexed question of the money, the amount is not important to the publishing house. I am not defending Lesyuchevsky and Karpova. But since the work was not written in return for the publishing house's money, and since there are no losses to be made good because of nonpublication of the novel, there is no need for further money to be paid. Everyone present, including you, Lydia Korneevna, know that the people are waiting for works that will explain this period from various points of view. The people must be helped to analyze this period and to arrive at well-thought-out conclusions—especially that any repetition of those times would have to be opposed and fought.

Chukovskaya: I agree that literature must illuminate what happened in 1937 in a profound way and from every angle. But this is beyond the powers of a single work. Only our literature as a whole can do that. And that is why we must not stop printing Solzhenitsyn. On the contrary, many more books about that time need to be printed, including my novel. When these works reach the reader, they will help clarify that period from every angle. On "ideological distortion," I have portrayed the main things correctly. When we talk about 1937, the problem is not individual distortions, but the mass annihilation of people. And it is very necessary to show how the mechanism of destruction worked. Solzhenitsyn did not show that. His aim was quite different, and he dealt with a different period. You said that my novel was too photographic. Perhaps that is so. But there are photographs—for example, from the battlefield—that are very important for an understanding of what happened. I wanted to show a heroine who was not able to comprehend the reality. The majority were like that. If people at that time had understood what was going on, many things would have been different. Literature about 1937 is indispensable for us in the struggle to reach a correct understanding. I wish to say once again that before the meetings between government leaders and the intelligentsia, the publishing house personnel had no negative attitudes toward my novel. On the contrary.

Respondent: As I listen to Chukovskaya and the representative from VOAPP, it seems that everything they are saying is good and correct. But if certain employees of the publishing house made a mistake and the Central Committee plenum corrected them, and they recognized their error, we cannot fail to take this into account. If the court rules in favor of the suit, it will satisfy the author's pride. This will be wrongly interpreted by others and will create a negative precedent. The publishing house must be protected against a flood of such manuscripts.

The judges withdrew for consultation, returned after ten minutes, and announced their decision: to rule in favor of Chukovskaya's suit and to fine the publishing house 540 rubles, for the royalty, plus 32 rubles for court costs. The defendant could appeal the ruling to a higher court within a period of ten days.

[No. 9, June 1965]

"Profound Truthfulness," But Not Publishable

BY ALEKSANDR TVARDOVSKY

The anti–anti-Stalinist line that emerged in 1965 soon hardened into official policy. By 1967, as we see here in Tvardovsky's private letter to the memoirist Suren Gazaryan (born 1903), there was no longer any question of publishing candid literature about the terror, not even in the once great bastion of Party anti-Stalinism, Novy mir. Before his own arrest in 1937, the Armenian Gazaryan, a veteran police official, was head of the economic section of the Georgian NKVD. After ten years in prison and camps, he was legally exonerated in the early 1950s and eventually settled in Moscow, where he worked as a literary editor. Gazaryan wrote his unusual memoirs about his years as a NKVD official and prisoner, This Must Not Happen Again, between 1958 and 1961, in the loyalist spirit of Khrushchev's de-Stalinization.[1] Unable to find a publisher in Moscow, he signed a contract in 1964 with a publishing house in Soviet Armenia, where censorship was sometimes more lax. Not in this case; the publisher broke the contract in 1965. Tvardovsky read Gazaryan's manuscript in 1967 as a private person rather than as editor of Novy mir. By then, the still high-ranking Tvardovsky, embattled and pessimistic, had become a reader and probably a source of the rapidly growing body of samizdat literature.

March 13, 1967

Dear Suren Oganesovich [Gazaryan]:

I had the opportunity to read the manuscript of your memoirs *This Must Not Happen Again,* and they left a powerful and significant impression on me. I should say that I have read quite a few memoirs dealing with that dreadful period in the life of our society which we designate by the term "1937" (although you are right that this concept does not apply to one year alone). But of all the works I have read, I would have difficulty naming one comparable to yours. Profound truthfulness is coupled in them with a restraint that precludes any deliberate heavy-handedness in describing fearful things, any desire to shock the reader. (This would be an easy desire to understand: one has undergone God knows what ghastly sufferings and torments and feels that not enough impression will be made on those who have not experienced these things, and without even realizing it, one lays the colors on too thick. Your work, I repeat, does not suffer from this.)

---

1. "Eto ne dolzhno povtoritsia" (manuscript; Moscow, 1961). A copy is in the West.

It is also worthy of comment that you are apparently a man of exceptionally strong character, capable of withstanding terrible tortures without committing a forced act of dishonor. At the same time, you do not dress yourself up as a classic hero, protected against physical and mental torment by the armor of clichéd conventionality. Rather, you appear to the reader as an ordinary person, an equal to the reader, who like anyone else, may feel pain and fear, bitterness and agonizing loneliness. In this respect, the chapters describing your interrogation and subsequent solitary confinement are especially powerful. Hence the reader's undeniable confidence in you and in everything you relate. Hence also the very high degree to which the book affects the reader, as the reader seems to live through, in his own experience, all the sufferings that the hero of the book, the author, had to undergo.

It is not necessary, I think, for me to explain to you that today there can be no question of your memoirs being published. But I do not doubt for a moment that, like certain other works, they will unfailingly become known in the world and serve the cause of Communism, that is, the education of people, especially young people, in the spirit of human values. These reminiscences, despite all that is grim and sometimes horrifying in them, do not lead one to despair, do not depress the reader with the feeling that there is no way out. On the contrary, they strengthen the reader by their power of will and force of character; they ennoble the reader.

Yes, it must never happen again. For these forms, these methods, these techniques absolutely destroy the final goal, place the very idea of Communism in jeopardy. And those who argue in favor of forgetting everything, not "opening up old wounds"—and we still have them among us—such people, knowingly or not, want to keep those methods and techniques in reserve.

Your book is an act of duty, a great service, and in its own way a feat of heroism. For it to be written, the urge to write was not enough. Tremendous will power and concentration were needed, and a readiness to let everything pass through one's soul again that had already left such cruel marks upon it. Finally, it required much labor, exertion, the expenditure of one's psychobiological forces.

For all this, thank you, Suren Oganesovich.

I cannot fail to mention—although in reading the manuscript I was not watching for this and did not consider this particularly important—that from a purely literary point of view the memoirs are quite exceptional, with their fine sense of proportion, preciseness, rightness of detail, natural rhythms of real speech, and indefatigable clarity of thought.

I wish you good health and contentment in the knowledge that you have accomplished a great and noble task.

Yours,
Aleksandr Tvardovsky
[No. 30, March 1967]

Varieties of Neo-Stalinism

The various aspects of neo-Stalinism were recorded, with growing alarm and undisguished repugnance, in Political Diary. *Four brief examples are printed below. Each takes the form of a commentary by Roy Medvedev and thus requires no special introduction, though a postscript is in order. The obscure Valery Skurlatov has passed again from public view, but his fascistlike ideas still have many advocates in the Soviet Union, inside and outside the Party. Sergei Trapeznikov (born 1912) remains in his powerful position and was finally "elected" to the Academy of Sciences. The literary careers of Feliks Chuyev (born 1941) and Ivan Shevtsov (born 1920) continue to flourish.*

Brezhnev's Aide

Sergei Trapeznikov is a prominent figure in the Party Central Committee. He is not only a member of the Central Committee, but from 1965 to the present he has headed its department of science and educational establishments. Thus, he is the highest authority in the country in the fields of science and education. In the past, he worked as an assistant to Leonid Brezhnev in Moldavia, and he is credited with exercising great influence on Brezhnev, at whose recommendation Trapeznikov was assigned to the Central Committee and the Higher Party School.

Immediately after Trapeznikov assumed this responsible post, he acquired notoriety because of his public speeches, which contained little else but veiled appeals for the political rehabilitation of Stalin. In his speeches, he called into question the decisions of the Twentieth and Twenty-second congresses. He also demanded that our newspapers stop publishing articles and obituaries in memory of Party and government leaders who perished under the Stalinist tyranny—articles that he contemptuously referred to as "funeral notices." It was Trapeznikov who for several years sought to have many of Stalin's works included in the curricula of our secondary schools and universities, contending that they were of "more than ephemeral value for Marxist-Leninist theory."

During his seven years at the Central Committee, Trapeznikov has not only shown himself to be a Stalinist and reactionary; he has also given proof many times of his extreme ignorance, especially on questions of Marxism-Leninism and Party history. In 1966, he declared his candidacy for the position of corresponding member of the Soviet Academy of Sciences. But many well-known scientists opposed his candidacy, and he suffered a scandalous defeat in the elections. He was rejected by a majority of the votes, and the retaking of the vote, which [Academy President] Mstislav Keldysh insisted upon, did not help him.

It seemed at the time that such an obvious "no-confidence vote" would mean the end of Trapeznikov's Central Committee career. And, in fact, a search was begun for some sort of new appointment for him. In the end, they settled on the post of minister of education, which was then vacant. But at a Politburo meeting this scheme was vigorously rejected by Aleksei Kosygin [chairman of the Council of Ministers]. It is generally known that Trapeznikov's outward appearance is highly unattractive. "He will frighten the children," said Kosygin.

Thus, the question of transferring Trapeznikov was never resolved and, against all expectations, he remained as head of the same Central Committee department. In 1969, he was an unsuccessful candidate for full membership in the Soviet Academy of Pedagogical Sciences. His candidacy, already announced in the papers, was withdrawn at the insistence of [Politburo member] Mikhail Suslov. [Then Soviet President] Nikolai Podgorny also spoke repeatedly against Trapeznikov in private conversations and at official meetings with limited attendance. But, to this day, Trapeznikov enjoys the support of Brezhnev, who oddly enough has disregarded the numerous protests against retaining this odious figure in a leading position on the Central Committee.

Incidentally, Trapeznikov suffers from graphomania, and the many books he has published in the last seven years abound in the crudest distortions and mistakes. But the book that came out in 1971, *At the Turning Points of History* [as translated into English: Moscow, 1972], is something of a masterwork in this genre. Even in the department he heads, people were going around with his book from office to office, reading different passages out loud and doubling over with laughter.

[1971, no. uncertain]

Valery Skurlatov • *"A Code of Morals"*

[Roy Medvedev's introduction:] Recently, strange as it may seem, the Central Committee of the Komsomol, together with the Komsomol's Moscow Committee and certain other municipal and regional committees, have become centers of an extreme Russian nationalist and chauvinist movement. Under the guise of "patriotic" or "military-patriotic" education, these centers are propagating views that are not only incompatible with Marxism but simply absurd from the point of view of the interests of a multinational state such as the USSR. As early as the end of 1965, a plenum of the Komsomol Central Committee was held in Moscow to take up questions of the military-patriotic education of the young. Before the plenum, it was suggested that Komsomol apparatus personnel prepare various proposals and projects for discussion. One of those who took part in this effort was Valery Skurlatov, who held a responsible position in the propaganda department of the Komsomol's Moscow Committee and who was a Ph.D. candidate in philosophy. He wrote up and mimeographed his suggestions, using the title "A Code of Morals." Several copies of this "Code" circulated outside the Komsomol Central Committee apparatus, and the whole affair became widely known. Skurlatov was removed from the Moscow Committee and given a Party reprimand; he now works at the Information Institute of the Academy of Sciences. His "literary work" is not, however, the product of some extremist's delirious fantasies. To a certain extent, the "Code" reflects the atmosphere of semimilitary discipline and nationalism that is now being inculcated among leading personnel of the Komsomol. Below we print the text of Skurlatov's "Code of Morals" with some small omissions.

1. Morals or social behavior are determined by the answers to such fundamental questions as "What is the meaning of life?" and "In what do my duty to my country and my place in the fate of my people consist?" Only after answering these questions can we speak of the inculcation of a true conviction of the justice of one's cause and of one's behavior. The education of youth must be begun with a discussion of these questions, adducing material from the lives of famous people and great revolutionaries. In this process we must decisively distance ourselves from the head, from rational egoism, and place in the center of our concern the heart and voice of the blood.

Self-sacrificing love for the motherland, for our comrades, and for our cause, the act of the soldier who covers the breach in the fortifications with his own body —these cannot be explained by rational egoism. On the contrary, all skepticism, nihilism, and betrayal are from the head, from egoism of all stripes, and revolutionary consciousness is always primarily marked by passion, by the heart. For this reason, it is necessary constantly to educate youth in an atmosphere of revolutionary romanticism, striving for a revolutionary ideal in an atmosphere of sacrifice of the "I" for the sake of the beloved "we."

2. The sociopolitical ideal must not be represented as one of well-fed petit-bourgeois prosperity, as a life without shocks, without struggle to the death. Only in the face of mortal danger is the nature of man revealed, and the inimitable uniqueness of his personality; only on the horizon of death is the joy and pride of the master of life revealed, who drinks fresh blood for thirty years; the fear of death and alienation is the slave's, who for three hundred years feeds on carrion.

Youth must be oriented toward a permanent mortal struggle not only for today and tomorrow, but for the day after tomorrow. This struggle must be connected with the cosmic mission of our people. The struggle for the cosmos and the struggle for man are inseparable. The cosmos is the favorite cause of [our] youth, and [represents] their longing for heroic deeds. For this reason, as the sociopolitical ideal is precisely determined, first place must be given to the revolutionary transformation and rigorous maintenance of our own people and our own cosmos and, lastly, to the transformation of all mankind.

3. A moral "categorical imperative"—a distinctive "moral code" of the heart —must be an organic part of the sociopolitical ideal. As distinct from the moral code of the head, the true moral code must give first place to duty to one's ancestors and descendants, duty to one's own people. Where the dead are not respected, the living will not be respected either. Love for the motherland is the best antidote for skepticism, nihilism, and dissoluteness. Love for the motherland gives meaning to life, saves people from loneliness and desperation, and directs man's entire behavior. Love for the motherland is the necessary and sufficient condition for citizenship. A cult of the ancestors must be established, because "lack of respect for one's ancestors is the prime index of savagery" (Pushkin). Every person must be saturated by the cult of his own clump of native earth, soaked with the sweat and blood of his fathers.

4. The "categorical imperative" must establish—until it becomes instinct— what is good and what bad in the moral sphere. Nihilistic theories of the "glass of water" type must be emphatically eschewed. At first, a long campaign must be conducted in favor of our ancestral moral and physiological values of virginal purity and honor, to persuade young people of the criminal nature of premarital sexual intercourse. We must not stop even at promoting ancient peasant customs: painting gates with tar, public showing of the sheet after the wedding night, corporal punishment of women who give themselves to foreigners, branding and sterilization of them.

5. To ensure the moral purity of the people, we should encourage various forms of stratification of a caste type—like the rules of military honor, codes for the physician, the teacher, the schoolchild, and so forth.

6. We must not concern ourselves with so-called sex education, or provoke interest in the question of sex. Sex is an intimate matter: here everything must be worked out privately. Interest in sexual questions must be suppressed in favor of encouragement of interest in romance, in revolution, in travel, and especially in the romance of science and creativity. Sex must be sublimated in creativity.

7. From the earliest years, youth must never be coddled. Corporal punishment must be introduced. The whip is the best teacher. A blow to the body hardens the soul. A set of measures for the militarization of youth from primary school on must be thought out: regular military games, planned marches, battle training, and the cultivation of laws of soldierly comradeship and chivalry.

8. There must be merciless rooting out of traitors, criminals, fornicators, smart alecks, and feckless people. There will be no order among the people unless each crime is followed by a fierce retribution: two eyes for an eye, two evils for each evil—since the criminal must be punished twice, once for his crimes against himself and once for those against the people. Drunkenness, prostitution, hooliganism, and juvenile delinquency will be destroyed by an atmosphere of comradeship, chivalry, and soldierly discipline.

9. Sport must be encouraged from the earliest years, and young people attracted into sport by all means; technical forms of sport are to be

especially cultivated. Competition tempers the individual and builds character.

10. There is no baser calling than to be a "thinker," an "intellectual," a smart-aleck scribbler. And there is no nobler calling than to be a soldier. The intellectual is the slave of dead reason, and the soldier is the lord of life, who subjects the world process to his will. Man's fate is equal to his strength and to his breeding; he who is born a slave remains a slave and one of the vanquished his life long; he who is born a master will be a victor even in death. And so that the people will not be corrupted and become slaves and robots, it is necessary to resurrect and assert forever the cult which is health giving and leads to true immortality—the cult of the soldier.

[No. 18, March 1966]
Translated by Stephen P. Dunn and George Saunders

Feliks Chuyev's Poem on Stalin

Many poems on Stalin by Feliks Chuyev are known in literary circles. Most of them circulate in manuscript among the Stalinists. In one of these unpublished creations Chuyev exclaims:

> I never grow tired / of the call:
> Put Stalin back / on the pedestal!

The censors have now grown more lenient toward Chuyev, and as a consequence, he managed to have the following poem published in *Molodaya gvardiya*. [2]

> Some day—I know that it shall be—
> Somebody's hands shall set to work.
> And such a building shall be built.
> Not built so much as raised on high!
>
> It will have portraits, hundreds, thousands
> Sevastopol's commanders, Duga's,
> Holding binoculars and maps,
> In boots and sheepskin coats and hats.
>
> Grandeur and glitter it may have,
> But that will not gainsay the truth.
> Heroes there'll be—Smolensk and Tula
> And Stalingrad, called Stalingrad.
>
> May all who enter feel their dependence
> On all that's Russian, of our dear land,
> And in the midst, Generalissimo Stalin,
> Surrounded by his marshals grand.

2. *Molodaia gvardiia*, no. 12, 1968, p. 212.

Once, at a party, where other poets were present, Chuyev proposed a toast to Stalin and was slapped in the face (it is said that Bella Akhmadullina struck him with her slipper). But this semiliterate Stalinist blockhead apparently receives more than just slaps for his endeavors.

We should note that *Molodaya gvardiya* has now added to its primitive nationalist platform ("dependence on all that's Russian") a pro-Stalin plank.

[No. 53, February 1969]

Shevtsov's Novels

In the spring of 1970, the publishing house Moscow Worker brought out a new novel by Ivan Shevtsov entitled *In the Name of the Father and of the Son.*

Shevtsov is the author of the short novel *Scum,* a libelous little book lacking in any talent but well known from the scandal it created. His new "novel" is written in the same vein, and even *Oktyabr* refused to publish it. However, Shevtsov's sponsors, of whom the most highly placed is said to be [then Politburo member] Dmitry Polyansky, provided some assistance in having the book published. It was after a phone call from Polyansky that Moscow Worker put the "novel" into production.

There is no point in analyzing the various types of slanderous fabrications and insinuations in the novel. It is not hard to see that we are dealing not only with a compulsive writer devoid of all talent but a ferocious neo-Stalinist, anti-Semite, and Black Hundredist—and presumably a psychopath with paranoid tendencies as well. Nevertheless, we cannot simply pass over the fact that such a novel was published and that Shevtsov obviously enjoys the protection of the Moscow Party Committee and of Polyansky, who is responsible to the Politburo for the work of the leading institutions and agencies of the Russian Federation.

Shevtsov had been trying to have his "novel" published since the fall of 1969, but even the Central Committee's cultural division opposed it, although in other cases that body was not noted for its adherence to progressive positions. Far from it. A reflection of this struggle in the "upper echelons" could be seen in a [sharply negative] review of Shevtsov's book that appeared in *Komsomolskaya pravda* on April 9, 1970.

The newspaper *Sovetskaya Rossiya,* which in recent months has more and more turned into a mouthpiece for the most reactionary groups in the Party and government apparatus, nevertheless intervened on the side of Shevtsov. It called the review by Mikhail Sinelnikov in *Komsomolskaya pravda* "hooligan" and printed several letters by its own readers in support of Shevtsov's novel.

The bookstores had not yet sold out of *In the Name of the Father and the Son* when another "novel" by Shevtsov appeared on their shelves, with the title *Love and Hate.* This book was published by the State Publishing House for Military Literature in an edition of 200,000 copies. It is obvious that in this case the leaders of the Political Administration of the Soviet Army were acting as Shevtsov's sponsors. *Love and Hate* is, if anything, even more malicious than his previous writings. Nikita Khrushchev is portrayed under the guise of deputy minister N. M. Fenin, and Khrushchev's son-in-law, Aleksei Adzhubei [editor of *Izvestia* under Khrushchev], is easily detected in the guise of Fenin's relative, editor of the magazine *Novosti*. In this piece of writing, too, Shevtsov reveals himself as a reactionary, a graphomaniac, and an anti-Semite.

[No. 68, May 1970]

Establishment Intellectuals Protest to Brezhnev

The Soviet dissident movement was born in the second half of the 1960s in a flurry of samizdat petitions. Representatives of educated society, their civic conscience awakened during the years of de-Stalinization, circulated dozens of letters, which gathered thousands of signatures, protesting neo-Stalinist trends in officialdom. Many of these petitions appeared in Political Diary. *The two printed below, letters addressed to Brezhnev in 1966 and 1970, are especially interesting. As their official titles and honors indicate, the signers represented an important segment of the Soviet intellectual Establishment. A number of these people, notably Andrei Sakharov, were subsequently compelled to become outright dissidents or émigrés. But in 1966–70, they tried to speak to the Brezhnev government in a comradely or loyalist voice. Whether from conviction or as a tactic, they treated "the pro-Stalin campaign" as something apart from Brezhnev's own leadership and threatening to his domestic and foreign policies. The second petition was spurred by a major literary, political scandal related to the upcoming ninetieth anniversary of Stalin's birth in 1969—the publication of Vsevolod Kochetov's novel* What Do You Really Want?. *Kochetov (1912–1973) was Tvardovsky's neo-Stalinist counterpart and a weighty official personage—editor of the conservative Party journal* Oktyabr *and at one time a candidate member of the Party's Central Committee. His novel was read as a neo-Stalinist program that posed a special threat to the liberal-minded intelligentsia.*

Dear Leonid Ilyich [Brezhnev]:

Recently, in several speeches and published articles, there have appeared tendencies aimed essentially at the partial or indirect rehabilitation of Stalin.

We do not know to what extent these manifestations, which have become more frequent as the Twenty-third Congress approaches, have solid support behind them. But even if the only matter involved is a partial reversal of the decisions of the Twentieth and Twenty-second congresses, this is cause for profound concern. We consider it our duty to bring to your attention our views on this question.

To this day, we do not know of a single fact or argument that would lead one to think that the condemnation of the personality cult was in any way incorrect. On the contrary, one can hardly doubt that a substantial body of fact concerning Stalin's truly shocking and horrible crimes—information that would confirm the absolute correctness of those congress decisions—has not yet been made public.

There is another issue, however. In our opinion, any attempt to whitewash Stalin entails the danger of creating serious fissures within Soviet society. Stalin not only bears the responsibility for the deaths of countless innocent persons, our lack of preparedness for the war, the departure from Leninist norms in Party and government practice, but also by his crimes and misdeeds he perverted the idea of Communism so greatly that the people would not understand and would not accept any retreat, even a partial one, from the decisions concerning the personality cult. No one can erase these decisions from his memory and consciousness.

Any attempt to do so would cause only widespread consternation and discord. We are convinced, for example, that the rehabilitation of Stalin would provoke great unrest among the intelligentsia and would cause serious complications in the attitudes of young people. As is true of the informed Soviet public in general, we are concerned about the youth. No special explanations or articles will be able to force people to believe in Stalin again. On the contrary, such things would produce only anger and distress. In view of our country's complex economic and political situation, it would obviously be dangerous to risk all this.

It seems to us there is another, no less serious danger. Stalin's rehabilitation is not only a domestic issue but an international one as well. Any step toward rehabilitating him would unquestionably bring with it the danger of a new split in the world Communist movement, this time between us and the Western Communist parties. They would interpret such a move as above all a capitulation by us to the Chinese. The Western Communists would never agree to that.

This is a factor of major historical significance, and we cannot simply strike it from the books. At a time when we are threatened, on the one hand, by greater activity on the part of the American imperialists and, on the other, by the Chinese leaders, to risk a break or even complications with the fraternal parties in the West would be extremely unwise.

Not to take up too much of your time, we have limited ourselves to mentioning only the most telling arguments against any rehabilitation of Stalin—above all the danger of a split. We have not mentioned what great complications a retreat from the Twentieth Congress decisions would cause for our cultural representatives who maintain international contacts, especially in the movement for peace and in the area of international cooperation. All the gains made in these areas would be jeopardized.

We cannot do otherwise than state what we think. It is absolutely clear that a Central Committee decision on this matter could not be regarded as merely a routine decision. In one way or another, it would have historical significance for our country's destiny. We hope this will be taken into account.

Academician L. A. Artsimovich, Lenin Prize and State Prize laureate.
O. N. Yefremov, director in chief of the Sovremennik Theater.
Academician Pyotr Kapitsa, Hero of Socialist Labor and State Prize laureate.
Valentin Kataev, member of the Soviet Writers' Union and State Prize laureate.

P. D. Korin, People's Artist of the USSR and Lenin Prize laureate.

Academician M. A. Leontovich, Lenin Prize laureate.

Academician Ivan Maisky.

Viktor Nekrasov, member of the Soviet Writers' Union and State Prize laureate.

V. M. Nemensky, member of the Soviet Artists' Union and State Prize laureate.

Konstantin Paustovsky, member of the Soviet Writers' Union.

Yu. I. Pimenov, People's Artist of the RSFSR and State Prize laureate.

Maya Plisetskaya, People's Artist of the USSR and Lenin Prize laureate.

A. A. Popov, People's Artist of the USSR and State Prize laureate.

Mikhail Romm, People's Artist of the USSR and State Prize laureate.

S. N. Rostovsky (Ernst Henry), member of the Soviet Writers' Union and Vorovsky Prize laureate.

Academician Andrei Sakharov, three times Hero of Socialist Labor, Lenin Prize and State Prize laureate.

Academician S. D. Skazkin.

Boris Slutsky, member of the Soviet Writers' Union.

I. M. Smoktunovsky, member of the Soviet Film Makers' Union and Lenin Prize laureate.

Academician Igor Tamm, Hero of Socialist Labor, Nobel laureate, Lenin and State Prize laureate.

Vladimir Tendryakov, member of the Soviet Writers' Union.

G. A. Tovstonogov, People's Artist of the USSR, Lenin and State Prize laureate.

M. M. Khutsiev, Honored Artist of the RSFSR.

S. A. Chuikov, People's Artist of the USSR and State Prize laureate.

Kornei Chukovsky, member of the Soviet Writers' Union and Lenin laureate.

[No. 18, March 1966]

Dear Leonid Ilyich [Brezhnev]:

We are appealing to you in regard to a recently published literary work that has greatly alarmed us all. Only some of the undersigned are members of the Writers' Union and work in literature professionally. Others are scientists, artists, and veteran Party members. But we are all lovers of Russian literature. The power of that literature always lay in its vital and unbreakable tie with society. The honor and better interests of that literature are just as dear to scientists and artists as to manual workers and to writers themselves. We are certain that many others share our opinion on this question. That is why we think it right that we bring our view to your attention.

Every one of us was shocked to read Vsevolod Kochetov's novel *What Do You Really Want?* in the September, October, and November 1969 issues of the magazine *Oktyabr.* We will not dwell on the fact that as literature the work is devoid of merit. That is the problem of the editors and publishers. The crucial thing is that it can hardly be called a *Soviet* work.

Kochetov's novel really does defame and discredit our society. It is a malicious caricature of reality. And it is published in the official Soviet press at a time when our opponents both in the West and in China have taken the offensive against us along the entire ideological front, when everything possible, from their point of view, is being done to promote unhealthy conditions in our society. Kochetov's novel helps those who are engaged in this effort, and it is impossible not to speak about it.

At a time when our entire country is preparing for the celebration of the Lenin centenary, Kochetov suddenly raises the banner not of Lenin but Stalin. Every unprejudiced reader of this novel has been struck by that more than anything else. Everyone knows that the cult of Stalin was emphatically condemned at the Party's Twentieth and Twenty-second congresses and that the Twenty-third Congress [in March 1966] reaffirmed those decisions. Nevertheless, the main theme of Kochetov's novel, pervading every chapter in one form or another, amounts to nothing but the glorification of Stalin. The message we are given is that after the condemnation of the Stalin cult, Soviet society began to degenerate and that the degeneration continues to the present day. That such a charge is made in this year of Lenin's centenary is plainly not accidental. At a time when the thoughts of our country are on Lenin, Stalin is held up to the people in an attempt to turn them little by little from the Leninist path. We are outraged at this. For the past fifteen years, there have been no such novels in the Soviet Union.

And that is not all. Kochetov does not hesitate to campaign openly in Stalin's behalf and call for the restoration of the Stalin cult through the mouth of a supposedly reeducated Russian SS man (Saburov). Saburov is the central figure in the novel and Kochetov obviously sympathizes with him. Saburov, the Hitlerite, literally states, for example, "What is so criminal about being a Stalinist?" Another character in the novel, the American intelligence agent Portia Brown, refers to the "Stalinists" as "the opinion makers for a broad public."

How is this to be understood in view of the decisions of Party congresses and our dearly bought experience of history? Since when have SS men, even "reformed" ones, been our teachers? We do not believe that anyone gave Kochetov the right to revise decisions of the Party. But this writer uses the arguments of Hitlerites in the year of Lenin's centenary to try to put Stalin back on a pedestal.

The pro-Stalin campaign is the source of other themes in Kochetov's novel, whether stated in the text or merely implied. At a time when the Party is urgently calling for unity and a closing of ranks in Soviet society, Kochetov plainly seeks to sow dissensions among different layers of our society, to stir up hatred and distrust between them. A reading of the novel clearly reveals the author's aim of deliberately inciting manual workers against the Soviet intelligentsia, who are portrayed as a layer of parasites producing nothing of material value (no "bread").

This at a time when the scientific and technical revolution continues at its tempestuous pace and the enormous public importance of the work of the Soviet intelligentsia, especially the growing army of scientific and technical personnel, has become evident to all but the most hardened obscurantists.

We consider it impermissible for anyone to insult the Soviet people, of whom the Soviet intelligentsia are a part, and it is especially impermissible at this critical moment in history, when our opponents in other countries are placing their bets on the very hope of internal discord in Soviet society. Kochetov cannot fail to recognize that unity between the manual worker and the mental worker is now more important to our state than ever before. Nevertheless, he incites one against the other. The novel also contains a crude and unsavory caricature of the Soviet younger generation. The author selects no better model of Soviet youth than a handful of "papa's sons" and good-for-nothings who live high in the company of foreign tourists and flaunt their political apathy and degeneracy. Kochetov has a "young Soviet poet" enter into intimate relations with the intelligence agent Brown. It is well known that another strategic wager being played by the anti-Soviet forces today is the "generation gap" in the USSR. What effect will a novel like this have on young people, other than to widen the gap?

A third well-known factor that the imperialists are gambling on is a split in the world Communist movement. A contemporary Soviet writer cannot fail to realize how important the unity of this movement is for our future. Kochetov, we assume, reads the papers. The recent international conference of Communist and Workers' parties focused all of its attention on unity. However—hard as it is to believe—here too Kochetov sows the seeds of discord. He smears the largest Communist Party of Western Europe, the Communist Party of Italy, accusing leading figures in that party of self-seeking and immorality, and even of previous membership in Mussolini's fascist movement.

Kochetov's novel is shot through with such unsuitable outbursts. At one point, he besmirches the peace movement because some "sirens of peace and love, both foreign and domestic" had tried to "palm off" upon him, as an emblem to replace the hammer and sickle, the "Biblical dove."

In another passage, he attacks (without naming it) the famous [Soviet] antifascist film *Everyday Fascism,* which was a documentary exposé of the Nazis. This at a time when fascism is trying to make a comeback in one country after another.

Under the banner of a struggle against bourgeois ideology, Kochetov in fact encourages contempt for the genuine treasures of Russian and world culture that we all recognize. He insults Soviet literary criticism, arguing through one of his heroes that statements against his own writings are "not of Soviet, but of foreign make." That is not so. It is Soviet citizens who are outraged by his novel.

Some passages in the novel can be understood only as thinly disguised attacks on the present Party line. Others are hardly disguised at all, and virtually call for a "great cultural revolution" in our country. It seems to us no accident that as far back as 1965 the Maoists lauded one of Kochetov's novels as a work that confirmed Mao's thesis on class contradictions in Soviet society.

We leave aside the fact that this writer almost always carries poor taste to the limit—for example, the way he rather obviously promotes himself (in the guise of "the writer Bulatov"). "What a mind!" his beloved heroine exclaims ecstatically, referring to Bulatov-Kochetov. But the low literary level, in our opinion, is a third-rate matter compared to the *political* content, the aspect of the novel that prompts us to write you. It is an unworthy piece of writing. It is not a Soviet work. It brings discredit to our literature, and does us great harm both at home and abroad.

We do not think the novel should be banned. After existing for half a century, Soviet society has no need for such measures to protect itself and to progress further. Even such types as Kochetov should not be gagged. But we think it would be a good thing if the Party and the Soviet press expressed their opinion about a work of this kind.

Signed by twenty-five prominent Soviet intellectuals,
including six academicians (Lev Artsimovich,
Roald Sagdeyev, Vladimir Engelgardt, Arkady
Migdal, Bruno Pontecorvo, and A. Alikhanyan);
Three writers (Sergei S. Smirnov, Semyon Rostovsky
[Ernst Henry], and Yevgeny Gnedin); and two
Old Bolsheviks (Polonsky and Pyotr Nikiforov).

[No. 64, January 1970]

Anti-Stalinist Poems

BY BORIS CHICHIBABIN, ANDREI VOZNESENSKY, AND ALEKSANDR TVARDOVSKY

Poets have written some of the most powerful condemnations of the Stalin years. Several of these poems, by Yevgeny Yevtushenko, Boris Slutsky, Tvardovsky, and others, were published under Khrushchev. Not surprisingly, anti-Stalinist poems continued to appear later in the 1960s in response to the resurgence of pro-Stalin attitudes. They could not, of course, be published, and they circulated instead in samizdat. The three examples below comment, from the perspectives of different generations, on the ways in which Stalin's legacy lives on in Soviet society. Boris Chichibabin (born 1917) is a little-published poet who lives in Kharkov in the Soviet Ukraine. Andrei Voznesensky (born 1933), who lives in Moscow, was one of the most popular Soviet poets of the 1960s and 1970s, and, in the opinion of many critics, the most gifted. (Their two poems originally circulated without titles.) We have already met Tvardovsky, whose "Memory" forms the third part of his epic poem By Right of Memory. (The second part appears above in Chapter 1.)

BORIS CHICHIBABIN · "Stalin Is Not Dead"

Do not rejoice too early
And let some other oracle proclaim
That wounds do not reopen,
That evil crowds don't rise again,
That the dead enemy no longer calls
And that I risk to seem retarded.
Let him orate. I firmly know that
Stalin is not dead.

As if the killed alone had mattered
And those who vanished nameless in the North.
The evil he implanted in our hearts,
Had it not truly done the damage?
As long as poverty divides from wealth,
As long as we don't stop the lies
And don't unlearn to fear,
Stalin is not dead.

As long as morons who hate Jews
Are not yet tamed in our country,
The splendid, well-groomed khans,
The brutal clerks of power,
As long as the briber remains cocky,
The red-tape artist unperturbed
And the informer is rewarded,
Stalin is not dead.

Isn't it according to old habit
That they are prone
To choke with cutting ropes
All that is young and new?
The road to glory is not even.
As long as, to the joy of the well fed,
The riffraff baits the Pasternaks,
Stalin is not dead.

Doesn't Stalin's spirit hide in us,
Cowardly and predatory both,
If we don't look for truth
But, rather, fear the new?
I'll throw myself on falsehood
And shall not yield to that which was.
But what to do when inside us
Stalin is not dead?

I pledge to the merry banner
To fight for justice honestly,
Keep to the steep and salty road
In combat with the evil brood,
Not to deroute nor to retract
Nor to surrender to fatigue
As long as I will breathe and
Stalin is not dead.

[No. 28, January 1967]
Translated by Vera Dunham

ANDREI VOZNESENSKY · *"Children of the Cult"*

Let's not beat around the bush,
No more nonsense.
We are the children of the cult.
We are its flesh and blood.

   We have been raised in the fog,
   Ambiguous indeed,

Inside gigantomania
And scarcity of mind.

We are mestizos, mixtures
Of unlike traits—
Of daring and of dogma,
Pretense and innovation.

We are the witnesses of that event
Which ripened into a storm,
Replete with honest faith
And full of filthy treason.

We did not even know
The nature of the game.
The villages died out.
The cities became black.

And like a flaming horseshoe
There burned at dawn
The wreaths made of barbed wire
Over the heads of the camps.

The coats of our fathers
Were pierced by bullets
Not by medals, twice punished
For Issik-Kul, the sands, the mines.

And the gray medals,
The pendants made of lead
Were hung from souls,
From hearts like heavy weights.

We are the people of the
Crossroads, led one by one,
Swaying like thin switches
In the September wind.

We are the fallen leaves.
We are the music of the shackles.
We are the courage of the amnesty
And of the locks torn down.

Doors flung open.
Felled observation posts.
And the rage of New Heresy.
And the brightness of what's right.

[No. 28, January 1967]
Translated by Vera Dunham

ALEKSANDR TVARDOVSKY · *"Memory"*

They're wrong to think that memory
Hasn't an increasing value
Or that the weeds of time grow over
Any real past event or pain.

That on and on the planet rolls,
Measuring off the days and years,
That nothing is taken out of the poet
If he stays silent because of the specter
Of a ban, despite what sears his soul.

No. Duty commands that everything now
That hasn't been said be said in full.
Try telling your curious Communist daughter
You can't speak because of your inner censor.

Explain why and by whose authority
The events of that era, anonymous
And of unsavory memory, were all
Placed in the category "restricted."

What special congress, never scheduled,
Decided for us, unannounced,
That a veil be drawn precisely
Over this memory that will not rest.

And who decided that certain pages
Cannot be read by adult folks
Lest our prowess be diminished
And honor fade around the world?

Or that we gladden the enemy's heart
When we report on the past out loud,
That for our victories we were obliged
To pay a price extremely high?

Is the enemy's backbiting new to us?
Aren't all the strengths we have in the world,
With all the virgin soil we've turned up
And watered with our sweat and blood,
Enough to cover such a cost?

Or is our cause just idle daydreams?
Our glory just some empty talk?
Then the silent monks are right,
Then all is vain, both prose and verse,
It's all just made up out of our heads.

Then it would not be any wonder
That the just voice of memory
Should prophesy trouble in our future:
Whoever is eager to bury the past
Won't get along well with what lies ahead.

But I say—we live in different times.
I no longer have the right to more
Postponements. The load must come off my chest.
There is still time, with no further delay,
To clothe this silent pain in words.

The pain which secretly now and then
And for long stretches burdened our hearts
And which we drowned out with the thunder
Of clapping to honor Stalin the Father.

In every meeting hall this thunder
Roared at full force, but this is why:
We were not clapping and applauding
Only for that particular Father.

It always seemed that at his side,
Having passed on the earthly succession,
There stood the man who disliked ovations
Or who at least knew their true value.

The one whose image, forever living,
The world preserved beyond destruction,
The one of whom the Father humbly
Termed himself the mere disciple.

Vulgarly we linked their names
And glorified the two as one
And entered both into the annals
As though the essence was the same.

And then the fear that we all know
When bad times place us by a deathbed
Taught us to maintian our silence
In face of evil on the rampage.

Impelled us, voiceless as we were,
To yield up to the special section
Our right to think. And since that time,
Like echoes of some ancient pain,
Thoughts hardly ever came to us.
Rather we asked for the will supreme.
"Give us the godhead's revelation."

A special sigh was always ready,
The limit of our daring souls,
"If Lenin came back from the grave
And saw how things have worked out . . ."

But we can't just wash our hands
Of what has happened or will happen.
And Lenin's not about to judge us.
He was no god when he lived among us.

And you who are perhaps so eager
To return the blessed past,
You go ahead and call for Stalin.
He was a god. He could come back.

This Father-God is easy to conjure
Here in our sublunar sphere.
Nothing so much attests to that
As his present-day Chinese duplicate.

[No. 60, September 1969]

The Charms of the Whip
BY RAISSA LERT

Stalinism fused, or subordinated, revolutionary Bolshevism to the old traditions of the tsarist Russian state. Which component predominated under Stalin,
Bolshevik or tsarist, is a disputed interpretative question. But there is no question
that this historic fusion became a major pillar of the Stalinist system in the 1930s
and 1940s, and that it helps account for the strong Russian nationalist complex-
ion of Soviet Communism even today. It also remains a potent appeal of neo-
Stalinism, as demonstrated by the neo-Stalinist Russophile movement inside the
Party itself since the late 1960s. Grouped around several Communist journals and
official antiquarian societies, this cultural and political movement is the subject
of Raissa Lert's polemical analysis. Lert (born 1905) was a Party member from
1926 to her expulsion in 1976, and an official newspaper and radio journalist from
the 1920s until her retirement in 1962. Since the late 1960s, she has been an
important samizdat essayist and editor. Lert was a political associate of Roy
Medvedev for several years and editorial secretary of his Marxist samizdat journal
of 1975–76, Dvadtsatyi vek (Twentieth Century). After disagreements with
Medvedev over dissident politics, she became a founding editor of a new samizdat
journal, Poiski (Searches), eight issues of which appeared in 1978–80, despite the
arrest of several other editors. Lert was still a Party member when she wrote this
1970 polemic against the historical underpinnings of neo-Stalinist ideology. Calling upon original Bolshevik attitudes, her arguments reflected the thinking of
many Party anti-Stalinists in the 1960s and 1970s. (Her essay has been abridged
considerably here; major deletions are indicated by ellipses.)

> Within this book, simplicity and grace
> Combine to show us, without fear or favor,
> The necessity of rule by tyrants
> And the charms of the whip.
> —Pushkin on Karamzin's History of Russia

An article by Sergei Semanov, entitled "Values, Relative and Eternal," has
taught me an astounding new fact. It seems that the real social revolution in our
country took place not in 1917 but in 1937!

In case you think I am making a bad joke, here word for word is what was
printed on page 319 of the Komsomol magazine Molodaya gvardiya (The Young
Guard), no. 8, 1970.

"Now it is plainly evident that the turning point in the struggle against the destructive and nihilistic elements occurred in the mid-1930s. How many foul words have been heaped upon this historical epoch, after the fact! It would be a good thing if all those who sigh for the lost 'golden age' which supposedly reigned in the literary and artistic salons of the 1920s, those who do not see anything in our culture and national life beyond those salons, were to remember that it was precisely *after the adoption of our Constitution* [that is, the so-called Stalin Constitution of 1936], which gave legal sanction to the immense social changes in our country and society, that *the equality of all citizens before the law came into being.* And that was a tremendous accomplishment. The practice of subdividing people, according to various categories, when they applied for jobs, for government or army service, or for admission to higher educational institutions, disappeared forever. All honest working people in our country, from that time on, were merged into a single, monolithic whole. It seems to me that to this day we do not realize the full significance of the colossal changes that occurred at that time. *And these changes had the most beneficial effect on our cultural development"* (emphasis added—R.L.).

There you have it. To this day we do not recognize. And if it weren't for Semanov, holder of a Ph.D. degree in history, and the editors of *Molodaya gvardiya*—it's a frightening thought!—we might still not recognize what the year 1937 meant in our history.

But now we know—the equality of all Soviet citizens before the law. Our only regret is that our candidate in historical sciences neglected certain historical realities. He didn't give a graphic demonstration of how this equality of citizens was put into effect concretely in that blessed year of 1937. Having been an observer and to some extent a participant in this historical event (I was thirty-two in 1937), I will take the liberty of filling in this gap.

In 1937, I was working on the newspaper of the Moscow Committee of the Party, *Rabochaya Moskva* (Workers' Moscow). I remember that when we put an article by some Party secretary, or factory manager, or director of a theater, or writer in an issue of the paper, we were never sure that the author might not be arrested the very same night as an "enemy of the people." And we were never sure that we—or our editor—would show up for work the next morning. In this sense, the equality under the law was remarkable.

In the 1920s, those who feared arrest were prominent ex-officers of the White armies or former Mensheviks and Social Revolutionaries; in the late 1920s and early 1930s, former Trotskyists, "bourgeois" engineers and specialists, and many peasant individualists (those who refused to join the collective farms—not just kulaks, by any means). Beginning in 1937, every citizen in the country—without regard to sex, age, social origin, social position, or party affiliation—could expect the arrival of the Black Maria [police van]. The composition of the prison-camp population confirmed the "equality of all citizens."

Party congresses could have been called in the camps at will—or writers' congresses, military councils, or conferences of academicians, inventors, stage directors, Stakhanovite workers, or exemplary collective-farm workers. The beneficial effect of prison equality upon our cultural development was expressed in the fact that all these people, unless they were camp trusties, shoveled dirt or felled timber—all of them, academicians and collective farmers, writers and lathe operators, marshals of the army and painters alike. What greater equality could there be?

Another one of Semanov's statements sounds very odd when tested against the historical realities. "The practice of subdividing people, according to various categories, when they applied for jobs, for government or army service, or for admission to higher educational institutions, disappeared forever."

It is true that social restrictions were abolished by the 1936 Constitution adopted in December 1936. Under the *law*, it was provided that anyone who passed an examination could be admitted to a university-level institution and anyone with the necessary skills and professional training would be accepted into a job. But at the same time that the Constitution was adopted, *legality* was abolished. If questions of life and death were decided without reference to the law, how much easier it was to disregard the law where civil rights were involved. In place of the old restrictions came a multitude of new ones. Their number grew with every year, closing more avenues to more and more people. What didn't they include in these new "subdivisions according to category"? There was nationality, oppositional activity, travel abroad, having relatives abroad, relatives who had been arrested, or friends or acquaintances in occupied territory. And so on and so forth.

The previous practice of dividing people according to social categories was not hidden in any way. It was the openly proclaimed class policy of the Party and government. The new restrictions were hidden like a shameful disease, because they were *illegal*. The categories became secret; they remained unspoken and were never given as reasons for the rejection of an applicant. A complex system and special apparatus were needed to implement these personnel policies. The "departments in charge of cadres," abnormally swollen, acquired enormous power. Previously they had modestly occupied themselves with the registration of personnel. Now the actual decisions on hiring and promotion were not made by the director of an institution but by the head of the cadres department, who in fact was not subordinate to the director. Not talent, not training, not ability, but a clean record, good personal connections, and skill at following orders and keeping one's mouth shut—that was what counted.

What this led to I know especially well from the field with which I was involved—journalism. In the 1920s, the period when the Soviet press was just developing its strength, a brilliant array of journalists emerged, such figures as Aleksandr Zorich, Mikhail Koltsov, Grigory Ryklin, and Taras Kostrov. Try to name anyone of equal greatness who came to the fore in the second half of the 1930s. There were none, and there could not have been. The arrests helped to rid us of editors who were cultured and independent minded. The poorly qualified but obedient people who were placed at the editor's desks dreaded responsibility (and with good reason!). They ran to the "higher-ups" to check on every line. It was in the latter half of the 1930s that editors in fact stopped editing—some "instructor" or other became the sole authority, who approved all plans for each issue, page, and section, and who personally "corrected" everything—whether poetry, news stories, or fiction. It was in the latter half of the 1930s that the antidemocratic method of writing pieces *for* the author took root and spread to mammoth proportions. Authors were relieved of the chore of expressing their own opinions. All they had to do was sign articles already prepared by the editors and simply laid before them. Is it surprising that, despite all this hectic activity, there was hardly anything worth reading—and virtually the only difference between one newspaper or magazine and another was the layout?

The same culture-destroying standardization process went on in literature, the theater, cinema, painting. It was in the latter half of the 1930s that such creatively unique and irreplaceable theaters as Vsevolod Meyerhold's, the Kamerny Theater headed by Aleksandr Tairov, and several others were dissolved. Measures were taken so that the Theater of the Revolution (later renamed the Mayakovsky Theater) would resemble its previous self as little as possible, and so that nothing in the Vakhtangov Theater would remain to remind us of that man of inspired frenzy, Yevgeny Vakhtangov; in short, so that all theaters would be the same. The arrests and denunciations of Meyerhold and other theater personalities of course contributed greatly to this standardization process.

As for literature, it is enough to take the first five volumes of the *Literary Encyclopedia* to get an approximate (highly approximate!) count of its losses. In these volumes, I found *(a)* 138 writers of whom it was said curtly, "Illegally repressed, posthumously rehabilitated"; *(b)* 22 writers of whom this was not said (possibly because there still was no information on them when the first volume was compiled), although on the basis of certain biographical data there is reason to suspect they fell into this category; *(c)* 40 writers who were victims of repression but survived the camps and prisons, losing "only" seven, or ten, or seventeen years of their lives. A total of 200 prose writers, poets, critics, and literary scholars! And these are only people whose names begin with the letters *A* to *P* (halfway through the *P*'s); and only those who were put in the encyclopedia. The available data indicate that a total of about 600 members of the Writers' Union suffered repression. That does not include those who had not yet become members. Or those who were not writers at the time of their arrests but could have become writers (some who survived, as we know, did develop that way).

A blow of truly monstrous proportions was dealt [also] to the literature and culture of the fraternal [non-Russian] peoples of our country during those years (both to those whose culture was just coming into being and to those whose culture was more ancient than that of the Russians). Some small nationalities lost virtually all of their lovingly nurtured intelligentsia—or at any rate, their most outstanding intellectual representatives. . . .

The list of martyrs is far from ended, but to continue would be too painful. I think the beneficial effect of the year 1937 on our culture is sufficiently clear. At any rate, we now have some idea of the deliberate process that went on throughout the 1930s—the destruction of national cadres who had been trained under Soviet power in the preceding years.

Now let us turn to another cultural sphere—one that the Semanovs have lately claimed the exclusive right to defend. I have in mind the study and preservation of ancient monuments, especially those of Old Russia.

We know that the Soviet government, from its very first days, took steps to preserve such monuments. Nevertheless, many were destroyed or fell into disrepair during the years of civil war and famine. This is a pity and a shame, but it is understandable. There were many factors at work: the anger of the masses that had been building for centuries and that was unleashed against the monuments and household objects of the tsars and great landowners; the counterrevolutionary activity of the clergy in the early years of Soviet power; the lack of resources in the ruined country; and the low cultural level of some local leaders, along with the impetuous ultraleftism of others. All these things played a role, and many treasures from our cultural history perished as a result.

But the Church of Christ the Redeemer in Moscow was not destroyed in the early years of the revolution. It was demolished calmly, according to a plan approved by Stalin, in those same blessed years, the 1930s. And the Church of the Savior in the Pine Woods, the Monastery of the Miracles, the Monastery of the Ascension, and the Grand Hall of the Granovity Palace—all in the Kremlin in Moscow—were demolished then, too, with Stalin's blessings and directly at his command. And in place of the Ascension Monastery came the useless and talentless architecture of the Kremlin Theater.

And even in those days protests were heard. In particular, Vladimir Nevsky, an Old Bolshevik and then director of the Lenin Library, protested against the destruction of these monuments of Russian culture. But all in vain. The architectural monuments perished under the blows of the wrecking balls. Nevsky perished in the camps.

Semanov wins the title for cynicism in dating the flowering of our culture from 1937. One wonders how this "historian," so concerned about the Russian people, its history, and its "eternal values," could so easily cancel from Stalin's account the smashing of Russian culture, both of the Soviet and the earlier period?

But he manages. And in so doing, gives himself away. Because, in fact, he doesn't care one bit about the Russian people or Russian culture. What is precious and important to him is the idea of Russian great-power chauvinism, an idea Lenin fought against to the end of his life; the idea that the Soviet state is the direct successor to the historic traditions and principles of the state system of the "Great and the Little and the White Russians." And it was none other than Stalin who gave Great Russian chauvinism a new lease on life. And compared to that, what is a Monastery of the Miracles? Or manuscripts that perished? Or lives that were lost?

Now it is clear how the apology for 1937 that we have quoted found its way into an article pretending to have a philosophical aim, and what place the Stalin repression has on the scale of "eternal values." After all, it was only after the smashing of Soviet historical science, accomplished by Stalin in the 1930s, that it proved possible to falsify history in such a way as to rehabilitate tsarism! For, over the course of many years, disciplined "ideologists," on Stalin's orders, were actually busy—under the pretext of glorifying the Russian people—at the task of rehabilitating tsarism. Semanov, Viktor Chalmayev, and other "neo-Slavo-philes" have good reason to harbor gratitude for Stalin.

The forced incorporation into Communist ideology of the idea of national exclusiveness, of a chosen people, which is an idea totally alien to Communism, was made easier by the circumstances of the war against the fascist aggressors. Chauvinism fed parasitically on the natural feeling of national pride (and the people had something to be proud of). It exploited that feeling in order to rewrite history completely. Alexander Nevsky, Yuri Dolgoruky, Ivan the Terrible, and Ivan Kalita were added to the assembly of saints on the grounds that "their life's path proved to be historically progressive." At the same time many national-liberation movements (Shamil, and so on) were slandered. There was virtually no deed of the tsarist army, administration, or diplomatic corps that was not white-washed by these obedient timeservers, who became quite proficient at blending a mishmash of Marxist phraseology and chauvinist ideology. A legend arose that still has currency today—the legend of the "voluntary" incorporation into the Russian empire of all the oppressed peoples whose subjugation was accomplished with rivers of blood. Gone from the pages of histories, novels, and textbooks was the tsarist Russia that was a prison house of nations, the gendarme of Europe and the hangman of revolutions, the empire that oppressed its colonies and at the same time was dependent on foreign capital. History began to be painted in unbearably rosy hues. It was considered a crime to glorify the khans and beys who fought against tsarism, but when those khans and beys came to serve under "the great white tsar"—and forced their own people to submit to the tsar—the title "progressive" was magnanimously bestowed upon them (as though they had foreseen the coming of the October Revolution and the Union of Soviet Socialist Republics).

O happy, happy childhood days of the Semanovs, Chalmayevs, Mikhail Lobanovs, and the others, never to return! How can they help loving and cherishing those days? It was then that Great Russian chauvinism was proclaimed by Stalin to be the one and only, infallibly true ("eternally valid"!) Communist ideology, and any disagreement with it was anti-Communist and anti-Soviet. Internationalism was left for ceremonial occasions only, a phrase that could be paraded out when needed. It was all arranged very simply. And this, incidentally, is the main danger in having one, uniform ideology imposed from above. One's view of the world is not elaborated and reinforced through conflict with those who disagree. It is handed down ready-made, like religious dogma, and under the cover of this dogma anything you please can be included, anything that the ideological lawgiver finds useful for the moment. And when beckoned by a crook of the lawgiver's finger, dissenters—Black Hundredists, let's say—having no other way of propounding their views, gladly rush to join the ruling ideology, make themselves comfortable within it, and over the course of time fundamentally revise it. That is where they come from—the Sofronovs with their hymns to the Cossack whip, the Feliks Chuyevs with their aggressive nationalism, and finally, the candidates in philosophical and historical science who seek to provide a "Marxist basis" for "the necessary fact of rule by tyrants and the charms of the whip."

Taking a firm stand in the Stalin-and-Pobedonostsev [that is, reactionary tsarist] tradition, Semanov lashes out frenziedly against the historian Mikhail Pokrovsky, one of the earliest Bolsheviks, who wrote the first Marxist history of Russia. Here is what Semanov says about the works of Pokrovsky, whose most active period was, as Semanov stresses, in the 1920s.

"Pokrovsky and his followers established a real monopoly on historical science at that time and dealt very stringently with dissenters. Pokrovsky and his school put a large minus sign in front of all of Russian history and rewrote that history on the principle of 'reverse logic.' Thus, in the work of Peter the Great, who transformed Russia, Pokrovsky saw only drunkenness and syphilis. His essays on Russian history (which would more properly be called essays in anti-Russian history) hardly mentioned [the tsarist military heroes] Suvorov and Kutuzov, the epic of Sevastopol in 1854–55, and many other persons and events, which became *(and remain!) sacred* for any patriotic citizen" (emphasis added—R.L.).

It is true that Pokrovsky wrote history, not sacred scripture. Neither Peter I, nor Suvorov, nor Kutuzov, nor even the [revolutionary] Decembrists and [revolutionary] members of People's Will (nor, I would venture to say, the Bolsheviks either) were icons for him. They were historical figures of their times, with all their unique and peculiar features. And he saw no need to hide from the reader the blood and grime that any country's history is full of (ours being no exception). One would expect any real scholar to work this way. And why exactly should Peter I or Suvorov—for all their talents—be *sacred* in a socialist country? Historians should not make objects of worship even out of those who led the people's struggle for freedom and independence. Their duty is to describe and portray them truthfully. But what, pray tell, makes Aleksandr Suvorov sacred for us? His campaigns of conquest against Turkey? His war against the French Revolution? The subjugation of Poland? The capture of Pugachov? . . .

But [the fact is that in regard to Pokrovsky] Semanov lies. If we read Pokrovsky's four-volume *History of Russia from the Earliest Times*, we find a chapter seven signatures in length devoted to "The Reforms of Peter." One may or may not agree with Pokrovsky's appraisal of the Petrine reforms in this chapter, but how can anyone argue, without resorting to the crudest lies, that Pokrovsky saw nothing in Peter's work but "drunkenness and syphilis"?

Here we come to a question of ethics, and not just ethics in theory but the rules of moral conduct, with which Semanov claims to be so concerned in his advocacy of eternal spiritual values. Why is it impermissible to speak the truth and call Karamzin the "Herodotus of the Russian nobility" (this being no discredit to Karamzin, since Herodotus is considered the "father of history"), but perfectly permissible to slander Pokrovsky by calling him an "anti-Russian historian"? . . .

There is a peculiar law that the more someone pounds his chest and shouts about "eternal values" and "lofty and unchanging virtues of the soul," the less he remembers the simplest human values. Such as elementary honesty.

Among the values Semanov lists as eternal, unchanged, and *unchanging* regardless of circumstances is—national character. I do not know whether he means this to apply to all nations (he does not discuss that), but he considers the national character of the Russian people something given once and for all, eternal, and embodied in a single psychological type. The truth is that this is just one step away from racism, for if a nation has only one psychological type, eternal and changeless, the only explanation for it is "the blood," racial heredity. It is also true that the Semanovs and other "keepers of the hearth" do a disservice to the Russian people, rob it and impoverish its history and character when they proclaim it to have remained unchanged from the earliest times to the present day. They deny the Russian people a wealth and variety of psychological types and above all the capacity to remake themselves in the process of making their own history. . . .

Why does Semanov have to dredge up the ancient theory that the cardinal virtues of the Russian people are submissiveness and patience? Why is it that Russian history and Russian literature provide him with only two types of heroes —the great leader who brings victory to the Russian state (for what purpose and at what cost being unimportant); and the modest and unassuming rank and filer, who dies for the state, as befits his station. It's as though, at the wave of a scepter, all the fighters for freedom have disappeared from Russian history, all its scientists and thinkers ("intellectuals," as Semanov scornfully labels the intelligentsia), and all the artists and poets persecuted by the tsarist autocracy. Why is this?

I see that many questions have piled up. It is time to answer them.

The fact is that, although Semanov is indignant about certain hints and allusions critical of Russian history, which are supposedly found in the works of some contemporary writers, he himself is very much inclined toward illusions about the past, inclined to apologize for tsarism. In works denouncing Ivan the Terrible and Nicholas I, he detects an insult aimed at the present day. The explanation for this does not lie in the peculiarities of his literary vision but in the specific nature of his political thought. Since for Semanov the entire history of the Russian imperial state—from Vladimir Svyatoslavovich [the original

Prince of Kiev] to Joseph Vissarionovich[Stalin]—is a single, smooth, uninterrupted process of strengthening the state authority, since "the old maintains the
new" and "the past is inseparably linked with the present," it is logical that any
exposé of our slavish past, any truthful word about the tyranny of the Russian
princes, tsars, and emperors, about torture and the rack, the suppression of
freedom of speech, the lack of equality for the many nationalities inhabiting this
territory, the Semanovs regard as "antistate activity." He does not call, as one
might expect, for deeper study of the history of our country, including its ancient
past. (Who could object if he did that?) What he calls for is the creation of a
historical iconostasis, for the exclusion from history of everything that is not
grand and ostentatious, that fails to inspire veneration. He argues that the most
important criterion of value—and not relative value either!—in social
phenomena is whether or not they contribute to the strengthening of our state
system.

In his opinion, contemporary Soviet man "feels himself to be the heir of his
forefathers, the *legitimate and grateful continuator of their cause in the construction and creation of our great state*" (emphasis added—R.L.). How, then, can he
help feeling indignation at the "carping critics" and "nihilists"? After all, neither
Stenka Razin, nor Yemelyan Pugachov, nor Chaadayev, Pestel, and Pushkin, nor
Belinsky, Herzen, and Chernyshevsky, nor Nekrasov and Saltykov-Shchedrin, nor
Zhelyabov and Sofia Perovskaya, nor Plekhanov, nor Leo Tolstoy [rebels and
social critics under tsarism]—none of them helped to construct the edifice of the
Great Russian Empire. On the contrary, they undermined and helped to destroy
it! It is natural that Semanov does not trace his genealogy back to these "forefathers." He feels himself to be (and wishes all Soviet young people to feel likewise)
not their descendant but the descendant of Ivan the Terrible, Peter I, Catherine
II, and—who knows? anything is possible—perhaps even Nicholas I? After all,
like it or not, the Decembrists were troublemakers, but Nicholas I made his
contribution to the might of empire. He conquered the Caucasus, extended the
frontiers of the state, put down the Hungarian revolution, turned Russia into a
prison house, and held all of Europe in fear. Of course, his reign, which began
with the gallows, ended with the defeat in the Crimean War. But it's all right
to skip this, leaving the reader aware of only one thing from the entire Crimean
War—the heroic defense of Sevastopol.

By "skipping over" everything in our history that contributed not to "the
strengthening of the state" but to the strengthening of revolutionary consciousness, Semanov is pursuing one very clear and definite aim. He is trying to
discourage inquiring minds and to educate the youth in the spirit of something
I recall from my childhood years in the tsarist schools—the "prayer after study."

"We thank Thee O Lord and Creator, for Thou hast helped us by Thy Grace
to attend to our studies. Bless our superiors, our parents and teachers, who guide
us in the knowledge of goodness and give us strength and fortitude to continue
Thy teachings."

These "teachings," first smuggled into Soviet historiography by Stalin (by whose orders both ancient and modern history were rewritten) and now successfully expanded by the Semanovs, are based on the most ordinary, standard, everyday great-power chauvinism imaginable, the kind that any Arakcheev, Pobedonostsev, or Stolypin [tsarist ministers] could subscribe to. The contribution to these teachings added by certain contemporary candidates in history amounts to this: on the one hand disguise them with empty phrases about Communism and revolution and, on the other, some skillful parasitic feeding on a certain moral questioning among Soviet youth today, a search for a spiritual ideal, a grappling with the dilemma of good and evil, which every generation must resolve for itself anew. The Semanovs find it advantageous that an intense interest has arisen among young people today in ancient Russian art, architecture, and music—an interest that in itself is quite commendable. (This interest arose, we should remark in passing, as a reaction against the stereotyped grayness of standardized canvases, the dreary rectangles of contemporary urban design, and the cheerful radio songs, whose lyrics and melodies are totally lacking in originality.) To give the genius of Andrei Rublyov [the ancient icon painter] its due, while sneaking in the poisonous idea of national exclusiveness unnoticed in all the commotion; to go into raptures over the architecture of Kizhi Island, while preaching the idea that the Russian state is eternal and imperishable; to gaze wonderingly at the blades used by Suvorov's "miraculous heroes," without asking how many freedom-loving heads, of Russians and non-Russian alike, were severed by those blades—that is the line of attack and those are the tactical methods of the Semanovs.

These methods must be known and understood, and we must debunk them, because naive people may think the writings of the Semanovs are patriotic. It isn't so. They are antipatriotic. Like any form of great-power chauvinism, they provoke intensified nationalism among the smaller nationalities, inspire mistrust and suspicion of the people in whose name (without any authorization!) the Semanovs announce for all to hear, that it is the leading nation, the very best, and that its entire history is sacred (including its subjugation of other nations). Not only do such ideas not contribute in any way to the promotion of internationalism; they do not even strengthen the state. . . .

There is no single or eternal form of patriotism; nor can it be an absolute value, as Semanov contends. First, there are as many forms of patriotism as there are nations and states; second, patriotism is one of the loosest and most relative of concepts. Who, for example, was truer to his homeland—the repentant Dostoevsky or the unrepentant émigré Aleksandr Herzen? I am not trying to compare their talents or to discuss the torments of their souls. There can be no doubt that both of them ardently loved Russia. Who, then, was truer to Russia: Dostoevsky, who endorsed the [official tsarist] formula "Orthodoxy, Autocracy, and Nationality"? Or Herzen, who refused to return to his homeland?

In my opinion, Herzen. And in yours?

Whose patriotism is "the highest virtue of the human soul," that of the [wartime] defeatist Lenin or the defensist Pavel Milyukov? Of Romain Rolland or Raymond Poincaré? Joan of Arc or Napoleon Bonaparte? Garibaldi or Mussolini? [The German Communist] Thälmann or Hitler? In any country, among any people, you find two kinds of patriotism: one is chauvinist and racist, it asserts the supremacy of one's own nation over others, and calls—under various pretexts!—for their reduction to the status of wards or dependents; the other is revolutionary and emancipatory, it fights for the freedom of one's own and of other nations—"for our freedom and for yours" [slogan of Czechs protesting the 1968 Soviet invasion]. You cannot base yourself simultaneously on Vladimir Lenin and Konstantin Pobedonostsev.

It would seem that everything is clear. Semanov's article (like a number of other articles in *Molodaya gvardiya*) represents a consistent and logical development of Stalin's great-power chauvinism and in a hidden way polemicizes against Lenin, from start to finish. But the polemic is not only with Lenin—it is with Plekhanov, and Chernyshevsky, and Herzen, and Radishchev, and all the Russian revolutionary thinkers who opposed the mighty fortress of Russian autocracy and who never "felt themselves" to be the "legitimate and grateful continuators" of its cause. It is not so often in our periodical press that one can read an article that reveals so definitively and so openly *the direction in which Stalin misled our ideology.*

To be sure, Semanov never mentions Stalin. He simply quotes him without attribution and pays him homage for the glorious year 1937. To be sure, Semanov does not openly polemicize against Lenin. He furtively conceals Lenin's pronouncements on the national question. His only open attacks are on contemporary "intellectuals," "nihilists and revisionists"—again without naming them by name. For example, he uses the term "enemies" (shades of that golden age, the second half of the 1930s!) for those contemporary writers and historians who have investigated Russia's past in depth and have dared to see in it both ignorance and gloom and reaction. And he denies such writers and historians the right to love their country. . . .

Since for Semanov the history of Russia is not an object of scientific investigation, but something "sacred"—all of it, including its pogroms and gallows and torture chambers, its tsars and its priests—he courageously defends the entire Russian state system, wholesale. But it is the leaders, the warriors, the defenders of the system, and the singers of its praises, whom Semanov considers the sacred names of Russian history. Not those who sought to bring it down, those who fought the state, our moral and spiritual giants. He finds the roots of the Soviet socialist state system somewhere in the midst of the ages, either in the age of Peter the Great, or in the dungeons of Malyuta Skuratov [Ivan the Terrible's police chief], or even earlier in Kievan Rus.

We will leave it to the reader to judge how accurate and inspiring that way of tracing our genealogy is.

And so everything is understood except for one problem. Why was this article printed in *Molodaya gvardiya,* the organ of the Central Committee of the All-Union Leninist Communist League of Youth?

Historians some day (preferably some day soon!) will answer this question. In full. Leaving nothing unsaid.

[No. 75, December 1970]

The Killing of Novy mir:
In Lieu of an Obituary
by A Reader

This chapter concludes with an important event. Tvardovsky's twelve-year editorship of Novy mir came to an end on February 10–11, 1970, when the authorities fired his longtime editorial associates and forced his own resignation. Since that event, a fierce dispute has raged over the political role of the journal in the 1950s and 1960s. For many anti-Stalinists, including its former editors and the anonymous author of the following essay, Novy mir had been, in addition to a publication of high literary standards, the Party's bastion of democratic reformist ideas, a great heroic voice of "Communism with a human face," in the harsh conditions of Soviet authoritarianism and censorship. For other people, such as Solzhenitsyn, the journal's onetime protégé who repudiated its loyalist reform ideas, Novy mir had already acquired, well before Tvardovsky's ouster, "a permanent stoop from endless compromise" and suffered a "spiritual death."[3] Nonetheless, the dispute, which is really a fundamental conflict between different perspectives on the Soviet system, underscores the political importance of the crushing of Tvardovsky's Novy mir; it abolished the last center of official anti-Stalinism. This article "in lieu of an obituary," printed here with only small deletions, circulated in samizdat shortly after the events of February 10–11. Solzhenitsyn later suggested, in a scathing attack on the article, that it was written by one of the dismissed editors, an allegation denied by the deputy editor.[4] Whatever the case, the author evidently was close to the purged editorial board. The article's viewpoint was echoed by a mourner at Tvardovsky's official funeral twenty-one months later: "Is it possible that no one is going to say that we are burying our civic conscience here?"[5]

These heroes ardently desired but one thing—that a deathly silence should reign amidst which their own voices would sound all the more loudly and that the level of social consciousness should fall so low that even people of their caliber would seem to be stars of the first magnitude.
—Marx and Engels[6]

---

3. Compare Vladimir Lakshin, *Solzhenitsyn, Tvardovsky, and Novy mir* (Cambridge, Mass., 1980), and Aleksandr Solzhenitsyn, *The Oak and the Calf* (New York, 1980).

4. Solzhenitsyn, *The Oak and the Calf*, pp. 282–83; Lakshin, *Solzhenitsyn, Tvardovsky, and Novy mir*, p. 83.

5. Quoted in ibid., p. 174.

6. Author's note: K. Marks and F. Engels, *Sochineniia*, vol. 8, p. 335.

Who can read our newspapers today? Evidently only someone who has the patience to plow through the tons of empty verbiage and dross that seems to have the power to repel even the shallowest simpleton willing to swallow anything. Only someone who has learned how to detect and extract from the heaps of verbiage the subterfuges of semisilence and the outcroppings of living, unconsoling, and unclouded truth. Only someone who has learned to divine, behind these devices, the biting, salty truth that has not been watered down. Only someone who in this way knew how to pick out the crumbs of information in our papers and had a chance to decode the ever-so-modest "chronicle" buried in the pages of *Literaturnaya gazeta* on February 11, 1970, and to decipher nothing less than the news of the death of our best and most beloved magazine, the great friend of all progressive socialist forces in the country, the magazine that bravely and honestly told us the truth, genuine, irreplaceable, and free of quotation marks. As if by chance and just in passing, this "chronicle" mumbles something about reassignments of personnel: some were "relieved of their duties" and others "confirmed in their posts." In the process, Tvardovsky's name is mentioned as though he were one of those who carried out this act of strangulation, as though he wished to remain *without* those "relieved" and *with* those "confirmed."

It was not enough that a miserly few lines stripped of any import were printed with the intention that they be noticed as little as possible. On top of that, the factual element in them was surrounded by lies. It is a barefaced lie that Tvardovsky agreed with the decision, the departure of many of his leading collaborators. In fact what they aimed at, by dismissing these people, was to force *him* to leave, to bring about *his* dismissal. The shot was carefully calculated to ricochet and hit a target they pretend they were not aiming at, at all! It is a lie that Tvardovsky agreed to this. Could anyone agree to such a thing? He did not agree to work on the magazine with people who are known to be totally alien to the spirit of *Novy mir,* people who agreed, after painting themselves up as "members of the editorial board," to participate in the strangulation of the magazine.

The calculation was careful, and now we learn—but, so far, from foreign radio broadcasts only (because *Literaturnaya gazeta* is holding its tongue)—that Tvardovsky has submitted his resignation as a protest against the changes in the editorial board and that his resignation has been accepted by the Writers' Union and the Party's Central Committee.

Literaturnaya gazeta has recorded for the ages the list of those who took part in the shameful meeting that decided the fate of *Novy mir.* They were Konstantin Fedin, Sergei Baruzdin, Konstantin Voronkov, Sergei Mikhalkov, Vladimir Ozerov, Leonid Sobolev, Nikolai Tikhonov, Aleksandr Chakovsky, and K. Yashen. They acted at the bidding of figures behind the scenes, a small but active group of Stalinist extremists who will stop at nothing to revise and eradicate the line of the Twentieth Congress, to restore all the vilenesses of Stalinism. (The political program of this group, closely attuned with Maoism, was popularized in the novels *What Do You Really Want?* by Kochetov and *In the Name of the Father and of the Son* by Shevtsov, which openly propagate ideological police-state attitudes and a universal barracks existence.)

Our most honest lips have ceased to speak. Arbitrary bureaucratic rule, which wants the reign of silence, has temporarily triumphed. But let us note how this was done: it was done on the sly, with the hope that by the time we realized it, it would be too late. The "chronicle" was inserted in the paper with such feverish haste that it appeared only in the last part of the press run, distributed only in Moscow. They wanted to confront everyone with the accomplished fact and were terribly afraid that all would be lost if they could not forestall angry reactions.

But their *political cowardice* was revealed most strikingly in the fact that they dared not make an open and unambiguous announcement that the journal was suspended, the editorial board dispersed, and Tvardovsky dismissed. That would have meant showing all the world their real impotence and inability to counter the mighty spiritual influence of the magazine by *spiritual* means, their helpless incapacity to answer ideas with ideas. An open act of administrative intervention would have meant acknowledging the ideological invincibility of *Novy mir*'s Truth. That is why force was masked with petty details; the main thing was totally covered up; the rest was presented as some minor triviality in a listing of recent events not worth diverting one's attention for.

Deprived of *Novy mir,* many of us will now gain a better understanding of what it represented. It was the most consistent and unfailing mouthpiece we had for the tendency that revived after 1953, and especially after 1956, a tendency favoring the development of socialism free of the deformations rooted in the heritage of many centuries of Russian feudalism. It was our most outspoken voice —within the limits allowed by an increasingly thick-headed and mistrustful censorship—the voice of the people's conscience. A voice that proclaimed the irrepressible and indestructible capacity of the people to struggle for genuine socialism—and this after the decades of deadening silence and Stalinist barracks existence. It was the surest symbol of moral and human awakening, the most faithful implementer and defender of the Twentieth Congress line, which condemned the monstrous abominations and crimes of barracks pseudosocialism (such as we now see raging in China).

Everything genuine, everything of more than ephemeral value in our imaginative literature, literary criticism, and topical writing, crystallized and formed itself around *Novy mir*. It truly became the central storehouse of our finest treasures, illuminating all of our intellectual and moral life. This treasure house by itself outweighed everything done in the last decade and a half by all the other magazines taken together. This made *Novy mir* a phenomenon of exceptional importance, far more than "just another one of our magazines." *Novy mir* took to heart the fundamental issues, the kind that submit rather poorly to formulation in the language of outworn clichés. And it is on clear thinking about such problems, free of all dogmatic blinders, and on true and reliable solutions that *our historical destiny as a whole* depends. Will our country have an openly resounding voice like this—a voice of truth, "And the truth should not depend upon whom it has to serve" (Lenin, vol. 54, p. 446)? Or will it not? On the answer to that question will depend whether our country comes out of economic depression and the political blind alley into which the Stalinist extremists are trying to drive it, whether there will be an end to spiritual self-devastation, so that we can truly take a socialist road that can be a progressive historical alternative to the world of capital.

Among *Novy mir*'s merits, we cannot fail to emphasize that it knew (and by its example taught others) how to value the truth above all—the truth of science, of art, of morality, a truth that is singular in all its complexity and unfalsified concreteness. *Novy mir* knew how to value the truth and taught others to value it above any expedient use—even with the noblest considerations by those "whom it has to serve." This means freedom to an equal degree from *positive fanaticism,* which shackles thought with the chains of self-satisfied apologetics and replaces creative problem solving with unilinear "firm determination" (if only everyone votes "for"); and from *negative fanaticism,* which is blinded—sometimes even more than the positive kind—by its bitterness and nihilistic faultfinding that acknowledges no problems (if only everyone votes "against"!). Free critical thinking is alien to all forms of fanaticism. And it is precisely that kind of thinking—soberly objective, courageously restrained, full of moral responsibility—that we have found up to now in every issue of *Novy mir.* Thus, it can be said that the people of *Novy mir* served as a model of commitment to ideas and principles—commitment to ideas not in the sense of the ideological language that has suffered the grossest inflation and that is used equally by the skilled and cynical mimic-chameleons and by the compliant bootlicker-fetishists. But in the humanist sense of the individual's control over the ideational content of one's own life. Such control has a great need for objective and historically concrete self-awareness, the lack of which cannot be replaced by any handsome posing before one's mirror at home.

The suppression of *Novy mir* is an attempt by a handful of spiritual bankrupts to eliminate from our moral and intellectual life, from the life of the people and Party, the voice of truth that gives expression to all the socialist and progressive forces in the country, the Twentieth Congress tendency. This is an attempt to turn the country back to barracks despotism, to a state of moral and intellectual voicelessness and the silence of the grave. But there is a good chance that this attempt to bring tragedy back to us will itself turn into farce. It would be a good idea for us to think over the results and lessons of the *Novy mir* experience in order to better understand ourselves and the problematical historical work before us. That is the task of the day. . . .

We have learned that the journal that still has the same cover as the suppressed *Novy mir* was given the order to "be no worse" than its predecessor. But this no longer depends on those who give the orders! This depends on what we —the writers and readers—decide, whether we will support this masked farce or uncompromisingly reject it.

In the same way, in the final analysis, it depends on us whether our land will fall under the *reign of silence*.

[No. 66, March 1970]

4

Currents of Soviet
Opinion and Dissent

P OLITICAL TERROR *creates an "inner censor" in citizens, even in normally gregarious members of the Russian intelligentsia. A bitter, and realistic, anecdote stated six axioms for survival under Stalin:*

> *1. Don't think!*
> *2. If you think, don't speak!*
> *3. If you speak, don't write!*
> *4. If you write, don't publish!*
> *5. If you publish, don't sign!*
> *6. If you sign, recant!*[1]

Of course, some people did think, speak, and even write critically during the terror, but only in the utmost privacy and, as the expression went, "for the drawer." As a result, the Soviet Union under Stalin seemed to be a country without public opinion apart from the state's, and where government itself was a monolith of single-minded functionaries.

By the end of the 1960s, for reasons that need no further discussion here, many Soviet citizens had overcome their "inner censor." The long silence of the intelligentsia, or at least its most critical segment, came to an end. The result was

---

1. Medvedev, *On Socialist Democracy* (New York, 1975), p. 316. Medvedev says these precepts "were very popular among the timid rank and file of the Party." But their history and substance indicate that they originated with the intelligentsia.

samizdat as a mass phenomenon—a torrent of opinionated, typescript words in rebellion against censorship in general. Thousands of uncensored documents, from bootlegged stenographs to political and literary writings, like those in this book, were in circulation, and thousands more were in the making. Samizdat became an important aspect of Soviet political and intellectual life. For some nonconformists in the cities, it even became an alternative to official Soviet culture, a kind of counterculture. A popular Soviet anecdote tells of a frustrated grandmother who finally resorts to typing the whole of Tolstoy's War and Peace, *which is available in bookstores, "because my grandson won't read anything that isn't samizdat."*

Politically, samizdat literature expresses much more than simply protest against the government. It expresses the multicolored realities of uncensored Soviet opinion, including fundamental disagreements inside the Establishment and among dissenters themselves. The items in this chapter have been chosen from dozens in Political Diary *to show some of the diverse sources of samizdat and some of the many currents of Soviet opinion.*

Viewpoints on Leadership and Politics

In the 1950s and early 1960s, Khrushchev's anti-Stalin campaigns inadvertently had encouraged public criticism of the Soviet past. The fall of Khrushchev and the new leadership's attacks on his "harebrained" policies then spurred criticism of current governmental practices. These three documents—a worker's letter to Kommunist, an account of a meeting of Moscow University students, and a teacher's letter to Kosygin—are examples of the upsurge of public outspokenness in 1964–66. Not all of this political criticism should be interpreted as "dissent" in the sense that the word acquired later in the 1960s, but rather as expressions of what we call public opinion. Nonetheless, it is significant that even the most loyalist and pro-Party of these documents, the two letters, were sharply critical of official practices and, in the Soviet context, strong advocacies of democratic reform. Indeed, they are evidence that a current of democratic opinion existed inside the Party itself.

ANATOLY SBITNEV • *Letter toKommunist [Journal of the Central Committee]*

I am a rank-and-file Communist, a worker at a factory in Ulan-Ude. The events occurring in our country, or rather the attitude of people around me toward them, have forced me to write this letter.

Over the years, working in factories and serving in the army, I have become convinced that a leader, no matter what post he holds, can achieve success only when his authority among his subordinates is unshakable. The conversations one hears among the people, and the anecdotes about certain leaders of our Party and government, have led me to wonder, Is the authority not only of certain leaders but of the Central Committee as a whole at the level it should be?

Over the years in which our Party has fought for the interests of the working class, a number of recognized leaders have emerged from its ranks. Their authority became solidly established among the masses and can still be felt today, forty-seven years after the founding of the Soviet state.

But what results did Khrushchev's policies achieve in strengthening the authority of the leader who serves as chief of state and ultimately the authority of the Central Committee, as the highest governing institution of our Party?

Following the Leninst principles of Party leadership, our Party expelled the anti-Party group [that is, Molotov and his Politburo allies in 1957] from its ranks. At first glance, it seemed that the Party had restored Leninist principles. But this was only at first glance. Khrushchev criticized Stalin for imposing the personality cult, but did the same thing himself. At present, the masses know a great deal about the reasons for Khrushchev's withdrawing from the posts he held. And did he really withdraw? Or was it perhaps a step forced upon him by pressure from the majority. The mass of the people tend to believe the latter.

That the glorification of Khrushchev was greater than that of Stalin was seen by all, but that Khrushchev operated according to Stalinist methods in solving problems can only be guessed at; still, it isn't that hard to figure out in view of the way the things Khrushchev introduced or advocated are being reversed. But Khrushchev made a mistake carrying out those policies: he turned the masses against himself. The people felt that the material standard of living was getting worse and it was harder to live, that sooner or later Khrushchev was going to bring the country to ruin with his giveaway policies. Judge for yourself. How can a working person fail to realize this when one kilogram of sausage costs 5 rubles, 54 kopeks, and the average worker earns 3.5 rubles a day? When food prices are not going down but, instead, are going up, while wages go down. Just you try and convince a miner that living is getting better when seven or eight years ago [before the devaluation of the ruble] he earned 4,000–7,000 rubles a month and now he earns only 100–300. Anger and disagreement with the policies being followed in the country were increasing. This was intensified by the actions of local authorities who tried to win fame by going all out for those policies, to get ahead by stepping over the bodies of others, putting on pressure, issuing orders, ruining the collective farms and overworking the industrial plants to the point of breakdown. The result of all this was that within the Central Committee there arose not only the necessity but also the possibility of taking measures to put an end to "the feverish activity of Khrushchev and his loyal retainers." This time the masses were not surprised by what happened. They foresaw it and considered it inevitable, for they believed in the strength of our Party and knew that the Party would find strength to recognize its own mistakes and correct them.

Great credit for what happened of course goes to the masses. The "hearty" welcomes the workers arranged for Khrushchev at various plants and in various cities in the recent past spoke eloquently of their attitude toward Khrushchev and the policies he was following. And that could not have gone unnoticed; it was necessary to pay attention to that, because the strength of our Party lies in its support among the masses.

Now, when our people have gone through the experience of fighting not only against internal enemies but external ones as well, now that they have built socialism and raised their own level of political literacy—under these conditions the working class will understand the decisions of the Central Committee correctly. The mistakes of individuals, even if they are leaders. cannot shake the faith of the majority of the masses in the Party's cause, the Party that has led the masses in the struggle for their just cause. But this alone is not enough to assure us that in the future the masses will not lose this confidence.

Our party needs leaders of the kind described by Lenin [referring to Sverdlov], whose mere word is "sufficient to secure an unchallenged and final settlement of a question, without conferences, and without a formal vote; so that everyone feels convinced that the question has been settled on the basis of such profound practical knowledge and organizational intuition that not only hundreds and thousands of advanced workers but also the masses in general accept that settlement as final."[2]

Such leaders are not brought to us from outside; they must be developed and trained within the Party. And the training must take place in the center, but in such a way that all members of the Party can observe the functioning of every candidate for the high posts of central Party leadership.

I deliberately emphasize *every candidate*. Because that is exactly the point. There should not be just one, but several, so that the masses and not only the central leadership can compare them and choose the one who is really capable of becoming a leader. There is a conclusion to be drawn from this. Our press must cover the activity of all members of the government and Central Committee more broadly and in more detail. Then the masses will be able to observe not only the functioning of the Central Committee as a whole but of each of its members as well. This will not only strengthen the authority that has already been won but will greatly increase it. In that situation Party members will be sure, when they elect a comrade to one or another post, that the comrade in question will justify their confidence. Then I, too, would agree with the argument "Leaders may be removed, but we remain; we are their betters in the sense that we vote them in."

But how can I agree with that if I am certain, when I vote for a representative to a Party conference, that the comrade I might vote for is no better informed than I about the activities of the person for whom he will have to vote, in turn, in my name for the higher bodies of the Party—when he knows only what he'll be told about that person at the conference? As for such posts as chairman of the Council of Ministers and chairman of the Presidium of the Supreme Soviet, election to those posts should be based on voting by the entire population. In that event, all will feel they know who they are voting for, and if one of the comrades who is elected commits errors, that becomes our fault. And when you know that you yourself are partly to blame for mistakes that are made, you won't say, "Who in the world knows who's right and who's at fault up there?"

Direct participation in electing the country's leaders—that is what the masses need.

[No. 3, December 1964]

---

2. Sbitnev's footnote: V. I. Lenin, *Polnoe sobranie sochinenie*, vol. 38, p. 78.

Students Speak Out: A Report by Roy Medvedev

A seminar for university-level instructors was held on April 12, 1965. Nikishev, deputy minister of education, spoke. The following is a partial summary of what he said.

Recently, certain unhealthy moods have been evident among students. For example, a well-attended debate took place not long ago at the school of mathematics and physics at Moscow State University on the topic "Cynicism and Social Ideals." Many unauthorized persons attended the debate, indicating that the event was planned to attract a broader public.

Those who spoke from the floor did not give their real names. In Nikishev's words, the speeches were defamatory of the Soviet Communist Party and leading Party figures. In seeking to explain the reasons for cynicism and cynically minded people, some speakers argued that the Party and its leaders were themselves to blame for the fact that mistrust, skepticism, and rejection of authority prevail among young people. It was said openly that no one tells the young the truth, including the newspaper called *The Truth (Pravda),* which should be renamed *Lies.*

Examples were given showing that since the ouster of Khrushchev the press said one thing and reality indicated another. [These speakers] said that the entire written history of the Party was a fraud and that Stalin was not the only one responsible for the liquidation of Lenin's closest associates. Mikoyan, Suslov, Nikolai Shvernik, and others were also to blame. No one is telling the truth about the removal of Leonid Ilyichev [Khrushchev's spokesman in ideological and artistic affairs] in the press or in oral reports. Truthful statistics on the economy are never given. It was the same at the March plenum [of the Central Committee]. All dumped the blame on Khrushchev and kept out of the way themselves.

The leaders in Stalin's time and his successors were in no way different from the Nazis. One of those who spoke—an artist—said they should all be mowed down with machine guns. There was also a study circle at Moscow University that discussed and analyzed our past, identified those guilty of the misdeeds of the Stalin era, and laid responsibility for the past on present leaders, who were said to be responsible for the present situation in the country.

After the debate mentioned above, ten Moscow University instructors were called in to see Nikolai Yegorychev, secretary of the Party's Moscow Committee. Among them was Georgy Platonov, a professor in the philosophy department. They were all asked this question: "How could you have allowed such anti-Soviet actions at Moscow University and not take counteraction? Didn't you have the academic qualifications, titles, degrees, books, and materials necessary to expose and refute those who spoke? How can we allow a Soviet university to be made into a platform for anti-Soviet speeches?"

The rector, Ivan Petrovsky, admitted that the debate had been disorderly and should not have been permitted. One of the instructors stated, "I am an astronomer; the stars are the focus of my attention. That is why I did not consider the students' speeches a problem; I assumed that it was simply an exchange of views, a heated argument."

I [Roy Medvedev] have been told that the main speaker at the Moscow University debate was a certain Kuznetsov—a freelance artist who worked for the Novosti Press Agency. He spoke for an hour and a half on the crimes of the Stalin era. Instructors who tried to oppose his views were in effect driven from the platform because the circumstances were such that the audience itself, with its shouting and yelling, decided who would speak.

[No. 7, April 1965]

V.K. [A University Teacher] • *Letter to Premier Kosygin*

February 1966

During the last few years, a great many questions for the Soviet people have piled up—questions to which they have not received any direct answers in the press, on the radio, or in the speeches of our Party and government leaders. It is not surprising that many of our people have begun to look to foreign radio broadcasts [in Russian] for answers to their questions.

Of course, this is not the best solution. Allow me to formulate and pose to you several of the questions that are awaiting reply. I am deeply convinced that one of our chief woes is the tendency to cover up and suppress discussion of many aspects of our life. This creates lack of confidence among the people toward the government and undermines the moral solidarity and unity of Soviet society.

The Twentieth and Twenty-second Party congresses revealed the flagrant crimes committed by Stalin and many of his retainers—crimes that were especially horrendous because of their senseless cruelty. The killing of millions of totally innocent Soviet citizens, of which Stalin, Yezhov, Beria, and their accomplices were guilty, undermined people's faith in the revolutionary infallibility of the Party and struck an irrevocable blow to its moral authority. There remains only one way to restore confidence—to punish publicly those guilty for the Stalinist tyranny, regardless of the posts they hold, to carry out a Party purge, and to publish in full everything relating to this most difficult period in our country's history. Why hasn't this been done? Why are attempts being made even now to restore Stalin to his former glory? Isn't it obvious that any step in this direction will only lead to a further loss of confidence in the Party and government leadership?

Have you and other leaders of the Soviet government given sufficient consideration to the difficult moral position in which our young people find themselves, including the majority of Komsomol members? A substantial section of the youth cannot believe in the truths that we believed in, and this loss of faith in the spiritual values of the past allows the attitudes of despair and disenchantment, now fashionable in the West, to penetrate into the ranks of our young people by the most varied channels. Do you understand that the struggle for the youth is the struggle for our future, and that the situation cannot be saved by propaganda of any kind as long as that propaganda is not based on the truth? The policy of passing over in silence and glossing over the shortcomings as well as the crimes of the Stalin-cult period is creating a gulf between the Party leadership and the youth.

Why is it that many excellent books, whose publication would only help to advance the cause of Communism, are forbidden? Why isn't Hemingway's best book, *For Whom the Bell Tolls,* published here? [A censored edition was published in 1968.] And why is Eugenia Ginzburg's autobiographical tale [*Journey into the Whirlwind*], which is known to thousands of Soviet citizens in its manuscript form, also denied publication? Do you understand that this refusal to publish—solely because these books depict both the good and the bad in our life truthfully and without embellishment—does terrible harm to the Soviet Union? Whose needs are served by this kind of censorship?

The foundation of socialism is equality and fraternity among all citizens, the refusal to allow any discrimination whatsoever. Why is it, then, that to this day collective farmers in many parts of our country are denied the right to have an [internal] passport and thereby restricted in their rights and movement? Isn't this an insult to these Soviet citizens and doesn't it conflict with our constitution? [According to reforms of 1976–77, internal passports, which are required in order to travel and to change residence in the USSR, were to be given to collective farmers as well, though it remains unclear whether this reform has been fully implemented.]

The experience of the years since our revolution has shown that the chief danger in a young socialist society is the rise of "strong-willed" leaders who aspire to one-man rule and are intolerant of any criticism. Under a one-party system, with extremely strict party discipline, such leaders can easily eliminate those who get in their way and can become unlimited dictators. That's how it was not only with Stalin but also with Khrushchev. Shouldn't we draw the conclusion from this that more democratic procedures should be introduced in the countries where socialism has been victorious? I do not mean the introduction of a multiparty system but the democratization of the Communist Party itself, free and public discussion and debate, and the chance to criticize any Party leader openly, either in print or orally. There is no need for harsh, semimilitary discipline in the present circumstances; it is even harmful. The Soviet people have changed greatly, and we do not have any internal class enemies within the country— neither the bourgeoisie, the landlords, the kulaks, nor the aristocracy—against whom a bitter struggle has still to be waged. Along with democratization of the Party, privileges must be abolished for Party members, both the rank and file and the leadership. (For example, the right to hold high government posts is reserved exclusively for Communist Party members for some reason.)

The system of elections to the Soviets must be changed. Under the present system, only one slate of candidates is listed on the ballot and the outcome of the elections is thus foreordained. The Soviet voter should have the right to decide which of two or three candidates is the best. Why doesn't the Soviet government let candidates be nominated freely and a free choice be made among them? This would help all of our Soviets to function better, including the Supreme Soviet.

In the Soviet Union, by comparison with other socialist countries, there is a very large disparity between the highest and lowest wage levels. Alongside salaries exceeding 500–600 rubles a month, we find a large category of people who are paid no more than 40–60 rubles a month (for example, laboratory assistants in many scientific institutions, typists, and others). It is virtually impossible to live on such wages, and this obliges people in the lowest categories to seek ways, both legal and illegal, to supplement their earnings. Shouldn't wage scales for all industrial and office workers earning less than 60 rubles a month be reviewed at the earliest possible time and ways be found to narrow the gap between the minimum and maximum wage?

Why does official anti-Semitism still exist in our country, albeit in highly camouflaged form? It is enough to look at the lists of deputies in the local and republic-wide Soviets, as well as the Supreme Soviet, to see that there is hardly a single Jewish name among them. Exceptions are sometimes made, but only for the most outstanding figures in science, literature, and the arts. There are hardly any Jews among top Party officials or Party secretaries, not only in regional committees, but also in city and district committees. A conciliatory attitude toward such a horrendous evil as anti-Semitism absolutely cannot be permitted in today's world.

It is essential to expand freedom of scientific research not only in words but in deeds, to put an end to the dictatorship of certain individuals in science, and to stop the interference in scientific disputes by Party officials who are not qualified, however high the posts they hold. Supervision by the state in the realm of scientific theory is absolutely impermissible. This has been demonstrated by the unhappy experience of state support for the fallacious ideas of Olga Lepeshinskaya, Gevork Boshyan, Lysenko, and several other biologists and by the refusal for many years to recognize the theory of relativity and cybernetics. Don't you agree that full freedom of scientific research should become a central principle of policy for us?

I would like to note in passing that the same principle can be extended to literature and the arts. Methodological control is undeniably necessary in this sphere, but its main area of application should be in encouraging the development of good taste; it should not take the form of state support for a single school of art or literature and the prohibition of all others.

I earnestly request that my letter be given careful consideration and, above all, that it be understood. It is motivated solely by a desire to see the USSR not only the strongest socialist state but also the most advanced in all respects.

[No. 25, October 1966]

The Struggle for Soviet Ideology: Marxists vs. Slavophiles

Outwardly, official Soviet life—especially the Communist Party, censored press, and Marxist-Leninist ideology—may seem to be, as is often said, mono-lithic. The inner reality is quite different—a world of conflicting political groups, programs, and even ideologies. The following document testifies to one of the fundamental conflicts behind the official facade. It is a partial transcript (abridged here) of a fractious meeting of Soviet literary critics, all of them in good official standing, held in Moscow on April 25, 1969. Their quarrel was about the neo-Slavophile movement that emerged in official circles, centering around several important Party and state journals and newspapers, in the late 1960s. Under the conditions of Soviet censorship, literary criticism is often a way of expressing larger ideological and philosophical ideas. Thus, several young literary critics, including Viktor Chalmayev (born 1932) and Anatoly Lanshchikov (born 1929), became leading spokesmen of the new Slavophilism, with its un-Marxist emphasis on Russia's separate and unique destiny, anti-Western and often religious nation-alism, and the peasantry as the real source of eternal values. Their Soviet oppo-nents accused neo-Slavophiles of "anti-Marxist" views, but the movement actu-ally developed within the official ideology, revising and refilling Marxist-Leninist categories with the older philosophical ideas of nineteenth-century Slavophilism. The result was (and remains) a profound conflict inside official Soviet ideology, which has since acquired even larger public dimensions.[3] It can be interpreted, on one level, as a Soviet repetition of the conflict between Westernizers and Russophiles that divided the nineteenth-century intelligentsia. On another level, it relates to the growing conservatism and nationalism of the Brezhnev adminis-tration and to the dispute between those who see Stalin's reign as a betrayal of Russian Marxism or Bolshevism and those who defend it as part of a greater Russian tradition. In either case, the conflict between present-day Marxists and Slavophiles arose out of the widespread ideological malaise created by Stalinism and de-Stalinization, the "loss of faith" discussed above by the university teacher V.K., or what one speaker here calls "the spiritual vacuum that has developed in our country."

Kogan: Lanshchikov argues with Yuri Surovtsev, accusing him of putting words in Chalmayev's mouth. But the truth is that Chalmayev himself constructed a totally fantastic theory. Surovtsev is charged with "hunting up" such reactionary

---

3. See, for example, A. Yakovlev, "Protiv antiistorizma," *Literaturnaia gazeta*, November 15, 1975.

predecessors for Chalmayev as [the nineteenth-century philosopher] Konstantin Leontyev, who is also then said not to have been a reactionary at all. Lanshchikov argues in his article that Chalmayev has his own methodology. But we thought the problem was that Chalmayev fell into a number of unfortunate and incorrect formulations and slips of the tongue, and made some outright errors, for which he was being reprimanded—so far quite mildly. Lanshchikov acknowledges certain "excesses of method" on Chalmayev's part. But is method really what we are talking about here?

Fyodor Levin: The problem is that definite ideological tendencies are in these articles [by Chalmayev and others]. Lanshchikov is a professional critic. But in his polemic he reveals the same ideological tendencies. Things should not be made to look as though Surovtsev was the only one who disagreed with Chalmayev. Fyodor Chapchakhov's article in *Literaturnaya gazeta* appeared soon after Surovtsev's. These articles exposed Chalmayev's incorrect ideological tendencies. Chalmayev and his supporters do not see any class struggle in Russian history; they derive Marxism, through various clever stratagems, from [the seventeenth-century priest] Avvakum, as though the [real sources] of Lenin had never existed. They disregard all the popular revolts and revolutions, take no notice of Herzen, the revolutionary democrats, and so on and so forth. On the other hand, Chalmayev quotes from Leontyev. This is a total abandonment of Marx and a different conception of history.

In his debate with Surovtsev, Lanshchikov evaded all these ideological questions. He praised Chalmayev for his *intentions*. We have no suspicions concerning Chalmayev's intentions. After all, we are not investigating the individual case of Chalmayev. But you, Lanshchikov, are hiding behind the question of his intentions.

When Chalmayev speaks out against philistinism, lack of principle, and faddishness in literature, that is good. But when he discovers the wellspring of our history in the patriarchal peasant, when the working class and intelligentsia clearly do not exist for him, that is bad. You have evaded the most important thing in Russian history. I understand that you have been published in the same magazine as Chalmayev, in *Molodaya gvardiya*, and you feel an obligation because of that.

Chalmayev has laid bare his entire conception here. But, unfortunately, it also peeks through now and then in the articles by Mikhail Lobanov and Pavel Glinkin. An effort to efface Marxism is under way, and that is what disturbs me. What we are dealing with here is a certain ideological disorientation, a series of anti-Marxist articles. The wheel has slipped out of our hands.

(Comment from the floor: the magazine *Zhurnalist* has knocked it out of our hands.)

Levin: No, *Ogonyok* (The Little Light) has seized the wheel. And not only in literature but in literary policy as well. For example, Viktor Petelin recently wrote in *Ogonyok* that everyone persecuted Mikhail Bulgakov [in the 1930s] and only Stalin supported him. And, in *Molodaya gvardiya,* Grigory Konovalov declared that Stalin was a military leader of genius. It makes you throw up your hands to read all this.

Vadim Kozhinov: On Lanshchikov's article. I do not entirely agree with it, but his polemic with Surovtsev and Chalmayev is very interesting and serious. Of course, the arguments are unfortunately not about the most important thing, about literature's relation to life. The arguments are about something else.

Right-wing extremism has been defeated. The danger now comes from left-wing extremism. The danger no longer comes from the banks of the Elbe but from the banks of the Ussuri.

1. Right-wing extremism (fascism?) has plainly been compromised and is therefore less dangerous.

2. Left-wing extremism is attractive to young people, and in the West they are infected by it (Marcuse and others). Left-wing extremism dresses itself up in leftist phraseology. For that reason, it is now more dangerous.

Actually the threat is from both the West and the East. And for that reason the concluding part of Lanshchikov's article is very important.

Lanshchikov: (Expresses his thanks for the criticism which will help him in his work.)

My article appeared in the second issue of *Molodaya gvardiya.* But this issue went to the printer in November 1968, before I was able to read the articles by Pyotr Strokov or Chapchakhov in *Literaturnaya gazeta.* As for Chapchakhov, I congratulated him on a fine article. (To Vadim Sokolov, who had raised the question of morality.) You have not shown who is right. It irritates me when people start denouncing *Molodaya gvardiya* and the tendencies in its articles, without proving any of their points. That is what offended me about Surovtsev's article. You didn't understand the main thrust of my article. On the other hand, there are critics who are allowed to do anything. Let them show us a list of the critics who have the right to decide who is correct and who is blameworthy. We are all vulnerable to some extent. *Zhurnalist* rails against *Novy mir,* but *Novy mir* also curses at *Zhurnalist.*

(Comment from the floor: But there are general criteria!)

Lanshchikov: General criteria! What general criteria? Who laid them down? We don't need them.

Simon Dreiden (Leningrad): Nikolai Utekhin's article, which has been mentioned here, is on the borderline between politics and provocation. This slander is systematically disseminated in millions of copies in our country. Such mass media as *Ogonyok* and other publications are dishonestly being used for this purpose. What is the central danger today? The attempt to disavow what was said at the Twentieth Congress and to revive the Stalin cult. I am a historian. But there is a whole range of undeniable facts about the personality-cult era that I cannot publish, or even write about. Our failings are held up as a positive example. One article, another, and then a third has been published, expressing a similar trend. But where are the replies to them?

Feliks Kuznetsov: It seems we are going beyond the bounds of possible criticism here! I have already decided in my own mind, if I may say so, what these articles are. A certain tendency has appeared, which has been made a mass tendency. Some editors and critics have arbitrarily taken upon themselves the right to make literary policy, with aspirations toward Party supervision over literature, having a monopoly with their own understanding of Party-mindedness in literature.

However, we should not forget that the discussion is not with enemies but with fellow men of letters and that they have simply failed to define their attitude precisely enough toward certain problems. Sergei Lisitsky has written an article about Andrei Bitov from which it is clear that a serious discussion about the class element and the general human element is necessary, and that Bitov must be criticized, but in a different way. For Lisitsky, neither Bitov nor literature has any importance. What is important to him is to demonstrate that *Zhurnalist* is pursuing its own ideological line in literature.

Still, distinctions must be made. The articles in *Ogonyok* are one thing; the articles by Chalmayev and Lanshchikov are another. Their articles constitute a very serious phenomenon and require a serious approach. It's not the same thing as *Zhurnalist.*

Until recently we had two poles in literature, *Novy mir* and *Oktyabr.* Now we are observing the emergence of a third pole in literature and in public life. I am aware of this third pole. It has already taken shape around *Molodaya gvardiya* and *Nash sovremennik* (Our Contemporary). It is not a purely literary phenomenon. It is the product of certain profound processes. You can't deal with this phenomenon with a dozen people on *Literaturnaya gazeta,* as Levin proposed. This problem will be solved much more slowly, certainly not all at once. It is a phenomenon that clearly flows from the existing conditions and has its own spiritual roots.

Lobanov resolves all conflicts under the aegis of "spirituality." Ivan Drozdov in *Zhurnalist,* number 3, called his own article "The Downfall of the Unspiritual Word." There is obviously a tendency here, a desire to fill the spiritual vacuum that has developed in our country. Attempts are under way to find some central principle of spirituality, and this is one of the directions in which the search is going. This tendency finds support among students and intellectuals. They are looking for an answer in a direction that is customary in the history of Russian social thought: the popular and national foundations of our life.

In the nineteenth century two basic trends clashed on the battlefield, two concepts of spirituality. One was represented by the ferment of the 1830s and 1840s, the Westernizers, the revolutionary democrats, the Narodniks [Populists], and the Marxists. The second traditions stemmed from the Lovers of Wisdom and Chaadayev, and passed through our young Slavophiles, Vladimir Solovyov, Konstantin Leontyev (who incidentally does not fully belong to this category), through [the 1909 book] *Vekhi* (Landmarks)—which, I should remind you, bore the subtitle "Essays on the Russian Intelligentsia"—and through Berdyaev, Fyodorov, and Fedotov, if we are to include [late nineteenth- and early twentieth-century Russian] bourgeois philosophers.

It is not so simple just to skip over this second line. I am convinced of this now, after rereading the authors mentioned. This second trend used to hammer away at the trend represented by our Marxist intelligentsia, which descended from the Westernizers and democrats. They argued that the Westernizers did not express the Russian national line in any way. Actually, at the heart of the second tradition lies Russia before Peter the Great and its patriarchal principles.

The third position now forces us to stop and think. It is extremely interesting in the way it poses certain questions. What exactly does the national and popular tradition [of Russia] represent now, in our day? Looked at from this angle, Chalmayev's article was necessary, for it is impossible not to think about all these questions. The whole problem is the *way* they think about them. How do they reconcile their position with our contemporary reality? How to combine Chalmayev's position with Marxism? How can these things go together even from the methodological angle, let alone the viewpoint of Marxist dogmatists. In Chalmayev, one senses beneath the surface a scornful attitude toward the revolutionary-democratic tradition. This other line is closer to him than that of the revolutionary democrats.

It would be good if Chalmayev and his cothinkers answered some questions: about their view of these traditions and the present-day sources of the national-popular element; and—an even more serious question—How does the national and popular principle manifest itself in contemporary life?

You assume that it is manifested in the peasantry (as the Slavophiles thought in the nineteenth century). But the peasantry today is not at all the same. What we have here is an unrealistic, bookish conception of the people. You don't know the peasant of today. You get everything out of books. In order to ground all these questions in present-day reality, we must start thinking for ourselves, and not go back to the nineteenth century for our ideas.

Today you can't get away from the October Revolution.

(Kogan comments from the floor: That's for sure—there's no getting away from it.)

Kuznetsov: You can't get away from the October Revolution, from the fact that the country was Europeanized long ago. It is time to understand that our misfortunes are not from socialism but from not enough socialism, not from Europe but not enough Europe.

We believe that your intentions are good. But they must be placed on real foundations. Otherwise, be consistent and go all the way to God! Go to the patriarchal peasantry as an ideal. And that means, unavoidably, to go first of all to Orthodoxy (as opposed to the Catholic, Western way). Go all the way, then, to religion and idealist philosophy. From your point of view, Peter the Great destroyed the Orthodox trend, which is to say, the "truth of the people."

You want always to keep the people in mind. But first you should check to see what the people themselves want. To return to the past? Or the opposite, to have something new come their way? You must understand that traditions cannot be preserved forever and without change.

I am against sticking labels on people. I am in favor of people's having a thorough discussion, entering into an open debate—one which, I am convinced, you would not win. The truth is that the revolutionary democrats cherished the national traditions of the people no less than you.

Lanshchikov (his second and more interesting speech): You ask what we are seeking. We seek a lost ideal! Our young people do not find any ideal. This troubles even the Komsomol Central Committee. More exactly, ideals aren't discovered once and for all; they change from generation to generation. A literature that does not search for an ideal has already begun to mark time.

What is irritating about the criticism of [Stalin's] personality cult is that many years have passed and we are still criticizing the same old thing. We can't just criticize the cult. We also need positive ideals. We are all in favor of our country's being the bearer of a progressive ideal. Our country has a special road. Dostoevsky spoke of that. And that is precisely why the revolution was achieved in our country.

(Comment from the floor: That's Berdyaev's conception!)

Lanshchikov: There is a grain of rationality in everyone's thinking—in Berdyaev's too. But in our country, after thirty or forty years, people are suddenly opening up Berdyaev, Leontyev, and others. It's understandable that people might be carried away by them. After all, these thinkers could have had correct ideas—they were not self-seeking people who wanted to destroy everything.

Let's speak plainly. People shouldn't have ideas imposed on them that they never expressed. No one made an ideal out of [the primitive peasant]. We don't have any real literature about the intelligentsia, with the exception of Vasily Kurochkin's "The Freak." Whenever they write about the intelligentsia, there's a standard pattern: one is a careerist, the other's okay.

It is true that neither Fyodor Abramov nor Boris Mozhayev nor Vasily Belov [fiction writers whose subject is the present-day Soviet countryside] represents the ideal. But this is literature. And not literature of the village either (no one in the villages reads it), but literature for the intelligentsia. What have they given us, these writers? Through them we have restored our language. In quality, they come close to nineteenth-century literature. If you want to know, this trend began with Solzhenitsyn. Before Solzhenitsyn, there was Sholokhov's *Quiet Flows the Don.* And we didn't know Bulgakov or Andrei Platonov. Now we have discovered them. I think Bulgakov said more about the cult, and said it better, than anyone else in his *Master and Margarita.* We see the failings of village prose. But through it we are moving toward genuine literature.

On religion. I will say bluntly that if the role of [Russian] Orthodoxy is to be denied, I don't know what then remains of Russia. Should she have stayed forever in pagan backwardness? Orthodoxy can no more be dismissed than can Catholicism in Europe. We must use Dostoevsky's way of analyzing things: Where is there truth and where falsehood? (And there is truth on every side.) If the discussion began to take this line. . . . But it isn't able to take this line!

We do not idealize the peasantry, although our Russian literature came from the peasantry. We want to return to the source, not in order to remain there, but in order to proceed from its morality, from its ideal, and move ahead to build something new. The mission of our people is much more lofty than we now grant (think?). Words will come (are expected?) from us.

[No. 55, April 1969]

The Real State of the Economy
BY ABEL AGANBEGYAN

Philosophy is not the only subject hotly disputed inside Soviet officialdom. Economic policy has been a chronic source of bitter conflict between reformers and conservatives since the 1950s. This confidential report on Soviet economic problems was delivered by Academician Abel Aganbegyan (born 1932) to a group of Leningrad editors in June 1965, and recorded by someone present. Aganbegyan, one of the first Soviet specialists in mathematical economics, is director of the Novosibirsk Institute of Economics and Industrial Organization, a branch of the Academy of Sciences, and a leading proponent of fundamental change in the hypercentralized economic system inherited from Stalin. His outspokenness was characteristic of reformers during the late Khrushchev years, but also as late as 1965, when the Brezhnev-Kosygin leadership announced what turned out to be a short-lived and ill-fated program of economic reform. Aganbegyan's report, despite its somewhat dated statistics, is still of considerable interest. His candid and knowledgeable discussion of the array of serious economic problems—inflation, unemployment, industry's structural inefficiency and declining growth rate, laggardly technology, the malfunctioning of the planning mechanism, the crisis in agriculture, the crushing burden of defense expenditures—contrasts vividly with the way the Soviet press still analyzes, denies, or simply ignores these problems, which persist today. (Many of the problems described by Aganbegyan led to the government's decision, in the early 1970s, to try to import foreign technology on a large scale.) Nor should Aganbegyan's flat assertion that CIA estimates in the mid-1960s were "an absolutely accurate assessment of the situation in our economy" go unnoticed.

In the last six years, the rate of growth of our economy declined by a factor of approximately three. In agriculture, there was approximately a tenfold decline (from an 8 percent annual growth rate to 0.8 percent). During this time, the increase in turnover declined by a factor of approximately four. And the rise in real income of the Soviet population also leveled off greatly during these years —real income being extremely low in general. (At present, the average per capita income stands at 40–45 rubles per month.) Since 1958, according to a number of indicators, absolute growth has also slowed. The most remarkable thing about all this is that the slowdown was completely unexpected!

In 1958, our economists predicted that an economic downturn would soon begin in the United States and the other leading capitalist countries. Our specialists' most optimistic predictions put the annual growth rate in the United States at no higher than 2.5 percent. But, in fact, the annual rate of expansion in the United States, beginning in 1958, proved to be 5 percent. (And we must keep in mind that the U.S. economic potential is twice as great as ours.)

During the same years, we experienced a decline in the effective accumulation of productive resources. The annual increase in industrial output keeps growing smaller. The gap between the potential for technical progress and the realization of that potential has increased.

Our industrial structure is the worst and most backward of all the industrially developed countries. Our plans for the introduction of new technology (not very good ones, incidentally) are fulfilled by no more than 70 percent.

In the most important sector of heavy industry—machine-tool production—there are about two million machine tools. In quantity, this is equivalent to the American, but only half of our machine tools are operational; the other half are either not in use or in repair. Our fixed productive assets are not utilized as well as those of the capitalist countries. We have an enormous underutilization of capacity in the machine-tool sector.

Half the timber processed in the USSR is lost; from the remaining half, we produce three times less than in the United States, five times less than in West Germany, and eight times less than in Sweden.

In recent years, there has been an enormous build-up of reserves held by industrial enterprises; stocks of goods amounting to three billion new rubles have accumulated. This is more than occurs in a crisis year in the West. Moreover, in the West during a crisis there is, on the one hand, an enormous quantity of goods that go unsold and, on the other hand, customers are short of money. But in our case there is, on the one hand, an excess of goods and, on the other, a continual increase in the amount of money the population has! Even the repeated price rises of the last few years have been unable to stop this process. The rise in prices in the USSR is inflationary in nature.

At present, the question of employment is a very serious problem (in the West they call it joblessness). In the coming five-year period an army of ten million young people looking for work will be upon us, and jobs will have to be found for them. Meanwhile, in the last two years, we have observed a significant rise in unemployment in our country. This applies especially to small and medium-sized cities. On the average, in such cities, 20–30 percent of the population capable of working and looking for work cannot find employment. In the major cities, this process has affected approximately 8 percent of the population.

The situation is not good as far as the effort to raise living standards is concerned. We are lagging very far behind the projected figures in this area. In practice, there has been a decline in the standard of living in the last few years. This is another sector in which the targets of the seven-year plan have not been met.

Everything we have outlined above is extremely disturbing, because this is not just a matter of the state of our economy for the moment. It is an overall tendency, and that is much worse! Nothing like this has ever happened in the USSR before! We can tell approximately when the severe slump began, but no one now knows when the overall tendency began or when it will end!

What is the cause of this tendency?

The objective causes are external. A great share of our resources is spent on defense. It is very hard for us to keep pace with the United States, since the outlays of the two countries for defense are approximately equal but our economic potential is only half of the American. Of approximately 100 million in the USSR who work, about 30–40 million are employed in the defense industry.

We have a permanent disadvantage in trade with other countries. Essentially what we sell are raw materials, because many countries (including socialist countries) are reluctant to buy finished products from us, because their quality is not very high. Because of the poor organization of the extractive industry, backwardness in technology and production methods, and so on, it usually costs us more to extract one ton of raw materials than we can earn when we sell it abroad. (Of course, we must be governed by the general world prices.) But the external causes are not the main ones in our difficult economic situation.

The main causes are internal. They can be divided into two groups. The first group of causes are related to the wrong direction of the country's economic development. The second group have to do with the disparity between the requirements of modern life and our system of planning, incentives, and management.

GROUP ONE

For many years, we have stuck to the course of superindustrialization. Even in recent years when the need for this disappeared, the same course continued. While this went on, artificial restraints were kept on sectors of the economy not having to do with heavy industry, to their detriment. As a result, there was a continual process of unequal exchange within the country.

Agriculture. The collective farms annually produce a net income, expressed in value terms, of 22 billion rubles. Of this sum, the state takes 11 billion—1 billion through taxes and 10 billion through the "price scissors" [the discrepancy between industrial and agricultural prices]. The remaining 11 billion is plainly insufficient to reimburse the collective farmers for their labor after equipment is paid for, after assets are assigned to the capital fund of each farm, and so forth. Calculations have shown that under present conditions a collective farmer earns on the average one ruble, fifty kopeks per day on the collective farm, as opposed to three rubles, fifty kopeks on his private plot. Is it worth it for him to work on the collective farm? Of course not! In the present state of affairs, if people were allowed to leave the villages, practically no one would stay there.

The money the state obtains from the collective farms is primarily invested in heavy industry (a large part of it in the coal industry, etc.). There is no necessity for this any longer, because, for example, we produce more coke than the United States. But to smelt one ton of steel, we use three times as much coke as does the United States. Natural gas is not delivered to metallurgical plants (there are no pipes, but the main problem is poor planning). Thus, we keep expanding the coal industry, and it devours enormous resources. In the USSR, construction projects regularly fall behind schedule, and construction organizations as a rule do not make efficient use of the assets assigned to them.

GROUP TWO

Our system of planning, incentives, and management in industry was established in the 1930s. Subsequently the labels were changed, but everything continued to be based on administrative methods in planning and management. The extreme centralism and lack of democracy in economic matters has had a very negative effect on our economy.

How are plans drawn up? They are drafted by the regional economic councils [which have been abolished] and the union republics; then they go to the nationwide State Planning Commission, which in practice discards them and substitutes its own plan, often having nothing in common with the (somewhat) realistic plans of the economic councils and union republics. The State Planning Commission's plan usually requires rates that are three times higher than those desired by the regional bodies.

Price and value relations. The regulating role of price and of value relations is virtually absent in our economy. Centralized distribution is the main thing. Our system of economic levers has nothing in common with the plan. It is against the interests of the economy.

In fact, there is a contradiction between the interests of the state and those of the enterprises. There is absolutely no balance in the State Planning Commission's plan, and it is impossible to establish a balance, because it would require that 4,000 product categories be balanced, and this would require $\frac{4000^3}{2}$ man-hours. The plan is left without a balance in the most primitive way, for if a balance was made, it would be impossible to accomplish anything—if some product was lacking, that would lead to the complete collapse of the economy. But that does not happen.

We totally lack information. No one really knows what is going on in the economy. The figures published by the Central Statistical Administration are inflated. And so our planning and economic management goes on without any true information about the situation.

The Central Statistical Administration cannot cope with the task assigned to it with the statistical data-processing equipment it has. It does not have a single electronic computer, and it is not planning to acquire any!

It is extremely difficult for economists to do their work, owing to the absurd secrecy surrounding many statistical data. For example, we obtain many figures, such as the quarterly average wages for workers in certain branches of Soviet industry, from American journals sooner than they are released by the Central Statistical Administration.

Incidentally, the polemic that developed in the pages of the Soviet press last year between our Central Statistical Administration and the U.S. Central Intelligence Agency was foolish, because the Americans gave an absolutely accurate assessment of the situation in our economy, whereas Stavrovsky sought to prove the impossible. Many of the statistics published by the Central Statistical Administration prove, upon analysis, to be simply absurd. Thus, our statistical agency argued that we brought in a harvest of 8 billion poods of grain. This is a lie! We never brought in that much. If that were so, we would have sold grain abroad, but the fact is we were buying grain! In Novosibirsk, we made a fairly exact estimate of how much grain is needed to meet the food requirements in the USSR, including the necessary amount for technical needs. Furthermore, since our press stated that much of the grain is fed to cattle and hogs, we added this quantity. The result we obtained was approximately 4.5 billion poods, but supposedly we harvested 8 billion! Where did the rest go? Not only did we not sell any abroad; we bought some! The Central Statistical Administration counts the grain in the storage bins, but evaporation reduces it by 10 percent while it lies in storage. The agency also estimates maize when it is ripe, not dry. And so on. That is how these figures are obtained.

Our economists have made a number of different proposals for reorganizing the entire Soviet economy. The regional economic councils are to be eliminated. Trusts, concerns, firms, associations, and the like are to be established that will be fully independent. There will be ministries for each sector, but their functions will be different. They will not get in the way of the managers. The government is currently working out these questions.

[No. 11, August 1965]

Scientists and the Danger of Nuclear War
BY ANDREI SAKHAROV AND ERNST HENRY

Like the "repentant noblemen" who founded the oppositionist intelligentsia in tsarist Russia, a number of privileged Soviet citizens abandoned official careers to become active dissidents in the late 1960s. None was more eminent than Academician Andrei Sakharov (born 1921). Since the samizdat appearance of his soon famous "Memorandum" in 1968, published abroad as Progress, Coexistence, and Intellectual Freedom *(New York, 1968), a long analytical plea for the democratization of the Soviet system and peace in world affairs, Sakharov has gone from the exalted status of one of the country's highest-ranking physicists —he is often called the "father of the Soviet hydrogen bomb" because of his scientific discoveries in 1948–50—to the persecuted life of leader of the democratic dissident movement. The government that for many years showered him with extraordinary honors and privileges finally banished him from Moscow in 1980 and continues to threaten him with worse. This dialogue between Sakharov and Ernst Henry (pen name of Semyon Rostovsky), a well-known official writer on political subjects, is notable for several reasons. (Henry's contribution to the dialogue has been abridged considerably here.) Their discussion was organized privately in 1967 on the theme of "World Science and World Politics," apparently to prepare a newspaper article written jointly by Sakharov and Henry later that year and banned by the Party Central Committee. Sakharov tells us that this document represented an important stage in his political development.[4] Though his views have changed substantially during his years in opposition, his thoughts here on nuclear testing, antimissile systems, and arms control remain particularly timely and authoritative. Finally, Sakharov's dialogue with Henry took place just before his emergence as an outspoken dissident and thus is another example of the sometimes thin line between an independent-minded official and an ostracized dissenter.*

The shadowy and fascinating Ernst Henry (Semyon Rostovsky) deserves a special introductory note. Now about seventy-three years old, he was a Russian Comintern agent on the Central Committee of the German Communist Party until Hitler came to power in 1933. Posted to the Soviet embassy in London between 1936 and 1951, under yet another alias, he became the Soviet contact for the espionage ring of Philby, Maclean, Burgess, and Blunt. Apparently, Henry was summoned to Moscow, along with Maclean, in 1951 and arrested. When he

4. *Politicheskii dnevnik*, I, 197; *Sakharov Speaks* (New York, 1974), p. 36.

emerged from prison in 1953, he was a bitter anti-Stalinist. Between 1965 and 1970, after establishing himself as an official Soviet publicist, Henry played an active role in organizing anti-Stalinist protests among intellectuals in the Soviet Establishment, wrote a widely circulated samizdat essay blaming Stalin for the victories of German fascism, and even developed ties with some dissidents, while remaining a writer in good official standing. His quasi-dissident activities apparently ended in the early 1970s, causing still more speculation about his enigmatic role in Soviet politics.[5]

Ernst Henry: I would like to share some thoughts with you and raise some questions. How do you see the role of scientists in current international politics? Don't you think the time has come for them to demand a greater voice in world affairs.

Never before in the history of humanity has so much depended on scientists. But the fact is that the role of scientists in world affairs by no means corresponds to their importance in modern society, to the relative weight of the exact sciences in the production process and in public administration.

Do you agree that scientists today should participate in the most active way not only in technical, economic, and cultural matters but also in world politics? I know you not only as an outstanding scientist but also as a courageous individual with a vital imagination, one who always thinks for himself and who would not be content to gnaw at your own ball of cheese. What is needed, in your opinion?

Andrei Sakharov: I will begin with an example that has already become part of history. In 1963, the well-known treaty ending nuclear-weapons testing in the atmosphere, under water, and in outer space was signed in Moscow. The Moscow treaty stopped the poisoning of the atmosphere that was dooming more than a hundred thousand of our contemporaries and descendants every year. It slowed down the arms race, and helped clarify the political position of a number of countries. It can rightly be regarded as the first step in the escalation of peace in the 1960s. I should remind you that the basis for the signing of the Moscow treaty was laid by an extensive, worldwide campaign among scientists and intellectuals in which such prominent representatives of science as Joliot-Curie, Linus Pauling, and Albert Schweitzer took part. This was an undeniable confirmation of the effectiveness of scientists and intellectuals in trying to solve the most important political problems.

It is the job of progressive scientists and intellectuals all over the world to discuss all problems openly and without prejudice, including the most sensitive ones. I have no doubt that science in our country and the West can help the cause of escalating peace, and help it in the most substantial way.

5. See Medvedev and Medvedev, *In Search of Common Sense* (forthcoming); and "Anthony Blunt's Soviet Spymaster Is Unmasked," *The Observer* (London), December 2, 1979.

Henry: How exactly? I know that you are a scientist and not a diplomat. What, in your opinion, are the specific ways in which this cause—the most important for humanity today—can be supported?

Sakharov: A number of very important proposals have been spelled out by the Soviet government, the governments of the other socialist countries, and the World Peace Council. I and several of my colleagues are especially concerned at present about the problem of a so-called moratorium on antimissile defense systems. This is the very problem that Comrade Aleksei Kosygin touched on recently at a press conference in New York, observing that it must be studied not in isolation from the problem of disarmament but as part of the whole question of universal disarmament. This question has hardly been discussed as yet in the Soviet press. It belongs to the category of highly sensitive matters that are difficult to discuss openly, but it is more important than ever to begin such a discussion.

As everyone knows, the United States and the Soviet Union possess enormous stockpiles of strategic missiles with thermonuclear warheads. The two countries are, speaking figuratively, armed with nuclear "swords." The construction of an antimissile defense system would mean adding a "shield" to the "sword." I think that such an expansion of nuclear missile armament would be very dangerous.

Henry: Why?

Sakharov: This is why. Under present political and technological conditions, such a "shield" could create the illusion of invulnerability. For the "hawks" and "madmen," a shield would increase the lure of nuclear blackmail. It would strengthen their attraction to the idea of a "preventive" thermonuclear strike. Don't you think there are crazy politicians and generals who would seize on the creation of such a "shield" to argue that thermonuclear war could serve as a modern "continuation of politics by other means"—to use the formula of Clausewitz?

Henry: I have been writing for years about such irrational politicians and generals in the capitalist world. Of course you are right.

Sakharov: But if Clausewitz's formula were applied across the board in our day and age, we would be dealing not with the "continuation of politics by other means" but with the total self-destruction of civilization, despite the existence of a "shield." The destruction of hundreds of millions of people, the genetic deformation of future generations, the destruction of cities and industry, transport, communication, agriculture, and the educational system, the outbreak of famine and epidemics, the rise of a savage and uncontrollable hatred of scientists and "intellectuals" on the part of civilization's surviving victims, rampant superstition, ferocious nationalism, and the destruction of the material and informational basis of civilization—all this would throw humanity centuries back, to the age of barbarism, and bring it to the brink of self-destruction. This is a gloomy prognosis, but we can't just brush the facts aside.

Here is one of them. We can roughly estimate the number of victims of one thermonuclear explosion. The area of fires from the explosion of a typical thermonuclear device—say, of six megatons—and the force of the explosion are three hundred times greater than those of the Hiroshima bomb, and the area of destruction is forty-five times greater. The detonation of such a warhead over a city would create a 200-square-kilometer area of fire and total destruction. More than a million people would meet agonizing deaths under the ruins of buildings, choking on brick dust and dying from burns. Radioactive fallout renders an enormous area, thousands of square kilometers, uninhabitable by living things for a great many years afterward. These figures should be multiplied by the number of explosions to be expected in a general thermonuclear war. (Of course, one must allow for the fact that not all the warheads would explode in heavily populated areas.)

Henry: Approximately how many atomic blasts might there be?

Sakharov: The argument that thermonuclear devices are too expensive is a myth. In any thermonuclear weapons system, the warheads are the cheapest component. The highly industrialized atomic powers can, for all practical purposes, produce as many of them as they need. Therefore the estimate of 100,000 thermonuclear explosions for five nuclear powers is not at all impossible. For such stockpiles to be built, it is enough to have several years of war fever or twenty to twenty-five years of "calmer" cold war. Part of such an amount of time has already elapsed.

Henry: In other words, it's true that the nuclear powers have accumulated enough destructive force to kill a hundred billion people—thirty times the number inhabiting the globe? And instantaneous destruction is a foregone conclusion?

Sakharov: Yes, that's right.

Henry: Then I have a question: Is it possible, in your opinion, to construct an effective antimissile defense system against a powerful enemy?

Sakharov: At the present level of military technology, no. Not one of the nuclear powers is able to spend many times more resources—material, intellectual, and financial—on its "shield" than an enemy of comparable strength can spend on its "sword." Where there are approximately equal outlays, the "shield" is only effective as a way of heating up the arms race and forcing the enemy to drain its budget. Today the technology of offensive weapons is far more advanced than that of defensive systems. In general, the situation is as follows. A major nuclear power can choose several dozen key enemy targets or regions and concentrate hundreds of missiles with multimegaton warheads on those targets. They can protect these missiles from the effects of the nuclear explosions of the enemy's antimissiles (except in the case of a direct hit, in which case one antimissile missile is lost for each attack missile destroyed, or each decoy missile). They can also protect them from laser beams and other known means of antimissile defense. They can saturate the enemy's skies with tens of thousands of decoy missiles, which are cleverly made to move and function like armed missiles, and thereby exhaust the enemy's antimissile defenses. And they can employ a wide variety of maneuvers, interference techniques, and camouflage. The simplest method, tactically, for breaking through an antimissile system and destroying the enemy's tracking stations is to flood certain enemy sectors with attack missiles in such density as to overstrain the network of missile-detecting stations, the antimissile-missile launching stations, highly complex computerized stations, and so on.

In past wars, the use of new tactical or technical devices proved highly effective at first, even when a simple antidote was quickly found. But in thermonuclear war such initial effectiveness may be decisive. And who knows how many unexpected innovations each of the sides may have waiting in its secret laboratories?

A vivid example of the way in which many years of work on an antimissile system can be instantly canceled out is the American early-warning system. This network of stations stretching over thousands of kilometers, which cost the United States enormous efforts and resources, became obsolete with the appearance of Soviet orbital missiles, which can come at their targets from any direction. The early-warning stations were, in effect, taken from the rear. Besides that, the unwieldy antennae on these stations are highly unstable and can literally be blown over by distant blasts.

Henry: That's clear. Now let's return to the question of the possible use of an antimissile system by an aggressor as a means of attempting, with impunity, to destroy the enemy or bring him to his knees.

Sakharov: In general, the illusion of impunity is just that—an illusion. Such a condition cannot occur. But what we must emphasize above all is that a preventive strike by an aggressor against the antimissile installations of an enemy of equal strength, with the expectation of impunity, is not very realistic. The country under attack still has a large number of missiles in "hard" underground launching pads or on submarines or on camouflaged mobile launching devices. It still has its choice of a counterblow. Escalation of the war can turn to the aggressor's disadvantage; its antimissile system will not save it. The impotence of such systems is especially evident in a nuclear war in which radioactivity becomes the main weapon, and the victim of aggression, on the brink of defeat, may resort to such a war.

Henry: The supporters of the arms race in the United States, as we know, are opposed to a general disarmament agreement. What they count on is the exhaustion of the Soviet economy, which they do not think can sustain the additional burden of an antimissile system.

Sakharov: Such military-economic prognoses are always risky. One should not suppose that the USSR is obliged to copy exactly the Pentagon's military-spending pattern or make the same decisions on technology. In particular, it must be kept in mind that every ruble or dollar spent on strengthening the "sword" compensates for a much larger sum spent by the opposing power on its "shield." Furthermore, I would like to stress that an effective defense against a massive attack by a powerful enemy is impossible. The achievement of more modest objectives, which are nevertheless crucial for saving lives, defensive measures against a surprise thermonuclear attack on a smaller scale (one having the aim of provocation, for example)—such things are entirely possible and necessary.

Henry: That's clear. No one has—or could have—a real guarantee of safety in the event of thermonuclear war. After 700,000 years of existence, the human race is actually threatened with extinction on the eve of its greatest forward advance in history. A spark in any part of the world can start a fire; the fire can lead to a global explosion; and the explosion, to the end. Can the world keep living this way, with history becoming transformed into one vast chain reaction? An agreement on global peaceful coexistence and universal disarmament has become the problem of problems for everyone.

Sakharov: All of us know that the socialist camp bases its policies on that very proposition.

Henry: And what if the American political leaders wish to keep playing with fire in the same old way?

Sakharov: Then the American people must have their say—with the intellectuals and scientists by no means the last in line.

Henry: Here we have come back to our starting point—the role of scientists in contemporary world affairs. It seems that scientists can make a great contribution, a very great one, to the cause of peace. They can demand—and demand insistently—that the drift toward further escalation of imperialist aggression be stopped. All that is needed is the will.

Sakharov: The fact is that American scientists—with the exception of those lost to the military-industrial complex—understand the total senselessness, cruelty, and criminality of the Vietnam War. They understand that bright hopes for the reduction of world tensions are being jeopardized by this war. The historic responsibility of American scientists and intellectuals at this critical juncture in world history is very great. If they deny their active or passive support to the war machine, if they can help explain to the American people how much more important the preservation of peace is than any or all American domestic problems, the war machine will begin to lose its power and more favorable circumstances will emerge—for ending the American aggression and allowing the national-liberation movement to develop freely. The role of scientists and progressive intellectuals, their ways of thinking and acting, will be enormously enhanced throughout the world. Shoulder to shoulder with the working class and in opposition to imperialist reaction, nationalism, and adventurism, the scientists and intellectuals must become aware of their power as one of the most important bulwarks of the idea of peaceful coexistence.

[No. 30, March 1967]

Viewpoints on the Possibility of a Soviet-Chinese War

Few, if any, topics agitate Soviet public opinion more than that of hostilities between the Soviet Union and the People's Republic of China. By the late 1960s, the former alliance between these two Communist giants, so dissimilar in other ways, had dissolved into intense political, ideological, cultural, and finally military enmity. Both sides built up forces along their 4,000-mile border, and military skirmishes broke out in 1969. In collecting for Political Diary, *in 1969–70, opinions about Soviet-Chinese relations and the prospect of an all-out war, Roy Medvedev explained that the subject was "being discussed in the USSR not only in the General Staff headquarters and Politburo, but in much broader circles, among intellectuals, workers, former military personnel, and elsewhere." Medvedev encountered seven "basic viewpoints," which are printed below in abridged form. It is significant that all of the viewpoints, except the devoutly international- ist perspective of the Old Bolshevik, took for granted animosity between the two countries and expressed no sympathy for China. This confirms other evidence that the Soviet populace and government share a general fear of and hostility toward China. On related questions, however, opinions differ sharply. One advo- cates, for example, "preventive war," while another insists that such an action would be the "greatest war crime in history." And, as in the United States, conflicting lessons are drawn from the experience of World War II.*

1) The View of N., a Research Fellow and Specialist on China

The war hysteria now being whipped up in China is mainly for domestic reasons, meant for internal consumption. There is no real threat of a major war now, nor will there be for a long time to come. The situation in China is such that the leaders of that country feel a powerful compulsion to maintain the myth of a military threat in order to keep the masses under submission and to justify the low standard of living. This has been the situation for a long time. It is well known that, in the late 1950s, China caused a conflict over the islands in the Gulf of Taiwan. In the early 1960s, the Chinese leaders provoked military clashes with India. Now they are provoking disputes along the Soviet border and building up the myth of a threat from the north. But even though China has several dozen atomic and hydrogen bombs, it is not ready for war and does not want an all-out war. China does not yet have long-range or medium-range missiles, and it has few modern planes, tanks, and other arms.

It should be kept in mind, N. adds confidentially, that our government also

has certain internal difficulties, and some of our leaders would find it advantageous if attention were diverted to an external threat. For that reason the Soviet
reaction to this or that border violation has been harsher in a number of cases
than it was in previous years.

*2) The View of K., a Doctor of Sciences; G., a Highly Placed Ministry
Official; and I., an Officer in the Reserves.*

At present, China is not ready for a major war. It is interested only in creating
tensions, which will help it not only to divert its people's attention from domestic
difficulties but actually to prepare for a major war in the future, and to do so at
a forced pace. As soon as China has built up sufficient military force for a major
war, as soon as it has an adequate stockpile of atomic and hydrogen bombs and
missiles, it will certainly start a war, and first of all a war with the Soviet Union.
When Hitler came to power in Germany in the 1930s, a major war in Europe
became inevitable. Germany's war against the USSR also became inevitable.
Now, in the same way, war with China is inevitable. And the reason for this
inevitability is demographic. China is overpopulated; it may already have a billion
people. The Soviet East has vast sparsely inhabited areas that China wants to
take.

A war with China five or ten years from now would be very hard for us and
might end disadvantageously, since China has such a great numerical superiority
over us in our eastern territories. In place of the present internal disorders, there
may come unity under a military-style totalitarian dictatorship. Fanaticism and
chauvinism will increase. In the face of this mortal danger, we should seriously
consider the possibility of a preventive war against China. It is now, when China
is not ready for a major war, that we must strike a blow, possibly with conventional
weapons, at the main centers of China's atomic and missile industries and destroy
its main missile bases. Then we could create an impenetrable stretch of territory,
an impassable zone, by building extensive fortifications and contaminating the
zone by using chemical and radiological weapons. If China used atomic devices
against our cities in Siberia, the Far East, and Central Asia, we too would have
to make an atomic strike against China's main cities. This is a hard decision, but
there is no other way of preventing a new Tartar yoke.

3) The View of N., a Historian and Doctor of Sciences, and B., a Writer.

No preventive war of any kind against China can be permitted. A preventive
war is a war of aggression. If we started a preventive war against China, all the
Western countries and Japan would come to the aid of China, the victim of
aggression. War between the two largest socialist countries would deal a death-
blow to the world Communist movement and to socialism in general. A strike
against two or three of China's military centers would not destroy its military

potential, which includes missiles and nuclear weapons. The Soviet Union is not ready for a war in its eastern part. We do not have roads or the economic resources to render a border more than 7,000 kilometers long impassable. War with China would set back our economy and bring ruin to our country. An invasion of China is unthinkable; our army would become hopelessly entangled there. The use of chemical or radiological weapons cannot be allowed for moral reasons. A nuclear strike there would destroy not only a great many Chinese but also a large part of the population of Japan, half of India, Vietnam, and Southeast Asia in general, as well as a significant portion of the Soviet Far East. Humanity would never forgive us for such a catastrophe. This would be regarded as the greatest war crime in history. No one would pay any attention to arguments about a possible future war by China against the USSR as a justification for preventive war now.

If even the smallest chance for a peaceful solution to the problem exists, it must be pursued. Under no circumstances should the Soviet Union be the first to start a major war with China. Such a war is not inevitable. China is preparing for war, but it is not by any means bound to start one. Over a five- or ten-year period a great many things can change inside China and in the world. We must prepare for possible aggression by China, but we must rule out any preventive strike as a means of warding off such aggression. This would be madness. Moreover, anything we destroy in China we would have to rebuild ourselves, since the ultimate aim of war with China would have to be the establishment of a friendly regime there, to which we would provide economic assistance.

4) View of V., an Old Bolshevik

A century or two from now, when socialism and Communism exist all over the earth and all borders and territorial disputes will have lost their significance, when there is full freedom of travel and people will be able to live wherever they wish—our Soviet Far East and part of Siberia and Kazakhstan will be settled by Chinese, not Russians. Without the help of the Chinese, we will never open up these vast regions. Many parts of European Russia, as we know, have not yet been brought into full use. When we had good relations with China, many hundreds of thousands of Chinese worked under contract in the cities of Siberia and the Soviet Far East. China constitutes a vast reservoir of labor, and it would not be wise to overlook this resource in attempting to open up Siberia and the Far East.

But since all questions of borders and territorial claims will have lost their significance in a hundred years, it makes no sense to start a war today over such questions and risk the annihilation of hundreds of millions of Chinese and tens of millions of Russians and other nationalities in our country. War with China would take more lives than the entire population of Siberia and the Soviet Far East. Moreover, these areas would probably be devastated, since China might use atomic weapons there even without medium-range missiles. Therefore, war or an attempt at a military solution should be avoided, if necessary at the price of territorial concessions, so long as this allows us to prevent a large-scale conflict.

5) View of S., an Academician

The Soviet Union cannot unilaterally agree to territorial concessions. Any move toward preventive war, in which our country would be seen as the aggressor by almost all the world, is equally inadmissible. War with China is a possibility, but the USSR should never be the one to start it. Under no circumstances should we invade Chinese territory. If China starts a war, it will apparently be impossible to avoid the use of atomic weapons at the front lines, i.e., tactical atomic weapons. The use of strategic weapons for an all-out blow at the enemy's home front cannot be permitted. This would be an act of lawlessness. After all, practically the entire Soviet population signed the Stockholm petition against the use of atomic weapons. Similarly, there are resolutions of the Supreme Soviet against such action. On the other hand, in the event of war, the USSR could not hold the Far East or sections of Eastern Siberia because in those areas China is many times our superior in numbers. This being the case, the USSR should make a strategic retreat and establish a line of defense on the inland side of Lake Baikal. China could not successfully invade Soviet Central Asia or Kazakhstan, because these are heavily populated areas and China would have to send its troops over mountains and through deserts. The seizure of part of our eastern territory by an aggressive China would bring it no advantages from an economic point of view; a war would cost it dozens of times more. We can expect in the future that these issues could be worked out by political negotiations.

6) View of M., a Scientist, and T., a Writer

The Soviet Union can make certain concessions in discussing minor border disputes. In many cases, the border follows a line that is not convenient for China. It goes along the Chinese side of the Ussuri River, for example, instead of down the center channel. In a number of cases, small changes in the border along the Amur and in Kazakhstan are feasible, to adjust for traditional cattle-driving trails, and so on. But no major territorial concessions to China are possible at this time. That does not mean that war with China is now inevitable. In the mid-1930s, a major war could have been avoided in Europe if timely measures had been taken to establish collective security. Hitler would not have dared to start a war under those circumstances.

The Soviet Union is now isolated. We find our relations with Europe and America strained, and we are involved in the Middle East conflict. All this emboldens the provocateurs in Peking. They take advantage of the fears the European countries have of us in order to strengthen their own military potential. West Germany and several other capitalist countries are in fact helping the

Chinese produce missiles and atomic bombs. Even the United States government has begun to make certain contacts with China.

War with China is possible but not inevitable. Demographic factors do not play the decisive role at present. It is not enough for us to strengthen our border and increase the military potential of the eastern part of the USSR, while hoping for internal changes in China. We must also pursue an energetic policy aimed at establishing collective security in Europe and throughout the world. We should take steps to improve relations with West Germany and the United States. Although the chief blame for the worsening of relations does not lie with the USSR, a certain amount does depend on us.

Of course, we can carry out a new foreign policy and elaborate new foreign-policy perspectives only if we succeed in preventing the restoration of the Stalin cult within the USSR and the strengthening of the Stalinist currents. The revival of a tough and dogmatic Stalinist line would inevitably mean a strain in our relations with Western Europe and with all other countries, including our allies in the Warsaw Pact and Yugoslavia.

7) View of R—v, an Officer

In his opinion, no Chinese army, even the most numerous, could occupy Siberia or the Soviet Far East, in light of the Soviet Union's present technical superiority. With minimal losses on our side, the Chinese divisions could be destroyed by missiles and planes and other technical means. There would be no hand-to-hand fighting or frontal assaults of any kind. From this point of view, the sparse population and vast expanses of Siberia, its severe climate, and so on are advantages for the Soviet Union in a war with China. Military men, however, insist on the building of a railway [the Baikal-Amur Line] north of Lake Baikal in order to deepen the zone of potential strategic defense. In R—v's opinion, Soviet armies would be able, in the event of war with China, to break through any Chinese defenses and march through that country "with fire and sword," destroying all its main strategic centers. But the Soviet armies would not be able to hold any Chinese territory, and would not try. After such a sweep through China, they would return to their Soviet bases.

[Nos. 63 and 68, December 1969 and May 1970]

A Deported Nation Appeals to President Mikoyan

Dissident ranks were broadened in the 1960s and 1970s by the frustrated grievances of various minority groups in the multinational Soviet Union. The plight of Soviet ethnic Germans, one of the small nationalities brutally deported en masse from their Volga River region during the war of 1941–45, is another example of the relationship between the Stalinist past, inadequate changes by successive post-Stalin leaderships, and the rise of civil-rights and emigration movements. Descendants of Germans who had settled in Russia in the 1760s under Catherine the Great, the Volga Germans were falsely accused of collaborating with the Nazi invaders and forcibly exiled to Central Asia in August–September 1941; their "autonomous republic," a constitutional entity that recognized their historic homeland in the USSR, was abolished. Stalin's deportation of small nations, which had victimized several million men, women, and children, was repudiated by Khrushchev at the Twentieth Party Congress. Nevertheless, the Volga Germans (like the Crimean Tartars) were denied any legal redress until a decree of August 29, 1964, formally rehabilitated them and restored their civil rights. The decree did not, however, give them the right, obtained by several other deported nations, to return to their homeland; in effect, it left these two million people in perpetual exile. This circumstance brought a delegation of Volga Germans to Moscow for a meeting, on June 7, 1965, with Soviet President Anastas Mikoyan (1895–1978) and Aleksandr Shelepin, another Politburo member and a deputy premier. The document below is a partial transcript of that extraordinary meeting. Mikoyan, himself an Armenian and member of Stalin's leadership during the deportations, again refused their appeal to return to a reestablished Volga German republic, while admitting that this "would be the best solution to the problem." Apparently, the government worried about "enormous economic losses" that would result from resettling Russians who had fallen heir to Volga German land and from the departure of these industrious Germans from the troubled grain area of Central Asia. Whatever the full explanation, the outcome reflected the heavy hand of the Stalinist past on the Soviet present. Rebuffed in official channels, some Volga German leaders became active dissidents, while many of their people began to insist upon their right to emigrate permanently to West Germany.

F. G. Schessler: We have appealed many times to the Party Central Committee and to the Presidium of the Supreme Soviet for the reestablishment of our republic, but we have received no concrete responses. The charges against us have now been lifted, but the penalties remain in force. Settlement of our former territory began in 1794. Our ancestors paid four million rubles for it.

During the civil war, we fought for Soviet power at the side of the Russian people, and this land was given to us by law. Even now [long after our deportation], the rural areas of this territory are only 25–30 percent settled. Most of the villages lie in ruins. For a genuine rehabilitation, the Volga Republic must be reestablished. Only such a step would free us from the disgrace and distrust that is now our lot.

Bornemann: I come from Kotovo, a village in the Volgograd [formerly Stalingrad] area. Today, seventy Germans live in our village.

We have come here in order to have our illegally dissolved republic restored and to seek cancellation of decrees [still in effect]. It is true that the decree of August 29, 1964, partially reversed the decree of August 28, 1941. But why haven't the other decrees been withdrawn? Rehabilitation means not only restoration of our honor, but also reestablishment of our former position. That means the Volga Republic must be reestablished and we must have national equality.

The 1964 decree stated that the Germans had "put down roots" in their new homeland. This meant that the Kalmyks and other [deported] peoples from the Caucasus who were not able to "put down roots" were again granted autonomy; but the Germans, who had worked hard and "put down roots," were forbidden to return to their homeland. Our people are also disturbed by the fact that the decree was not published in the Russian newspapers. We want everyone to know the truth about the Soviet Germans.

G. G. Wormsbecher: Up until the war, the republic of the Volga Germans was one of the most advanced republics, both economically and culturally. But what is our situation now? All together, we have only two newspapers. There is not a single German school. Such conditions were not even imposed on us in tsarist Russia. All the peoples of the Soviet Union have their own state institutions, but not the Soviet Germans. This legitimately raises the question, Are we a Soviet people?

G. F. Kaiser: The decree of August 29, 1964, withdrew and canceled all the onerous charges under which the Soviet Germans of the Volga region had lived and labored. But all the onerous penalties against them remain fully in force. In fact, the following have not been canceled: *(a)* the second half of the decree of August 28, 1941, concerning the forced deportation of the Volga Germans; *(b)* the decree of November 26, 1948, on the permanent resettlement of Soviet Germans from various localities, providing penalties of up to twenty years at hard labor if they leave the area of enforced settlement; *(c)* the decree of December 13, 1955, prohibiting Soviet Germans from returning to their home areas, from which they were unjustly deported, their property, both collective and individual, being confiscated. Thus, the decree of August 29, 1964, did not change anything in regard to our national status.

Elementary logic suggests that the innocent should not be punished. The assertions in the second part of the decree, that the Soviet Germans have allegedly put down roots in their new places of habitation and that they have supposedly found a second homeland there, do not correspond to reality. People do not put down roots as a result of forcible deportation. And the establishment of an autonomous republic somewhere in the newly inhabited areas would not be a rehabilitation but permanent exile for us and all our descendants. Because of the deliberate dispersion of the Soviet Germans in small groups to various parts of the USSR, they have been denied their own national statehood and do not have their own deputies in the Council of Nationalities and the Council of the Supreme Soviet.

The territory for the reestablishment of the Volga German Autonomous Republic is on the Volga. This territory was developed through the labor of centuries by our ancestors; it was given to us by the great October Revolution. That is where Germans established Soviet power and where Lenin, with the decree of October 19, 1918, founded the first German autonomous republic within the Russian Republic.

K. D. Welz: We lived in our territory for two hundred years. We had all the characteristics of a nation. We had eleven deputies in the Council of Nationalities and three in the Council of the Union. We had five higher educational institutions and four hundred primary and secondary schools, a national theater, a publishing house, five republicwide newspapers and journals, and twenty local ones. Now we don't have a single school. We have only one newspaper, published in Moscow. But no Germans work on it; they aren't trusted. Even though we were not allowed to fight against the fascists, two Volga Germans who fell at the front were named Heroes of the Soviet Union. Some German families have been resettled as many as six or eight times.

Wersch: It is not just some little group of Germans that wants the republic reestablished. If we could collect signatures, we could bring in as many as a million (there are only two million Soviet Germans altogether). In spite of any and all persecution, we have not lost faith in the Party and government. On the left bank of the Volga, there is very little population, and many villages lie in ruins. There is an office for new settlers in Volgograd. But the people who arrive in the area quickly leave. Another hundred years would be needed to rebuild the economy that way. But we could revitalize the whole area in a few years. To this day, Germans are not given permits to live in the Volga region.

T. Khromova: What little was promised in the decree of August 29, 1964, is not carried out in the local areas. We are accused of nationalism. But the real nationalists are not those who are forced to demand their national rights but the ones who took away those rights and will not give them back.

Mikoyan: I think that the statements [given here] are sufficient. The Soviet Germans conducted themselves well during the war and after it, and they conduct themselves well today. They work hard. To keep agriculture going in the Virgin Lands now would be impossible without the Germans. You have a deputy in the Supreme Soviet—Becker. The number of deputies will now be increased. The Germans have been fully rehabilitated.

You raise the question of reestablishing the republic. We understand very well that that would be the best solution to the problem. But that is impossible, because we would have to take half a million people [from the Volga area] and resettle them. There is no reason to think that the Germans cannot live without a republic. After all, before the war, two-thirds of the Germans lived outside the boundaries of the republic. At this time, we cannot reestablish the republic. That would involve great difficulties. Not everything that has been done in history is correctable. No one confuses you with the West Germans. You are Soviet citizens and have the right to newspapers, schools, and so on.

In the present situation, we cannot move toward reestablishing the republic, because that would entail enormous economic losses. But as far as cultural needs are concerned, we can meet you halfway. As for individual offenses, there are people in the apparatus who act in an incorrect way. If you know of instances of mistreatment, you can give your information to the comrade sitting here [Shelepin]. We will intervene. We assume you will help us with these cultural measures. Good-bye.

From the German Delegation's Letter to Mikoyan and Shelepin after the Meeting: We are by no means satisfied with the results of the meeting. Our people did not send us to the government to get societies for amateur art and popular culture. They sent us to win full rehabilitation for two million people, the assertion of their equal rights with other citizens of the USSR, and the reestablishment of their state institutions.

A purely utilitarian attitude is being taken toward the Soviet Germans, and their national aspirations are being scorned. Lenin's policy on the national question is not being applied to the Soviet Germans, because that "might entail economic losses." The Germans who lived outside the republic did well only because the republic existed, because they had their own state institutions behind them, caring about them in every way, giving them cultural, educational, and economic assistance. The Volga German Republic was a foundry where cadres were forged for all the other German districts. We are Soviet people, Communists, not Bundists; we don't want cultural-national autonomy, but our own state institutions.

The German Democratic Republic [East Germany], since its founding, has had every kind of care and attention bestowed on it by the USSR, while the Soviet Germans are left to choke on the moral implications of the war. One might think the fascists had not been in Germany, but among the Soviet Germans. All the populations that were groundlessly accused and subjected to repression during the Great Patriotic War [World War II] were fully rehabilitated by the Twentieth Party Congress. Why, then, are the Soviet Germans treated as pariahs to this day?

And what would you have devoted your life to, Anastas Ivanovich [Mikoyan], if Beria during the dark days of his omnipotence had dispensed with Armenia? Who could ever agree with your argument that not all the mistakes made in history are correctable? It is true that mistakes cannot be corrected in relation to the dead, to those who were senselessly destroyed. But Soviet power lives and will live! And as long as a people that was treated unjustly lives, the mistake that was made can and must be corrected.

[No. 9, June 1965]

The Jewish Question in the USSR: Theses
BY MIKHAIL ZAND

Soviet Jews occupy a special place among the minority protest groups that have shaped dissident politics and enriched samizdat literature. As a result of domestic and international circumstances since the late 1960s, the "Jewish question" in the Soviet Union has been one of both nationality and religion, reform and exodus, internal affairs and foreign policy. Jewish demands to emigrate, heightened by the Israeli-Arab War of 1967 and by mounting official anti-Semitism, became a focal point of the democratic movement for human rights. Though modest Jewish success provoked anti-Semitic resentment among many Russians and depleted dissident ranks, their emigration campaign also "brought the very concept of rights to the consciousness of a vast number of people in the Soviet Union who had never before thought about rights."[6] The following analysis, which circulated widely and anonymously in early 1970, is a high-quality example of "Jewish samizdat." Mikhail Zand, who later emigrated and now teaches at Hebrew University in Jerusalem, has identified himself as the author. Zand's calm treatment of general and specific aspects of the Jewish question is unusually interesting, as is his argument that official discrimination is not mindless but part of a "policy of assimilation."

1) Jews living in the USSR are a part of the Jewish people, who, as a whole, are divided into those living in their state in Israel and those living in other countries—in the diaspora. To the extent that Jews living in the Soviet Union belong to that part of the Jewish people living in the diaspora, the Jewish question in the USSR can be viewed as part of the question of the Jewish diaspora. At the same time, the Soviet Jewish question is part of the problem of nationalities within the USSR.

2) The basic features of the Jewish question in the diaspora are:

    a) Discrimination.

    b) Assimilation.

3) The discrimination against Jews in the Soviet Union is a combination of all the basic forms of discrimination existing in the other countries of the diaspora, and includes official discrimination:

    a) There are percentage norms limiting acceptance to higher educational institutions and limiting employment opportunities.

---

6. Michael Meerson-Aksenov and Boris Shragin, eds., *The Political, Social and Religious Thought of Russian Samizdat* (Belmont, Mass., 1977), p. 586.

b) A circular has become known that declares those people not politically friendly to the USSR as undesirable for positions in the defense establishment, rocketry, nuclear work, and other secret undertakings. It is understood that this circular refers to Jews.

c) There is definite knowledge of discrimination against Jews in advancement in civilian work as well as in the military.

d) The road to diplomatic service, foreign trade, and the central party apparatus is practically closed to Jews.

e) Exit, whether for a work assignment or for tourism, is extremely difficult for Jews.

f) Wide international publicity has been given to the many cases in which Jews who have received invitations from relatives in Israel to come there and live have been denied the right to leave. By doing this, Soviet agencies violate Point 5 of "The Declaration of Human Rights" (the right of each person to live where he wishes), which was signed by the Soviet Union. They likewise violate the public promise of the chairman of the Council of Ministers of the USSR that those so desiring could join their relatives in Israel.

4) There are examples of unofficial discrimination in the USSR—ethnic, religious-confessional, ideological, and social.

For example, anti-Semitism in the Ukraine is much sharper and has more of a mass-movement character than in other republics of the Soviet Union (despite the decisive dissociation from it and struggle against it on the part of the nationalistically minded Ukrainian intelligentsia). This is obviously explained by the combination of an anti-Semitic tradition predating the USSR and administrative exploitation of this tradition.

Among these cases of intolerance, confessional in origin, we can also classify the swift growth of Judeophobic feelings among some of the youth of the USSR who come from Moslem backgrounds. Although most of these young people are not religious, Judeophobia in them stems from a feeling of Moslem solidarity. This is fanned by pan-Islamic propaganda, which closes ranks here with official pro-Arabic propaganda.

Judeophobia is part of the ideology of certain Nazi-type underground groups existing in the Soviet Union (whose existence is seen in the dissemination of anti-Semitic leaflets) and also of the almost legalized activities of the Great Russian chauvinists, the "men of the soil."

In regard to common, everyday anti-Semitism, every layer of Soviet society is diseased. Any Jew living in the USSR could tell of humiliations suffered in the most varied of situations—in the communal apartments, on the streets, in traveling, on store lines, in military barracks, or in city hospitals. Soviet laws calling for criminal punishment for such abuses are not applied. And the revitalization of anti-Semitic feelings is spurred in a large measure by the constant publication in the Soviet press of materials from Arabic sources concerning the "brutalities of the Israeli occupiers."

The national dignity of the Jew, a resident of the USSR, is no less mocked by an anti-Jew campaign that employs all the resources of mass propaganda. Like the one in Stalin's last years, this campaign is set up as a struggle against Zionism and not Judaism, and it even has the participation of some Jews. But this fact does not change the essence of the campaign. In all ages, Jewish apostates have participated in the persecution of Jews, using the weapons and the means of Judeophobia. The basic motivation for this campaign at the present is the sympathy of a significant portion of the Jews in the USSR for Israel, which is an uncompromising contradiction to the unconditionally anti-Israel foreign policy of the Soviet government. That this campaign is organized and directed from the top is indisputable, if only for the simple reason that nothing happens in the Soviet Union without the sanction of government and Party organs. Top-level direction is also apparent from the participation of highly placed government personnel. It is enough to recall the "witticism," expressed in the best tradition of Russian anti-Semitism, delivered by Foreign Minister Andrei Gromyko in a speech to the United Nations in 1967, about "the local bazaar." His deputy, V. Semenov, has written a book (under the pseudonym K. Ivanov and along with Z. Sheinis) entitled *The Government of Israel.* Yuri Ivanov, the leading specialist on Jewish affairs in the Central Committee apparatus of the CPSU, has also appeared as an author with *Beware of Zionism* and the contemporary *Protocols of the Elders of Zion.*

Discriminatory measures against the Jewish religion are well known: the closing of synagogues, the practical nonexistence of religious education, the ban on bringing in or producing objects for the cult. Under these conditions, the Jewish people as a community exist only as an object of discrimination, as all their rights and needs as a national community are rejected.

5) Discrimination is not a goal in itself. It is only the instrument of the rulers in their policy of assimilation.

6) Assimilation as a general feature of the life of Jews in the diaspora has a number of forms. Physical assimilation is expressed in the descendants of mixed marriages, the majority of whom include themselves in the basic population. In this case, the physical assimilation of Jews in the Soviet Union is wholly comparable to the physical assimilation of Jews in other countries of the diaspora. There are only three items that might be mentioned wherein this aspect of assimilation differs in the USSR from other countries of the diaspora:

a) According to Soviet law, at the age of sixteen, upon receiving their passports, children of mixed marriages must state their national affiliation. A growing, though still small, percentage of such children of Jewish descent are declaring themselves Jews as a gesture of protest against discrimination.

b) Administrative organs clearly do not wish to register such persons as Jewish. They categorically refuse to register as Jews those descendants of mixed marriages who acknowledge themselves to be Jewish after receiving their initial passports. Such behavior by the administrative organs undoubtedly exposes their interests in bringing the descendants of mixed marriages into the national fold, i.e., in hastening the tempo of physical assimilation.

c) Descendants of mixed marriages who do list themselves in one of the basic national groupings serve the interests of the administration, yet such people find acceptance into agencies and establishments, where the cadres are recruited according to special social and national "purity" and where the application has questions about the nationality of each parent, very difficult or even closed.

7) Linguistic assimilation is a general phenomenon in the countries of the diaspora. But an essential difference between the linguistic assimilation of Jews in the USSR and that of Jews in other countries has been its speed and the force used to accomplish it. The closing of Jewish educational institutions in the late 1930s, the reduction in the number of Jewish journals, newspapers, and theaters in those same years, the later liquidation of the remnants of Jewish cultural institutions, and the physical destruction of the most famous cultural activities of the Jewish people at the end of the 1940s and the beginning of the 1950s— these are the phases of a forcible linguistic assimilation of the Jewish population in the USSR whose native language was Yiddish. This has led to a situation in which the overwhelming majority of Jews in the Soviet Union has ceased speaking in its native tongue.

8) Cultural assimilation has gone through the same stages as linguistic assimilation. An essential factor in the artificial acceleration of this assimilation was the deliberate identification of Jewish culture with the Yiddish language. As a result, culture in Hebrew was destroyed in the Soviet Union already in the 1920s. In the 1930s, the embryonic Jewish culture in the Georgian language was liquidated. At the end of the thirties, the literature of the Bukhara Jews was suppressed.

At a time when Jews in most of the other countries of the diaspora have had the opportunity of developing their culture in the language of the country in which they live, Jews in the USSR since the 1920s have been deprived of the opportunity of continuing their culture in the Russian language, which has become their sole means of communication. Practically speaking, at the present time in the Soviet Union there is only one Jewish culture—the culture of mountain Jews in the Tatsky language, and it continues to exist only because the bearers of this culture are forbidden to consider themselves Jews.

9) The remnants of Jewish culture in Yiddish in the USSR have no chance for future survival, inasmuch as the sources nourishing this culture are drying up. The existence of one literary journal, the publication of a few books, and the work of a few traveling ensembles serve as a screen covering the real absence of Jewish culture in the USSR.

10) The religious community has always been a factor in determining who was a Jew. The idea of "Jewishness" coincided with the idea of "Judaism." But the situation changed after the Russian revolution. The general decline in religious life in the Soviet Union was expressed for the majority of the Jews either

in a direct break with the synagogue or in indifference to it. In the postwar years, however, the situation changed again. Discrimination, together with the liquidation of all forms of national existence for Soviet Jews, led to a state in which national feelings turned to the sole legally preserved institution—the synagogue. Against its wishes, and even with open fear, the synagogue became the center of Jewish spiritual life. But it could not answer the people's questions or satisfy their needs, for the following basic reasons:

a) The active enmity of the government to all religions (and perhaps particularly to Judaism as the religion of the "internal enemy") led the synagogue into a servile humility, a constant fear of repression and therefore to submissive acquiescence in all of the demands of the rulers, no matter how unjust they were.

b) The deep assimilation put a wall of linguistic and cultural estrangement between the synagogue and the Jewish people in the USSR. The Jew, ignorant of his own language and history, raised in traditions of Russian culture, and, finally, with no chance for help and leadership from the Jewish religious community, had to move by groping in the dark, like a blind man. It is not surprising that an intellectual of Jewish descent looking for religion frequently turns to [Russian] Orthodoxy, which, in the final analysis, signifies yet another step in the assimilating process.

On the other hand, there can be no doubt that the longing of Soviet Jews for the synagogue has not so much a religious as a national character. Thus, even complete religious freedom in itself, no matter how important and also how unlikely it is under the Soviet system, cannot solve the Jewish problem.

11) At the present time two extremes can be discerned in Soviet Jewry:

a) Those Jews who have lost, or almost lost, all national consciousness and strive for complete assimilation into the basic population.

b) Those Jews who have come to realize the complete impossibility of a national existence as Jews in the USSR and strive for repatriation to Israel. Between these two extremes are those who have not yet realized the inevitability of a choice between assimilation and repatriation.

12) The sole possible solution of the Jewish question in the conditions of the Soviet Union lies in this: that the first group be given the real possibility of assimilation into the basic population and that the second group be given the unconditional right to repatriate. The third group must make its own decision.

[No. 67, April 1970]

Solzhenitsyn and Censorship: Two Letters
BY GEORGY VLADIMOV AND VIKTOR SOSNORA

Outlying sources and allies notwithstanding, the political and intellectual center of Soviet dissent was (and remains) the urban intelligentsia. Several events in 1967–68, especially the Solzhenitsyn affair, political trials, Sakharov's "Memorandum," and the Soviet invasion of Czechoslovakia, shook the critical intelligentsia and created new protesters within it. The Solzhenitsyn episode focused attention on censorship, a question of special importance to the intelligentsia, and highlighted the relationship between that oppressive institution and the growing body of samizdat literature. Banned from publication, harassed by the KGB, and the target of an official campaign of defamation, Solzhenitsyn composed an open letter of protest, dated May 16, 1967, and mailed a copy to every delegate to the upcoming Soviet Writers' Congress. An eloquent and powerful indictment of the official literary scene, the letter called for an end to the campaign against him and, still more, the complete abolition of censorship as a "relic of the Middle Ages." Solzhenitsyn's letter was suppressed at the congress, and his own situation continued to worsen; he was expelled from the Writers' Union in November 1969. But more than a hundred Soviet writers rallied to his call in 1967. Many circulated their own protest letters, which formed still another volume of samizdat. Several of these letters appeared in Political Diary; *two are printed below with small deletions. Georgy Vladimov (born 1931), then an established writer of novels and stories, has since become a prominent dissident, head of the Moscow chapter of Amnesty International, and yet another Soviet author who can publish only abroad.* (Faithful Ruslan. New York, 1979.) *Viktor Sosnora (born 1936), a Leningrad poet, also has had to turn to samizdat and foreign publication. His caustic remarks on the many layers of censorship, state imposed and self-imposed, and on the "generation-gap argument" are particularly noteworthy.*

Dear Comrades!

I, like you, have received the letter of A. Solzhenitsyn and wish to make known my opinion on all the points in that letter.

I would venture to remind the congress that the main purpose of writers' congresses is not to deliver reports on our brilliant creative victories, or to hear the greetings of foreign guests, nor is it [to express] solidarity with the peoples of Africa and the struggling Vietnamese; it is first and foremost [to express] our solidarity with our own people, first and foremost to solve our own pressing problems, [for] without such a solution Soviet literature cannot go on living and developing. Without freedom of creativity, complete, limitless freedom to express any opinion on any aspect of the social and moral life of the people, [it cannot continue] however much we may curse this legitimate demand of every artist who has the slightest power of thought, the slightest sense of honor.

And I must say that such freedom does exist. It is put into practice, not in officially recognized, censored literature, but in the activities of so-called samizdat, of which you are probably well aware. Passing from hand to hand, from reader to reader, in typed seventh or eighth copies, are the unpublished works of Bulgakov, Tsvetayeva, Mandelstam, Platonov, and others alive today whose names I refrain from mentioning for fully understandable reasons.

Organize mass search raids, seize all the tapes, all the copies, arrest their authors and those responsible for their circulation—even so, at least one copy will escape, and having survived will be duplicated in even greater quantities, because forbidden fruit is sweet. This process whereby art is being liberated from all the fetters of "official directives" is developing and expanding, and to fight against it is as stupid and senseless as to ban tobacco or spirits.

I have read many works in samizdat and can say of nine-tenths of them with full responsibility that they not only *can* be published—they *must* be. There is nothing antinational in them—no artist in his right mind would ever think of it—but there is the breath of talent, brilliance, the radiance of unfettered artistic form, there is a love for man, an authentic knowledge of life, and at times echoes of pain and anger for the writer's fatherland, or bitterness and hatred toward its enemies who pose as friends and protectors.

Naturally, everything I have said above applies also to the unpublished works of Solzhenitsyn. I have had the good fortune to read almost all that he has written; he is the writer of whom my Russia is most of all in need, who is destined to glorify her in this world and to answer all our burning questions about the tragedy we have suffered. I know no other author who might have a greater right to this task and greater strength for it. I do not intend to insult the congress when I say that probably nine-tenths of the names of its delegates will not survive to cross the threshold of the century. But the name of Aleksandr Solzhenitsyn, the pride of Russian literature, will reach beyond them.

A ban on publication or performance, search raids and confiscation of his archive, "restricted" editions of works the author himself did not intend for publication, and, in addition, malicious slander against a military officer who fought through the whole war . . . it is painful, agonizing, shameful to read about. And this is going on in a proletarian state. This is going on in the fiftieth year of the Revolution. This is going on, lastly, in a civilized society in the second half of the twentieth century.

So I should like to ask the plenipotentiary congress: are we a nation of scum, sneaks, and informers, or are we a great people that has presented the world with an unrivaled galaxy of geniuses? Solzhenitsyn will fulfill his task; I believe that.

as firmly as he himself does. But ourselves, what of us? Did we protect him from the search raids and the confiscations? Did we push his works into print? Did we shield his face from the slimy, fetid hand of slander? Did we in our editorial offices and our boards at least answer him intelligibly when he sought an answer?

We were listening to greetings from [the foreign guests] Mr. Dürrenmatt and Mrs. Hollman at the time. After all, that was business too, just like solidarity with the struggling Vietnamese and the suffering Greeks. But time will pass, and we shall be asked; What did we do for ourselves, for our near ones for whom living and working were so difficult?

The letter by Solzhenitsyn has already become a document that cannot be evaded by silence—that would be unworthy of honest artists. I suggest that the congress discuss this letter at an open session, pass a new and unequivocal resolution on it, and lay this resolution before the government of the country.

Excuse the sharp language of my appeal—but after all, I am talking to colleagues.

Yours respectfully,
Moscow, May 26, 1967   G. Vladimov
[No. 33, June 1967]

To the Secretariat of the Writers' Union:

Aleksandr Isayevich Solzhenitsyn did not address his letter to me, and therefore I have only just read it and been astounded by it.

The newspapers published the rantings of literary imbeciles like Sholokhov, who is as allergic to sensitive literary questions as the Persian wild boar to the Phrygian flute. And the letter that ought to have been one of the main talking points at the congress was suppressed.

What good did that do? In two weeks, the letter has circulated in thousands of copies. In another two weeks, there will not be a single person in Russia who has not read it.

One of the writers who now represents decency and the conscience of the country—one of the few, at a generous estimate—was not chosen as a delegate to the conference. The reasons for this are quite definite and unambiguous: he is a writer who is always writing, always thinking, worrying, and suffering for others; he is an unperson: he is also an enemy to the bunch of idlers and flunkeys who, if they write at all (which very seldom happens), write only what they are urged to write by the authorities; and if they think, then only what the authorities have already thought out for them.

A professional writer, the pride of Soviet literature, a fiery fighter against an alien ideology, has to approach the director of the publishing house, as a ragged Hindu approaches his many-headed deity, not knowing which face the monster will turn to him, and what abuse it will bestow on the flower of the Soviet intelligentsia. The writer has all the obligations; the director has all the rights. But what is the director? An ideology merchant, a parasite on literature.

I have a good idea of the truly draconian censorship of the past. I see before me the [tsarist] writer-censors Nikitenko, Goncharov, Aksakov. These writers can be accused of a multitude of sins, but not of lack of literary talent or literary taste.

Is there a single censor at this moment who is a writer, or at the very least a literary expert? Remember Marx's early article on censors, discussing how little right an aesthetically illiterate person had to correct or suppress, say, Goethe's poetry. Like it or not, Goethe was a genius.

I also have a good idea of the censorship of today. This mysterious phenomenon is intangible, like an invisible surgeon in the operating theatre, but its surgical operations are real enough.

But not everything need be put down to the censorship.

The censor in chief, like Jesus Christ, has his twelve apostles, who watchfully protect and stoutly defend this responsible personage. We do not have just one guilty censor. We have twelve.

The first censor is the author himself, who censors his book to the utmost before taking it to the publisher. The second is the editor who receives the book. The third is the editor who is given the manuscript to work over. The fourth is the first reviewer. The fifth is the second reviewer. The sixth is the senior editor. The seventh is the whole editorial board. The eighth is the editor in chief of the Department of Belles Lettres. The ninth is the publishers' council. The tenth is the editor in chief of the publishing house. The eleventh is the director. The twelfth is the local office of ideological control—and SELF-CENSORSHIP is only the thirteenth bead on the rosary.

Of the 300 writers who received Solzhenitsyn's letter, not one plucked up the courage to read it out to the congress. Various euphemisms spring to mind, but the fact is they were all cowards.

The generation-gap argument is a load of rubbish. The generation gap is only a biological phenomenon. I am thirty-one. But there are no fewer bad eggs in my generation than in the older one. My generation is not my age group, but a group of talented and decent people—the generation of Paustovsky, Ehrenburg, Tvardovsky, Solzhenitsyn, Voznesensky, and Gleb Gorbovsky. It follows that the persecution of Solzhenitsyn is not the fault of the OLDER GENERATION or the YOUNGER GENERATION, but of ALL OF US and of our READERS.

The enemy in 1963 was not formalism.

That much has become clear now that all the so-called formalists have been more or less officially acknowledged. They have not changed their forms or their point of view since 1963.

The fight was against those with talent!

Gifted people always work for the good of their country, and the mediocre are always its enemies. The fight was led then, as always, by the mediocrities. The gifted have no need to fight anything or anyone; merely by being born they are the victors. All they have to do is fight for every hour of their existence. They have achieved doubtful fame through the twilight existence of their manuscripts, and been deprived of the opportunity of living as people and as citizens.

The best books at present circulating in manuscript are a golden treasury of

Russian literature. Concealing this treasure from the people is literary official-dom's unforgivable sin.

I am thirty-one. I have been writing professionally daily for the last fifteen years (by professionally I refer to quality, not publication).

I have published two books of verse, two books of 3,000 lines each. Like all books, mine were painstakingly castrated in anything from seven to twelve stages.

All the best things I have written are unpublished, although I have not kept any of them under the counter, and have submitted everything I have written to just about every periodical in the country.

My name is unknown, my voice is weak. But as a member of the Writers' Union I consider I have the right to ask the secretariat publicly to debate Solzhenitsyn's resolution and the letters replying to his letter. In my opinion, the secretariat is obliged to give its approval to this.

Respectfully,
Viktor Aleksandrovich Sosnora
[No. 33, June 1967]

To Hope or to Act: A Reply to Sakharov
BY ESTONIAN INTELLECTUALS

The samizdat appearance of Sakharov's now famous "Memorandum," in May–June 1968, spurred an intense programmatic debate among dissident and other critical-minded readers. The discussion revealed a wide range of political outlooks and formed another ongoing subject in Political Diary. *In publishing this reply to Sakharov, which was signed "numerous representatives of the technical intelligentsia of the Estonian Soviet Socialist Republic,"* Political Diary *criticized its religious perspective but recommended it as "an interesting document." The authors' primary concern is the "moral healing of our society" and expresses what is called, somewhat loosely, the movement for "ethical socialism," or "ethical democracy," among dissidents. The document's starting points are, however, familiar—the Stalinist past, neo-Stalinism, and the "spiritual vacuum" among Soviet citizens. Characteristic of the good-natured quality of dissident discussions at that time, which no longer is often the case, the Estonians strongly supported Sakharov's dissent, while sharply criticizing some of his basic ideas. It should be remembered that Sakharov's views were still cautious, generally loyalist, and reformist in 1968, and that he has since evolved into a more implacable and radical critic of the Soviet system.*

Sakharov's pamphlet is a noteworthy development in the context of our unofficial literature. The author, one of the creators of the Soviet hydrogen bomb and consequently one of those indirectly guilty of the nuclear impasse in which the world finds itself, discusses a number of the central questions of our time, showing great civic courage and anguish of soul. This indicates that our scientists are beginning to emerge from the narrowly specialized confines of their research, to think about the consequences of their scientific work, and to make a moral assessment of their own activity. They are at last beginning to recognize their own human responsibility for the death-dealing elements they have brought into the world.

Sakharov's pamphlet is divided into two parts: "Dangers" and "The Basis for Hope." They provide an analysis of the past, touch on the alarming problems in the world today, outline certain noble goals, and indicate the means for achieving them. All honest and thoughtful people in our society would subscribe to the basic postulates of Sakharov's essay.

In the present work, we will not discuss the things about which we agree with Sakharov; rather, we will focus attention on our differences and add our own ideas. The fact that Sakharov belongs to the world of science leaves its mark on his way of thinking. He unjustifiably places great hopes on scientific and technical means, economic measures, the good will of the leaders of our society, and the common sense of most people. And he sees the basic causes of the world crisis as lying beyond the borders of our society.

Here, too, the author is profoundly mistaken, and in this he shares the basic prejudice of our age. He sees external causes and prefers external, material means to an end, disregarding inner, spiritual, political, and organic means. In this connection we shall indicate three factors that, for us, are simultaneously ends and means.

A. The Moral-Philosophical Factor

The political upheavals that have occurred in our society during the twentieth century have resulted in the removal of Christianity as the basic ideological force in the life of our society and the destruction of our society's moral values. The new materialist ideology [Marxism] did not replace those lost values (nor could it replace them). A moral vacuum was created. This resulted in a splitting of the individual personality from the moral point of view. On the one hand, there is a sham morality, an external, hypocritically collective morality; on the other hand, there is an inner, subterranean morality, a primitively selfish and predatory one. This has produced a society with a mechanistic kind of solidarity on the surface, which in fact is based on individuals who are alienated from society, who fear those closest to them, and who feel alone and insignificant in the face of the gigantic machine of the state. In such an atomized society, the sad facts that justifiably distress Sakharov are inevitable. Moreover, they are an organic part of such a society.

At this point, we must emphasize the question, Aren't we holding the demonic figure of Stalin, with his trusted "cadres," responsible for too much? Society as a whole is actually responsible for these events! Didn't its inertia, indifference, servility, ignorance, and just plain cruelty provoke all the excesses of the personality cult? An idol is inconceivable without idolators. And that is not all. If a new "Stalin" were to appear, the same things could happen all over again. The moral and psychological foundations and the social base for such things still exist among us. Only the raising of the moral standard of our society, the intensification of conscious civic activity, and the wakening of a sense of personal responsibility can effectively prevent such a bloody bacchanalia.

To accomplish this, new moral values must be created first of all. Our society must either work out a new moral-philosophical doctrine or adopt someone else's; either way, one must be found and written down. It obviously does not now exist. But those who seek shall find. This is one of the conditions for the moral healing of our society and its development in a proper direction.

B. The Social-Political Factor

  1) Domestic

Our society now finds itself in a state of unstable political equilibrium. It is shaky and unsure. At any moment, some strong personality could come to power, establish a neo-Stalinist order, and plunge our country into a maelstrom of lawlessness and repression. And then the figure of ten to fifteen million victims of [Stalin's] repression, mentioned in the pamphlet, will be substantially increased. Only political freedoms (not just intellectual freedom) and civic activism can counteract neo-Stalinism. *The emancipation of a society is impossible without the active participation of the forces in that society.* Our society now needs the broadest possible democratization as much as it needs air to breathe. The right of the minority to opposition activity must be legally guaranteed. The activities of government bodies must be subject to control by the society. The agencies of government are not the born prerogative of the ruling bureaucracy. The Supreme Soviet should be a businesslike forum for the expression of differing views, not a mechanism for unanimity. Elections should be based on a multiparty system.

The most advanced people in our society, its most honorable and courageous elements, who have been subjected to repression because they dared to be themselves, dared to think and write independently, and dared to express their convictions, should be freed at once, from the writers Sinyavsky and Daniel to those who demonstrated on Red Square on August 25, 1968, against the occupation of Czechoslovakia (Pavel Litvinov, Vladimir Dremlyuga, and the others).

The national question must be settled in a just manner. The right of different nationalities to a sovereign and independent existence as a state must be guaranteed. The conception of class preference must be reexamined. All sections and layers of society should have equal rights. It is pointless to keep assuring us that the ideals of political freedom are alien to the peoples of the Soviet Union, that we have only material interests. If that is true for a certain section of the population, the task of our intelligentsia is not to adapt to ignorance but to educate the people in democratic ideals and raise their moral and political level. Only a democratic society can be a true school of humanism.

It is useless for certain pseudotheoreticians and accommodating slanderers to accuse our progressive intelligentsia of "Zionism" and "counterrevolution." It is not counterrevolution that is inscribed on their banner, but anti-Stalinism!

Twelve years have passed since the Twentieth Congress. We are waiting and asking our government for liberating reforms. We are willing to ask and wait for a while longer. But in the end we will demand and we will act! And then the tank divisions will have to be sent, not to Prague or Bratislava but to Moscow and Leningrad!

2) International

First and foremost, we are obliged to exercise self-criticism in assessing our own role in the world. After all, the doctrine of militant and aggressive Communism originated with us! The doctrine of peaceful coexistence itself was inspired not so much by humane considerations as by fear for our security and the requirements of the moment. Was it not our country that in the period from 1939 to 1949 annexed 100,000 square kilometers of territory and established military and political control over eight countries and 1,274 million square kilometers in Europe alone? At the same time, the territory of the other victorious powers in World War II hardly changed. All of this may gratify the great-power chauvinist feelings of some patriots of the kvas bottle, but it does not contribute in any way to the relaxation of international tensions and cannot be regarded as a matter of high moral caliber.

We should renounce the senseless accumulation of territory, the expansion of our influence as a world power, and our aggressive policy. We must help create a belt of neutral states on our borders under UN supervision, make peace with other powers, and shift the major part of our government resources from the war machine to cultural and economic work. Since we are responsible, not for half, but more than half the tension in the world, we should take the first steps and the biggest steps toward making peace!

C. The Material-Economic Factor

Economic development, even the most rapid, does not automatically improve society in some miraculous way, nor does it eliminate social evils. If one's aim is to transform human beings, this can be accomplished least of all through the stomach. A wolf with a full stomach doesn't turn into a lamb. If the end we are striving toward is the moral individual, the material-economic factor serves as a supplement to the first two factors and flows naturally from them. Our economists must have the opportunity for broad and free research and adoption from other models in order to find flexible economic forms based on compromise that can best assure satisfaction of the needs, not so much of the state as of each member of society. To orient the population primarily toward material demands as ends in themselves is a profound political error. Material demands can be justified only as a means for achieving moral ends, the ideal of the good, that which is so lacking in this world of violence and evil!

On the basis of what has been said above we consider it necessary to supplement Sakharov's proposals as follows:

1. Not only must the lack of contact between hostile powers be overcome; they must actually be brought closer together.

2. Not only must there be coexistence and cooperation but actual reconciliation.

3. Not only must we combat physical hunger but also moral deprivation.

4. Not only must there be laws on freedom of the press but also laws guaranteeing political freedoms for the individual.

5. Not only must Stalinism be held in check and exposed; it must be eliminated altogether.

6. Not just an amnesty for political prisoners but full freedom for all and guarantees that none will be persecuted for their convictions.

7. Not just a trimmed-down economic reform but fundamental economic changes.

And, above all, not only must external alienation be overcome but inner alienation as well.

In conclusion, we appeal to the leading minds of our society: Don't limit yourselves to technical and scientific fantasies, pleasant illusions, and the awakening of rosy expectations! Create new moral values! Work out new social, political, and economic ideals! Give us a program for action, in case our hopes and appeals for change should prove to be in vain!

[No. 48, September 1968]

Protest and Reprisal

*A chain reaction of protests, reprisals (including a series of trials in 1966–68),
and new protests sharpened the dissident movement's concern with civil rights.
The trial of four young dissenters in January 1968—Aleksandr Ginzburg, Yuri
Galanskov, Aleksei Dobrovolsky, and Vera Lashkova—was an important episode
in this connection. Convicted of "anti-Soviet" activities, their only offense had
been to compile and distribute samizdat materials, including a documentary
record of the Sinyavsky-Daniel trial of 1966. More than a thousand people now
protested the new trial, which brought further persecutions. Many of these
protesters, lacking the fame of a Solzhenitsyn or a Sakharov, faced reprisals out
of public view. Valeria Gerlin, a Moscow school teacher, was one of 170 people
who signed a petition to top Soviet authorities objecting to "gross violations of
the correct legal norms" in the Ginzburg-Galanskov trial and demanding that the
case be reopened. The petition also endorsed, in passing, another protest against
the trial, an open letter "To World Public Opinion" by the well-known dissidents
Larisa Bogoraz and Pavel Litvinov. (Bogoraz was then married to Yuli Daniel,
the writer sentenced to a long prison camp term in 1966.) Gerlin made the
following record of a meeting summoned by her trade union, on April 16, 1968,
to condemn and punish her. It is especially interesting as an example of a
protester's vulnerability at his or her place of work, but also for Gerlin's own
experiences as the daughter of a victim of Stalin's terror, her strong belief in
legality and "personal responsibility for history," the attitudes of her colleagues
at school, and the outcome of her case. According to* Political Diary, *the trade
union's "shameful" decision was upheld by the district Party Committee, but
both were overruled by a court to which Gerlin appealed. She returned to
teaching in another school, at her own request.*

Chairman: This trade-union meeting must decide on the question of dismissing
V. M. Gerlin, a literature teacher in the upper grades, who does not deserve our
confidence with respect to her ideological and political views.

A. V. Novozhilova: The trial of the four young writers occurred at the beginning of January, 1968. They were engaged in genuine anti-Soviet activity. Their
degree of guilt varied, but the charge against them was proved by irrefutable facts.
They were found to possess a printing device, dollars as well as Soviet money, and
anti-Soviet literature. In addition to his anti-Soviet activity, the accused Ginzburg
even had his articles published abroad. These four were arrant anti-Soviets, and
they received well-deserved punishment. Their trial was not completely open,

but, then, what importance does that have when the issues are so clear? They could not be permitted to make their anti-Soviet statements in the presence of Soviet people; they could not be permitted to force our people to listen to such slander. Perhaps there were other reasons why no one from the street was allowed to walk into the courtroom. But we don't have to know all the reasons. We must trust our institutions and not be suspicious of them. After the court's decision, Litvinov and Bogoraz-Daniel delivered a slanderous diatribe to the foreign press that contained anti-Soviet demands—a plea for freedom for defendants and for condemnation of the Soviet court which tried them. Several unstable members of the intelligentsia consented to join in sending this dirty letter to the West. Their signatures were added to those of Litvinov and Bogoraz-Daniel. A group of ideologically unstable people, they chose to defend recognized criminals. Our teacher, Gerlin, was among those who signed this letter. She is attempting to be at one and the same time a defender of anti-Soviet people and a teacher of literature. Such duplicity is intolerable. A person who wavers or doubts cannot be a guide in our ideology, cannot be a teacher, and cannot work in our schools.

V. M. Gerlin: Everything that is now happening to me is already familiar. I was condemned behind my back in 1949, condemned only because I am the daughter of a man who was shot in 1937. Today I am being condemned once again, or, more accurately, I have already been condemned behind my back, since a Party conference and the local trade-union committee have already made a decision without even bothering to hear my side. The decision of this meeting is preordained; the collective has to support an already adopted decision, and it is for this purpose alone that you are gathered. I am not afraid of this—things have been even worse. But I must discuss my actions and my reasons for them.

I became an orphan at the age of seven; my father, a Communist, was shot, and my mother was sentenced to eight years in prison for associating with an enemy of the people. She did not live long after having been rehabilitated. I was arrested when I was nineteen years old. My institute unanimously denounced me, together with two other "enemies," who have since been rehabilitated and today are teachers of Marxism. When I, too, returned to Moscow after being rehabilitated, there were a great many people who were ashamed to look me in the eye. These people simply accepted my guilt, never daring to question the decision of their superiors. Before branding somebody else a criminal, all who are living witnesses to the years 1937 to 1949 should remember the mass meetings that were held in those years and the demands made then for the shooting of Tukhachevsky and Yakir. Thousands of guiltless people were accused, "unmasked," and compelled to expose so-called anti-Soviet organizations, which allegedly existed even among children in kindergartens. I know that these were violations of the law. And I know that it is important for the honor of our state that the letter of the law be observed, since the *spirit* of the law is expressed in the *letter* of the law. For us, history is not in textbooks, not in dead pages—history is in our blood.

We must feel a personal responsibility for history, and we must, therefore, not be indifferent to violations of the law; we must sound the alarm every time we believe that the law of the Soviet state has not been precisely observed, since, on a statewide scale, legality and only legality is a means to justice. I do not understand people who lack civic courage, people who are not interested in justice or in the honor of our country. Just and lofty ideas find fulfillment only in just methods of application. Civil agitation to correct injustice is not only my right but my obligation—that was the motive for my act of signing the letter. My major objective was to protest the illegality of the court procedures.

Now, about the letter itself. I did not sign and would not sign the appeal made by Litvinov and Bogoraz-Daniel that was addressed to world opinion outside the USSR. I appealed only to state and judicial officials. I do not consider it proper for me to appeal over the heads of Soviet officials to world public opinion. In condemning me for being antisocial, you, for some reason, introduced quotations only from that letter by Litvinov and Bogoraz-Daniel, although my signature is on a different letter. My letter was directed (I emphasize once again) to the Supreme Court, Comrades Brezhnev, Kosygin, Podgorny, and to the lawyers of the accused. There is not a word in it about appeal to the foreign press. The demands made in this letter are sharply divergent from those of Litvinov and Bogoraz-Daniel. I do not ask that the accused be freed but only that their case be reconsidered "with genuine observance of all judicial norms including an open trial," and punishment of those persons who are truly guilty of violating legality —that is, the Moscow Municipal Court. The letter I signed does not raise the issue of the guilt of those tried; I do not take up this question in general. I am not competent to do so, since I cannot assume the functions of a court. But— once again—the exact and honorable observance of the law should interest every conscientious person. Every criminal, murderer, and lawbreaker in a legally con- stituted state, and most especially in a Soviet state, must be tried strictly accord- ing to the law, in strict observance of the law, and without any violation of the law.

Voice from the hall (the mathematics teacher, N. N. Nozhkina): And you think anti-Soviet persons should be tried according to the law?

Gerlin: Yes, anti-Soviet people, even war criminals.

Nozhkina: But they are our enemies! How is it possible to defend our enemies? They want to harm us, but we should observe the laws! We can't allow that! They wouldn't grant us the same privileges.

Gerlin: Shame on you! Your words are not only unworthy of a teacher, they are unworthy of an even moderately reflective person. I do not want to forgive our enemies but to judge them according to the law, and only according to the law. Our law is sufficiently strong and firm to punish any person who violates it, without our resorting to injustice. And if we do not observe the laws of our own country, how will we distinguish ourselves from our enemies? You are essentially invoking the lynchings and punishments of 1937! Where is the guarantee that, having illegally condemned the guilty today, the same court will not condemn the innocent tomorrow?

Nozhkina: We cannot judge criminals with justice! That would mean exonerating them all!

Gerlin: To condemn the guilty and exonerate the innocent is the meaning of law. A person who doesn't understand such obvious things should go through a course in elementary political theory.

Nozhkina: What does the fate of some criminals matter to you, how does it affect you?

Gerlin: I am not raising the question of their fate. I am talking only about observance of the laws in a lawful state. But to continue. The people who were ordered to expel me and who have already made that decision want to listen to nothing and understand nothing; they condemn me by repeating insistently one phrase from the letter I signed: "We fully support the authors [Litvinov and Bogoraz-Daniel] of the letter." But what does it mean to "fully support" Litvinov and Bogoraz-Daniel? In reading the letter, I understood, and still understand, this phrase in only one sense: we support the position of civic anxiety and alarm that resounds in the letter written by Litvinov and Bogoraz-Daniel. In other respects, the letter I signed is in conflict with that of Litvinov: it makes different demands and addresses different people. If the letters were in agreement, a new text with different demands would have made no sense, and it would have been enough to say "we fully support Litvinov and Bogoraz-Daniel." I agree that the phrase "we fully support" is susceptible to two interpretations. If I had composed the letter, or had the opportunity to edit it, I would not have allowed such carelessness in phrasing. The phrase either should not be there or should have read precisely: we share the concern of Litvinov and Bogoraz-Daniel over the violation of Soviet laws in a recent political trial. I insist, in returning to this matter, that the comrades bear in mind my explanation of this "criminal" phrase and take my interpretation and evaluation into account.

Comrades, I am not afraid of what will happen to me. Things were even worse for me in the past. I am thinking today not only of myself but of you. Because of you, I do not want a repetition of the situation in 1949. But what is happening now speaks for itself: this meeting, held after the decision to discharge me was made, confirms the sense of injustice that prompted me to sign the letter. Consider which is more important—a slovenly or even untruthful phrase contradicted by the actual contents of the letter or the purity and sacredness of Soviet law, without which our state is unthinkable.

Novozhilova: Why don't you want to admit that the Soviet government could have valid reasons, which it is not obliged to divulge to anyone, for not admitting just anyone to the courtroom?

Gerlin: The law itself stipulates the occasions when a trial may be closed to the public. But, since 1956, you and I and everyone must understand how dangerous it is to hold secret trials. Has history taught you, a historian, nothing? [The spy] Oleg Penkovsky's trial was transmitted over television, and no one questioned the legality of an open trial in that case.

Eidlin (history teacher):   Do you think the accused were guilty of being anti-Soviet?

Gerlin: I have already said that I cannot answer this question, since I am not a judge. Is it possible that you have not yet understood what is and what is not relevant to this matter?

Somebody: Why did you appeal to the Voice of America and the BBC?

Gerlin: I appealed to our government and judicial bodies. I am not responsible for what is broadcast on the BBC.

Voice: But the BBC transmitted it.

Gerlin: The BBC, but not me. I am not the BBC.

Andreev (vocational teacher):   Why do you always say "we," "we"? Who are these "we"? What organization are you representing?

Gerlin: I said "we" with only one meaning: we citizens (and that includes you) should be attentive to what happens in our country. I signed the letter, and I am responsible for my signature.

Andreev: Who gave you the letter to sign?

Gerlin: I do not consider that an ethical question, and I will explain why. Since I am being driven from my job because I signed the letter (and just for signing, without having given it to anyone else to sign), then the person who gave the letter to me would be subject to still greater persecution. These people did not wish to do anything bad, nor did they do anything bad, and I will not burden their fate.

Chairman: Who wishes to speak? *(Three minutes of complete silence.)*

Savelev (drawing teacher, deputy director of the pedagogical division):   Valeria Mikhailovna has spoken about humanity, about respect for mankind. Her feelings are well known to me. But there is something else that is not familiar to me: what does this children's collective have to do with what we have been discussing? But here's what I have learned. Until recently, nobody in the school knew or talked about such poets as Andrei Bely, Sasha Cherny, Akhmatova, or Gumilev. And now? Students who are not in her [Gerlin's] classes ask about these poets. Where have they learned about them? From children in her literature course. Nobody talked about these poets or read their verses before, but now they are read and reprinted. Why? They are even printed on the school's [mimeograph] machines. Why don't they just use what is in the library? Where did this unhealthy heightened interest come from?

Voice: Who signed first, you or your husband?

Gerlin: I did.

Nozhkina: If this trial had been held according to the legal norms, what would you have said then?

Gerlin: I would have said that justice had triumphed.

Nozhkina: How can one pin you down?

Voice: Why do you feel this indignation about political matters? You haven't written about criminal matters.

Gerlin: You're mistaken, I have written on criminal matters, but they didn't hound me from my job for that.

Andreyev: In effect, she signed the letter from Litvinov and Bogoraz-Daniel. Her letter was nothing more than an addition to Litvinov's letter. Aren't there any people other than you in this union who are honorable? Do you think you are the most honorable? Don't we have our own newspapers and institutions? But you didn't turn to them. That means that you have trampled on the very Soviet laws of which you speak. You didn't say who gave you the letter. You're saying only what's to your advantage. You're not telling the truth in saying that you were not the first to sign. You were one of the first.

Gerlin: The signatures are in alphabetical order.

Andreyev: And you are making a mistake when you speak about Soviet legality. If you received an appeal, you should have sent it to the proper place.

Gerlin: But I sent it to the Soviet government!

Andreyev: And then, you also declare that Litvinov's letter is a contribution to democracy. You tell us here that you didn't give out the keys to your apartment, while your husband says he did. Look, I keep my keys in my pocket, but where are yours? You are not telling the truth, you are opposing the Soviet state. We chose our judges so that we can have confidence in them, but you demand that they be punished. The letter was written from beginning to end by an anti-Soviet hand. Even among Party members there are some dishonorable people. Who told you about the decision of the Party meeting?

Gerlin: I ascertained this "government secret" myself: there was a Party meeting and, after that, a local committee meeting, which made the decision to fire me. It is obvious that this committee is not the first to meet.

Andreyev: Once again, you don't want to reveal the dishonorable people for whom you are covering up. Who told you about the meeting?

Gerlin: I have already explained.

Andreyev: A person who signed such a letter cannot work at our school.

Osipova: We all know and understand that the vocation of a teacher involves definite obligations. We all know Valeria Mikhailovna. She is a good teacher. We have to act properly, not crudely. I cannot help believing her explanations; I must take them into account. We must also respect the motives that prompted Valeria Mikhailovna. In reality, she feels strongly about the issue of legality, and she has a right to. Even if she made a mistake in not attributing the necessary importance to the first phrase in the letter—why must we punish her for one mistake? I want to make the following analogy. Lenin, in speaking against great-power chauvinism and nationalism in general, said that, while we must forgive nationalism in the oppressed nations, we must not forgive the chauvinism of the dominant powers. If our colleague erred, then her mistake is understandable. And it is necessary not to punish but to understand her. She did not sign the letter sent out by Litvinov and Bogoraz-Daniel—she signed a letter to the chief organs of the Soviet state. We must not ignore this fact. Let us first consider the matter, and then decide.

L. P. Semerova: We are faced with a very complicated situation. The hand of the enemy is apparent in Poland and in Czechoslovakia. The ideological struggle has grown particularly intense. Valeria Mikhailovna says that she is grieved about the laws and about human justice. The fate of the accused matters less to her than the manner and process by which the judgment was formulated. How can a Soviet person talk this way? When all this is transmitted abroad, it aids the hand of the enemy. We call on people to correct shortcomings, but why write letters? Why collect signatures? Why make this known to the entire world? These letters sully our state and our laws. Valeria Mikhailovna's words reveal that she thinks that she alone understands well and analyzes well and that other people do not understand! If a teacher does not have confidence in the righteousness of the state, he cannot be an educator. Pouring out filth in letters is forbidden. And why is there any need to talk about the past? It has already been evaluated, and there is no reason to bring it up again.

Ogorodnikov (physical-education teacher):   Alla Leonidovna said something here about chauvinism. For shame! What has this got to do with nationality?

Osipova: You misunderstood me!

Ogorodnikov: Perhaps I misunderstood you, but all the same! Alla Leonidovna is incorrect. Valeria Mikhailovna is trying to disown Litvinov's letter. But it doesn't work! It is impossible to disown one and sign the other. That is very clear. There are only two sorts of propaganda. Everything that is beneficial to Western propaganda is hostile to ours. Her political laxity makes Valeria Mikhailovna an untrustworthy teacher. I distrust her politically.

N. Ye. Smirnova (literature teacher):   I have heard many things here that must be refuted. First of all, why have almost all the comrades who spoke talked about the Litvinov and Bogoraz-Daniel letter? Valeria Mikhailovna did not sign that letter. She has convincingly demonstrated, facts in hand, that she had taken a different position from Litvinov and Bogoraz-Daniel, that her letter was addressed to the proper Soviet authorities, and that the motives that produced it were truly civic. A person takes a responsible step not because of fame or profit; he takes that action which his conscience as a citizen prompts him to take. If Valeria Mikhailovna did, in fact, make a mistake in not attributing the required meaning to the first phrase of Litvinov's letter, which has provoked such agitation here, she has explained this matter convincingly enough.

Vasileva (teacher in the primary grades):   Comrades, I, as a Communist, must declare bluntly that Valeria Mikhailovna signed a document of indisputably anti-Soviet content. Those comrades who are now discussing the letter of Litvinov and Bogoraz-Daniel are behaving correctly. We must discuss not only the slovenly formulation of the letter but, out of our sense of responsibility, the anti-Soviet content of this letter. Why did 220 persons sign such a letter? What is this, an expression of personal outrage? And you are trying to tell us that this is not offensive! Nor have you considered the complicated international situation, which is most important to us as ideologically experienced teachers. Comrades, I do not trust Valeria Mikhailovna to educate children!

Eidlin: I understand Valeria Mikhailovna. Her fate was not an easy one. But was she perhaps the only one who went through all that? Just yesterday, oppressed by her terrible story, I told it to my father. And I learned, unexpectedly, that my father had also suffered from the cult. He suffered in 1952. I never knew about this. I did not live with my father and did not see him. Although he suffered, he talked agitatedly about those who write dirty letters about our country to our enemies. My father educated me to be politically conscious and firm. But what have we here? Precisely the opposite: We have someone who is politically weak, which, to be quite frank, leaves me unmoved about her fate.

V. I. Nagornaya (physical-education teacher):   We made a mistake. At the local committee meeting, we made a decision without having listened to Valeria Mikhailovna. She is right—this should not have happened. We do not judge an act—we judge a person. What we deal with is not just paper but a person, and one must not only be able to read a paper, one must know how to listen to a human being. I knew nothing about the letter, I had no opinion before today. Today, I have listened to a person. I cannot doubt her. You think to yourself, why is it that this trial has provoked such distress, why have people been accused of violating the law? No one has answered this question for me. Why can't these facts be published? Perhaps then it would all be clear. And then some people talk about Valeria Mikhailovna's "literary circle." It has been meeting for less than a year. That is a short time to have caused the alleged changes in the children. The literary group could not corrupt the children. Besides, aside from literature, we have other subjects. There is physical education. And I, a teacher of physical education, say, I also educate, so you must remove me, too, then everyone.

Nozhkina: I am not convinced that Valeria Mikhailovna came to defend justice. This is a strange kind of justice. Alla Leonidovna and Valentina Leonidovna talked about her here, but they did not convince me. They did not convince me! If Valeria Mikhailovna herself were right, she should be able to convince me. Your opponents here have convinced me, but not you. I don't believe in your system of legality. The main thing, Valeria Mikhailovna, is that these events were a personal affront to you. Your signature was a defense of people you do not know. Should one defend criminals? What kind of justice is this? It is just to condemn criminals, but you defend them.

Ingerov (director of the school):   None of you, comrades, was uncertain about who would defend Gerlin. This matter must be taken into consideration. The list of defenders is not accidental, nor is it accidental that we could predict which names would be on it. It is time for these comrades to think about themselves. Where will such a position lead them? The collective does not wish to work with those who defend that view. Valeria Mikhailovna's speech should be discounted. The first and second letters are one and the same thing! It is useless to use tricks and traps! The same thing! It does not extricate you, it deceives no one! Valeria Mikhailovna has been quietly contemptuous of us all. Why did she say that everything was decided earlier? These statements and the statements of her defenders are all pitiful attempts. None of their little ways deceive us; it is useless to hint and hedge. Not one genuinely thoughtful person spoke up in Valeria Mikhailovna's defense. Today, the chief question, comrade defenders, is what attitude you intend to take from now on. We cannot permit you to follow a double policy. You have no right to introduce doubts into sixteen-year-old minds. A group was formed [around Gerlin] that is rushing unscrupulously to defend its comrades. Can we be sure that a [true] Soviet situation will be restored with Valeria Mikhailovna's departure? We unequivocally warn these comrades. Let them consider the matter first, then vote. We consider this a political matter. Valeria Mikhailovna should have been discharged earlier. A politically unreliable person should not be allowed to teach our children.

Chairman: Valeria Mikhailovna, you do not have the civic qualities and integrity that you have talked about. You are apolitical in many matters. The comparison with the cult of personality is itself an indication of great political ignorance. People who have a clear conscience and genuine civic feelings are completely secure. Why don't I feel exposed to danger? I have a clear conscience.

A motion has been made to ask the OMK to discharge V. M. Gerlin according to Article 48 of the KZOT, Code of Labor Law, on the request of the trade-union organization.

The voting results were as follows: out of a total of forty-two persons, five were opposed to dismissal, two abstained. In the OMK, the vote was slightly different: two or three against dismissal and one abstention.

Gerlin: I am very ashamed. I am so ashamed that I cannot raise my eyes. I am ashamed, ashamed for you, comrades. Because you cannot hear and understand, you cannot think, because many of you have shown yourselves to be even more unprincipled than I thought you were.

[No. 43, April 1968]

Confrontation at the Coffin
BY A WRITER

On those infrequent occasions when the Soviet state buries in honor a truly respected figure, the funeral becomes a political confrontation between antagonists inside, or on the fringes of, the Establishment. Professional bureaucrats, full of official pomp and mock respect, preside over genuine mourners who want to hear and speak truthful, heartfelt words. Repressed political animosities redouble and threaten to burst into the open. When the deceased is a beloved writer, as we learn from the following report, "a magnetic field of social protest invariably builds up around the coffin." Such events are a Russian tradition; the state habitually takes precautions. This account of the funeral of Kornei Chukovsky (1882–1969), the famous literary critic, translator, and writer of children's verse, circulated anonymously (signed "Litterateur") in Moscow after his burial in late October. It requires no further introduction.

The last man they were all scared of has now died. There is a long queue in the anteroom behind the stage of the Central House of Literature. We await our turn to be led out to the guard of honor and the coffin lying in state on the stage.

Most of the people present are those who are not working. Those who traditionally bring the proceedings to a close, who later figure in the newsreels and photographs—Boris Polevoi and Konstantin Fedin—appear only toward the end of the leave-taking. Lydia Korneyevna Chukovskaya is said to have provided the heads of the Moscow division of the Writers' Union in advance with a list of those whom her father did not want invited to the funeral. That probably explains the absence of Arkady Vasilev, Mikhail Alekseyev, and other members of the literary Black Hundred.

Very few Muscovites have come to pay their last respects—the newspapers did not mention the coming lying in state. There are few people, but, as at the funerals of Ehrenburg and Paustovsky, the militia cluster like flies. Besides the uniformed branch, there are a number of boys in mufti with morose, disdainful expressions. The boys began by taking over all the available chairs, letting no one linger or sit down. Dimitri Shostakovich, seriously ill, arrived. They did not let him take his coat off in the vestibule, and in the hall they forbade him to sit on a chair. There was a row.

The memorial service is in secular form. Sergei Mikhalkov stumbles through the high-flown verbiage, delivering it with highly inappropriate expressionlessness and indifference. Then there begins: "From the Soviet Writers' Union . . ."

"From the Russian Federation Writers' Union . . ." "From the Children's Literature Publishing House . . ." "From the Ministry of Education and the Academy of Pedagogical Sciences . . ." All this is read out with the same stupid pomposity with which the major domos must have used to summon the carriages of departing guests, Count So-and-so, or Prince Such-and-such.

Whom are we burying, anyway? Is it some official mandarin, or is it Kornei, the buoyant wit with his wry sense of the ridiculous?

Agnia Barto rattled off her "lesson." Lev Kassil performed a complex verbal pirouette designed to show his audience how close he personally had been to the departed. And only L. Panteleyev, breaking through the barricade of officialese, said a few clumsy and sad words about Chukovsky's popular image. Kornei Chukovsky's family had asked Lyubov Kabo to speak. But when, in the crowded room, she sat down at a table to make a few notes for her speech, KGB General V. N. Ilin (in civilian life, administrative secretary of the Moscow Writers' Union) approached her and said politely, but firmly, that she would not be allowed to. Why not? "A great many people would have liked to speak, but time is pressing. Kornei Ivanovich [Chukovsky] must be buried while it is still light."

The old story. They made haste to bury Boris Pasternak just like this. (On that occasion a leading member of the Literary Fund, one Nikolai Elinson, had snatched a spade from the hand of a dilatory gravedigger and had himself started to shovel the earth on the coffin.) At Ilya Ehrenburg's funeral, passes were issued "for his immediate circle." As a result, most of the dead man's friends could not come to Novodeviche cemetery, where, because of the "pressure of time," Boris Slutsky was denied the right to say his speech of farewell; and once again, last July, when Konstantin Paustovsky was being buried, his relatives and friends were unable to speak—it was necessary to hurry off to Tarussa. But then, on the Moscow–Tarussa road, these same "people in a hurry" had stopped the funeral cortege for half an hour to prevent the young people from getting at Konstantin Georgiyevich's [Paustovsky's] grave. The same provocatory trick was played over Anna Akhmatova's coffin. First of all, people were compelled to hang around the Sklifovsky Hospital morgue for over an hour in complete ignorance of what was happening; and then, all of a sudden, there was a lightning ten-minute farewell accompanied by constant proddings from the militia and Literary Fund bosses.

Why this fear of dead men? Well, you know, it's a tradition. This is how Russian writers have been buried for almost two hundred years. This base and cowardly ritual has been passed down from generation to generation of gendarmes and literary jailers, from [the tsarist officials] Benckendorf and Bulgarin to Ilin and Mikhalkov. The literary secret police always have sharp noses for the danger of any outburst of human feeling, any outburst caused by sudden grief. A magnetic field of social protest invariably builds up around the coffin of a great writer. The intelligentsia, who on ordinary days are distrait, disunited, and ground under by the difficulties of life, suddenly see themselves, beside the graves of those dear to them, as a society of brothers in thought and belief. At such times, they find official lies particularly hard to swallow. People want the word of truth, and even the silent become orators. The authorities, now and in the past, have never bothered to try a dialogue; they have merely sent police reinforcements to the writers' gatherings.

The body of Kornei Ivanovich is being carried out of the hall. In life, he was a head taller than most. Now his body seems enormous. Buses and cars make their way to [the artist colony] Peredelkino.

The funeral service takes place on the slope of the Peredelkino cemetery. It is muddy. We stick in the churned earth. Wet snow falls on bared heads. The crowd grows. The residents of Peredelkino gather in their quilted coats and gum boots. It is an odd crowd. There is no making out who predominates—the locals, the intelligentsia, or various ranks of the militia. In the middle of the human huddle is the upright lid of the coffin, black and red; a loudspeaker is on two posts.

From the loudspeaker issues the apathetic voice of Mikhalkov, sounding even deader and hollower than before. Worn clichés to the effect that young and old know and love Chukovsky. Then a similar speech by the chairman of the District Executive Committee in whose jurisdiction the village of Peredelkino lies, read from a text with a similar lack of expression. The words are garbled. There is no lively intonation, no sincere word, no personal recollection. "The Motherland will not forget . . . Meetings with him were always joyous occasions . . ."

Two steps from the platform stand the pine trees under which lies the genius of Russian letters, Boris Pasternak. We are burying Kornei Chukovsky, a great master of the Russian language; in the crowd are dozens of Russian writers, masters of words. And the officials on the platform grind out their speeches in meager and stereotyped journalese.

But suddenly a stir goes through the "bosses." Pavel Nilin has expressed the wish to speak. Ilin and Mikhalkov do not want to let him, but it is hard to argue with the obstinate Nilin. There he is up on the staging, wobbling on the insecure planking. He has raised his large hand. People turn silent and listen. For the first time today, human speech has been heard on this hillside. Nilin remembers: only a month ago he and Kornei Ivanovich had walked together in these fields. Kornei Ivanovich had wistfully thought aloud that if only he could last out this autumn, there would be light at the end of the tunnel. Nilin had replied that Kornei Ivanovich would last out this and many another autumn and spring; with his resilience of spirit and body, he would close the eyes of many who were still young. Chukovsky had laughed, glad that Nilin did not believe in his impending death.

And we, standing next to the speaker, were picturing Kornei Ivanovich laughing, leaning on his stout stick in the bare field. Everyone who knew him had often seen this picture: Kornei laughing, gesticulating, sometimes guffawing like a boy. Nilin was saying: we still have not altogether realized whom we have lost. A little time must pass before those of whom there are at the moment so few in our country, those who compose only a very small segment of the people— the intelligentsia—can realize whom they have left in the Peredelkino cemetery on this miserable October day. Nilin looked as if he wanted to add something, but he stopped abruptly, sobbed, flapped his hand, and left the platform.

The hammers sounded hollowly on the wood. The crowd moved up the hill, nearer the open grave. We push past fences and between bare bushes. The crowd has covered Pasternak's grave. It affords a good view of the last act of the funeral.

They were very different: animated Boris Leonidovich [Pasternak], going through life like a ship under full sail, and the shrewd peasant Kornei Ivanovich. They were not friends, although each of them in his heart had to respect the other. Death has erased the superficial and the accidental in the relationship of these two great teachers of ours, and we are left with the memory of these men whose very existence made this world more human, more hopeful and truthful. Now they shall lie side by side, and remain side by side in our memories.

The "boys" of the militia, hands in pockets, professionally surveying the surrounding scene, make for their cars. The human river flows off the cemetery hill slowly and unwillingly. People stop and gather in knots. Now the crowd has dissolved. Those who form its core become visible—those to whom Chukovsky is really dear: some fifteen writers and academics. They include Irina Grekova, Kabo, Boris Yampolsky, Valentin Asmus, Nilin, Grigory Svirsky, Emma Gershtein, Olga Chaikovskaya, and some old librarians and young university people.

Yes, one is loath to leave this hill. Through the pompous ritual, through the wordy wrapping, the fact itself begins to show: Kornei Ivanovich is no more. It is difficult to imagine Peredelkino, difficult to imagine life itself, without him.

[No. 63, December 1969]

From Intellectual Ferment to an Intellectual Movement
BY A. ANTIPOV

The initial wave of short, occasional samizdat documents, such as petitions, were supplemented toward the end of the 1960s by more analytical and program- matic writings. The following essay by A. Antipov (a pseudonym), dated January 1969, was one of the most widely circulated and discussed. Its subject is the phenomenon of samizdat itself (though Antipov does not use the word), which he treats as both an expression and forum of a new intellectual and political life in the Soviet Union. Since 1969, many of the more ambitious samizdat works called for by Antipov have appeared.

> Ideas can be rendered harmless only by other ideas.
> —Balzac

One of the most notable gains of the last twelve years [that is, since the Twentieth Party Congress] is that we have acquired a passion for conversation. When we run into one another, there is a lively exchange of news, rumors, and educated guesses. Much more rarely, we exchange fragments of ideas that have suddenly occurred to us and share each other's emotional responses to the politi- cal and cultural events in the life of our society. Discussions have become freer and freer; we have become more daring and more trusting, and to a large extent we have gotten away from superstitions.

The importance of these changes should not be underestimated, but there is also no point in exaggerating them. At first, after the dreadful silence of the Stalin era, this kind of communication unquestionably had positive meaning. It helped us to throw off, or at least to loosen, many of the shackles that had bound us; it led to the formation of circles in which people confided in one another; and it even produced a semblance of public opinion. It should be recognized, never- theless, that this necessary stage in the development of public opinion in our country has already been exhausted; we have gone beyond it. With the passage of time, conversations are degenerating more and more into monotonous chatter. Time and energy are wasted on chewing over the same old cud, spitting it up, and chewing it over again. It leaves a bitter taste in the mouth. Our freethinking is lazy and superficial; there is a flavor of gossip to the exchange of information; criticism verges on griping; and irony has the ring of sheer mockery.

Our task is to go forward from idle chatter to real thinking, that is, to work. We have talked enough on every subject that it's possible to talk to death over a cup of tea or glass of vodka. It is time to move from the dinner table to the writing table.

Our development into an intellectual phase requires an intensive exchange of ideas. Only under that condition will our society be able to become conscious of itself, to make a serious and objective assessment of the situation in our country and the world, to work out new goals, and to spell out realistic ways of achieving them. The job we are talking about will unquestionably require the efforts of many minds for a number of years. We need high-quality statistical material, solid research dealing with the economic, political, social, legal, moral, cultural, and psychological problems of our society, and objective studies of its history. We also need translations of works by foreign specialists. We must undertake a fearless study of our own social organism. This has become an urgent task that we can only do together, under conditions of lively and free discussion. We have mastered the art of speech; we must now learn to write.

The reader has the right at this point to ask the logical question: "What kind of fantasy is this? Where does the author think he's living? Does he know about the existence of the censorship?" Yes, the author knows that the censorship exists, and he is acutely aware that the life of ideas in our society must proceed to a large extent outside the sphere controlled by the censorship. In the last few years, we have witnessed the mass circulation of various materials in manuscript form—stenographic records, minutes of meetings, letters, memoirs, sociological and historical studies, even novels. This material has increased in quantity from year to year. Unfortunately, it has gone undiscussed, so that it is being lost, if not in silence, then in idle chatter.

It is no small merit of this type of literature, regardless of genre, that material intended for informal circulation is written without the feeling of an inner censor leaning over the author's shoulder, as in the case of a text written for regular publication. Researchers and writers of imaginative literature who are used to writing for the official press will probably not find it easy to take up the pen with unshackled hand. But the new and intense delight they will experience will more than repay them for the effort of learning this skill.

There is another important aspect of this matter—uncensored literature is producing a type of reader that is new for us. The writing of a reply, a critical analysis, seems likely to become the most normal and natural reaction to the reading of new material. The discussion proceeds with no one presiding. Everyone with something to say has his own rostrum from which calmly to present his point of view without interrupting anyone else. Pen and paper, courage and caution—those are all that is needed.

Significant writings will give rise in this way to a lavalike flow of critiques, critiques of critiques, and commentaries upon commentaries. We should note parenthetically that it would be desirable, in order to facilitate references, if each text were accompanied by a signature (pseudonymous, of course) and if it were broken down into small paragraphs provided with subheadings.

There is no reason to think that the method of circulating literature in manuscript form would in any way narrow the audience to which it is addressed. Plato, Euclid, and Plutarch enlightened their contemporaries and continue to enlighten us today, despite the fact that their works were produced long before the invention of the printing press. Books are older than printing. One must recognize clearly that the two great cultural advances—phonetic writing and the printing press—are not commensurate. The former was a tremendous conquest of human reason; the latter is an important technical improvement. Under present conditions, another clever device, of even more recent invention, has taken on special importance. The typewriter can do things that Gutenberg's press cannot.

It is also an important fact that writings in manuscript, as experience has shown, have a tendency to reproduce themselves. They do so not long after their appearance in the world—all by themselves and without the participation of their authors or any special organizations—reaching an optimal number of copies and essentially meeting the effective demand. Moreover, the number of copies proves to be approximately proportionate to the social value of the work.

Here the reader will rightly ask another question: "But does the author know what country he is living in? Does he know about the existence of powerful agencies that block the circulation of materials that have not gone through the censors?" Yes, the author knows of the existence of these agencies. But potency is not omnipotence. The power of the apparatus of detection must be answered with coolheadedness and circumspection. Every participant in the uncensored ideological life of our society is required to observe certain basic norms of personal and collective security. Even now, there are many conversations in which appropriate measures are being discussed—the foundations for a future unwritten code of behavior. We must think about these measures. We must reduce to the minimum the dangers to which citizens are exposed in exercising their legal rights under conditions of illegality.

We shall not make a fuss; we shall not fight for freedom of the press: we shall put it into practice.

[No. 55, April 1969]

5

August 1968: The Winter of Communist Reform

ON THE NIGHT OF August 20–21, 1968, the Soviet Union and four Warsaw Pact allies invaded Czechoslovakia to crush the experiment in Communist liberalization known as the Prague Spring. Unlike the similar invasion of Hungary in 1956, the overthrow of the reformist Czechoslovak government, headed by Alexander Dubcek, was a watershed event in Soviet political life as well. It heralded the full victory of antireformist and neo-Stalinist forces in Soviet officialdom, while dealing another heavy blow to reformers in the Soviet Party and liberal intelligentsia. The invasion also created new Soviet dissidents, extended protests to foreign policy, radicalized dissident attitudes and tactics—eight protesters staged a demonstration on Red Square on August 25—and brought yet another wave of official repression.

Developments in Czechoslovakia, a longtime bastion of Stalinist-style rule, had excited and divided Soviet political opinion since 1967. Soviet reformers watched hopefully as the Dubcek wing of the Czechoslovak Party peaceably ousted Antonin Novotny's hard-line leadership in January 1968, initiated market reforms in economic life, and took dramatic steps toward democratization, including more toleration of opposition and the abolition of censorship. They saw in the Prague Spring, with its avowed commitment to anti-Stalinism and "socialism with a human face," many of their own ideas and programs for change in the Soviet Union. Meanwhile, Soviet conservatives and neo-Stalinists viewed these developments as a direct challenge to their own position; their insistence *that the Prague Spring represented a dire threat to official Soviet interests, at home and throughout Eastern Europe, grew steadily more clamorous and menacing. A high official asserted even before the invasion, "If it becomes necessary, we'll shoot Dubcek."[1]*

Those Soviet reformers who continued to believe, even after Khrushchev's overthrow, in the possibility of anti-Stalinist change initiated from within the Party elite had a special stake in the Prague Spring. For them, "it proved that within the Communist Party there are regenerative forces that, within a short time, can produce formidable results in liberalizing the regime without renouncing the fundamental values of socialism."[2]

This was, of course, the basic perspective of Political Diary, *which sought to provide reformist ideas and inspiration for these "regenerative forces" in the Soviet Communist Party. Therefore, Czechoslovakia became, beginning in mid-1967, an increasingly important subject in its pages. Whole sections of successive monthly issues were devoted to Czechoslovak political developments, the programmatic statements of the Dubcek leadership, and official Soviet reactions. When the invasion turned hope into despair,* Political Diary *continued to report on the Soviet occupation, Czechoslovak resistance, and Soviet protests.*

The selections in this chapter are only a small sample of Political Diary's *coverage of these events. They are enough to show, however, that the fate of the Prague Spring was a great tragedy of Soviet reform as well.*

1. *Politicheskii dnevnik,* I, 423.
2. Medvedev, *On Soviet Dissent: Interviews with Piero Ostellino* (New York, 1980), p. 73.

"I Cannot Sleep"

BY YEVGENY YEVTUSHENKO

Yevgeny Yevtushenko (born 1933) was the most popular Soviet poet of the late 1950s and early 1960s. In poetry that was lyrical and declamatory, elegiac and civic, he seemed to speak for a new generation liberated from its own Stalinist youth.[3] His fervent anti-Stalinism and Communist idealism, expressed in such poems as "Winter Station," "Babyi Yar," and "The Heirs of Stalin," made Yevtushenko a kind of junior poet laureate (after Tvardovsky) of the Khrushchev years.[4] Yevtushenko's political outspokenness declined considerably, along with his great popularity, in the late 1960s and in the 1970s; despite subsequent skirmishes with Soviet authorities, he remains a writer in good official standing even today. His later career has led some people, including Western critics whose political courage has never been tested in such difficult circumstances, to forget Yevtushenko's courageous role in the years of de-Stalinization and to dismiss him as a timeserver. The following telegram protesting the Soviet invasion of Czechoslovakia, which Yevtushenko sent directly to Brezhnev, should help to revise this unfair judgment. (Note also that even at this late date, he associated himself proudly with the "tradition" of Solzhenitsyn.) Though Yevtushenko spoke only for himself, his telegram no doubt expressed the feelings of many Soviet intellectuals and artists who were not open dissidents.

I cannot sleep. I do not know how to live my life after this. I understand only one thing, that it is my moral duty to express my opinion to you. I am profoundly convinced that our action in Czechoslovakia is a tragic mistake. It is a cruel blow to Czechoslovak-Soviet friendship and to the world Communist movement. This action detracts from our prestige in the eyes of the world and in our own.

For me, this is also a personal tragedy because I have many friends in Czechoslovakia and I do not know how I will be able to look them in the eye, how I will ever dare to face them again. I tell myself that what has happened is a great gift to all the reactionary forces in the world, that we cannot foresee the overall consequences of this act.

I love my country and my people. I am a modest successor to the great tradition of Russian literature, of such writers as Pushkin, Tolstoy, Dostoevsky,

3. See his *A Precocious Autobiography* (New York, 1963).
4. See George Reavey, *The Poetry of Yevgeny Yevtushenko* (New York, 1965).

and Solzhenitsyn. This tradition has taught me that in some situations it is shameful to remain silent. I ask you to regard my views concerning the action in Czechoslovakia as those of a true son of this country, of the poet who once wrote the song "Do the Russians Want a War?"

[No. 47, August 1968]

A Refutation of the Soviet Invasion
BY ROY MEDVEDEV

In addition to Czechoslovak and Soviet documents, Political Diary *published its own extensive, unsigned commentary on the events in Czechoslovakia. All of it was written by Roy Medvedev, who provided readers with what they could not find in official Soviet publications—a fair and sympathetic analysis of the Prague Spring. Immediately after August 21, 1968, Medvedev's commentary turned into a critical examination of official justifications for the invasion and subsequent occupation. These justifications hinged on the old Stalinist assertion that only Soviet-style systems are truly socialist, and that alternative models are "antisocialist and counterrevolutionary" intrigues sponsored by domestic and foreign reactionaries—an imperial line of reasoning that extends from Stalin's threats against Yugoslavia in 1949–53, to Soviet warnings about Polish developments in 1981. Medvedev's analysis was a remarkably informed and effective repudiation of these Soviet claims and of the invasion itself. It is printed below in abridged form.*

Was the Invasion a "Defense of Socialism"?

On August 22, 1968, *Pravda* published a long editorial, "The Defense of Socialism Is the Highest International Duty," constituting the official Soviet version of the events in Czechoslovakia. Its purpose is to provide ideological justification for the invasion by Warsaw Pact troops of a friendly country that is a member of the Warsaw Pact. The editorial contains a great many erroneous arguments and obvious fabrications meant to disorient Soviet citizens.

For example, *Pravda* writes that the Soviet Communist Party has had an "understanding attitude" toward the decisions made by the Communist Party of Czechoslovakia (CPC) at the January 1968 plenum of its Central Committee. But *Pravda* says nothing about the mistakes and crimes of the Novotny group, which brought Czechoslovakia to its present state of political crisis. *Pravda* asserts that the Soviet Communist Party leadership has no desire to impose its views on the CPC concerning forms and methods of social control or the road to socialism. But the facts testify to the opposite.

During the past six months, we have tried to impose on the CPC our false understanding of events in that country, and when our point of view was rejected, we resorted to military action. Referring to the meetings with CPC leaders in Dresden last spring, *Pravda* admits that the Czechoslovak leaders insisted that they were in full control of the situation in their country. But the Soviet Party leadership "on the basis of all the available facts came to quite a different conclusion"—namely, that "the course of events was such that it could lead to a counterrevolutionary coup." This was a totally wrong conclusion, based not on an analysis of the facts but on hysterical appeals by the Novotnyites, who were being removed from their posts, and by their obvious allies in the Soviet embassy in Czechoslovakia. There was no danger of a counterrevolutionary coup either in the spring of 1968 or later—not if one is to speak of an immediate danger, at any rate.

Pravda comes down full force against the CPC's Action Program of April 1968, calling it "a legal platform for further attacks by right-wingers on the Party, the foundations of socialism, and friendship between the Czechoslovak and Soviet peoples." This too is blatant slander. Any form of democratization opens the way to criticism, including criticism by nonparty forces and groupings. In the majority of cases, however, such criticism is not only not dangerous to the ruling Communist Party but is even to its advantage.

Pravda declares that the massive personnel changes in the Czecho-Slovak Socialist Republic (CSSR) were undermining the very foundations of the social system there. But that is not so. The purge of Party cadres in Czechoslovakia was not on the same scale as that in Hungary and Poland, or in the USSR after the Twentieth and Twenty-second congresses and after Stalin's death. There was no de-Stalinization in the CSSR. Thus, a change of personnel was indispensable, and its actual effect was to increase the stability of the social system.

Pravda is unfair in its denunciation of the letter by a group of writers and other prominent Czechoslovak public figures that has been called the "Two Thousand Words" manifesto. This letter was not a platform for counterrevolutionary action. And in fact it was condemned by a presidium of the CPC Central Committee, the National Assembly of the CSSR, and the Party press. Under existing circumstances that was sufficient. But the Czechoslovak press could not apply the term "counterrevolutionary" to the majority of the authors of this letter, who are well known and highly respected by the Czechoslovak people. Among the signatories of this letter were national heroes of the CSSR, but *Pravda* stops just short of calling them "agents of Western intelligence services."

Pravda cites as examples of "dangerous counterrevolutionary actions" instances in which leaflets appeared at some factories. The Czechoslovak Party press itself wrote about these leaflets and criticized them. *Pravda*'s contention that "the country was overwhelmed by a vicious anti-Communist campaign organized by counterrevolutionary forces and obviously inspired by imperialist propaganda" is also slanderous. *Pravda* continues, "The party was being destroyed, its leaders were carrying things so far that the CPC was being transformed into an amorphous, ineffective organization, a kind of discussion club and nothing more." Actually, the CPC's moral authority was swiftly rising in 1968, and more and more new members were joining. (*Pravda* calls the removal of those responsible for the serious crimes of the Stalin era and the crimes committed in the CSSR in the late 1950s a "pogrom" and the moral equivalent of "having them shot.")

Pravda's contention that the CPC leaders "did nothing to defend Communist ideological positions" and that they had "renounced Leninism" is equally base and deceitful. Similarly twisted and totally unfair is *Pravda's* interpretation of the Czechoslovak leaders' effort to improve the functioning of their country's economy through an economic reform. This was actually a wise attempt to combine planning with market mechanisms. (Our own economic reform projected the same kind of thing in a different, more cautious form.) But *Pravda* portrays this to its readers as an attempt to *replace* planning by market mechanisms.

The CSSR made it easier for foreign tourists to enter its territory. Of this *Pravda* says, "The border of Czechoslovakia was in fact opened to foreign spies and saboteurs." But similar measures were taken long ago by Poland, Bulgaria, Yugoslavia, and Rumania. Even the USSR several years ago effectively opened its border with Finland, despite the fact that spies could enter our country disguised as Finnish tourists.

Pravda gives a biased and tendentious account as well of the activities of various political clubs and the revitalization of the non-Communist parties in the National Front of Czechoslovakia. It is true that during 1968 a number of small clubs and organizations have arisen in Czechoslovakia which are not controlled by the CPC and which the CPC has even spoken out against on several occasions. Most of these organizations favor socialism but have a different conception of how to build it than does the CPC. Two small parties within the National Front, whose presence was hardly even noticed in previous years, since they existed mainly for the sake of appearance, have revived and become active in new ways. Attempts have also been made to reestablish the Social Democratic Party of Czechoslovakia.

But what should the CPC have done under the circumstances? Immediately ban all undesirable groups? Dissolve all the newly emerging, tiny independent organizations? Dissolve the People's Party and Socialist Party, which had been in the National Front for twenty years and whose local committees were being reactivated? Such a policy would have been the crudest possible political mistake. An embryonic opposition was indeed arising in Czechoslovakia. But this was advantageous for the CPC itself. The CPC's position and influence were so powerful that it was not threatened by any opposition.

Thus, the correct thing for the CPC to do was to engage in an ideological polemic and political debate with most of the political associations and clubs that emerged in 1968, and that is what it did. And if the question of suppressing some active counterrevolutionary organization had come up, the Czechoslovak government, rather than the Party, was in the best position to decide such matters. The entry of a Warsaw Pact army of 600,000 was not required to accomplish that.

By violating Czechoslovak sovereignty, affronting the government of the CSSR and the leadership of the CPC, and offending the national sensibilities of the Czechs and Slovaks, we have weakened, not strengthened, the positions of socialism in that country. Our action in Czechoslovakia was not the "defense of socialism" but a blow against socialism in Czechoslovakia and throughout the world.

(August 24, 1968)

Was There a Danger of Military Intervention by NATO?

The official Soviet justification for the military intervention by the five Warsaw Pact countries insists, first, that there was an immediate danger of domestic counterrevolution and, second, that there was an immediate danger of an invasion by NATO forces. Several Soviet propagandists now argue approximately as follows: "If the Soviet and allied troops had not entered Czechoslovakia, the divisions of the *Bundeswehr* and of NATO would have been there within three to five days." It requires little effort to refute this version of events.

First, it should be noted that no evidence of imminent military intervention by NATO has been presented to Soviet public opinion. There are no facts or arguments that we can analyze—only bald assertions, which count on the majority's traditional blind acceptance of official communiqués. But the whole world knows that in the period preceding August 21 there were no significant troop concentrations along Czechoslovakia's western border—not even enough to overrun the Czechoslovak army's border defenses. The only forces NATO had near the Czechoslovak border were several *Bundeswehr* divisions and some American military units. There was no mobilization under way in West Germany. On the contrary, military maneuvers that had been scheduled along the border of Czechoslovakia were shifted to another area to avoid complications.

As everyone knows, Czechoslovakia is a member of the Warsaw Pact and is linked with the other socialist states by additional friendship and mutual-aid treaties. No Western power or alliance could plan an isolated invasion of Czechoslovakia, or East Germany, or Hungary. Every Western strategist knows that if such an invasion took place, their forces would be met by the armed might of the entire Warsaw Pact. In other words, a new world war would begin. The same would be true if our forces invaded West Germany, for example. But no Western politician is going to risk a world war today merely to support some isolated counterrevolutionary groups in Czechoslovakia. The Western powers could not bring themselves to intervene in Hungary in 1956, where counterrevolutionary forces were incomparably stronger than in Czechoslovakia. Moreover, the Nagy government had announced Hungary's withdrawal from the Warsaw Pact and appealed for aid to the Western countries. The only aid given was to organize and arm reactionary Hungarian émigré units and send them over the border into

Hungary. But before August 21 there were practically no armed émigré Czecho-slovak units in West Germany or Austria.

If there really had been a danger of armed intervention from the west, Warsaw Pact troops could simply have been sent to the border regions of the CSSR in consultation with the Czechoslovak government. West Germany is the only NATO country bordering Czechoslovakia, and our troops could have occu-pied the key sectors along this border within an hour or two, advancing from East Germany. One wonders why it was necessary to send parachute troops to Prague and Bratislava.

It is quite obvious that the American political leaders, the German militarists, and the entire NATO leadership were watching the course of events in Czecho-slovakia quite closely. And, of course, they not only followed events but tried in every way to push them in a certain direction, seeking, above all, to split the socialist camp in Europe. To this end, our Western opponents not only gave as much support as they could to open counterrevolutionary groups in Czecho-slovakia; they also tried, if only verbally, to support reforms that remained within the framework of socialist democracy and that actually did not weaken but strengthened socialist society in Czechoslovakia. To the Western strategists, the decisive thing was that these reforms displeased many of the leaders of the other socialist countries and drew harsh criticism from them.

We ourselves support various nationalist capitalist movements in a similar way when they are directed against the American and Western European imperi-alists. And not only when underdeveloped countries are involved. We support de Gaulle's initiatives against the United States and NATO. But in such cases, both for us and for our opponents, it is only a matter of political and economic support. In some cases, there is also military support, for example, in the Middle East. But the situation that developed in Czechoslovakia excluded the possibility of direct military intervention by the West. Therefore, it is absurd and ridiculous to argue that the Warsaw Pact troops prevented a new German occupation. No one in that country believes these primitive inventions.

(September 22, 1968)

The Real Dimensions and Danger of Domestic Counterrevolution

The other argument of official Soviet propaganda is that by the summer of 1968 a counterrevolutionary situation had developed and the threat of a counter-revolutionary coup was imminent. The antisocialist forces in Czechoslovakia, so go the arguments in our press, were very strong: they had hundreds of thousands of armed underground supporters; they had taken control of the greater part of the mass media; and a substantial section of the youth and intelligentsia was under their influence. The counterrevolutionaries in Czechoslovakia, led by a single central organization, were closely linked with foreign intelligence agencies

and émigré organizations. All of these anti-Soviet, antisocialist, and counterrevolutionary forces were preparing for the seizure of power, and we had to strike a
"preventive" blow to frustrate their conspiratorial plans.

Of course, it was not enough to argue the strength of the counterrevolution
to justify our intervention in Czechoslovak internal affairs. A second argument
was necessary—the alleged weakness of the socialist authorities in Czechoslovakia. Our newspapers wrote that the leadership of the CPC Central Committee had temporarily fallen into the hands of right-wing revisionists who, instead
of putting up a real fight against the counterrevolution, were allowing it to seize
one position after another. As for the Polish and East German newspapers, they
openly accused the CPC of having lost power and claimed that the authorities
there no longer controlled the situation. It followed that only outside intervention
could save socialism in Czechoslovakia and prevent it from being transformed
into a jumping-off point for further attacks on the socialist countries.

The CPC leaders, as we know, disputed our allegation. They argued that
there was no real danger of a counterrevolutionary coup. They admitted there
was an intensification of antisocialist propaganda but denied our claim that the
counterrevolution had penetrated all the Party and government institutions and
had seized control of the mass media. They said that the Party, the workers'
militia, the army, and the security police were vigilantly defending the socialist
system and that therefore there was no need for intervention by Warsaw Pact
forces.

Were there counterrevolutionary and antisocialist forces? Yes, it is a known
fact that after 1948 quite a few former capitalists and landlords continued to live
in Czechoslovakia. Unlike Hungary and Romania, Czechoslovakia did not take
part in the war against the USSR, and there was not the same kind of bitter
underground and semi-underground civil war as in Poland and Yugoslavia. Hence
there was no substantial emigration. There had been quite a few small and
medium-sized capitalists and property owners—kulaks and owners of small busi-
nesses, commercial establishments, private housing, and so on. The revolution
took away these people's private property and privileges, and it would be strange
to expect that they would support socialism or socialist reforms. Undoubtedly
there were small, semilegal and legal groups and organizations that rested on this
social base, took antisocialist positions, and were oriented toward the Western
capitalist countries. The serious errors committed by the preceding CPC leadership, headed by Antonin Novotny, gave considerable sustenance to antisocialist
propaganda and antisocialist moods in Czechoslovakia.

The changes in the Party and government leadership and the de facto abolition of censorship allowed antisocialists to express their views more openly and
frankly. Many antisocialist tendencies and groups surfaced and even began to
rally their forces and organize. This is undeniable. At the same time, there is no
question that the new CPC leadership's decisive reversal of the crimes and errors
of earlier years, the proclamation of the new Action Program, the honest practical

implementation of the fundamental principles of genuine socialist democracy, the restoration of legality, and the elaboration of a program of economic reforms aimed at rapidly improving the economic situation—all of this was pulling the rug out from under the antisocialist and counterrevolutionary forces and strengthening the real authority of the CPC and its leading role. It was obvious that as the new Action Program [of April 1968] was more and more put into effect, the influence of the antisocialist forces and anti-Communist propaganda would steadily decline.

The CPC held the decisive positions in the state apparatus and therefore would have found it easy to stop antisocialist propaganda and activity. However, the CPC Central Committee preferred not to bring in the security police, workers' militia, or army right away. They chose to use political and ideological methods to counter their opponents, and in that specific situation they were absolutely correct.

We do not know how the political struggle in Czechoslovakia would have unfolded, but most of the evidence shows that the CPC knew how to retain its leading role in the country without resorting to violence and without banning other groups. The intervention by the Warsaw Pact forces changed the entire political atmosphere in Czechoslovakia, and in some respects weakened the position and authority of the CPC.

The official Soviet view of the counterrevolutionary danger was based on several extremely flimsy premises. First, we greatly exaggerated the strength of the counterrevolution. Among the "antisocialists" we included not only real opponents of the Communist Party and socialism but also many prominent figures in the CPC, writers, journalists, and other representatives of the youth and intelligentsia of Czechoslovakia who did not oppose the leading role of the CPC or the socialist system. Some of these people actually made political errors. It is not hard to find elements of nationalism in their speeches and articles. And some were excessively harsh in their criticism of the entire twenty years of the "Novotny era," from 1948 to 1968. It was possible and necessary to polemicize against such people (without, of course, resorting to the kind of rude and violent tone used in our press in the last few months), but it was totally wrong to call them all antisocialists, reactionaries, and, later on, even counterrevolutionaries. This was a typically Stalinist technique—to transform a struggle against dissidents within the Party into a struggle against "enemies of the people."

Most of the journalists and writers who appeared on radio and television in 1968, and who edited Literarni listy, Mlada fronta, and many other newspapers and magazines were members of the CPC, who had worked in the same jobs under Novotny. In the spring of 1968, they began to write and speak differently from before. In so doing, they committed many errors, and some of them went too far to the right or left. But this was no reason to call all of them counterrevolutionaries or demand that the CPC leaders immediately put a stop to their activities.

The case of Jan Prochazka is typical. We often wrote about him in past years as a prominent representative of the Czechoslovak Communist intelligentsia, leader of the Czechoslovak Writers' Union, and member of the CPC Central Committee. In late 1967, he was removed from the leadership of the Writers' Union and from the Central Committee. In early 1968, he once again became deputy chairman of the Writers' Union. In his articles in 1968, he made quite a few mistakes, and our press called him a "right-wing revisionist" and a "nationalist." (*Literaturnaya gazeta*'s articles about Prochazka contain even more errors and overstatements than his writings did.) By September 1968 *Pravda* and *Izvestia,* along with *Literaturnaya gazeta,* were calling Prochazka a counterrevolutionary, even a "ringleader of the counterrevolution."

In general, our press has been rather irresponsible in the way it has thrown around the terms right-wing revisionist, antisocialist, and counterrevolutionary in the last few months. Thus, many people who have taken absolutely correct Marxist-Leninist stands (and justly criticized many of our actions from this point of view) have been called right-wing revisionists. And many Czechoslovak intellectuals who actually did fall temporarily into "left," "right," or nationalist deviations under the influence of the present situation have been called counterrevolutionaries and antisocialists. Since the leadership of the CPC Central Committee continued to maintain ties with Prochazka and Pelikan and Jungmann—and even with Ota Sik and Jiri Hajek, who held prominent posts in the Czechoslovak government—we began to write in our newspapers and magazines that the "right-wing revisionists" had established ties with "counterrevolutionaries and antisocialists" and thus a counterrevolutionary situation had arisen in that country.

Such an analysis, in which any journalist or Party leader we didn't like was immediately placed in the category of "right wing" or "antisocialist," constituted the crudest kind of error. It prevented us from soberly assessing the real forces of the counterrevolution in Czechoslovakia and whatever real danger there was to the socialist conquests won by that country. There were no grounds for pinning the label "counterrevolutionary" on the famous Czechoslovak travel writers Hanzelka and Zikmund, the Olympic champion Zatopeka, and dozens of others who are extremely popular there.

And this is not to mention the outright lies that have apparently been deliberately inspired in our newspapers in the last few weeks. We have dismissed the universal indignation shown by the Czechoslovaks toward the crude and illegal actions by the five Warsaw Pact countries as the product of "counterrevolutionary intrigue." When crowds of Czechoslovak citizens expressed their outrage at our forcible removal of their legally elected leaders—Alexander Dubcek, Josef Smrkovsky, and others—we called these crowds "counterrevolutionary bands directed by West German *Bundeswehr* specialists." The mobile radio stations of the Czechoslovak army, which kept the population informed about the situation in the country and the decisions of the government and National

Assembly, we called "underground counterrevolutionary radio stations." *Pravda* published an article on August 28 entitled "Hidden Facts Come to Light," which claimed that the Fourteenth Congress of the CPC was convened in Prague by some underground counterrevolutionary organization that had long existed in Czechoslovakia.

Here is how *Izvestia* described the situation in that country before the invasion by Soviet troops: "Across the wide-open borders there streamed a flood of emissaries from West Germany, in the guise of 'tourists, economic experts, representatives of West German banks and corporations, correspondents,' etc. Money, arms, radio equipment, and copying machines for antisocialist literature came by the same route. There were reports that 'instructors' from West Germany took a direct part in establishing underground bases and conspiratorial apartments in Czechoslovakia and in training counterrevolutionaries in the techniques of subversive warfare, including armed struggle. . . . Fighting groups of saboteurs and terrorists were put together with the active participation of West German agents, for example, in the districts of Ceske Budejovice, Kladno, and Cesky Krumlov. Armed units were being organized in Prague and other cities, consisting primarily of students and adolescents."

This entire terrifying picture of a counterrevolutionary coup in preparation painted by K. Petrov, supposedly based on information in West German newspapers, is nothing but slander. And these lies appeared in our press on September 21, that is, a month after the Warsaw Pact troops entered Czechoslovakia. Why haven't our troops, who sealed the borders on the night of August 21, captured any of these West German "instructors" or other leaders of these "saboteur and terrorist groups"? Why did we have to make concessions to Dubcek, Cernik, and the other leaders and restore them [temporarily] to power in Czechoslovakia?

Many of our newspapers and magazines followed an extremely primitive logic. Since the Soviet troops who invaded Czechoslovakia were met with hostility, that means the counterrevolution was at work. And the larger the scale of the protests, the greater the alleged influence of counterrevolutionaries. For example, *Pravda*'s special correspondent A. Murzin recently wrote, "When you observe the events [in Czechoslovakia] you understand better and better that the hidden enemies of socialism and the most ferocious anti-Soviet elements have been undermining the socialist foundations in Czechoslovakia for a long time. And when the troops of the fraternal socialist countries came to the aid of the Czechoslovak people, reactionaries gave vent to all of their malice and hatred for socialism and for Soviet-Czechoslovak friendship. By playing on peoples' feelings, raising irresponsible slogans, issuing deliberately harmful orders, provoking, and slandering, they succeeded in disorienting a section of the populace and creating disorders."

Such a version of the events in Czechoslovakia after the invasion is totally wrong and mistaken. In fact, the quick response of the Czechoslovak populace to the arrival of these uninvited troops, their organization of radio and television broadcasts, production and circulation of newspapers and leaflets protesting the occupation and the arrest of their elected leaders, the organization of the Party Congress, the renaming of villages and the removal of street signs—this avalanche of popular protest and outrage was not and could not have been organized in twenty-four hours by some counterrevolutionary group. This was the work of the Party and government of Czechoslovakia, its army, and its legal press, radio, and television. And at the head of this protest were not counterrevolutionaries but members of the Communist Party and Young Communist League and of the workers' militia. And if there was any single center in Czechoslovakia directing the resistance, it operated not in the name of foreign intelligence agencies but of the legally elected Czechoslovak government, the National Assembly.

Of course, there were quite a few spontaneous actions and expressions of mass indignation; some were even led, apparently, by underground counterrevolutionary organizations. It's entirely possible that many of the terrorist acts against Soviet soldiers and officers were provoked precisely by such counterrevolutionary groups, whose work was made easier by our crude intervention in Czechoslovak internal affairs. But the main wave of protest, the demonstrations of outraged citizens, the strikes, and acts of defiance—all of this was controlled by the existing central Party organization.

And this is entirely natural and logical. The CPC would not have fulfilled its duty to its people if it had taken any other position, if it had failed to call on its people to put up nonviolent resistance, if it had asked them to submit to this coarse violence.

Imagine for a moment that Chinese paratroops had descended on Moscow some night on Mao Zedong's orders, quickly occupied all government buildings, arrested Brezhnev, Kosygin, Podgorny, and other Soviet leaders, and flown them to Peking, proclaiming them to be right-wing revisionists, counterrevolutionaries, and antisocialist elements. How would the Soviet people react to such an invasion? How would the Party and government leaders who remained at large conduct themselves? Would they perhaps begin to praise the "glorious helmsman"? After all, the Chinese newspapers write even now about the Soviet peoples' great love for Mao. We would have to assume that the Soviet people and all our organizations and publications would act in a way very similar to the way the Czechoslovaks acted when, on the morning of August 21, they found their country occupied by foreign troops. They would not have rushed to help the invading forces suppress their own "counterrevolutionaries and right-wing revisionists" but would have directed their anger against those troops—who, of course, would not be to blame, since they would only be carrying out orders. And, of course, many of our soldiers recognized the irrationality and harmfulness of their orders only after August 21.

Some of our ideologists, having been totally disoriented on the question of counterrevolution in Czechoslovakia, have advanced another very odd and very dangerous concept. We have in mind the concept of "peaceful" counterrevolution. This was most clearly expressed in a long article by S. Kovalev in the September 11 *Pravda,* under the title "On 'Peaceful' and Nonpeaceful Counterrevolution." Kovalev writes as follows:

"In the new stage of historical development, when socialism has become a world system and the might of imperialism has been seriously undermined, there are bound to be substantial changes in the tactics of the antisocialist forces. Reaction has begun to use 'quiet' or 'peaceful' forms of struggle (at least at the outset) against socialism. This is confirmed in particular by the course of events in Czechoslovakia, where the antisocialist forces, disguising their counterrevolutionary aims, have contended that they are not opposed to socialism in general but are only against 'bad' socialism and are for 'good' socialism. But what they call 'bad' turns out to be the true and genuine socialism that has been won by the working people, and 'good' is right-wing, reformist 'democratic' socialism, which represents a turn back toward the bourgeois system.

"The tactic of 'peaceful counterrevolution' (in the initial stage) is a very crafty tactic, because it counts on deceiving the masses within the country by citing the need to 'improve' socialism in the alleged interests of the people and misleading light-minded people in foreign countries."

What can we say about this "very crafty" theory, which is very far removed from genuine Marxism-Leninism? If we were guided by Kovalev's theory, any criticism that was really aimed at improving socialist society could be called "peaceful counterrevolution." For who is to distinguish between sincere and insincere criticism? Wouldn't it be the same conservative bureaucrats who remain in Czechoslovakia and in other socialist countries?

Second, even if we assume that "peaceful counterrevolution" would at first criticize only "bad" socialism and defend "good" socialism, would the best argument against counterrevolution in such a case be the use of tanks, guns, and paratroops? Wouldn't the resort to crude force mean that we have no other arguments to defend true and genuine socialism? And don't actions like the ones we took in Czechoslovakia play into the hands of the real counterrevolutionaries, both the peaceful ones and the nonpeaceful ones? And don't these actions show that there do exist in the world both good and bad kinds of socialism—or real and pseudo socialism, to put it more accurately. No, we're not about to say that Soviet socialism is "bad" and today's Czechoslovak socialism is "good." In both countries, elements of genuine socialism are mixed in with pseudo socialism. It is not so simple to separate one from the other, and the effort to do so is not helped by tanks and paratroops, especially those from some other country.

Third, we cannot fail to comment that Kovalev's "new" conception is not at all new. It is only a new presentation of the old theory of Stalin and Molotov presented at the February–March 1937 plenum of the Central Committee of the Soviet Communist Party. We should recall that Molotov and Stalin spoke then about the new disguise assumed by the "enemy of the people"—he carried a Party card in his pocket and spoke of improving socialism and correcting difficulties, but in fact he was harboring plans to restore capitalism. Let us also recall how much the acceptance of that false theory cost our people and the entire world Communist movement.

To sum up our discussion of the question of counterrevolution in Czechoslovakia, we would repeat that although there was a certain danger of counterrevolution, we greatly exaggerated that danger and committed an error that was far more dangerous to socialism throughout the world than any counterrevolutionary intrigues in Czechoslovakia or other socialist countries could have been. On September 4, 1968, a cartoon appeared on the back page of *Literaturnaya gazeta*. It shows a fool getting ready to hit a fly on a windowpane with a hammer. Those who ordered the Warsaw Pact armies into Czechoslovakia, a force of 600,000 troops and nearly 2,000 tanks, risked the destruction of far more than just some window glass.

(September 24, 1968)
[No. 47, August 1968 and no. 48, September 1968]

Russia's Shame
BY ALEKSANDR IVANOV

A great many ordinary Soviet officials and citizens seem to have supported the invasion of Czechoslovakia for reasons that had little to do with socialism. They defended the action as a legitimate expression of Russia's national interests; the Soviet Union, they insisted, was entitled, for its own national security, to maintain subservient regimes in Eastern Europe, which it had liberated in World War II. The following polemic by Aleksandr Ivanov (probably a pseudonym) is an assault on this kind of raw Russian nationalism, which the author associates with Stalinism. The version printed here is extracted from a longer article, dated 1968–69 and entitled "The National Shame of Great Russians (On the Forthcoming Ninetieth Anniversary of J. V. Stalin's Birth)." Unlike neo-Stalinists who equate Soviet Communism with Russian nationalism, or dissidents such as Solzhenitsyn who argue that Stalinism is a Communist evil without any roots in Russian tradition, Ivanov condemns the invasion as a Stalinist blasphemy of both Communism and Russia. To emphasize this point, he identifies himself as "a member of the Soviet Communist Party and a Russian."

August 1968 was one of the most shameful manifestations of the campaign [to restore Stalinism in the Soviet Union]. What a dark and forbidding object lesson for all future generations—this forcible exporting of the remnants of pseudo socialism into Czechoslovakia on the superhypocritical pretext of defending that country's development toward socialism! Stalinist pseudo socialism—precisely because it is dying out everywhere in our country, because it already smells of the grave, because the ground is giving way under its feet—rushed hysterically to save *itself* by the most extreme means. It seeks to postpone the burial of the barracks spirit for the very reason that it has been thoroughly aired out almost everywhere. It can try to save itself only by drowning out the implacable tolling of the bell of history with the clanking and clatter of tank treads.

So here we see the Stalinists of our huge country, frightened to death, trying to drown out with the clatter of tank treads the voice of those Communists who in tiny Czechoslovakia were a bit too hasty in trying to cleanse the *human face* of socialism of the trappings of pseudo socialism. They drown out and suppress revolutionary efforts rather than bury these barracks-spirited encrustations upon true socialism. With the blow of the iron fist, they have, for the moment, saved themselves and the Czech Stalinists—ridiculously small in numbers!—from the irreversible forward march of socialism.

As Lenin said in 1921, "The main thing is . . . to take maximum initiative, to show maximum self-reliance and maximum audacity." One needs no special theory to see that this was the very thing the [reformist] Czechoslovaks set out to do, with greater audacity than anyone, in January 1968. It is enough just to look at what actually happened. The only thing the Czechoslovak Communists might be reproached for from our, Communist, point of view is a certain hastiness and disregard for coordinating their efforts with the general, gradual movement toward de-Stalinization that was going on everywhere in our country—in spite of the outward appearance of restoration. They could also be reproached because they didn't attach any importance to the *froth* of abstract and sometimes irresponsible phrasemongering [among some Czechs and Slovaks], which although it was not decisive in Czechoslovak society was nevertheless used by our Stalinists to discredit and smear what was really going on there.

What could be more shameful for us? We declared a revolution—the continuation of the revolution, its further development—to be a counterrevolution! The implementation of the socialist principle that says, as Marx and Engels put it in the *Communist Manifesto,* that the free development of each is the condition for the free development of all, was declared to be—antisocialist! True Communists, who creatively hastened the process of socialist development, of bringing the socialist revolution to fruition—we declared them to be "revisionists"!

August 1968 was a blow at the *practical reality* of socialism and at the Communist movement throughout the world. It was a blow against the ideas of socialism, against genuine Marxism, against the prestige of Communists in the eyes of all progressive humanity, because this blow was struck in the name of socialism and its ideas. It would be hard to think of anything else that would have so substantially served the interests of preserving antagonistic class society in general and state-monopoly capitalism in particular—preserving its foundations in the capitalist countries and their remnants in our own country.

But it was our own "young and green" soldiers who carried out this reactionary deed. They did it without knowing or asking *who* they were going after, *who* they were crushing—whether it was a counterrevolution or a revolution. This blind and obedient willingness to follow any order, this unwillingness to consider the significance of one's own actions and to take responsibility for participating in such an action—that is our national shame, the national disgrace of our times!

Those people who do not feel *great* shame over August 1968 are not Great Russians. They are Russians only in their language and in certain external appearances acquired without any effort of will, merely reproduced superficially, and therefore lacking in any value.

The stamp of historical shame is on our brow. We should understand that, all of us Russians. And the first to set the example of great awareness of this shame, greatly heeding the call of conscience, should be every genuine Communist, every Leninist, who is true to the Communist ideal, not the "ideal" of the Stalinist barracks.

We cannot cleanse ourselves of this shame simply by setting ourselves apart from it. After all, we are responsible for the enormous harm done to Czechoslovakia's development toward Communism, for all the consequences of our reactionary intervention.

Today, there is only one road that we can take. And that is to try to attain the level of the *Czechoslovaks'* initiative, to carry on what *they* began, without of course repeating their mistakes. Only by coming up to their level, and by achieving a general coordination of the [anti-Stalinist] movement, can we set matters right.

Before us stands the difficult, very difficult road of making reparation.

[No. 63, December 1969]

6

Toward a Moscow Spring?

THE STALINIST PAST *still hovers over the Soviet present, as we have seen in previous chapters. We end, in this chapter, with prospects for the future.*

Those Soviet citizens who want a more liberal or democratic order, whether they are officials or dissidents, must confront the same question that divided their counterparts in nineteenth-century tsarist Russia: Is meaningful reform possible in such a tenaciously authoritarian, habitually repressive system, and where liberal ideas seem to have little support in the nation's historical traditions or in present-day society?

As a result of counterreforms and new repressions by Khrushchev's successors, many liberal-minded Soviet citizens have lost their reformist hopes of the 1950s and 1960s. They now believe that the Soviet system is hopelessly ill conceived and corrupt, that reform cannot come from within the ruling Communist Party or under the banner of its Marxist-Leninist ideology, that only an entirely different kind of political system can produce a better future. But unlike Russian radicals in the nineteenth century, most of these people, including even avowed dissidents, recoil from the logical conclusion of their pessimism. Having experienced one revolution, they fear another no less than they dislike the existing system.

These people are trapped, it seems, in a political cul-de-sac, without faith in the possibility of reform or any desire for revolution. Among those who have not abandoned politics altogether, some now advocate a spiritual, usually religious, transformation within individuals; others bravely devote themselves to protesting official abuses of civil liberties. Both outlooks are important trends in the Soviet Union today. But neither offers any kind of real programmatic perspective, any way toward even a modest degree of Soviet liberalization, even on a theoretical level.

That is one important reason why the reformist idea persists in the Soviet Union, despite its setbacks since the mid-1960s. Another is that reformers take a longer view of the process of change. They see the limited reforms of the Khrushchev years (and by analogy, reforms in Eastern Europe) as evidence that enlightened forces do exist in high Party circles, that these officials will, in the right circumstances, respond positively to the country's social and political problems, and that Communist ideology can inspire a more humane socialism. In this longer view, the defeat of reform since Khrushchev, while a bitter disappointment, is only a stage in an ongoing struggle for change inside the Soviet system.

Any prospect of liberal change in the Soviet Union therefore depends upon the gradual creation of a larger, more stable, and more confident body of enlightened, or reformist, opinion inside the Party and state bureaucracies. For many years, this essentially educational goal was pursued most vigorously, inside the Soviet Establishment, by Novy mir, the official monthly journal edited by Tvardovsky. Its editors, themselves officials and Party members, believed in the possibility of movement toward a Soviet "democratic socialism" that would be "human through and through." In a necessarily guarded and censored form, Novy mir promoted political and economic ideas—many of them similar to those of the Prague Spring—that could shape political opinion and find a constituency "in the corridors of power."[1]

Political Diary sought to perform the same function, but in an uncensored and thus bolder way. Ideas and policies only adumbrated in Novy mir were stated explicitly in Political Diary. Because the latter was a samizdat publication and proponent of democratic freedoms, its pages were open to different political perspectives. But the main purpose of Political Diary was to present reformist ideas that were "loyal and will not shock," that "can and should appeal to 'consumers' within the Party and state apparatus."[2] In this way, Political Diary hoped, even during the winter of Soviet reform, to contribute to an enlightenment of Soviet officialdom and to inspire the government to go beyond sporadic "thaws" to an authentic Moscow Spring. Many aspects of this agenda for liberal-democratic reform from above are expressed in the selections that follow.

---

1. Vladimir Lakshin, *Solzhenitsyn, Tvardovsky, and Novy mir* (Cambridge, Mass., 1980), pp. 66–67, 80–81.
   2. See the document by Okunev (Karpinsky) below; and Medvedev, *On Socialist Democracy* (New York, 1975), p. 313.

Words Are Also Deeds
BY L. OKUNEV (LEN KARPINSKY)

This programmatic essay circulated in samizdat under the pseudonym L. Okunev. It is a remarkable document in two respects. First, it develops an elaborate theory and strategy of Soviet liberalization from within, arguing that changes in social education, the nature of production, and communications have made possible a coalition between liberal reformers inside and outside the Soviet Establishment. Second, the author's real identity is direct proof that democratic Marxist reformers can emerge in high Party circles, but also that their position often is perilous. "L. Okunev" is actually Len Karpinsky (born 1925), a former high Party official and the son of Vyacheslav Karpinsky (1880–1965), who was a prominent Old Bolshevik and friend of Lenin.[3] In the 1960s, Len Karpinsky was one of the national secretaries, or leaders, of the Komsomol Central Committee and then, in 1966–67, a department head and member of the editorial board of Pravda; he served also on the commission appointed to draft a new Soviet constitution. Although he lost his position at Pravda in 1967, for having coauthored an article calling for less censorship in the Soviet theater,[4] he was made a director of Progress Press, a large and important Soviet publishing house, where he served until the early 1970s. While working at Pravda, Karpinsky became the center of a small group of prominent Party intellectuals and officials—most of them were journalists and relatively young—who agreed on the need for liberal-democratic reforms in the Soviet system. The group existed until 1974, when Karpinsky and the others prepared an unofficial volume of essays—or perhaps it was to be the first issue of a regular journal—on the theme of creative Marxism and liberalization. The KGB intervened at this point, evidently on Politburo orders. The group's manuscripts were confiscated and its members subjected to various reprisals. Karpinsky himself was expelled from the Party in 1975, after a long fight; he now works as a bibliographer in a Moscow library.[5] He wrote this reformist manifesto, which is couched in Marxist terms and in the style of an internal memorandum to like-minded officials, in the late 1960s, while he still held a prominent Party position. It is printed here in abridged form.

---

3. Okunev's identity and other information about Karpinsky is divulged in Medvedev and Medvedev, *In Search of Common Sense* (forthcoming).

4. L. Karpinsky and F. Burlatsky, "Na puti k prem'ere," *Komsomol'skaia pravda*, June 30, 1967. According to *Political Diary* (no. 34, June 1967), the attack on Karpinsky and Burlatsky, and their dismissal from *Pravda*, occurred on Brezhnev's orders.

5. Medvedev and Medvedev, *In Search of Common Sense;* and "Norvezhskii zhurnalist ob oppozitsionnoi gruppe v KPSS," *Russkaia mysl'*, September 25, 1975.

The author of this work proceeds from the assumption that Lenin's famous dictum "Words are also deeds" has acquired new importance in present-day [Soviet] conditions. The author believes that because the language of the program of the Party democrats is loyal and will not shock, it can and should appeal to "consumers" within the Party and state apparatus. Our words can become their deeds.[6]

Distrust and skepticism are typical of the intellectuals' frame of mind in a period of reaction. They doubt themselves, and those close to them, question the worth of their own nation, and have no confidence in the success of any good cause or, especially, the effectiveness of words, which are the prime weapon of thinking people. No one would deny that there are weighty reasons for such moods. After 1964, the time of active reflection upon our social chimeras (in permitted doses in the press, and without any limits in "dinner-time conversations") was followed by weariness at the endless round of talk, the impotence of it all, and the de facto defeat of the supporters of the Twentieth Party Congress.

This defeat conformed to a certain logic that requires further examination. For whatever reason, hardly anyone now gives the past the attention it deserves. It is as though it was all wasted time, when in fact it was a time of *fundamental acquisitions,* a time when the irreversible process of the disintegration of Stalinism began.

A section of our scientific and ideological intelligentsia have put their feet back inside their "children's slippers," the joys of professional work and self-sufficient apolitical attitudes—which prove to be comfortable in a philistine sense as well. However, many of those in whom we are particularly interested are continuing the agonizing search, although hardly any see light up ahead. Not the least reason for this is that they conceive of the possibilities for change in outworn categories and stereotypes, solely in terms of historical analogies.

But history is a great innovator. And that includes the forms it "invents" for social revolutions. Unlike all the famous revolutionary transformations of the past, the coming change in our country could be made, to a decisive extent, by words alone. An idea that has taken hold among the masses can now become a "material force" in almost the direct and literal sense.

To put it in conventional terms, our forefathers (the Decembrists) sought to change the forms of rule by nothing less than bringing the regiments out onto Peter's Square; and our fathers and grandfathers called "the iron battalions of the proletariat" out into the streets. But the revolutionary of today must bring forward ideas that hit the mark and put them into circulation through the channels of information. The storming of the Winter Palace, as a method of revolutionary action, was a continuation and reenactment of the storming of the Bastille. The storming of our bureaucratic "fortresses" will be *radically* different.

---

6. The last two lines of this paragraph do not appear in *Political Diary*'s version of this document. They did appear in a longer version and are quoted in Medvedev, *On Socialist Democracy,* p. 313.

Those fortresses will begin to crumble under the blows of thought itself, expressed in words rather than embodied in rows of armed soldiers, insurgent crowds, columns of revolutionary sailors, or a volley from the cruiser *Aurora.* We will not have to call for "taking up the axe"; our work will be to "store up" weapons that operate in unprecedented ways.

This kind of "idealism," whose *realism* was demonstrated to the full in Czechoslovakia (in the so-called creeping revolution, or counterrevolution, as its enemies call it), could profitably be discussed, and should be, in terms of all the objective and tangible concepts and propositions that it represents.

Reactionary periods are periods of intellectual doubting and "renunciation." History is drowned in fatalistic predetermination. Nothing but curses hang over it. An eternal hopeless round with no way out is all that anyone looks for. "In the Netherlands the revolution ended with the hereditary stadtholder; in England, with the protectorate; in France, with Thermidor and (twice) the empire." Added to this are the special curses of Russian history—the dead-end centuries of the Tatar yoke, the bloody heritage of Ivan the Terrible, the work of Peter the Great that all went awry, the godforsaken barracks life under Emperor Paul and Nicholas I, the torture rack and the smoke of burning books, the defeat of the Decembrists, the execution of Stenka Razin and of Pugachov, the killing of Pushkin, the exiling of Herzen, the Siberian confinement of Chernyshevsky, the wall of misunderstanding around the Narodniks. And the castration of October—the castration by Stalinism: the "tsarist," the slavish mentality of the people . . . Simple and clear, clear and simple! Lodged in the past is everything that now is and everything that shall be. History is denied any *historical* development.

There are fashions in everything; and the interpretation of history is no exception. As for our bureaucratic despotism, it is hardly correct or productive to trace its origins to the traditional Russian autocracy and even less so to reduce it to a simple continuation of fatally unalterable tradition. Even if our "ugly heritage" did play a role, it is not at all helpful to substitute a bare reference to that heritage for a concrete understanding of the particular causes and laws of operation behind the growth of bureaucratic (non)socialism. No matter how attractive was the innovative conception of a revolution that "upset the pattern," no matter how correct Lenin was against the Mensheviks when he argued for the possibility of a socialist transformation in "reverse historical order," we have not succeeded in avoiding the more distant consequences of this reversal of historical logic. We have not circumvented its "more deeply laid mines." In my opinion, Marx and Engels had the most precise "bearing" on what those consequences would be.*

There is no need to try to show that the underdevelopment of the Russian proletariat was just as great as that of the German workers, which gave Marx

*Editor's note: Here the author quotes Marx at length on the dangers of a premature proletarian revolution in 1850.

pause, and that the artisans' prejudices and petty-bourgeois acquisitive aspirations, strengthened by the war, were also more than ample among the Russian workers. Our system is what you might call the nonproletarian (petty-bourgeois) truth torn from proletarian lips; it is an extraction, a deepening, and a governmental crystallization of everything backward, of the bigoted, antisocial, shopkeepers', and petty-bourgeois mentality that survived in the proletariat and was blown up out of proportion [by Stalinism] in our peasant country.

Bureaucratic "socialism" arose as history's revenge for the reversal of its normal order. It was the realization "immediately" not of our hopes but of "specifically petty-bourgeois" hopes and aspirations and encrustations upon the upper surface of the labor movement, including the *immediate expectations* of the proletarian masses—as against their fundamental historical interests. After a stubborn and bloody battle against those who tried to defend the long-term interests of the proletariat, the loss of countless heads (unfortunately not only in the physical sense), a social regime triumphed that was "proletarian" in *form* but petty bourgeois in *content.* (The fact that this turn of events was not obligatory is shown by developments in socialist Yugoslavia, where the bureaucratic forces have suffered one defeat after another and where, despite internal difficulties of *another* kind, the country is moving in the direction of a "positive abolition of private property" on the basis of the self-management principle.)

Here one could of course drag in—after the fact, but with some justification —the tradition of Russian autocratism. But is that what is involved? Isn't it more correct to say that this petty-bourgeois, barracks-minded throw-off from the proletarian movement is similar to the autocracy only in its external features, having *totally* different class foundations and an *absolutely* different specific content? The *costliness* of the abrupt leap in historical development that has devoured our last several generations has nothing in common with mystical predetermination. We simply had to pay the cashier of history extra for the speed and remoteness (Asiatic roundaboutness) of the socialist route we took.

It is very important to evaluate the way things turned out for us on the basis of the development itself, which is not reducible to any earlier schema. This approach allows us to see not only the principles and laws by which the system was consolidated but also those that will bring its disintegration and destruction. It allows us to see its *transitory* character.

It is our profound conviction that the "reserves" of capitalism within our system are now "finished from within." The "fifteen, twenty, or fifty years of civil war and international conflict" that Marx spoke of have gone by. To be sure, this is the situation within a system that has its good and bad points. The system is suspended over an expanse of washed-out soil, held up exclusively by its own "blocks and tackles," its own apparatus of absolute rule, which lacks any serious social basis. It cannot convince anyone of its fertility and only hangs on by the instinct of self-preservation. The farce of neo-Stalinism we are passing through is just the outward expression of the "uneasy forebodings" the petty tyrants feel. They long for the old regime, the "Stalin fortress," but they find only decrepit foundations too weak to support such a structure.

What feeds these "bold" conclusions? It is primarily a matter of the new and different population. The concept of a "Soviet people" and "new Soviet individuals" who have organically fused their personal fates with socialism is not just an empty phrase dreamed up by some propagandist (cheap skepticism notwithstanding). But it is universally understood today that the fusion is not with *this kind* of "socialism." A characteristic trait of the general popular consciousness today is what we might call "experimental" protest—a refusal, on the basis of the promised and long-suffered-for ideas of socialism, to accept the partial manifestations of socialism in the reality we know so well. Even the social apathy most often infecting the youth testifies, as a rule, to a deeper sense of the falseness around us. Such sayings as "It's like that everywhere" or "It's always that way" represent a negative return to fundamentals, a generalization with a minus sign, but nevertheless a *generalization*.

Of course, human refuse of various kind has emerged around this axis, but on the whole this type is not numerous. On this point we must acknowledge that certain forms of "subterranean adaptation" have emerged on a massive scale. There is an underground system of social relations opposed to those of the state bureaucracy. It enables people to work, be paid for their work, to buy what they need, and simply to exist. But this petty-swindler, Mafia-like system, which was forced into existence and is based on a homemade type of production without government subsidy, has defensive and not profiteering aims. It was invented as a way of subsisting under present conditions. Such surrogate production and exchange cannot satisfy anyone.

We cannot fail to take into account the new cultural level of the people, the fact that they are educated and capable of grasping scientific concepts. There is no need to put such ideas in the form of agitational devices to "engage" the heavy "gears" of illiterate and undeveloped thought among the rank and file of the revolution. From now on, scientific propaganda is itself the best type of agitation. The appeal to a person's intellectual conscience—not to social instinct but to social reason—is acquiring decisive importance. In addition, time has introduced fundamental corrections into the traditional conception of "the people" at one pole and a handful of enlightened and enlightening intellectuals (or imperious manipulators of the popular consciousness) at the other. The intelligentsia, the pole of enlightenment and knowledge, has itself become an essential and rapidly growing part of "the people."

But it is not just a matter of quantitative characteristics. A substantial share of the total social product now comes from the realm of scientific creativity, the phases of "research and development." And this, as we know, is closely linked with the transformation of science directly into one of the productive forces. Scientific creative work has not only expanded but is becoming *predominant.*

With certain qualifications, it can be said that an enormous part of the intelligentsia constitutes precisely the working class (the "composite worker," or collective worker, in the primary social sense of the term) which Marxism links with the historic mission of this section of humanity, a mission predetermined by its position in production and by the way the labor process evolves. The authors of the *Communist Manifesto* declared that of all the social classes, only the proletariat had the ticket to the future and was able to progress. But does anything remain of this statement if by the proletariat we understand as before only those who suffer the torments of physical labor and "basic manufacturing"?

We should speak not of the "deproletarianization of production" but of the "intellectualization" of the working class, its loss of such distinguishing features as routine and exhausting physical labor, its monotonous reproduction of the same results to "preserve" the creative fruits of the thinking elite, its isolation in separate "partial" operations that narrow the sphere of social communication. The chief manifestation of these inspiring changes can be seen in the rise of new professions based on profound internal alterations in industrial operations, the rise of mental inputs to predominance over physical inputs, and the replacement of mechanical and stereotyped labor by creative work, with its characteristic search for new solutions to problems.

Of decisive importance in this type of work are such stimuli as the possibility for self-expression, creative initiative, ideal aims, individual projects and conditions in which such projects can be carried through, the desire to solve the contradiction between the known and the unknown, between what is true and what is false in reality, and the need for unlimited information and autonomous development. Through science and information, the working person is linked with all aspects of social life, assimilates its influences, and experiences its condition as "his or her own." Social-spiritual factors come to the fore; hence, democracy as the only suitable mechanism for free creativity becomes an essential social condition and an elementary prerequisite for efficient production.

Numerous facts confirm that all the small-scale journalistic "exposés" of the various unfortunate situations in our economy merely express in "atomized" and distorted form the main contradiction: between the conscious and social nature of modern labor and its partial, bureaucratic, and "blind" form of organization. Of course, we are speaking only about a trend, but it is one that has already made itself felt quite insistently. Our sociologists have not yet studied the structure of production and society sufficiently, and have not learned enough about the people of today and their labor, to be able to see clearly that two fundamentally different spheres and types of activity now exist.

In one sphere, mechanical uniformity prevails as before. Through regular reproduction of the social product, society obtains its daily requirements, the particular number of items, meters, kilograms, and so on, of various goods that it needs. So far, this accounts for the bulk of what is produced. For this kind of practical work, the administrative cliché "No results without the whip" has a certain relevance. Such work can still tolerate administrative forms that consist of universally applicable and assertive commands. It still accepts organization of the type that was cast in uniform molds poured and set long ago and that requires undeviating adherence. Here discipline seems to be and in fact primarily is a matter of obedience; civic duty is the capacity for superendurance; ideological principle is loyally following the book; and patriotism is stubborness and devotion to carrying out orders. It is not hard to see that all the apologists for our system have grown up on this principle of mechanical repetition and permanent stereotypes rooted in old-fashioned factory life; that their thoughts and feelings are nourished precisely from this source.

But, alongside the traditional sphere of labor, a new one is quickly growing up, the product of scientific and technical progress. This is a sphere of creative, nonstandardized operations and decisions that cannot be reduced to one another. Aside from research institutions, whose creative importance is increasing day by day, every plant now faces the task of continually improving the labor process itself. It is enough to leaf through the plans for new equipment for factories or, say, the contracts between plants and research institutes to see that apparently the standardized and measured stride of industrial life can no longer conceal the caprices of constant alteration. Isn't this why, alongside the ponderous administrative pyramid which customarily sees to it that the quantitative program is carried out, parallel organizational structures have arisen everywhere in the factories, structures corresponding to the new creative needs? Their main features are flexibility, mobility, and the capacity to react instantaneously to changing situations.

What is now needed is an integrated creative group that can thoroughly lay down the complex configuration of new rearrangements—with new plans and new systems of operations. How will the new arrangement affect previous and subsequent operations? Here subordination no longer has a place. The designer is on a par with the technologist, and the technologist with the production worker. They are all colleagues.

This is a prototype of the future relations of scientists and experimenters in which the abilities, knowledge, and ideas of one will serve not as a limit upon but as a continuation of the abilities, knowledge, and ideas of another. As the factory people themselves put it, "One person may not think of one thing and another may not think of something else; but together we work it all out." This is the historical limit to managerialism, even for the most highly qualified managers. The limit is that so much of the mental and organizational culture of labor must be mastered that the point of total absorption is reached.

What is most valuable in the new creative associations, as in human groups in general, is the combination of dissimilar merits, "dissent," as it were, among cothinkers, people who approach the common task in different ways. Organization ceases to mean establishing stereotypes, and its overall effectiveness is based on the full revelation of all the merits and strengths of each member. Consequently, this technique of organization resembles the process that it directs.

From what circles are they recruited—these young organisms that seem to be growing in the womb of the old? From the same source of human and professional material, the only one. From among all those who, in the ordinary course of relations with one another in their posts, constitute an ordinary collective working in the old way. But now these people are placed together not in the usual cell-by-cell arrangement, hidden from one another on the differentiated-labor model. Instead, they have dug new, supplementary "communications trenches" through to one another. And in the event of sharp conflicts in which their creative interests, reflecting real needs and the vital disturbances of reality, clash with the duties of their posts (which often reflect nothing but themselves), these people fight their way through a barricade of doubts and torments to take the side of life and to truly become themselves.

An enormously important complementary process from the other direction is also under way. It is a cliché to stress the role of the modern means of mass communication. Our official propagandists themselves never suspect how close they are to the truth when they liken the country and its population to a single audience that has been called together, which hears and sees and learns together and is capable of *thinking* together. Today, the power of the information media is used mainly to produce "mass society" with its standardized thinking and the unpardonable manipulation of the popular mind. But a completely different kind of solidarity and a different kind of unity are not excluded. Freedom of speech and the press would today mean much more for the spread (or, more precisely, for the shaping) of a new social conception than decades of the most persistent journalistic propaganda or the most selfless agitational "going to the people" that occurred in the last century and at the beginning of this century.

The central point in our argument is that *fundamental* changes are taking place in the "everyday life" of today's society—similar to those once signified by the rise of articulate speech, that especially *practical* factor in human relations and powerful objective lever in the formation of the human race. The idea is that of the rise of some "second signal system" of social existence that would become an unquestioned physical reality and part of the social organism, capable of regulating its "vegetative system." Our tanks in Prague were, if you will, an anachronism, an "inadequate" weapon. They "fired" at—ideas. With no hope of hitting the target. They "dealt with" the Czechoslovak situation the same way that at one time certain reptiles "dealt with" the coming of the age of mammals. The reptiles bit at the air, gnashing their teeth in the same ether that was literally seething with the plankton of renewal. At the same time, fettered by their natural instincts, they searched for "hidden stocks of weapons" and diligently occupied the postal and telegraph offices. With a fist to the jaw of thinking society, they thought they had knocked out and "captured" its thinking processes.

Let us bring in a certain analogy (to be sure, nothing more than an analogy) with the technical theory of explosions. There are two methods. One is to apply powerful thermal pressure to the material, so that when an outside or secondary factor causes it to flame up, it explodes. The other is the projection of vibrations aimed at producing a resonance within structures that are under strain and barely holding together, with the result that they disintegrate. It is easy to understand that we are interested in the second analogy.

What could the "strained" Novotny regime in January 1968 oppose to the "vibrational beams" set off by the Czechoslovak Writers' Congress and then transmitted into the leadership of the Party, 95 percent of whose apparatus considered the main brake upon socialism in the country to be the lack of democracy (as revealed in a *Rude pravo* questionnaire)? Exactly nothing. The manifesto "Two Thousand Words," which probed the gaps of bureaucratic omniscience, for all its confused and chaotic character, totally paralyzed the defensive powers of the bureaucracy. The regime began to come apart at the seams before all eyes—and to such a dangerous extent that the very instruments of social control were being lost. It turned out that, apart from the methods of absolute rule, the system did not represent anything; no one stood up for it. And had it not been for the intervention of our reptiles, who restored their local relatives to their former places, we would probably have a totally different socialist Czechoslovakia by now. The "second signal system" of social action demonstrated its superiority in principle over the "unconditioned reflexes" of the bureaucratic machine. The experience of Czechoslovakia—this Paris Commune of the twentieth century—is crucial for us.

The problem is to make a concrete analysis of the concrete tendencies and sociopolitical forces in our country. And, first of all, to understand the character and inner motive forces of what we have thus far called in a general negative sense "the bureaucracy."

Of course, when we say that bureaucracy is the guiding principle of the Party and state administrative apparatus, we do not have the right to extend this assessment to all persons in positions of authority in the country. One cannot ignore the following relevant factors: the powerful moral legacy of socialist ideas and the grandeur of the goals under whose aegis the society continues to work and live; the slow, restrained, but steady replenishment of the "bureaucracy" by elements that have a qualitatively different cultural level, who do not allow socialism to be taken on faith (especially energetic specialists who have suffered from bureaucratic lead strings and from the absurdity, clumsiness, and inefficiency of the machine); the ever increasing fusion between the administrative apparatus and the scientific and technical elite, who bring with them certain progressive tendencies; the pressure of real difficulties, which tends to crack the "monolith" of the apparatus and to turn even died-in-the-wool bureaucrats toward the search for solutions; and, finally, the subterranean pressure of public opinion, which cannot be removed in the Stalin manner by the arrest of several thousand or even tens of thousands of intellectuals. The people itself is becoming the intelligentsia.

The Stalinism of the 1930s and 1940s was the work of rotten elements who relied on the blind enthusiasm of the majority of the population and the selfless devotion of the best and most honest believers among the new crop of cadres. Present-day Stalinism is also the work of rotten types, but it is sinking into a bottomless pit of popular indifference and distrust and losing the support of the best young cadres who honestly believe in socialism. This does not mean, of course, that the Stalinist moods are totally alien to the popular mind. Some workers still long for the absolute, unchallengeable, and deified boss as an all-powerful protector against low-level oppressors, a board of appeal against local predatory fiends.

In general, Stalinism represents (to some extent) the powerless worker's longing to settle the score for his day-to-day humiliations with the help of some harsh justice from the top. Impotence seeks a higher power to avenge itself. But this kind of "Stalinism" is a form of criticism of the bureaucracy, a form of antibureaucratic hatred. In history, there are many cases in which progressive social attitudes are born in the garb of reactionary utopias. Stalinism today feeds on its own "excrement." The masses are escaping from its fundamental deformities and worst consequences, while reminiscing about the mythical boom time of its youth.

The new times are percolating into the apparatus and forming a layer of party intellectuals within it. To be sure, this layer is thin and disconnected; it is constantly eroded by cooptation and promotion and is thickly interlaced with careerists, flatterers, loudmouths, jesuits, cowards, and other products of the bureaucratic selection process. But this layer could move toward an alliance with the entire social body of the intelligentsia if favorable conditions arose.

This layer is already an arm of the intelligentsia, its "parliamentary fraction" within the administrative structure. This fraction will inevitably grow, constituting a hidden opposition, without specific shape and not aware of itself, but an actually existing and widely ramified opposition at all levels within the administrative chain. Everything will depend on the possibility of linking up the "internal" forces (within the bureaucracy) and the external ones (of the people as a whole) that favor renewal, a reunification of the intelligentsia with its "bureaucratic" component.

To make politically ossified elements dance to one's own tune was an idea of the young Marx that we completely share. We are not talking about any "willful" (or voluntarist) creation of contradictions but simply about expressing them and giving them shape. We can discuss at some length three groups of contradictions —first, between the administrative bureaucracy and the people as a whole; second and in particular, between the bureaucracy and the "social" (i.e., nongovernmental) intelligentsia; and, finally, between the bureaucracy and the layer of "bureaucrats" who have an interest in creating optimal conditions for work within the context of the scientific and technical revolution. Since the system has penetrated all spheres of life, to the lowest level of production and the individual worker at that level, these may be regarded as contradictions within the system itself. The "growing points" and the contending forces reveal themselves within the heart of the system. The coming together of all forces for progress is an objective process—and the task of our words is to accelerate and express this consolidation.

Let us consider several aspects of the transformation process itself and some possible models. A certain likeness to a parliamentary road to socialism may be imagined. At the initial stage of the movement, the role of parliament would be played by the existing voices within the hierarchy. Events might then unfold in several different ways.

The ideal case would be the actual development of a Party-wide (then inevitably a nationwide) discussion—both oral and printed. Such a discussion in our opinion is indispensable and is probably the only road for achieving change. It in fact constitutes the modern form of the revolutionary process through "a second signal system." Only a broad discussion would immediately and surely paralyze bureaucratic absolutism and serve as its undeniable negation. It would give an insuperable advantage to the elements committed to ideas, the principled elements who have something to say. In a discussion, the means of transforming reality would coincide with the essence and aims of such transformation: fundamentally, a discussion would serve as a prototype of the social situation that would come to prevail in the Party and the country.

Since it would be destructive in relation to the bureaucracy, a discussion would have to be an intensively constructive effort, showing that it bears within itself the "building blocks" for a new system. Discussion is the only way in which profound social changes could be ensured without disruption of the normal processes of production and exchange, avoiding any breakdown or collapse in essential social relations. This and this alone would ensure the swift precipitation and consolidation of all the healthy forces in the Party, and their drawing a line separating themselves from their own criminal past; that is, it would make possible an "opening back" to the values of October and the people's confidence in socialism.

Before such a discussion, a Marxist current within the Party cannot be recreated; it will be organized only in the course of the discussion. Discussion is the demonstrably legal and recognized norm of activity of any Marxist party. Discussion ensures the most numerous possible army for the revolution, one that is not easily subject to destruction by grapeshot or tanks or prisons or any other means of political and physical annihilation. The central tasks in a discussion would be to extend and deepen it constantly in the direction of consistent socialist conclusions; to promote the complete defeat and definitive burial of Stalinist conceptions in the social sciences and the consciousness of the masses; and to struggle energetically against even the smallest hint of antisocialist or simply antisocial deviations.

[In the absence of such a nationwide discussion, there is another possibility,] an intermediate one, so to speak. Here, the fundamental problems would be discussed only at the top. A certain expansion of democratic freedoms could occur if the discussion shifted in that direction. This should be utilized energetically to propagandize in favor of the tasks of renewal, to point out constantly the halfheartedness of the steps that had been taken and the necessity for further changes. As the process developed, it would inevitably reach a new limit, after which the same need for a general discussion to clear the air would again arise. If the process were curtailed, we would return to the original situation, with all the consequences that would entail.

At this point, all that would remain to us would be to take consolation in the fact that our cause had not perished, that it had "awakened" new layers within the Party intelligentsia who would repeat the attempt with more success. It would be enough that we had shared the role of preservers and transmitters of the "heresy" of Marxism.

But even if things came to that, we would not be lacking in practical goals. The poet dreamed that the pen would become mightier than the sword. We think that this dream is more and more coming true, and that the realm of Soviet political life is no exception.

[No. 68, May 1970]

Reformist vs. Radical Marxism:
MEDVEDEV ON GRIGORENKO ON SAKHAROV,

Marxist critics of the Soviet system can disagree profoundly among themselves. Partly as an outgrowth of Khrushchev's de-Stalinization campaigns, a
number of dissident Communist groups appeared in the 1950s and 1960s whose
political analysis and programmatic views were more radical than reformist. One
of these groups, the "Union of Struggle for the Revival of Leninism," was
founded in 1963 by former Major General Pyotr Grigorenko (born 1907). Grigorenko is a remarkable figure in the history of Soviet dissent. After a long and
illustrious military career in the Soviet army, he was arrested for the first time
in 1964, for protesting Khrushchev's own regime, expelled from the Party, demoted to the rank of private, and confined to punitive "psychiatric" wards
intermittently over the next thirteen years. In poor health, he finally left the
Soviet Union in 1977 and now lives in the United States. Grigorenko played a
major role in the dissident movement during the 1960s and 1970s, lending his
prestige and powerful presence to many civil-rights causes. Though he apparently
no longer believes in any kind of Communism, his radical Marxism-Leninism of
the 1960s was a challenge not only to official dogma but to Marxist reformers,
who want to change the system gradually, not replace it. Roy Medvedev's critique
of Grigorenko's views, occasioned by the appearance of Sakharov's reformist
"Memorandum" in 1968, can be read as a confrontation between these two kinds
of oppositionist Marxism. The document has been abridged here.

Former Major General Pyotr Grigorenko, who openly proclaims himself a
representative of the "Communist opposition" to the present regime, has sent
a letter to Academician Sakharov about his "Memorandum." Grigorenko's document is quite interesting if one wishes to analyze the currents and shades of
opinion in our social and political life that are not reflected in the official press.

Grigorenko is a representative of one of the extreme opposition currents. He
is inclined to exaggerate rather than minimize all the failings of our government
and to make sharper rather than milder statements in formulating his criticism.
He sees the present-day Soviet state as the enemy, and there cannot be anything
positive about the enemy.

This is the main weakness in his position, as with most extreme currents. Even
when Grigorenko is right in his conclusions, they remain the property merely of
a small group of people, because they do not correspond to the level of consciousness of most oppositional-minded intellectuals, let alone the majority of the

people. Such extreme tendencies, both of the left and of the right, can only come to the fore in a country under extreme circumstances, when there is an extreme crisis. But we have a long way to go before such a crisis, and whether there will ever be one is uncertain. Therefore, it is better to point out only some of our failings to the people and to succeed in eliminating those failings, thereby opening the way for real forward motion, than to indulge in hyperbole about those failings and win a following among only a small handful of discontents disposed toward exaggeration.

But let us return to Grigorenko's letter. At first, he writes about Sakharov's article as a work of genius, because "it presents every thinking person with what seem to be his or her own thoughts, which had long been in existence but which before this had not found finished formulation, and it does this in an ingenious manner insofar as the expression of the burning issues of social thought is concerned. That is exactly how your article is being received."

After a short introduction, Grigorenko goes on to comment on specific points in the text. He agrees that the scientific method of administering society has not yet become a reality in our country. But this method "cannot become a reality if there are no scientists in the leadership, not a trace of any, and if the leaders are all bureaucrats and timeservers. . . . Plainly, what needs to be changed is not the method but the administrative system itself. Plainly, it must be reworked so that it will not tolerate bureaucrats or timeservers within it and that, if some should appear, they would automatically be expelled just as ruthlessly and inexorably as a living organism does with any foreign matter."

Citing Sakharov's words about the working class as the most active and organized layer of Soviet society (this passage was revised in later editions of Sakharov's article), Grigorenko gives his own opinion about the Soviet working class, an opinion that is tendentious in the extreme. After the civil war [of 1918–21], in Grigorenko's opinion, the working class was partly a declassed element, diluted by those who poured in from the ruined villages, and it continued to be diluted in that way. "From 1927 on, and especially in the early 1930s," writes Grigorenko, "the traditional working class was swamped by the disorganized and elemental flood of ruined and terrified peasants in such a powerful process that it is simply absurd to speak of the working class as a progressive force. What organized action was this 'working class' capable of? Only unquestioning submission to the authorities. . . . They were willing to work night and day, to accept any obligation, to vote for having any 'enemy of the people' shot, as long as they and their families were left in peace." Grigorenko continues: "I do not think I need to tell how the character of the working class changed during World War II. Hungry and emaciated women and children, not to mention the tens of millions of *zeks,* can hardly be called the most organized and conscious layer of society." "And finally," he adds, "let us take the present-day working class. All the most active, enterprising, and thoughtful elements within it are taking up studies, going to school, and entering the ranks of the intelligentsia or ending up on trial for their convictions and swelling the numbers in the prison camps."

These arguments are compacted of extreme exaggeration; certain tendencies that are actually present but that constitute only one aspect of reality are made out to be the total reality. It is true that in the 1930s the villages added millions of people to the ranks of the working class. Having arrived in the cities, however, and having entered the environment of large-scale industry, these people acquired certain skills. Not only did they bring their petty-bourgeois shortcomings into the working class; they took on many worthwhile qualities and themselves changed in many ways. Likewise, during the Patriotic War the working class did not consist only of hungry women and children. There was a hard-core working-class nucleus that in its own way brought the newcomers along and trained them. It is incorrect to suppose that nowadays all thinking young people are leaving the working class and joining the intelligentsia. It is even less correct to write that all remaining thoughtful workers end up behind bars. The positive and negative qualities and aspects of the working class and its role in contemporary society should neither be overestimated nor underestimated.

In expressing his views on foreign policy, Grigorenko demands that all foreign-policy matters be put under the control of the masses. "No secret agreements," he demands. "International organizations should be democratized and be given the right to function publicly and independently of the government. Moreover, their duty is to criticize government actions on all points where they disagree and seek the removal of the government if it fails to work toward the relaxation of international tensions." And so on.

There are many unrealistic demands here. We should certainly strive for a correct and honest foreign policy. And it is necessary that specific bodies be established to oversee foreign policy (for example, such institutions as the commissions of the Supreme Soviet should be given a more active role). But, for the time being, our foreign policy cannot be made fully public or placed under the control of the masses in the broadest sense of the word. . . .

There are many exaggerations elsewhere in Grigorenko's letter (along with a number of totally justified observations, of course). For example, Grigorenko writes that the Party is rather like the hierarchy of the Catholic Church at the height of the Inquisition and the Jesuit movement. He also holds the opinion that the competition between socialism and capitalism has not ended in a temporary stalemate, as Sakharov thinks, but in defeat for us.

According to Grigorenko, "It is natural, therefore, that in order for us to overcome our difficulties, we must seriously analyze not only our past evolution but also the experience of capitalism. Apparently, we will have to borrow some things from capitalism. And not only in the sphere of technology and production engineering but in the realm of solving social problems and organizing the economy. Our economic system is like a living organism that is totally lacking in capillaries. All the arteries and veins that are under direct pressure work more or less normally, but there is no blood supply to the periphery. In the capitalist world, small traders and artisans perform the function of capillaries, but in our country they were swept away and nothing was put in to replace them."

The comparison is interesting but again inexact. It can't be said that the "capillaries" were "totally" destroyed. Some elements remained in spite of everything. Today, in some southern cities, as much as 50 percent of certain food products reach the population through the collective-farm markets. It is another matter that the "blood supply" to the periphery needs substantial improvement and that, to accomplish that, we must have recourse to an expansion of private initiative.

Further on in his letter, Grigorenko cites several examples of flagrant mismanagement by the Stalinist administration (the building of the Palace of Soviets on the site of the Church of Christ the Redeemer after it was blown up; and the Volga–Baltic canal project). But his conclusion that the present bureaucratic administration is altogether incapable of managing economic affairs is too categorical and final. "The most frightening thing of all," he writes, "is that the gigantic and many-tentacled bureaucratic octopus we have analyzed here is constantly spreading and its size constantly increasing, so that it more and more stops up the vital pores of the social organism and drains it of its vital fluids."

It cannot be denied, however, that the present administrative apparatus performs a certain useful function in managing the economy and running the society. It can and should be reduced and made more efficient, a system of control and feedback should be introduced, and so on. But even under a gradual process of democratization many sections of the present apparatus and a large number of the people in it would have to be used. After the October Revolution, we must recall, it was necessary to hire most of the former employees of the former state apparatus to work for the Soviets, especially at the middle and upper levels. Still more will we have to rely on the present apparatus in the process of socialist democratization. The best form of democratization, by the way, would be a gradual evolution and not a rapid or abrupt leap that would disrupt the balanced functioning of many processes and therefore entail certain dangerous possibilities.

However, an evolutionary transition to new forms and methods (both the managers and those who are managed must become accustomed to democratic ways, incidentally) requires not only pressure from below but wise and systematically planned measures from above. Up to now, no such thing exists. Those at the top are more inclined to "tighten the screws." This causes a heightening of tensions in the society, especially in relations between the administrative apparatus and the intelligentsia.

Grigorenko also exaggerates the scale of violence in present-day Soviet society. "Our society," he writes, "continues to suffer colossal losses simply because the monstrously swollen apparatus of coercion does not wish to sit around doing nothing. It 'keeps busy.' And with its 'busy work' it removes large numbers of the most valuable and indispensable people from the production process and from public life for long periods of time and sometimes forever." Fortunately, things have not actually gone that far, although, of course, we must be intolerant of the particular arbitrary and lawless acts about which Sakharov writes, several further examples of which Grigorenko provides.

Grigorenko proposes that management of the country's economic life be placed in the hands of scientists and the "owners of the means of production," that is, the producers themselves. This again is not quite right, because scientists in the precise sense of the word should occupy themselves with science, including managerial science. The actual, immediate management of economic processes in most cases should be in the hands of specially trained administrators who would utilize recommendations from scientists as well as computerized problem-solving machines. Of course, such administrators would be under the control of workers' councils or other organs of workers' self-management.

Grigorenko suggests that only some branches of the economy should be planned on a nationwide scale: energy, industrial raw materials, basic food sources, transportation, communications, and new industries. "Neither razor blades nor nylon shirts," he writes, "should be planned in the currently understood sense of the word. The existing branches of industry should produce according to the demand that arises, and the products should be realized on the basis of free market relations. The only central 'planner' for these sectors should be scientific statistics, and in each individual sector there should be industrial associations.

Further on, Grigorenko advocates the gradual withering away of the state in both domestic and foreign affairs. The withering away should go faster than the convergence of countries with differing social systems. Unfortunately, Grigorenko has not avoided exaggeration here either. He writes, for example, "In regard to preparations for the defense of the country, our government has played *only* a negative role." Why the word *only?* He advocates the organization of "direct popular participation" in the creation of an impregnable, strictly defensive military system. "It is evident," he writes, "that such a system could only be one in which the armed forces were more and more merged with the people themselves, that is, in the final analysis would be 'the armed people organized on a socialist basis.' "

Thus, Grigorenko proposes the complete abolition of the state even before the existence of two hostilely opposed social systems has been overcome. Of course, this is utopian. If such a system were adopted, the people would find it necessary all the same to establish certain specialized agencies to manage the exceptionally complex military system required by modern warfare, to safeguard military and state secrets, to protect military and other important installations, to carry out intelligence operations, etc., etc. And the totality of these agencies would constitute a state.

"Everyone knows," writes Grigorenko, "that the security agencies have long been employed in nothing but a war against the people, against its progressive forces, and in view of that, have the same function in our body politic as a cancerous tumor in a living organism." Here, too, the words *nothing but* are inappropriate, as is the cancer simile. We are far from being inclined to idealize the present security agencies, but Grigorenko's kind of criticism can do us no good. Grigorenko's lines on the militia are also extremely biased.

At the end of his letter, Grigorenko goes totally astray. He writes that the state is nothing but a parasite blocking all the pores of society and threatening to stifle it completely. As for officials working in the state apparatus, "throughout the ages they have belonged to the class of exploiters," in his opinion. This primitive view seems wrong to me even in regard to a substantial segment of the officials in a bourgeois state, who sometimes perform highly important and necessary social functions, ultimately contributing thereby to social and economic progress. Businessmen themselves are not merely parasites and exploiters, as is shown by the relatively rapid development of capitalist production in the past twenty-five years.

"As a result of the October Revolution," Grigorenko writes, "a state machine arose that in principle was of the same kind that had existed before, but it was refined to a previously unheard-of extent." What does he propose be done in the near future to combat this state? "The most urgent task within the power of our still weak progressive movement is to organize petition campaigns on an ongoing basis. The activities of the Crimean Tatars in the fight for equal national rights has convinced me of the exceptional effectiveness of such campaigns. At any rate, public opinion can be organized on this basis; people cease to feel isolated and defenseless in the face of official arbitrariness; and the authorities themselves gradually become used to feedback, which they had grown completely unaccustomed to during the years of Stalin's tyranny."

We see that after formulating extremely radical demands "for the abolition of the entire present-day state" and writing off all the employees of the state as exploiters, Grigorenko places extremely narrow limits on the possibilities for our society at present to wage a battle for democratization of the state and social system. In fact, the forms and techniques that can be used in this struggle are far more varied. Petitions of various kinds are not the main or most important form of struggle now. And it is not only "unaffiliated" citizens who can and must take part in this fight but also every honest member of our state and Party apparatus.

[No. 47, August 1968]

A Reformist Program for Democratization
BY ANDREI SAKHAROV, ROY MEDVEDEV,
AND VALENTIN TURCHIN

What follows is one of the few reformist programs for democratization ever to appear in the Soviet Union. Its appearance in samizdat, in March 1970, marked the fullest, but also the last, major reformist statement addressed to the leadership by a group of prominent dissidents. Drafted by Sakharov, and delivered personally by him to government offices, the document was cosigned, after some revisions, by Medvedev and Valentin Turchin (born 1931), a well-known physicist, civil-rights activist, and samizdat writer.[7] Their program brought together many ideas about political and economic reform that had circulated for years in the Soviet Union and Eastern Europe. It called for a far-reaching democratization of the Soviet system as the only "way out of the difficulties now facing our country," but its specific proposals were intentionally gradualist, socialist, and loyalist. Addressed to "respected comrades" Brezhnev, Kosygin, and Podgorny, then the three main Soviet leaders, each proposal was formulated as a reform that would be "acceptable" to and benefit the government, and that could be implemented under its auspices. Sakharov, as noted earlier, soon abandoned hope in this kind of reformist appeal, as did Turchin, who was forced to emigrate in 1977. Medvedev now remains alone in the Soviet Union as an important dissident spokesman for reform from above. A few of their secondary proposals were subsequently implemented by the Soviet government, no doubt for other reasons. (Later in the 1970s, the Soviet Union stopped jamming most foreign radio broadcasts, signed the international copyright convention, and began to give internal passports to the peasantry.) But the major proposals for democratization are, of course, still unfulfilled.

Respected Comrades:

We are appealing to you on a question of great importance. Our country has made great strides in the development of production, in the fields of education and culture, in the basic improvement of the living conditions of the working class, and in the development of new socialist human relationships. Our achievements have universal historical significance. They have deeply affected events throughout the world and have laid a firm foundation for the further develop-

---

7. The history of the document is told in Medvedev and Medvedev, *In Search of Common Sense.*

ment of the cause of Communism. However, serious difficultie¯ and shortcomings are also evident.

This letter will discuss and develop a point of view that can be formulated briefly by the following theses:

1. At the present time, there is an urgent need to carry out a series of measures directed toward the further democratization of our country's public life. This need stems, in particular, from the very close connection between the problem of technological and economic progress and scientific methods of management, on the one hand, and the problems of freedom of information, the open airing of views, and the free clash of ideas, on the other. This need also stems from other domestic and foreign political problems.

2. Democratization must promote the maintenance and consolidation of the Soviet socialist system, the socialist economic structure, our social and cultural achievements, and socialist ideology.

3. Democratization, carried out under the leadership of the Soviet Communist Party in collaboration with all strata of society, should maintain and strengthen the leading role of the Party in the economic, political, and cultural life of society.

4. Democratization should be gradual, in order to avoid possible complications and disruptions. At the same time, it should be thoroughgoing, carried out consistently in accordance with a carefully worked-out program. Without fundamental democratization, our society will not be able to solve the problems now facing it and will not be able to develop in a normal manner.

There are reasons for assuming that the point of view expressed in the above theses is shared to one degree or another by a significant part of the Soviet intelligentsia and the advanced section of the working class. This attitude is also reflected in the opinions of student and working youth, as well as in numerous private discussions within small groups of friends. However, we believe the most appropriate thing is for us to set forth this point of view in coherent written form, in order to facilitate a broad and open discussion of these most important problems. We are in search of a positive and constructive approach that will be acceptable to the Party and government leadership of the country; we seek to clarify certain misunderstandings and unfounded apprehensions.

Over the past decade, menacing signs of breakdown and stagnation have begun to show themselves in the economy of our country, the roots of which go back to an earlier period and are very deep-seated. There is an uninterrupted decline in the rate of growth of the national income, and a growing gap between what is needed for normal development and the actual new capacity put into use. A great mass of data is available showing mistakes in the determination of technical and economic policy in industry and agriculture and an intolerable procrastination about finding solutions to urgent problems. Defects in the system of planning, accounting, and incentives often cause contradictions between local and departmental interests and those of the state and nation. As a result, new means of developing production potential are not being discovered or properly put to use, and technical progress has slowed down abruptly. For these very reasons, the natural wealth of the country is often destroyed with impunity and without any supervision or controls: forests are leveled, reservoirs polluted, valuable agricultural land flooded, soil eroded or salinized, and so on. The chronically difficult situation in agriculture, particularly in regard to livestock, is well known. The population's real income in recent years has hardly grown at all; food supply and medical and consumer services are improving very slowly, and with unevenness between regions. The number of goods in short supply continues to grow. There are clear signs of inflation.

Of particular concern regarding our country's future is the lag in the development of education: our total expenditures for education in all forms are three times below what they are in the United States, and are rising at a slower rate. Alcoholism is growing in a tragic way, and drug addiction is beginning to surface. In many regions of the country, the crime rate is climbing systematically. Signs of corruption are becoming more and more noticeable in a number of places. In the work of scientific and scientific-technical organizations, bureaucratism, departmentalism, a formal attitude toward one's tasks, and lack of initiative are becoming more and more pronounced.

As is well known, the productivity of labor is the decisive factor in the comparison of economic systems. It is here that the situation is worst of all. Productivity of labor in our country remains, as before, many times lower than that in capitalist countries, and the growth of productivity has fallen off abruptly. This situation causes particular anxiety if one compares it with the situation in the leading capitalist countries, in particular with that in the United States. By introducing elements of state regulation and planning into the economy, these countries have rid themselves of the destructive crises that plagued the capitalist economy in an earlier era. The broad introduction of computer technology and automation assures a rapid rise in the productivity of labor, which in turn facilitates a partial overcoming of certain social problems and contradictions (e.g., by means of unemployment benefits and by shortening of the work day).

In comparing our economy with that of the United States, we see that ours lags behind not only in quantitative but also—most regrettable of all—in qualitative terms. The newer and more revolutionary a particular aspect of the economy may be, the wider the gap between the USSR and the USA. We outstrip America in coal production, but we lag behind in the output of oil, gas, and electric power; we lag behind tenfold in the field of chemistry, and we are infinitely outstripped in computer technology. The latter is especially crucial, because the introduction of electronic computers into the economy is a phenomenon of decisive importance that radically changes the outlines of the production system and of the entire culture. This phenomenon has justly been called the second industrial revolution. Nevertheless, our stock of computers is *1 percent* of that of the United States. As for our utilization of the electronic computer, the gap is so great that it is impossible even to measure it. We simply live in another age.

Things are no better in the sphere of scientific and technological breakthroughs. Our role in this area has not advanced either. Rather, the contrary has been true. At the end of the 1950s, our country was the first in the world to launch a satellite and send someone into space. By the end of the 1960s, we had lost our lead in this area (as in many others). The first people to land on the moon were Americans. This fact is one of the outward manifestations of the gulf that exists and is continually growing between us and the Western countries all along the line in scientific and technological work.

In the 1920s and 1930s, the capitalist world went through a period of crises and depressions. During this period, we utilized the upsurge of national energy engendered by the revolution to build up our industry at an unprecedented rate. The slogan raised at that time was "Catch up with and surpass America." And we actually caught up with America in the course of several decades. Then the situation changed. The second industrial revolution began, and now, at the beginning of the 1970s, we see that not only have we not succeeded in catching up with America, we are falling more and more behind it.

What is wrong? Why have we not only failed to be the pioneers of the second industrial revolution but in fact found ourselves incapable of keeping pace with the developed capitalist countries? Is it possible that socialism provides fewer opportunities for the development of productive forces than capitalism? Or that in the economic competition between capitalism and socialism, capitalism is winning?

Of course not! The source of our difficulties does not lie in the socialist system; on the contrary, it lies in those peculiarities and conditions of our life that run counter to socialism and are hostile to it. The source lies in the antidemocratic traditions and norms of public life established in the Stalin era, which have not been decisively eliminated to this day.

Noneconomic coercion, limitations on the exchange of information, restrictions on intellectual freedom, and other examples of the antidemocratic distortion of socialism that took place under Stalin were accepted in our country as an overhead expense of the industrialization process. It was believed that they did not seriously influence the economy of the country, although they had very serious consequences in the political and military arenas, in the destinies of vast layers of the population, and for whole nationalities. We will leave aside the question of the extent to which this point of view is justified for the early stages of development of a socialist national economy; the decline in the rate of industrial development in the prewar years rather suggests the opposite. But there is no doubt that since the beginning of the second industrial revolution these phenomena have become a decisive economic factor; they have become the main brake on the development of the productive forces in this country. As a consequence of the increased size and complexity of economic systems, the problems of management and organization have moved to the forefront. These problems cannot be resolved by one or several persons holding power and "knowing everything." These problems demand the creative participation of millions of people on all levels of the economic system. They demand the broad exchange of information and ideas. In this lies the difference between a modern economy and the economy, let us say, of the ancient Orient.

However, we encounter certain insurmountable obstacles on the road toward the free exchange of ideas and information. Truthful information about our shortcomings and negative manifestations is hushed up on the grounds that it "may be used by enemy propaganda." Exchange of information with foreign countries is restricted for fear of "penetration by an enemy ideology." Theoretical generalizations and practical proposals, if they seem too bold to some individuals, are nipped in the bud without any discussion, because of the fear that they might "undermine our foundations." An obvious lack of confidence in creatively thinking, critical, and energetic individuals is to be seen here. Under such circumstances, the conditions are created for the advancement up the rungs of the official ladder not of those who distinguish themselves by their professional qualities and commitment to principles but of those who verbally proclaim their devotion to the Party but in practice are only concerned with their own narrow personal interests or are passive timeservers.

Limitations on freedom of information mean not only that it is more difficult to control the leaders, not only that the initiative of the people is undermined, but that even the intermediate level of leadership is deprived of rights and information and that these people are transformed into passive timeservers and bureaucrats. The leaders in the highest government bodies receive information that is incomplete, the rough spots glossed over; hence they are also deprived of the opportunity effectively to utilize the authority they have.

The economic reform of 1965 was an extremely beneficial and important start toward resolving key problems of our economic life. However, we are convinced that purely economic measures alone are not enough to fulfill all its tasks. Furthermore, these economic measures cannot be fully implemented without reforms in the sphere of management, information, and open public discussion.

The same can be said regarding such promising undertakings as the organization of complex industrial associations with a high degree of autonomy in economic, financial, and personnel matters.

Whatever concrete problem of the economy we may take up, we very soon will come to the conclusion that its satisfactory solution requires a scientific resolution of such general problems of socialist economics as the forms of feedback in the managerial system, price formation in the absence of a free market, and general principles of planning.

There is much talk these days about the need for a scientific approach to the problems of organization and management. This is true, of course. Only a scientific approach to these problems will allow us to overcome the difficulties that have developed and to realize those opportunities for controlling the direction of the economy and of technical-economic progress that in principle the absence of capitalist property relations allows. But a scientific approach demands full information, impartial thinking, and creative freedom. Until these conditions are established (not for certain individuals but for the masses), talk about scientific management will remain hollow.

Our economy can be compared to traffic moving through an intersection. When there were only a few cars, the traffic police could easily cope with their tasks, and traffic flowed smoothly. But the stream of traffic continually increases, and a traffic jam develops. What should be done in this situation? It is possible to find the drivers and replace the traffic police, but this will not save the situation. The only solution is to widen the intersection. The obstacles hindering the development of our economy lie outside of it, in the social and political sphere, and all measures that do not remove these obstacles are doomed to ineffectiveness.

The vestiges of the Stalin era are having a negative effect on the economy not only directly, because they preclude a scientific approach to the problems of organization and administration, but also indirectly, because they reduce the creative potential of people in all fields. But under the conditions of the second industrial revolution, it is precisely creative labor that becomes increasingly important for the national economy.

In this connection, the problem of relations between the state and the intelligentsia cannot be left unmentioned. Freedom of information and creative work are necessary for the intelligentsia because of the nature of its activity and its social function. The intelligentsia's attempts to increase these freedoms are legitimate and natural. The state, however, suppresses these attempts by employing all kinds of restrictions—administrative pressures, dismissals from employment, and even court trials. All this gives rise to a social gulf, an atmosphere of mutual distrust, and a profound lack of mutual understanding, making fruitful collaboration difficult between the Party and state apparatus, on the one hand, and the most active layers of the intelligentsia, i.e., the layers that are most valuable for society, on the other. Under the conditions of modern industrial society, in which the role of the intelligentsia is constantly increasing, such a gulf can be described only as suicidal.

The overwhelming majority of the intelligentsia and the youth recognize the need for democratization, and the need for it to be cautious and gradual, but they cannot understand or condone measures of a patently antidemocratic nature. And, indeed, how can one justify the confinement in prisons, camps, and insane asylums of people who hold oppositionist views but whose opposition stands on legal ground, in the area of ideas and convictions? In many instances, no opposition was involved, but only a striving for information, or simply a courageous and unprejudiced discussion of important social questions. The imprisonment of writers for what they have written is inadmissible. It is also impossible to understand or justify such an absurd and extremely harmful measure as the expulsion from the Soviet Writers' Union of the most significant popular writer [Solzhenitsyn], who has shown himself to be deeply patriotic and humane in all that he does.

Equally incomprehensible is the purging of the editorial board of *Novy mir*, around which the most progressive forces in the Marxist-Leninist socialist tendency had rallied.

It is indispensable to speak once again about ideological problems. Democratization, with its fullness of information and clash of ideas, must restore to our ideological life its dynamism and creativity—in the social sciences, arts, and propaganda—and eliminate the bureaucratic, ritualistic, dogmatic, openly hypocritical, and mediocre style that reigns in these areas today.

A course toward democratization would bridge the gulf between the Party and state apparatus and the intelligentsia. The mutual lack of understanding would give way to close cooperation. A course toward democratization would inspire a wave of enthusiasm comparable to that which prevailed in the 1920s. The best intellectual forces in the country would be mobilized for the solution of economic and social problems.

Carrying out democratization is not an easy process. Its normal development would be threatened from one direction by individualist and antisocialist forces, and from the other by the supporters of a "strong state" and demagogues on the fascist model, who might try to exploit for their own ends the economic problems of our country, the lack of mutual understanding and lack of confidence between the intelligentsia and the Party and government apparatus, and the existence of petty-bourgeois and nationalist sentiments in certain sectors of our society. But we must recognize that there is no other solution for our country and that this difficult task must be worked out. Democratization, conducted on the initiative and under the control of the highest official bodies, will allow this process to be realized in a systematic fashion, taking care that all levels of the Party and government apparatus succeed in adopting a new style of work, differing from past work by its greater openness and fuller public airing of views, and its broader discussion of all problems. There is no doubt that the majority of apparatus officials—people educated and trained in a modern, highly developed country— are capable of making the transition to a new style of work and will very soon recognize its advantages. The sifting out of the few who are incapable of this change would only contribute to the general good.

We propose the following draft program of measures, which could be realized over a four-to-five-year period:

1. A statement from the highest Party and government bodies on the necessity for further democratization and on the rate and means of achieving it. The publication in the press of a number of articles discussing the problems of democratization.

2. Limited distribution (through Party organs, enterprises, and institutions) of information on the situation in the country and theoretical works on social problems that at the present time would not be made the object of broad discussion. Gradual increase of access to these materials until all limitations on their distribution have been lifted.

3. Extensive, planned organization of complex industrial associations with a high degree of autonomy in matters of industrial planning, technological processes, raw material supply, sale of products, finances, and personnel. The extension of these rights to smaller productive units as well. Scientific determination, after careful research, of the form and degree of state regulation.

4. An end to the jamming of foreign radio broadcasts. Free sale of foreign books and periodicals. Adherence by our country to the international copyright convention. Gradual expansion and encouragement of international tourism in both directions (over a three-to-four-year period), expansion of international postal communications, and other measures for broadening international communications, with special emphasis in this regard on Comecon countries.

5. Establishment of an institute for public-opinion research. The publication (limited at first but later complete) of materials indicating public attitudes on the most important domestic and foreign policy questions, as well as of other sociological materials.

6. Amnesty for political prisoners. An order requiring publication of the complete record of all trials of a political character. Public supervision of all prisons, camps, and psychiatric institutions.

7. Introduction of measures to improve the functioning of the courts and the procuracy and to enhance their independence from executive powers, local influences, prejudices, and personal ties.

8. Elimination of the designation of nationality on [internal] passports and questionnaires. Uniform passport system for the inhabitants of cities and villages. Gradual elimination of the system of passport registration, to be accomplished simultaneously with the leveling out of economic and cultural inequalities between different regions of our country.

9. Reforms in education: increased appropriations for elementary and secondary schools; improving the living standard of teachers and increasing their autonomy and leeway to experiment.

10. Passage of a law on information and the press. Guaranteeing the right of social organizations and citizens' groups to establish new publications. Complete elimination of prior censorship in every form.

11. Improvement in the training of leadership cadres in the art of management. Introduction of special managerial training programs on the job. Improvement in the information available to leading cadres at all levels, increasing their autonomy, their rights to experiment, to defend their opinions, and to test them in practice.

12. Gradual introduction of the practice of having several candidates in elections to Party and Soviet bodies on every level, even for indirect elections.

13. Expansion of the rights of Soviets; expansion of the rights and the responsibilities of the Supreme Soviet of the USSR.

14. Restoration of the rights of those nationalities deported under Stalin. The reestablishment of the national autonomy of deported peoples with the opportu-

nity for them to resettle in their homeland (in those cases in which until now this has not been done).

15. Measures directed toward increased public disclosure of the work of governing bodies, commensurate with the interests of the state. Establishment of consultative scientific committees to work with the government bodies at every level, such committees to include highly qualified specialists in the different disciplines.

This plan must, naturally, be viewed as a draft plan. It is clear also that it must be supplemented by a plan for economic and social measures worked out by specialists. We emphasize that democratization alone in no way solves the economic problems but will only create the prerequisites for their solution. Without these prerequisites, the economic and technical problems cannot be solved. We have occasionally heard our friends abroad compare the USSR to a truck whose driver is pressing the accelerator all the way to the floor with one foot, while with the other foot he is simultaneously pressing down on the brake. The time has come to use the brake more wisely.

The proposed plan proves, in our opinion, that it is fully possible to outline a program of democratization that is *acceptable* to the Party and government and that, even at the first stage of approximation, *satisfies* the vital needs of the country's development. Naturally, a wide discussion and thoroughgoing scientific, sociological, economic, and sociopolitical research in actual practice will introduce vital corrections and additions. But it is important, as the mathematicians say, to prove the "theorem of the existence of a solution."

It is also necessary to dwell for a moment on the international consequences of our taking a course toward democratization. Nothing could be more favorable to enhancing our international authority and strengthening the progressive Communist forces in the world than further democratization, accompanied by increased technical and economic progress in the first socialist country in the world. Undoubtedly, the possibilities for peaceful coexistence and international cooperation would grow, the forces of peace and social progress would be strengthened, the attractiveness of Communist ideology would increase, and our international position would become more secure. It is particularly important that the moral and material position of the USSR in relation to China would be strengthened and that we would have increased possibilities for influencing the situation in that country indirectly (by example and by economic and technical aid) in the interests of the people of both countries.

A number of correct and necessary foreign-policy steps by our government have not been properly understood, because the information provided to citizens on these questions is very incomplete and because, in the past, obvious inaccuracies and tendentiousness were evident in the information provided. This, naturally, is not conducive to building confidence. One such instance involves the question of economic aid to underdeveloped countries.

Fifty years ago, workers of war-ravaged Europe extended aid to those who were starving to death in the Volga region. The Soviet people are no more callous and self-centered. But they must feel confident that our resources are being expended for genuine assistance, for resolving serious problems, and not for the construction of pompous stadiums or the purchase of American cars for local officials. The situation in today's world and the opportunities and tasks facing our country demand broad participation in economic assistance to underdeveloped countries in collaboration with other countries. But for the public correctly to understand these problems, verbal assurances are not enough; what is called for is fuller information and democratization.

Soviet foreign policy is fundamentally a policy of peace and cooperation. But the failure to inform the public fully arouses discontent. In the past, there were certain negative features in Soviet foreign policy that bore a messianic and overly ambitious character and prompted the conclusion that imperialism does not bear the only responsibility for international tensions.

All these negative aspects of Soviet foreign policy are closely linked with the problem of democratization, and this link has a dual character. There was a great deal of unrest over the absence of democratic discussion concerning such questions as arms aid to other countries—for example, to Nigeria, where a bloody war was going on, whose causes and course the Soviet public knows very little about. We are convinced that the UN Security Council resolution on the Israeli-Arab conflict is a just and reasonable one, though perhaps it is not concrete enough on several points. But there is uneasiness over whether our position does not in fact go substantially beyond this document and whether our position may not be too one-sided. Is our position on the status of West Berlin realistic? Is our effort to extend our influence to areas far beyond our borders always realistic, considering the difficulties in Sino-Soviet relations and the serious problems in our country's economic and technical development? Such a "dynamic" policy may be necessary, of course, but it must accord not only with the basic principles of our country but also with its real possibilities.

We are convinced that the only realistic policy in the age of nuclear weapons is a course toward more far-reaching international cooperation; persistent search for lines of rapprochement in scientific-technical, economic, cultural, and ideological areas; and the rejection in principle of weapons of mass destruction. We take this opportunity to express our opinion that it is advisable for the nuclear powers to make unilateral and joint declarations of principle that they will not be the first to use weapons of mass destruction.

Democratization will be conducive to a better public understanding of foreign policy and the removal of all the negative features in this policy. This, in turn, will wrest the "trump card" from the hands of those opposed to the democratic movement.

What is in store for our nation if it does not take the course toward democratization? The fate of lagging behind the capitalist countries and gradually becoming a second-rate provincial power (history has seen cases of this); the growth of economic difficulties; increasingly tense relations between the Party and government apparatus, on the one hand, and the intelligentsia, on the other; the danger of ill-considered moves to the left or right; exacerbation of national problems, because the movement for democratization emanating from below in the national republics inevitably assumes a nationalistic character.

This perspective becomes particularly ominous if one also takes into account the danger of Chinese totalitarian nationalism (something we regard as a temporary phenomenon from a historical point of view but as an extremely serious one for the next few years). We can counter this danger only if we widen or at least maintain the existing economic and technical distance between ourselves and China, increase the number of our friends in the world, and offer the alternative of cooperation and aid to the Chinese people. This becomes an obvious necessity if we consider the numerical superiority of this potential enemy's population, its militant nationalism, the length of our eastern borders, and the sparse population of our eastern regions. Therefore, the economic stagnation and the lag in our rate of growth, coupled with an unrealistic (often overambitious) foreign policy on all continents, can lead to catastrophic consequences for our country.

Respected comrades! There is no way out of the difficulties now facing our country except a course toward democratization, carried out by the Soviet Communist Party in accordance with a carefully worked-out plan. A turn to the right —that is, a victory for the forces that advocate a stronger administration, a "tightening of the screws"—would not only fail to solve any of the problems but, on the contrary, aggravate them to an extreme point and lead our country into a tragic impasse. The tactic of waiting passively would ultimately have the same result. Today, we still have the chance to take the right road and to carry out the necessary reforms. In a few years, it may be too late. The recognition of this is a necessity on a nationwide scale. The duty of all who see the causes of these problems and the road to their solution is to point out this road to their fellow citizens. Understanding the need for, and possibility of, gradual democratization is the first step along the road to its achievement.

[No. 66, March 1970]

Détente, Disarmament, and Soviet Democratization
BY MATHEMATICIAN N.

It is appropriate to end this book with a selection that reminds us that developments inside the Soviet Union can affect all of us. By the early 1970s, Soviet dissidents were embroiled in a bitter debate among themselves over what has become known as détente between the United States and the USSR. Having lost all faith in the possibility of reform from inside the Soviet political system, many dissidents began to insist that the United States withhold crucial aspects of détente, including an arms limitations treaty and economic credit, until the Soviet government liberalized its domestic policies, especially in the area of emigration and other civil rights. Other dissidents argued, however, that this kind of linkage, which sought to impose internal Soviet reform through foreign pressure, would backfire and imperil all Soviet reformers as well as détente. The crux of the debate is the nature of the relationship between Soviet domestic politics and world affairs, a question that also divides Western observers. In which international circumstances is the Soviet government more likely to carry out meaningful reforms at home—those of détente or those of cold war? The anonymous author of this final selection comments on the question in an interesting way, even though his discussion of the "New Left" in American politics is dated. He takes for granted that democratic reform can be initiated only inside the Soviet political system, but he argues that such an internal development, by changing both American and Soviet perceptions, would lead to a new era of détente and even disarmament. The essay printed here is an abridged version of one chapter from his book-length manuscript entitled "Disarmament and Democracy."

What steps should the Soviet Union take to achieve disarmament? *The only way to achieve disarmament is to democratize Soviet society.* That is, there is a high probability that as Soviet society is democratized more and more, it will be easier and easier to arrive at a disarmament agreement. And there is a low probability of achieving disarmament without democratization.

Let me now proceed to the proof of this assertion. First of all, we may conclude from the experience of past years that no matter what form relations between the USSR and the United States took—whether they grew better or worse—the arms race never abated. I believe that no matter what foreign policy we pursue, without internal changes we cannot achieve disarmament. In the best of cases, certain measures to limit the arms race may be won, but important as that would be, it is insufficient to eliminate the threat of war. The problem is that the existence of nuclear-armed missile systems makes it possible to strike a blow without any visible preparation. Because of this, the military doctrines of both the United States and the Soviet Union allow for the possibility of a sudden outbreak of war during a period of relaxation of international tensions. Thus, an absolutely essential condition for agreement is mutual trust; that is, changes must be brought about in the social psychology of the population and the ruling circles in the United States, because no atmosphere of trust can be established when anti-Communism and anti-Sovietism exist on such a mass scale as they do now.

How would democratization in the USSR affect political life in the United States? I have already written about the mechanism of anti-Communism that operates among the intellectuals and is based on an image of Communism as an ideology that belittles the importance of the individual. This is linked with anti-Sovietism, since the Soviet Union is viewed as a totalitarian state in which the individual has no rights. This view of the USSR is based on a distortion created by bourgeois propaganda, which plays upon the fact that the level of democracy in the USSR lags behind the requirements of real life.

Democratization in our country would knock the trump card out of the hands of the bourgeois propagandists. Intellectuals who oppose the regimentation of the individual under state-monopoly capitalism would begin to regard a Soviet society in which the individual was able to flourish (I am an optimist) as a model to follow. It is not by accident that I am discussing the position of the intellectuals at length, because their role and influence is constantly increasing as the scientific and technical revolution continues and as their numbers swiftly grow.

It is not only the attitude of intellectuals that would be changed by democratization in the USSR. (Incidentally, the intelligentsia in the United States is quite heterogeneous; there are conformist groups that don't care a bit about democracy even in the United States, never mind in the Soviet Union; but the leading current is the one I have described.) In recent years, with the comprehensive automation of production, the character of labor for highly skilled workers has changed. They are freed from routine and wearing labor; broad possibilities for creative activity are now open to them. Because of this, there is among these layers a growing interest in problems of democracy, particularly economic democracy. It is natural that within these more advanced layers of the working class—and their number and importance are likewise growing rapidly, apace with the scientific and technical revolution—anti-Sovietism would drop sharply as political and economic democracy in our country developed. There would also be a noticeably better attitude toward the USSR in bourgeois-liberal, religious, and pacifist circles.

It would be a mistake to think, however, that the American military-industrial complex, that rabid foe of disarmament and democratization, would surrender its positions without a fight. This is especially true because, after democratization in the USSR, mass anti-Communism and anti-Sovietism would still persist among the extreme right-wing layers, which are the social base for the various fascist movements in the United States. We should recall that ten million people voted for George Wallace in 1968. A fierce political struggle over a peace agreement is bound to develop inside the United States between the advocates of moderation and the aggressive circles. This struggle is already under way in a certain form, but after democratization in the USSR it would proceed under circumstances substantially more favorable for us, since the attitudes of the masses toward Communism and the Soviet Union would change.

A vanguard role in this struggle could be played by the New Left. In writing about the New Left, I suggested that this movement needs to turn its efforts in a new direction, to take the place of its opposition to the Vietnam War. It is clear that the fight for disarmament could be this new direction. But at present the anti-Communism and anti-Sovietism of the New Left constitute an obstacle to that fight. If there were democratization in the USSR, the situation in the New Left would change fundamentally. Abandoning anti-Communism and coming to see that the creative Marxism which was able to bear such successful fruits in the USSR was the most progressive ideology, the New Left would be able to close ranks ideologically and organizationally on the basis of this ideology and form a coalition with the more advanced trade unions and liberal organizations. This coalition could take control of the Democratic Party by driving out the right wing.

It is entirely possible for the moderate forces to gain full control of the Democratic Party and to win the national elections. One result could be a disarmament agreement between the United States and the Soviet Union. In describing the role the New Left could play in the fight for disarmament—along with democratization in the USSR—I should refer again to the fact that the New Left now stands at a crossroads. Because of this, it is important that democratization begin in our country as soon as possible, to help save the New Left from disintegration.

In this connection I should take note of one fundamental error made by Academician Sakharov. In his famous *Progress, Coexistence, and Intellectual Freedom,* he argues that it is impossible to prevent a war without convergence of the two systems on a socialist basis, which would require "not only wide social reforms but also substantial changes in the structure of ownership in the capitalist countries." Sakharov stands the problem on its head. It is not that disarmament will result from a convergence on a socialist basis, but that *after disarmament* favorable conditions would arise for social change. Of course, disarmament is inconceivable without the establishment of an atmosphere of trust. But that is something entirely different from convergence in the sense that Sakharov understands it. The capitalists do not want to perish in a thermonuclear war any more than other normal people. That is what makes disarmament possible, even with the continued existence of the capitalist system.

In discussing the international consequences of developments in the USSR, we cannot fail to mention the fact that as a result of such a process the situation could change abruptly in countries like France and Italy, which have exceptionally strong Communist parties and powerful democratic movements. And, as we know, these are NATO allies of the United States and could put pressure on that country to come to a disarmament agreement.

Nor, in discussing disarmament and the connection between disarmament and democratization, can we leave unmentioned the fact that not everyone in our country fully realizes the need for the speediest possible disarmament. Some of our ideologists are ready, for the sake of certain abstract and outdated dogmas, to apply the brakes to the expansion of cultural, scientific, tourist, and other ties between the United States and the Soviet Union (without which a disarmament agreement is inconceivable). Their psychology is somehow reminiscent of the position taken by the notorious American reactionary James Burnham, who wrote in 1947, "The destruction of mankind is preferable to the victory of Communism. Better dead than Red!"[8]

In this connection, let me take up the question of the American policy of "building bridges." This doctrine has a clearly expressed antisocialist thrust. Its aim is to break the socialist countries [of Eastern Europe] away from the USSR, to encourage divergent positions among those countries on various questions of economics, politics, and international relations, to weaken the influence of socialism in the world, and thereby to keep socialist ideas from growing stronger in the United States. To accomplish these ends, the theory of "building bridges" foresees an intensive economic, ideological, and cultural penetration of the socialist countries. The objective basis for the "bridge-building" policy is the tremendous economic might of the United States, the growing gap between it and the Soviet Union in a number of new industrial sectors, in scientific research, experiment, and design, and in industrial management. It is to the advantage of the smaller socialist countries to engage in economic cooperation with the United States, which can provide great financial, scientific, and technical aid. The U.S. ruling circles hope that one result of such aid would be a change in attitude toward the United States that would be reflected in the ideology and politics of those countries.

Naturally, we must combat the antisocialist essence of the "bridge-building" policy. But in so doing, we must remember that the methods for fighting socialism now coming into prominence are not military. It is not a matter of economic blockade or "containment" (isolating the Soviet Union) but, above all, the use of political and ideological influence. Thus, from the point of view of disarmament, this policy must be entirely welcomed, since the expansion of economic, cultural, and other ties weakens the influence of the aggressive circles in the United States. Moreover, we should combat the aims of the "bridge-building"

8. Translator's note: This quotation is retranslated from the Russian, since the author gives no reference to the English original.

policy not just by defensive means (limiting contacts with the United States); we should take the offensive ourselves. After all, a bridge is not a diode, conducting in one direction only. We can carry our socialist ideology into the United States over the same bridge.

But the utilization of the favorable opportunities provided by the "bridge-building" policy is inseparable from the democratization of Soviet society. We will not be able to catch up with the United States economically in the next few years. We should compensate for this economic disadvantage by introducing an immeasurably higher level of democracy, by creating the conditions for the fully rounded development of each individual. This would enable us to compete successfully with the United States for ideological influence in the world. For as we know, it is not by bread alone that men live. . . .

[No. 60, September 1969]

Appendix:

Contents of All Available

Issues of Political Diary

Almost eighty numbers of *Political Diary*, including occasional double issues, appeared between October 1964 and March 1971. What follows is a list of the contents of all issues now available outside the Soviet Union. (For a fuller explanation, see above, "Editor's Preface.") An asterisk denotes issues available only in typescript. All other issues have been published in Russian, in two volumes, by the Alexander Herzen Foundation (*Politicheskii dnevnik*. Amsterdam, 1972 and 1975). Copies of the unpublished typescript issues are deposited in the Slavic collection of Firestone Library at Princeton University. Some of their contents will be published in 1982 in Russian, in one volume of selections from *Political Diary*, by Chalidze Publications in New York City. The reader should bear in mind that titles listed in this appendix are literal translations from the Russian originals and therefore do not always correspond to titles used for items published in this book.

No. 1, October 1964*

1. The October Plenum of the Central Committee of the CPSU
2. Suslov's Report at the Central Committee Plenum and the Charges against Khrushchev
3. From Other Speeches at the Plenum
4. On Certain Changes after the Plenum
5. Some Details Concerning the Preparations for the October Plenum of the Central Committee

No. 3, December 1964

On Khrushchev's Release from His Duties in the Leadership
1. Anastas Mikoyan on the October Plenum of the Central Committee and on Khrushchev

2. A Letter from the Worker A. I. Sbitnev to *Kommunist*
3. On the "Cult" of Khrushchev
4. Khrushchev on the Stalin-Cult Period
5. Khrushchev as a Statesman and as a Person

On Responsibility for the Crimes of the Personality-Cult Period
1. Responsibility for the Repressions in Philosophy
2. From Maxim Rylsky's Poem *Winter Notes*
3. The Responsibility of Officials in Stalin's Camps
4. A Letter about Lev Sheinin Addressed to *Komsomolskaya pravda*

*No. 5, February 1965 (Partial contents)**

1. A. Rumyantsev's Article in *Pravda*
2. The Congress of the Writers of the Russian Republic. *Rinascita* on the Writers' Congress and the Painting Exhibit at the Manège
3. Anatoly Sofronov Speaks Against Rumyantsev's Article
4. N. Yegorychev on Solzhenitsyn and Yevtushenko—On Solzhenitsyn's *Ivan Denisovich* —On the Position of the Communist Parties of Latin America
5. Stories about Stalin
6. From the History of Soviet Literature, 1924

No. 7, April 1965

Foreword

Some Events of the Month
1. The Seminar of Propagandists of the Party's Moscow Committee
2. The Speeches of Pyotr Demichev and V. Snastin at the Editors' Conference
3. The Seminar for Teachers at Higher Educational Institutions: The Speech by Nikishev, Deputy Minister of Higher Education for the USSR
4. Once Again the Question of Stalin Is Raised

On Certain Articles, Letters, and Manuscripts
1. On an Article by Arthur Schlesinger
2. Marietta Shaginyan's Memoir *Pages from the Past*
3. From the Reminiscences of D. Vitkovsky.
4. From a Satirical Article by Saltykov-Shchedrin "Light-Minded People" from 1868
5. On Yevgeny Zamiatin's Article "The Goal"

From the Past
1. The Death of L. Martov
2. The Murder of Ignace Reiss
3. The Tragic Fate of G. I. Myasnikov and His Family
4. The SRs after the Revolution
5. Christian Rakovsky
6. The Opposition in 1927
7. Albert Einstein on the Results of Autocracy
8. The History of One of Mandelstam's Poems
9. The Twentieth Party Congress

No. 9, June 1965

Miscellaneous News
1. Conspiracy in Bulgaria?
2. Crime in Moscow
3. Rumors of Possible Changes in the Leadership
4. A Conference at the Ministry of Higher Education
5. Lydia Chukovskaya's Suit against a Soviet Publishing House

On Certain Books, Articles, and Manuscripts
1. Pyotr Kapitsa's Pamphlet *Science and Contemporary Society*
2. I. M. Danishevsky's Letter Concerning V. Peskov's Article "Fatherland"
3. On the Narrative Poem *Kolyma* and the Poetry of Yelena Vladimirova
4. A Letter to *Izvestia* from a Group of Prominent Historians
5. Excerpts from George Lukacs's Article "Problems of Coexistence in the Cultural Sphere"

The National Question in the USSR
1. The Strengthening of Nationalist Tendencies and Trends in the Ukraine
2. The Question of Reestablishing the Volga German Republic (From a Discussion between Anastas Mikoyan and a Delgation of Volga Germans, June 7, 1965)
3. On T. Kichko's Pamphlet *Judaism without Embellishment*
4. An Item in *L'Humanité* [on the Kichko Pamphlet]
5. An Anti-Semitic Novel by Anatoly Dimarov
6. On the Problem of Anti-Semitism in the USSR: A Letter by Boris Polevoi

From the Past
1. On the June 1957 Central Committee Plenum
2. On Khrushchev's Foreign Policy
3. On Khrushchev's Entourage
4. The January 1, 1918, Assassination Attempt on Lenin
5. From the History of Soviet Literature: Bukharin and Trotsky on Yesenin

[Additional Items from No. 9, 1965*]

1. On the Lag in Agricultural Production in the Non–Black-Earth Regions of the USSR
2. On Differential Rent under the Conditions Existing in Socialist Agriculture

*No. 11, August 1965 (Partial Contents)**

On Certain Current Events
1. On Yevtushenko's Narrative Poem "The Bratsk Hydroelectric Station"
2. Certain Instructions on Ideology
3. The Demonstrations in Armenia
4. The Strange Story of Arthur Miller's Play *Incident at Vichy*
5. The Proposed Soviet Economic Reform
6. Do We Have Unemployment?

On Certain Statements, Letters, and Manuscripts
1. Remarks by A. G. Aganbegyan, Corresponding Member of the Soviet Academy of
   Sciences, on Problems Concerning the Present State of the Soviet Economy
2. Ernst Henry's Letter to Ilya Ehrenburg
3. The Question of a National Language

From the Past
1. On the Glorification of Stalin
2. The Tragic Fate of the Singer Mikhailova
3. On Nadezhda Krupskaya
4. Stories about Stalin

Notes on Agricultural Production
1. Procurement Prices in the Years of the Stalin Cult
2. Changes in Procurement Prices, 1953–62

No. 12, September 1965 (Partial Contents)*

1. Rumyantsev's Article in *Pravda*
2. The Editor of *Pravda* Is Replaced
3. Is Gomulka Opposed to the Rehabilitation of Stalin?
4. Are the Rumors about Changes in the Leadership True?
5. The Arrest of the Literary Critic Andrei Sinyavsky and the Cancellation of Plans to
   Publish a Novel of Solzhenitsyn's
6. Central Committee Plenum on Economic Problems
7. Several Epidemics

On Fyodor Raskolnikov
1. Statements by S. Trapeznikov for the Rehabilitation of Stalin and against the Rehabilitation of Raskolnikov
2. Once Again on the Charges against Raskolnikov
3. Fyodor Raskolnikov, "A Psychological Portrait of Stalin"

On Certain Manuscripts, Articles, and Statements
1. A Retired NKVD Official on Eugenia Ginzburg's *Journey into the Whirlwind*

From the Past
1. Stalin and Machiavelli
2. More on Stalin
3. From the Tales of S. B. Brichkina

No. 17, February 1966*

On the Trial of the Writers Sinyavsky and Daniel
1. The Situation before the Trial
2. Once More on the Sinyavsky-Daniel Case
3. The Opening of the Trial, February 11
4. At the Trial

4. On the Nationalities of the Soviet North
5. On the Problem of the Karabakh Mountains Autonomous Region
6. Valery Skurlatov's "Code of Morals"

Problems of Socialist Theory and the History of Socialism
1. From the Book *Essence and Prospects of Socialism*
2. From the History of the Fourth International: Excerpts from Isaac Deutscher's *Prophet Outcast* and Some Comments

No. 19, April 1966 (Partial Contents)*

The Twenty-third Party Congress: Materials, Documents, Comments
1. On Certain Speeches at the Twenty-third Congress
2. From Sholokhov's Speech at the Congress
3. Lydia Chukovskaya's Open Letter to Sholokhov

No. 20, May 1966 (Partial Contents)*

On Certain Statements, Letters, and Manuscripts
1. Ernst Henry's Lecture at the Physics Department of Moscow University
2. Ilya Ehrenburg's Remarks

Notes on Economic and Sociological Topics
1. On the Standard of Living and Elements of Inequality
2. Competition between the Two Systems: On the Decline in the Annual Growth Rate in the Socialist Countries
3. The Overall Results of the Seven-Year Plan in Agriculture

No. 21, June 1966 (Partial Contents)*

1. On Pyotr Demichev's Instructional Report
2. The Discussion at the Marxism-Leninism Institute on the Draft of Volume 3 of the History of the CPSU

No. 24, September 1966*

Miscellaneous Reports and Comments
1. On Certain Books
2. Harold Koch Requests Asylum in the USSR
3. On Rural Trades
4. On the Taganka Theater
5. The Elimination of Vocational and Industrial Training in Secondary Schools

From Literary Life
1. Writers' Congresses in the Union Republics
2. From Vasil Bykov's Speech at the Fifth Congress of Byelorussian Writers
3. A. Karlyuk's Remarks
4. The Italian Communist Vittorio Strada on *Novy mir*
5. *Novy mir* on the Tasks and Aims of Literature

3. On the Attitude toward the Leaders of the Opposition in the 1920s
4. *Jenmin Jihpao* on the Discussion of Volume 3 of the *History of the CPSU*
5. On the World Communist Movement
6. The Official Chinese Press on the Twentieth CPSU Congress and Stalin
7. Sovietology
8. The Virgin Lands in 1965–66

From Literary Life
1. On the Guidance of Literature: Anatoly Lunacharsky
2. *Pravda* on *Novy mir* and *Oktyabr*

On Certain Letters, Articles, and Manuscripts
1. Nikolai Berdyaev's Article "On Fanaticism, Orthodoxy, and Truth"
2. Church Matters (The Letter of Eshliman and Yakunin)
3. On Certain Poems
4. On Thomas Jefferson

The Problem of Responsibility for the Political Crimes of the Past
1. From D. Melnikov's Article "West from the Elbe"
2. From Ernst Henry's Article "The Brown Plague on the Screen"
3. From D. Melnikov's Article "The Theory of All-Forgivingness"
4. The Position of *Oktyabr:* From a Short Novel by M. Lansky
5. The Journalist K. Bukovsky, of *Oktyabr,* Polemicizes against Zalygin and Ehrenburg
6. Some Comments on the Problem of Responsibility
7. On Aleksandr Fadeyev

From the Past
1. The Question of Red Terror in 1918
2. The Question of Terror in 1922
3. From Victor Hugo's Pamphlet *Little Napoleon*
4. On the Question of Hostages
5. On Yezhov
6. On the People's Militia of 1941
7. Nadezhda Krupskaya in 1938

Notes on Various Topics: Marx, Engels, and Lenin on the Jacobin Terror

No. 30, March 1967

The Major Political Events of the Month: On the Defection of Stalin's Daughter, Svetlana Alliluyeva

From Literary Life
1. A Discussion in the Secretariat of the Soviet Writers' Union on *Novy mir*
2. Aleksandr Tvardovsky's Letter to Suren Gazaryan

On Certain Political Discussions: A Dialogue between Ernst Henry and Andrei Sakharov
From the History of Soviet Literature
1. On Mikhail Bulgakov's Letter to the Soviet Government
2. A Party Meeting of Moscow Writers in March 1956 on the Results of the Twentieth
Party Congress (Excerpts from the Minutes)

From the Past
1. On the Struggle against "Cosmopolitanism" in Economics
2. From the History of the Brest-Litovsk Peace: Dzerzhinsky's Position.
3. From the History of the Conflict with the Opposition in 1925: An Unknown Letter
of Dzerzhinsky's

No. 31, April 1967

On Certain Current Events
1. The Conference of Communist Parties at Karlovy Vary
2. The Death of a Soviet Cosmonaut
3. Interest in the Narodniks among Soviet Youth
4. On Certain Myths
5. *Pravda* and *Izvestia* in the Capital and in the Provinces
6. On Certain Youth Organizations
7. Tvardovsky in Italy
8. On Eugenia Ginzburg's *Journey into the Whirlwind*
9. The Trial of Victor Khaustov
10. On Articles Dealing with the Victims of Stalin's Terror
11. Svetlana Alliluyeva's Press Conference
12. The New Currency Policy

From Literary Life
1. A New Story by Solzhenitsyn
2. An Article on Solzhenitsyn in a Slovak Newspaper

On Certain Articles, Letters, and Manuscripts
1. Grigory Pomerants, "On Pseudo Revolutionary Movements and the Intelligentsia"
2. From Frankland's Book on Khrushchev
3. From C. Wright Mills's Book *The Power Elite*
4. From a Collection of Articles by the Polish Marxist Andrzej Stawar
5. From Aleksandr Todorsky's Review of Nikolai Pogodin's Play *Loyalty*

On Gorky: Some Documents and Materials
1. Gorky and the Right SR Trial
2. On Gorky's Pamphlet *V. I. Lenin*
3. Gorky and Stalin
4. Trotsky's Article Criticizing Gorky

From the Past
1. On the Question of Bureaucratism

2. Trotsky and Lenin's Death
3. Stalin and Socialism
4. Lenin and the Central Committee in October 1917
5. Again on Bureaucratism
6. On the Slogan of Self-Criticism in 1928

No. 33, June 1967

Events of the Month
1. The Dismissal of Semichastny
2. On the Theses for the Fiftieth Anniversary of October
3. The Middle East Conflict and the Intelligentsia
4. Again on the Middle East War
5. On the System of People's Control in the USSR

From Literary Life
1. Yevtushenko on Sholokhov
2. Paustovsky and Solzhenitsyn
3. Eugenia Ginzburg's Book
4. Films
5. What Writers Expected From the Writers' Congress

On Certain Letters, Articles, and Manuscripts
1. An Exchange between Prof. I. Dashkovsky and Radio Commentator B. Stepanov
2. A. Khrabrovitsky's Letter to Sholokhov
3. Letters by Soviet Writers in Support of Solzhenitsyn's Letter (Pavel Antokolsky, Georgi Vladimov, Viktor Konetsky, and Viktor Sosnora)
4. On Solzhenitsyn's Letters to Mikhail Yakubovich
5. *Literaturnaya gazeta* on the Verse and Narrative Poems of V. Firsov

From the Past
1. Bureaucratism and Irresponsibility
2. On the Twenty-second Party Congress
3. Pavel Milyukov's Article on Bolshevism

*No. 34, June 1967 (Partial Contents)**

On Certain Current Events
1. The "Nekrich Affair"
2. Theater and Cinema
3. "Lecturer's Day"
4. The "Yegorychev Affair"
5. On Certain International Matters
6. Czechoslovakia
7. Cuba
8. A Strange Story (The Case of Burlatsky and Karpinsky)
9. Reports from the Middle East

Notes on Economic Questions
1. A Balance Sheet on Soviet Industrial Progress in 1967
2. The Volume of Goods and Services Produced in the United States in 1967
3. On the Annual Increase in Industrial Production in the USSR and Other Countries
4. On the Difference Between the Developed and Underdeveloped Countries
5. On the Training of Skilled Workers in the USSR
5a. On Population Shifts in the USSR (From Vl. Kantorovich's Article "Sociology and Literature," *Novy mir,* no. 12, 1967)
6. On the Social Structure in Soviet Secondary Schools (Ibid., p. 157)
7. On the Cultural Level of the Soviet Population (Ibid., p. 161)

Notes on Various Topics
1. "Rules" for Despots and Tyrants
2. What Is the Power of Prophets?
3. On Certain Recently Published Articles and Letters of Lenin's
4. On the So-called Freedom Obelisk
5. An Instructive Experiment
6. Ends and Means

No. 43, April 1968

Events of the Month
1. From the Speeches at the Nineteenth Moscow Party Conference
2. Reprisals Continue on the Administrative and Party Levels
3. A Chronicle of Certain Events
4. From a Report by Viktor Grishin, First Secretary of the Party's Moscow Committee
5. A Trial in Leningrad

On the Events in Czechoslovakia
1. The Plenum of the Central Committee of the Communist Party of Czechoslovakia (CPC): From Alexander Dubcek's Report
2. Speech of Cisar, a Secretary of the CPC's Central Committee, to the Plenum
3. From the CPC's Action Program
4. The Changes in the Government and the National Front of Czechoslovakia
5. The Italian Communist Party on the Events in Czechoslovakia
6. The Soviet Press on the Events in Czechoslovakia
7. On the Events in Poland

From Literary Life
1. Session of the Secretariat of the Moscow Writers' Organization
2. Vladimir Tendryakov's New Short Novel
3. A "Blacklist" of Writers
4. On the Film *Asya the Lame Woman*
5. Foreign Publication of *Cancer Ward:* Two Letters by Solzhenitsyn
6. Lev Ozerov on Yevtushenko
7. On Feliks Kuznetsov's Article "Criticism Begins with the Critic"
8. A Writers' Meeting in the Central House of Literature
9. *Novy mir* on Viktor Nekrasov's Book *In the Trenches of Stalingrad*

From the Literary and Theatrical World
1. The New Theater Season in Moscow
2. From Vladimir Lakshin's Review of Bulgakov's *The Master and Margarita*
3. The Letter by Leaders of the Soviet Writers' Union Supporting the Soviet Government's Actions in Czechoslovakia
4. From the Theatrical World: The Magazines *Ogonyok* and *Teatr*
5. On Vladimir Firsov's Narrative Poem *The Republic of Immortality*
6. *Literaturnaya gazeta* on Jiri Hanzelka

On Certain Books, Articles, and Manuscripts
1. On the Book by V. Berezhkov *Tehran 1943*
2. A Letter to the Presidium of the Supreme Soviet
3. From M. Markovsky's Letter to Academician Sakharov
4. From N. G. Kuznetsov's Memoirs *The War Years*
5. V. Khvostov and A. Grylev's Article in *Kommunist*
6. On Dennis Pritt's Article "Human Rights, 1968"
7. A Letter from Estonia to Academician Sakharov
8. From a Letter by the Writer R.
9. Letter to Academician Sakharov from Georges Pire, Winner of the Nobel Peace Prize in 1958

Articles and Notes on the Events in Czechoslovakia and around Czechoslovakia
1. Was There a Danger of NATO Military Intervention in Czechoslovakia?
2. On the Real Dimensions and Danger of Internal Counterrevolution
3. The Soviet Press on the Events in Czechoslovakia
4. The Soviet Army in Czechoslovakia
5. Some Preliminary Conclusions
6. On Certain Theoretical Questions
7. On the Reasons for the Intervention by Warsaw Pact Troops
8. Some Historical Analogies

Pages from History: The October 1956 Events in Poland and Reactions in Moscow

No. 50, November 1968

Major Events of the Month
1. Suspension of the Bombing of North Vietnam
2. Belovaya Restored to Party Membership
3. The Writer Aleksei Kosterin's Resignation from the Party
4. Talks between the CPSU and the French Communist Party
5. Kirill Mazurov's Report
6. The Election of Richard Nixon as President of the United States
7. The Funeral of Aleksei Kosterin
8. The Ministry for the Preservation of Public Order Reorganized as Part of the Ministry of Internal Affairs
9. The Disposition of Two Appeals to the Party Control Commission under the Central Committee
10. The Preparatory Commission for the International Conference of Communist Parties

11. On the Elections to the Soviet Academy of Sciences
12. Programmatic Declaration of the Hungarian Workers' Party
13. Programmatic Statement of the Spanish Communist Party

On Events in Czechoslovakia
  1. An Article in *Rude pravo* on the Slogan of a Working-Class Policy
  2. A Writers' Evening at the Central House of Literature
  3. From the Newspaper *Nepszabadsag*
  4. On Certain Articles in *Pravda*
  5. Inside the Czechoslovak Writers' Union
  6. Statement of the Active Party Members among Czech Writers
  7. The Fifty-first Anniversary of October in Czechoslovakia
  8. Brezhnev and Gomulka on the Events in Czechoslovakia
  9. Once Again on Yuri Zhukov's Article in *Pravda*
  10. On the Plenum of the CPC Central Committee
  11. On the Resolution of the Above Plenum
  12. Eugen Löbel's Interview in *Le Monde*
  13. The Improvement in Relations between the USSR and Romania
  14. Expanded [Soviet] Contacts with [Various] Prominent Czechoslovaks
  15. The Student Strike in Prague
  16. Czechoslovak Scholars Criticize the Soviet "White Book"

From Literary Life
  1. *Krasnaya zvezda* (Red Star) on Vasil Bykov's Short Novel *Running Attack*
  2. *Ogonyok* on the Magazine *Tvorchestvo* (Creativity)
  3. On Certain Literary Awards
  4. On the Magazine *Molodaya gvardiya*
  5. *Ogonyok* Attacks *Novy mir*
  6. From V. Chalmayev's Article "Inevitability"
  7. On E. Mikulina's Essay "Life As It Is"
  8. A Polemic between *Komsomolskaya pravda* and *Ogonyok*
  9. *Novy mir*, no. 9: Vladimir Lakshin's Article "The Sowing and the Reaping"
  10. The Critic F. Chapchakhov on Chalmayev's "Inevitability"

On Certain Books, Letters, Articles, and Manuscripts
  1. On Ladislav Mnacko's Novel *Taste of Power*
  2. From Yelizaveta Drabkina's Article "The Day after the Revolution"
  3. On the *Information Bulletins* of the Representatives [in Moscow] of the Crimean Tatar People
  4. Letter from the Soviet Writer Lev Kopelev to the Czechoslovak Writer Milan Kundera
  5. On Robert Conquest's Book *The Great Terror*
  6. Irzy Hanzelka and Miroslav Zikmund's "Special Reports"
  7. An Encyclopedia of the October Revolution
  8. On Ivan Svitak's Article "Scientism and Marxism"

Problems of Public Education
  1. Public Education in the USSR and the United States: A Comparison of Funding and Educational Systems

2. Admissions to Higher Educational Institutions in 1968
3. The Coming Revolution in Teaching Methods
4. Excerpts from Martsinkevich's Book (On Selection and Job Assignments for Young People)

Notes on Philosophical Topics: Contemporary Man and Questions of Faith and Religion
 1. The American Psychologist Erich Fromm on Religion
 2. Albert Einstein and Religion
 3. The Philosophical Credo of the American Scholar Curt John Ducasse
 4. From an Article by F. J. Curie "Reflections on the Humanism of Science"
 5. A Conversation with the Philosopher M.
 6. Communism and Religion: A Summary of Roger Garaudy's Article "How to Erect a Human Habitation"
 7. The Crisis of Modern Christianity (From the Article "The Church without God")
 8. On Personal Immortality: Lev Ozerov's Open Letter to Ilya Selvinsky, 1966
 9. Science and Religion (From an Article by Charles Towns)
10. From an article by Julian Huxley, "The Key to the Future Is Humanism"
11. On the Essence of Religion, and Communists and Religion: From the Remarks of the Philosopher Grigory Pomerants at a Discussion at the Institute of the Peoples of Asia

No. 53, February 1969*

On the Events in Czechoslovakia
 1. The Trade-Union Congress
 2. Ota Sik and Eduard Goldstücker
 3. *Literaturnaya gazeta* on Events in Czechoslovakia
 4. From a Speech by Cestmir Cisar
 5. From a Speech by Lubomir Strougal
 6. The Question of Czechoslovakia at the Twelfth Congress of the Italian Communist Party
 7. Publication of a Pamphlet Attacking Josef Smrkovsky
 8. An Interview with François Billoux
 9. The Czechoslovak Student Organizations and the Komsomol
10. The Position of the Czech Magazine *Reporter*
11. Miscellaneous Reports from Czechoslovakia
12. Two *Pravda* Articles
13. A New Tragedy at St. Vaclav Square
14. The Hungarian Magazine *Valsag* on Events in Czechoslovakia

New Attempts to Rehabilitate Stalin
1. New Poems by Feliks Chuyev
2. From N. G. Kuznetsov's Memoirs
3. On Marshal K. A. Meretskov's Book *Serving the People*
4. On the Book *Essays in the History of the CPSU*, a Textbook for Schools on the Fundamentals of Marxism-Leninism
5. An Article on Stalin in a 1969 Tear-off Calendar
6. L. V. Shirikov's Report at the Historical Archives Institute
7. On S. M. Shtemenko's Book *The General Staff during the War*

On Certain Articles, Letters, and Manuscripts
1. On Anti-Semitism in Fascist Germany (Excerpts from V. Kral's Book *The Crime Against Europe*. Moscow: Mysl Publishers, 1968, Translated from the Czech)
2. On the "New Left" in the United States (From an Article by Howard Parsons, "The American Philosophy of Life and the 'New Left' " in *Voprosy filosofii* (Problems of Philosophy), no. 6, 1968)
3. V. P. Efraimson's Article on the Genesis of Ethics
4. The Director of a Philosophy Institute in Hungary on the Present Situation in Philosophy
5. On the Social Philosophy of Herbert Marcuse (Abstracts of Two Articles in *Voprosy filosofii*)

Notes on Economic Questions
1. Per Capita National Income
2. On Certain Economic Concepts
3. The Space Program and Economy of the United States
4. On Economic Difficulties in India and China
5. The Increase in the National Income
6. On Forms of Management in Science and Industry
7. John Galbraith on the U.S. Defense Industry
8. From a Lecture by A. Galkin on Social Changes in the Advanced Capitalist Countries
9. The Working Class in the United States
10. From an Article by A. I. Levkovsky "Population, Food, and the 'Third World' " (*Voprosy filosofii*, no. 1, 1969)
11. The Socialist Countries and the United Arab Republic
12. From D. Wall's Book *The Challenge of the Third World* (London, 1968)
13. From M. Simonsen, *Brazil in 2001*
14. N. Moiseev's Article on the Problem of Managing the Economy
15. V. Chivilikhin's Essay "The Earth in Trouble"

No. 54, March 1969

1. Armed Clashes on the Sino-Soviet Border
2. A Conference of the Warsaw Pact Countries
3. Richard Nixon's First Major Decision
4. The Congress of the League of Yugoslav Communists
5. Concerning a Wall Newspaper
6. V. I. Gantman's Report on the World Situation
7. Destruction of the Winter Crops in the Soviet South

On the Situation in Czechoslovakia
1. An Article by Vasil Bilak
2. In the Czechoslovak Writers' Union
3. Jiri Hendrich
4. A Poll among Young people
5. Another Self-Immolation in Czechoslovakia
6. An Article in the Newspaper Evening Prague

7. From a Speech by Strougal
8. An Article in *Literaturnayagazeta* on Ota Sik
9. Provocatory Material Published in *Sovetskaya Rossiya*
10. Once Again on the Position of the Belgian Communist Party
11. The Position of the Mexican Communist Party
12. The Newspaper *Zprava* Continues Publication in Czechoslovakia
13. Czechoslovakia and the "Cultural Revolution" in China
14. Survey of the First Issues of the Magazine Politika

From Literary Life
1. N. Voronov's Short Novel *Youth in Zheleznodolsk*
2. A Conference on Military-Patriotic Literature
3. A Moscow-wide Conference of Writers
4. On the New Chapters of Sholokhov's Novel *They Fought For Their Country*

On Certain Letters, Articles, and Manuscripts
1. Academician Pyotr Kapitsa's Speech at a Session of the Presidium of the Soviet Academy of Sciences
2. On the Question of the Kirov Assassination: Material Published in *Les Lettres nouvelles*
3. Pyotr Yakir's Letter to *Kommunist*
4. Ernst Henry's Article "The Defeat of Right-Wing Social Democracy in the 'Third World'"
5. Excerpts from A. Luk's Book *On Wit and the Sense of Humor* (1969)
6. F. Shakhmagomov's Novel *"Mercury" vs. "Scorpion"*
7. A. Birman on the Opponents of the Economic Reform

From the Past
1. Nikolai Chernyshevsky on the Tsarist Bureaucratic Machine
2. On the Number of Soviet Prisoners of War
3. Repression within the NKVD
4. Lenin and the Anarchists
5. The Fate of Betal Kalmykov
6. Western Political Figures on the 1930s Trials
7. On Boris Pasternak
8. Paul Robeson and Itsik Fefer
9. On V. M. Bekhterev
10. Arrests after the War

No. 55, April 1969

On Events in Czechoslovakia
1. April 1–10: The Situation Worsens
2. April 17–20: Decisions of the Plenum of the CPC Central Committee
3. From a Speech by Lubomir Strougal

From Literary Life
1. At a Seminar for Literary Critics

2. Introductory Remarks by Vadim Sokolov
3. Discussion
4. Summary

On Certain Books, Articles, Letters, and Manuscripts
1. On Avtorkhanov's Book *The Technology of Power*
2. Antipov's Memorandum on Samizdat
3. Elsa Triolet's Article on Sakharov's Pamphlet
4. The Italian Communists on the Border Conflict between the USSR and China
5. The Unusual Fate of the Family and Relatives of Yakov Sverdlov (An Item by A. M—y)
6. On Anatole Rappoport's Book *Strategy and Conscience*

From the Past
1. From Konstantin Ordzhonikidze's Memoirs on His Brother Sergo
2. From the Memoirs of D. B—y (Industrialization. Ideology and Fanaticism. On Bukharin)

Articles and Notes on Various Topics
1. On Pitirim Sorokin and Some of His Writings
2. V. I. Lenin on Freedom of the Press and the Intelligentsia
3. On the October Revolution and the Political System It Produced (A Dialogue)
4. From the History of the Czech Military Legion in Russia

*No. 59, August 1969 (Partial Contents)**

On Certain Current Events
1. August 20: On Events in Czechoslovakia
2. August 21–31: Events in Czechoslovakia
3. From Ceausescu's Report to the Tenth Congress of the Romanian Communist Party
4. On the Personnel Changes in Azerbaidzhan
5. New Clashes on the Sino-Soviet Border
6. Again on the "Nekrich Affair"

On Certain Books, Articles, and Manuscripts
1. Once More on S. M. Shtemenko's *The General Staff during the War* (R. B. Lert, "Shtemenko vs. Shtemenko")
2. From an Article by A. Gulyga on Mythmaking
3. On A. E. Golovanov's Memoirs *Long-Range Bombing Mission*

*No. 60, September 1969**

On Certain Events in the World
1. September 1: The Situation in Czechoslovakia
2. An Interview with a Czechoslovak Journalist
3. On Soviet-American Rivalry in Space
4. The Situation in the Czechoslovak Writers' Organizations

5. Jiri Hajek's Position
6. September 29–30: The Situation in Czechoslovakia and the New CPC Plenum

From Literary Life
1. On an Article by A. Dementiev in *Novy mir*
2. *Ogonyok* Attacks *Novy mir*
3. From a Speech by Aleksandr Chakovsky at the House of Scientists in Obninsk
4. Tvardovsky's New Narrative Poem *(The Son Does Not Answer For the Father)*
5. Vsevolod Kochetov's New Novel

On Certain Articles, Letters, and Manuscripts
1. Some Articles from the Czechoslovak Press and Czechoslovak Samizdat
2. From the Discussion around Sakharov's Essay
3. From an Unpublished Book in Manuscript by the Mathematician N., *Disarmament and Democracy*

No. 63, December 1969

From Literary Life
1. On Solzhenitsyn's Expulsion from the Writers' Union
2. Around Kochetov's Novel
3. Results of an Opinion Poll of *Literaturnaya gazeta*'s Readers

On the Ninetieth Anniversary of Stalin's Birth
1. An Article in *Pravda*, "On the Ninetieth Anniversary of the Birth of J. V. Stalin"
2. An Article by A. Ivanov, "On the National Shame of the Great Russians"

On Certain Books, Articles, and Manuscripts
1. From an Article on Science by Yu. Schneider: On Certain Ethical Problems
2. A Second Volume of *Selected Samizdat Texts* Comes Out
3. On Aleskandr Chakovsky's Article "Writers in Today's World"
4. From the Unpublished Book Seven of Ilya Ehrenburg's Memoirs
5. From a Book by S. Klyuyev, *The Basic Elements of Economic Preparation for War*
6. An Anonymous Piece on the Funeral of Kornei Chukovsky
7. Mikhail Yakubovich's Reminiscences of Zinoviev (From a Tape Recording)

Notes on Various Topics: The USSR and China
1. An Anonymous Survey, "Six Points of View on the Question of a Sino-Soviet Conflict"
2. The USSR, the United States, and China (The American Point of View)
3. From Horst Pommerening's Book *The Sino-Soviet Conflict*

From Conversations on Political Topics
1. On Marxism
2. Lenin on Soviet Power and the Dictatorship of the Proletariat
3. The October Revolution and Other Revolutions
4. The October Revolution and the Worldwide Socialist Revolution

No. 64, January 1970

On the Events of the Past Month
1. Gustav Husak's New Year's Interview
2. The Renaming of Lugansk
3. Letter from a Group of Prominent Intellectuals to the CPSU Central Committee
4. The Sorry Business Involving the CPSU Central Committee's Theses [On the Hundredth Anniversary of Lenin's Birth]
5. The New Plenum of the CPC Central Committee and New Personnel Changes in Czechoslovakia

From Literary Life
1. The Prize Awarded to Sergei Smirnov
2. Lev Ginzburg's Notes
3. Concerning One of Sergei Mikhalkov's Fables
4. From *Novy mir*, no. 11, 1969: Man in the Society of the Future; Pisarev on Revolution; On Forms of Protest; The End and the Means

Nationalism and National Problems in the Modern World
1. Nationalism in the Balkans
2. From Louis Snyder's Book *The New Nationalism*
3. From Robert Laffont's Book *France*
4. Some Statistics

On Certain Books, Articles, and Manuscripts
1. On Andrei Amalrik's Manuscript "Will the Soviet Union Survive Until 1984?"
2. On the Manuscript Entitled "Time Does Not Wait"

Notes on Various Topics: Problems of the Soviet Economy
1. On Some Results of the Soviet Economic Reform
2. On the State of Livestock Farming in the USSR, 1966–69

No. 66, March 1970 *

Some Major Events
1. The Smashing of *Novy mir*'s Editorial Board
2. The First Response in Samizdat to the Smashing of *Novy mir* (An Article Entitled "After the Killing of *Novy mir:* In Lieu of an Obituary")
3. Around the Changes on the Editorial Board of *Novy mir*
4. From an Article by V. Mdzhavanadze in *Kommunist*
5. The Publication of Semyon Budyonny's Memoirs
6. Georgy Zhukov on the First Weeks of the War
7. Expulsions from the Communist Party of Czechoslovakia
8. The Coup in Cambodia
9. The Conference of the Writers of the RSFSR

Around Kochetov's Novel
1. From an Article by Yu. Golosov, "What Does Kochetov Really Want?"
2. From Raissa Lert's Article "He Wants to Go Back"

On Certain Letters and Manuscripts
1. Letter by Three Soviet Scholars (Sakharov, Turchin, Medvedev) to Brezhnev, Kosygin, and Podgorny
2. Statement by the Attorney in the Case of Pyotr Grigorenko

Notes on Various Topics: Economic Questions
1. An Overall Survey of the Economic Competition between Socialism and Capitalism, between the USSR and the United States, 1961–69
2. On the State of Agriculture and Its Difficulties
3. On Inflation in the USSR
4. Certain Demographic Data for the USSR
5. On the Economic Situation in Yugoslavia

Notes and Materials on History and on the History of Social Thought
1. On Hitler and Hitlerism: From an Unpublished Book by D. Melnikov and L. Chernaya *Public Enemy Number One*
2. From Bigelow's Book *Wars of the Rising Sun* (1969) (On Genghis Khan)
3. Aleksandr Herzen on Premature Socialist Revolution
4. From the History of Russian Social Thought: The Slavophiles and Konstantin Leontyev (A. L. Yanov's Article in *Voprosy filosofii*, no. 8, 1969, pp. 97–106)
5. Lavrov on the Views of Tkachev and the Tkachevists
6. Pisarev on the Nature of Dogmatism
7. New Ideas and Old Authorities: From an Article by Pisarev
8. Adolf Joffe's Letter to Leon Trotsky

Miscellaneous: On a Detective Story

No. 67, April 1970

Miscellaneous
1. On Personnel Changes in the Apparatus
2. On the Lenin Prizes for 1970
3. Lenin on Anniversary Celebrations (From the Memoirs of Professor I. Dashkovsky)
4. The Celebration of the Centenary of Lenin's Birth
5. Computers in the United States
6. Multiple-Warhead Missiles
7. The Launching of a Sputnik in China
8. The Jewish Question in the USSR

Notes on Certain Problems of Soviet Foreign Policy
1. General Observations
2. European Security
3. The Situation in Vietnam and Southeast Asia

From History
1. From the History of the Crimean Tatars
2. From the History of the Left SR Party and Its Leaders (The Notes and Statements of Irina Kakhovskaya)

No. 68, May 1970*

On Certain Events of the Month: Notes on Various Topics
1. Monuments to the Victims of the Stalin Repression
2. The Funeral of Molotov's Wife, P. S. Zhemchuzhina
3. A Two-Volume Edition of Brezhnev's Articles and Speeches
4. Astronaut Neil Armstrong in the USSR
5. Initial Results of the American Invasion of Cambodia
6. An Article by A. Abalkin in *Pravda*
7. A Seventh Point of View on the Sino-Soviet Conflict
8. Two Novels by Ivan Shevtsov
9. From Literary Life: A New Narrative Poem by Yevtushenko

On Certain Books and Manuscripts
1. From the Memoirs of Air Force Chief Marshal A. Novikov
2. From a Pamphlet by A. O. Baranov, *The Revolution in Military Science and Its Socioeconomic Consequences*
3. From an Essay by L. Okunev, "Words Are Also Deeds"
4. S. Mironov, "A Few Words at a Fresh Grave Site" [On *Novy mir*]
5. A. Bekhmetyev, "From My *Philosophical Notebook*"

An Essay: "The Mideast Conflict and the Jewish Question in the USSR"

No. 70, July 1970 (Partial Contents)*

On Certain Current Events
1. On Aleksandr Tvardovsky's Sixtieth Birthday
2. Publication of Kochetov's Novel in Byelorussia
3. On A. E. Golovanov's Memoirs
4. The Bust at Stalin's Grave
5. Slogans and Graffiti about Stalin in Georgia
6. Condemnation of Shevtsov's Novels
7. The Persecution of Communists in Syria and Iraq
8. The Session of the Supreme Soviet of the USSR
9. From L. I. Brodsky's Pamphlet *On the Ideological Struggle*
10. Man and the Automobile
11. From Literary Life: Yevtushenko's New Narrative Poem
12. Man and Nature: The Problem of the Caspian Sea

No. 72, September 1970

Events and Comments
1. The Victory of the Left-Wing Parties in the Elections in Chile

2. The Appointment of V. S. Tolstikov as Ambassador to China
3. Civil War in Jordan
4. The Trial of Natalya Gorbanevskaya
5. The Expulsion of Charles Tillon from the French Communist Party
6. Cholera in the Soviet South
7. The Lifting of the Quarantine

Notes on Economic Questions
1. The USSR and the Third World: The USSR's Place in Economic Competition
2. The Industrialization of American Agriculture
3. Agrobusiness Groups in the United States
4. On the Lag in the Soviet Paper Industry
5. On the State of Affairs in the Virgin Lands
6. Expansion of Automobile Production in the USSR
7. Japan's Economic Successes
8. On the U.S. Economy
9. Some Economic Problems of Soviet Industry
10. On the Term *National Income*

On Certain Articles, Books, and Manuscripts
1. D. Yu. Zorina's Article "Lenin's Fight for the Monopoly of Foreign Trade"
2. Vittorio Strada on Kochetov's Novel

No. 75, December 1970

On Certain Events of the Month
1. Condemnation of the Line of *Molodaya gvardiya*
2. On Solzhenitsyn's Nobel Prize Award
3. The Banquet in Stockholm
4. An Article in *Pravda*
5. Khrushchev's Memoirs
6. The Sino-Soviet Agreement
7. The Treaty between Poland and West Germany
8. The Moscow Human-Rights Committee
9. On the Events in Poland
10. A Trial in Leningrad

On Certain Letters, Articles, and Manuscripts
1. Semanov's Article in *Molodaya gvardiya*
2. Raissa Lert's "Treatise on the Charms of the Whip"

Materials and Documents on the Jewish Question in the USSR and Zionism
1. From an Article by A. Aranovich, "The Near and the Far" (Notes on the Jewish Question in the USSR)
2. From an Interview with King Faisal of Saudi Arabia
3. From an Article by Goebbels, "The Jews Are Guilty" (November 16, 1941)

On the International Communist Movement

Index

1994